WITTGENSTEIN, THEORY AND
THE ARTS

"This is an important book which ought to be read by anyone reflecting on the humanities or engaged in humanistic scholarship...points us in the right direction of a healthy comprehension of human beings, their art, and their culture."

Robert L. Arrington, Georgia State University

To date, Wittgenstein's later philosophy has had little influence on disciplines that practice the theory and criticism of the arts, such as film studies, literary studies, and history of art, and only limited influence on philosophical aesthetics. This important collection of original essays by philosophers and scholars of the arts seeks to cultivate a new reception for Wittgenstein's later philosophy by exploring its profound implications for the study of the arts, especially for 'theory' as a form of explanation routinely employed in that study.

Introductory papers outline the basic tenets of Wittgenstein's later philosophy and how it can be used to clarify the forms of explanation that are logically appropriate to the subject matter of humanistic disciplines. 'Theory', they conclude, is not one of these. More specialized case studies employ Wittgenstein's philosophical methods to diagnose conceptual confusions at the heart of well-known theoretical paradigms currently employed in the study of the arts, such as psychoanalysis, cognitive psychology, structuralism, and deconstruction. The volume also includes essays that address Wittgenstein's own remarks on art and aesthetics, the relationship of his philosophy to artistic modernism, and the interpretation of Wittgenstein best known to contemporary scholars of the arts, that of Stanley Cavell.

Richard Allen is Associate Professor of Cinema Studies at New York University. **Malcolm Turvey** teaches film history at Sarah Lawrence College. **Contributors**: Richard Allen, Charles Altieri, P.M.S. Hacker, Oswald Hanfling, John Hyman, Graham McFee, Louis A. Sass, Severin Schroeder, Ben R. Tilghman, Malcolm Turvey.

WITTGENSTEIN, THEORY AND THE ARTS

Edited by Richard Allen and Malcolm Turvey

London and New York

First published 2001
by Routledge
2 Park Square, Milton Park, Abingdon, Oxon, OX14 4RN

Simultaneously published in the USA and Canada
by Routledge
270 Madison Ave, New York NY 10016

Routledge is an imprint of the Taylor & Francis Group

Transferred to Digital Printing 2006

Typeset in Times by Taylor and Francis Books Ltd

British Library Cataloguing in Publication Data
A catalogue record for this book is available from the British Library

Library of Congress Cataloging in Publication Data
Wittgenstein, theory and the arts / edited by Richard Allen and Malcolm Turvey
p. cm includes bibliographical references and data
1. Wittgenstein, Ludwig, 1889 - 1951. I Allen, Richard, 1959 - . II Turvey,
Malcolm, 1969 - .
B3376. W5645 2001
192 -- dc21

ISBN10: 0–415–22875–1 (hbk)
ISBN10: 0–415–40825–3 (pbk)

ISBN13: 978–0–415–22875–6 (hbk)
ISBN13: 978–0–415–40825–7 (pbk)

TABLE OF CONTENTS

Part II
Theory and the arts

CONTRIBUTORS

Richard Allen is Associate Professor of Cinema Studies at New York University. He is author of *Projecting Illusion* (Cambridge University Press, 1995) and co-editor of *Film Theory and Philosophy* (Clarendon, 1997) and *Hitchcock: Centenary Essays* (BFI, 1999).

Charles Altieri teaches in the English Department at the University of California, Berkeley, where he is also the Director of its Consortium for the Arts. His most recent books are *Subjective Agency* (Blackwell, 1994) and *Postmodernisms Now* (Pennsylvania State University, 1998).

P.M.S. Hacker is Fellow of St John's College, Oxford. He is author of numerous books, among which are *Insight and Illusion: Themes in the Philosophy of Wittgenstein* (Oxford University Press, 1972; revised edition, 1986); *Appearance and Reality* (Blackwell, 1986); *An Analytical Commentary on Wittgenstein's Philosophical Investigations* in four volumes (volumes 1 and 2 together with G.P. Baker) (Blackwell, 1980–96). His most recent book is *Wittgenstein's Place in Twentieth-century Analytic Philosophy* (Blackwell, 1996).

Oswald Hanfling is Visiting Research Professor at the Open University. He is the author of numerous articles on Wittgenstein and his books include *Wittgenstein's Later Philosophy* (Macmillan, 1989) and *Philosophy and Ordinary Language* (Routledge, 2000).

John Hyman is Fellow and Praelector in Philosophy at Queen's College, Oxford. He is author of *The Imitation of Nature* (Blackwell, 1989) and editor of *Investigating Psychology* (Routledge, 1991).

Graham McFee is Professor of Philosophy at the University of Brighton. His major research interests, in addition to the philosophy of Wittgenstein, are in aesthetics, and in the philosophy of understanding. His principal publications include *Understanding Dance* (Routledge, 1992) and *Free Will* (Acumen, 2000).

Louis A. Sass is Professor of Clinical Psychology at Rutgers University, where he also serves on the graduate faculty in comparative literature and is an affiliate of the Center for Cognitive Science. He is author of two books: *Madness and Modernism: Insanity in the Light of Modern Art, Literature, and Thought* (Harvard University Press, 1992), and *The Paradoxes of Delusion: Wittgenstein, Schreber, and the Schizophrenic Mind* (Cornell University Press, 1994); he also co-edited *Hermeneutics and Psychological Theory*.

Severin Schroeder is Lecturer in Philosophy at Lady Margaret Hall and Christ Church, Oxford. He is the author of several articles on Wittgenstein, a monograph on Kripke's *Naming and Necessity* (*Über namensphilosophische Intuitionen*, Hänsel-Hohenhausen, 1992), and a book on Wittgenstein's private language argument (*Das Privatsprachen-Argument*, Schöningh, 1998). He has edited *Wittgenstein & Contemporary Philosophy of Mind* (Palgrave, 2001).

Ben R. Tilghman is Professor Emeritus at Kansas State University where he taught from 1967 to 1994. Previously he taught at Reed College, Western State College of Colorado, and the University of Wyoming. His publications include *The Expression of Emotion in the Visual Arts* (Martinus Nijhoff, 1970), *Language and Aesthetics* (University Press of Kansas, 1973), *But is it Art?* (Blackwell, 1984), *Wittgenstein, Ethics and Aesthetics* (State University of New York Press, 1991), and *Introduction to the Philosophy of Religion* (Blackwell, 1994).

Malcolm Turvey is former Managing Editor of the journal *October*, and has just joined the faculty of Sarah Lawrence College to teach film history. He has published articles on Wittgenstein, film theory and avant-garde film.

ABBREVIATIONS

Throughout this volume, the standard abbreviations for Wittgenstein's works will be used. They are as follows:

AWL	*Wittgenstein's Lectures, Cambridge 1932–35*
BB	*The Blue and Brown Books*
CE	'Cause and Effect: Intuitive Awareness'
CV	*Culture and Value*
LA	*Lectures and Conversations on Aesthetics, Psychology, and Religious Belief*
LE	'Lecture on Ethics'
LFM	*Wittgenstein's Lectures on the Foundations of Mathematics*
LPP	*Lectures on Philosophical Psychology 1946–1947*
LW I	*Last Writings on the Philosophy of Psychology: The Inner and the Outer*, Volume I
LW II	*Last Writings on the Philosophy of Psychology: The Inner and the Outer*, Volume II
NB	*Notebooks, 1914–1916*
OC	*On Certainty*
PG	*Philosophical Grammar*
PI	*Philosophical Investigations*
PO	*Philosophical Occasions 1912–1951*
PP	'Wittgenstein's Lectures in 1930–33' in *Philosophical Papers*
ROC	*Remarks on Colour*
RPPI	*Remarks on the Philosophy of Psychology*, Volume I
RPPII	*Remarks on the Philosophy of Psychology*, Volume II
TLP	*Tractatus Logico-Philosophicus*
Z	*Zettel*

ACKNOWLEDGMENTS

The editors are grateful to John Hyman for his comments upon the introduction, and Rahul Hamid for his editorial work. Thanks also to Tony Bruce at Routledge for his support for this project and to Muna Khogali for helping us to stay on course. Finally, the editors wish to thank Bridget Sisk and Sarah Wilcox for their moral support.

Charles Altieri (1976) 'Wittgenstein on Consciousness and Language: A Challenge to Derridean Literary Theory', *Modern Language Notes* 91(6): 1397–1423. © The Johns Hopkins University Press. Reprinted with permission.

1

WITTGENSTEIN'S LATER PHILOSOPHY

A prophylaxis against theory

Richard Allen and Malcolm Turvey

To date, Wittgenstein's later philosophy has had little if any lasting influence on humanistic disciplines that study the arts. The highly original conception of philosophy he pioneered in his later writings, and his realization of this conception in investigating the manifold uses of language in the stream of human life, are almost entirely unknown to scholars in fields such as film studies, literary studies, history of art and cultural studies. And while there are a few exceptions to this situation, they tend to foster misunderstandings of Wittgenstein due to their over-hasty assimilation of his work to philosophical trends that are currently prevalent in the humanities (most notably, various forms of scepticism). Meanwhile, although his later conception of philosophy is more familiar to Anglo-American aestheticians, it is not widely adhered to by them.

The primary goal of this volume of essays is to help in the task of rectifying this situation by making Wittgenstein's later philosophy better known and understood to scholars in these disciplines. For although Wittgenstein himself did not spend much time on the sort of philosophical questions they raise, or address the broader implications of his later philosophy for the humanities in general, he nevertheless has much to teach scholars who study literature, the arts and culture. As in other domains of knowledge, the powerful methods he employed in his later writings can yield considerable riches when applied to questions and problems of a properly philosophical nature encountered by such scholars. As many of the essays in this volume demonstrate, these methods can extirpate the conceptual confusions to which scholars of the arts succumb, and enable a perspicuous grasp of the distinctive concepts they use in studying artistic phenomena.

Just as importantly, Wittgenstein's later conception of philosophy, as well as his own investigations into the logical character of explanations of human behaviour precipitated by this conception, have far-reaching ramifications for the very practice of the humanities, for the way human beings as social, historical and cultural beings are studied. As one of Wittgenstein's former students, the philosopher G.H. von Wright, has argued, they can provide the foundations for a veritable philosophy of the humanities, one

1

that clarifies the forms of explanation that are logically appropriate to the subject matter of humanistic disciplines, thereby defining and defending the autonomy of humanistic understanding (von Wright 1993: 165).

This volume is designed to demonstrate both types of propaedeutic role that Wittgenstein's later philosophy can play in the humanities by focusing on one form of explanation routinely found in disciplines that study the arts, namely, theory. Theories, of course, come in many shapes and sizes, differing considerably in their scope, in the type of phenomena they purport to explain and the sort of evidence they employ, and in the ways they are created, tested and used. For example, a philosophical theory that attempts to flush out the necessary and jointly sufficient conditions for the application of a concept is different in all of these ways (and more) from a natural scientific theory, such as Newtonian mechanics.

However, despite this variety, theories tend to possess two basic features. First, they unify a range of apparently disparate, unconnected phenomena by postulating an underlying principle that these phenomena putatively have in common and that can explain their nature or behaviour. Second, the common, underlying principle postulated by the theory – whether it takes the form of an entity, process, force, concept, or something else – is at least initially hidden from view. It is these two features – the unification of apparently diverse phenomena, and the postulation of an underlying principle that cannot be immediately discerned – that theories typically share, despite their other differences. For example, philosophical theories of the concept of 'art' often attempt to explain all correct uses of this concept – despite any apparent diversity – by postulating underlying conditions that are necessary and jointly sufficient for its application; conditions which, these theories argue, are not necessarily known to many of those who actually use the concept of 'art', hence the need for a theory that flushes them out. Similarly, Newtonian mechanics attempts to explain the behaviour of all bodies in motion, despite their apparent diversity, by postulating the existence of underlying laws that govern their behaviour, laws that are not available to direct observation.

By a theory, we mean in this volume a form of explanation that possesses both of these features. Many of the chapters that follow are concerned with exposing and dissolving away specific conceptual confusions embedded in (and often motivating the very existence of) some of the most influential linguistic, psychological and philosophical theories currently circulating in disciplines that study literature, the arts and culture. But the volume is also intended to question the very prestige that theory as a form of explanation currently enjoys in these fields. For if the later Wittgenstein is right, then regardless of the specific conceptual confusions embedded in specific theories, theory itself is in most cases a logically inappropriate form of explanation for humanistic subject matter. In other words, humanistic subject matter is not, for the most part, amenable to theorization, if the central tenets of Wittgenstein's later philosophy are true. Several of the essays that follow touch on or examine this broader ramification of Wittgenstein's later thought, thereby taking steps toward the philosophy of the humanities envisaged by von Wright.

This volume is therefore designed to present the central tenets of Wittgenstein's later philosophy to a wide, inter-disciplinary audience within and across humanistic disciplines that study literature, the arts, and culture, and to focus on their implications for specific theories commonly employed in these fields, as well as theory itself as a form of explanation as we have defined it. It brings together the work of philosophers and scholars of the arts from a number of disciplines who are informed by the later Wittgenstein. It combines papers which give relatively abstract overviews of his later conception of philosophy and its relevance to humanistic studies (Chapters 2–3) with essays that put this conception into practice in dealing with concrete philosophical or conceptual problems raised by some of the theories of language (Chapters 7, 9 and 10) and psychology (Chapters 8 and 11) currently circulating in the study of the arts. And it includes contributions that ward off potential misunderstandings of his later writings fostered by some of the extant scholarship on Wittgenstein and art, by clarifying aspects of his own remarks on art and aesthetics (Chapter 4); the relation of his later philosophy to artistic modernism (Chapter 6); and to scepticism, a philosophical trend currently prevalent in the humanities (Chapter 5).

In order to set the stage for these essays, this introduction presents the central tenets of Wittgenstein's later philosophy by examining his rejection of theory, first in his philosophy of language and then in his philosophy of psychology. Finally, we go on to elucidate the broader ramifications of this rejection of theory as a form of explanation for the subject matter studied by the humanities, including literature, the arts and culture.

I

What is Wittgenstein's later conception of philosophy? There is now a huge secondary literature that addresses this question, as well as much debate among Wittgenstein's interpreters over its specific claims, its continuities and discontinuities with his earlier philosophy, and its wider ramifications. However, there is a widespread consensus amongst his most informed interpreters about one of its fundamental features, which is its rejection of theory as an appropriate method of philosophical enquiry.

Wittgenstein's rejection of theory is due, in part, to a sharp distinction he draws in both his earlier and later writings between philosophy and the natural sciences. Many modern philosophers have conceived of philosophy as continuous with science in a number of ways. For example, some have claimed that, because of its considerable achievements, scientific knowledge of nature constitutes the paradigm of successful knowledge in general. Hence they have argued that, in order to make progress, philosophy should employ the methods and forms of explanation characteristic of science, including its method of theory construction. In his 'On Scientific Method in Philosophy', for example, Bertrand Russell writes:

> A scientific philosophy such as I wish to recommend will be piecemeal and tentative like other sciences; above all, it will be able to invent hypotheses which, even if they are not wholly true, will yet remain fruitful after the necessary corrections have been made. This possibility of successive approximations of the truth is, more than anything else, the source of the triumphs of science, and to transfer this possibility to philosophy is to ensure a progress in method whose importance it would be almost impossible to exaggerate.
>
> (Russell 1953: 109)

Philosophy, according to this view, has the best chance of making progress by importing the method of theory construction used in the natural sciences. Like the latter, it should attempt to explain the phenomena it is concerned with by building theories piecemeal out of preliminary hypotheses deduced from the available evidence that are then rejected, confirmed or refined by future evidence. If it does, its theories will have a good chance, like natural scientific theories, of being successively closer approximations to the truth, thereby adding to human knowledge about the world. Indeed, Russell conceived of philosophy as itself a science, but a science of the most general facts of the universe.

Wittgenstein, however, both early and late, argued that this view fails to take into account the profound differences between philosophy and the natural sciences, and that science is not the only paradigm of explanation and knowledge. 'Philosophy is not one of the natural sciences' (TLP 4.111), he wrote in the *Tractatus Logico-Philosophicus*, his first masterpiece; and in *Philosophical Investigations*, his second, he claimed: 'It was true to say that our considerations could not be scientific ones' (PI §109). According to Wittgenstein, the subject matter, questions, problems and solutions of philosophy are fundamentally different from those of the natural sciences because they are not empirical in character. While the natural sciences aim to explain empirical phenomena, philosophy is concerned exclusively with something that antecedes and is separable from empirical inquiry: namely, questions of sense and meaning. While the scientist conducts empirical research into something unknown about the universe – such as the properties which constitute the nature of empirical phenomena, or the laws governing their behaviour – by formulating hypotheses, which are then confirmed, rejected or refined as more evidence becomes available, the philosopher is concerned with something that is known in advance of empirical inquiry: the meaning of the words and sentences that make up a language, including the language used by the scientist to undertake empirical research.

The basic distinction at stake here can be illustrated, provisionally, by invoking a simple, canonical example. The statement, 'a bachelor cannot be married', seems to state a general proposition about bachelors that is akin to a general empirical proposition such as, 'all cows eat grass'. However, it does not state a general fact, one that can be proven or disproven by empirical research in the way that the claim 'all cows eat grass' can be. Rather, the 'cannot' of the first sentence is logical, not empirical. Someone who understands the English language knows in advance of any empirical investigation that a bachelor cannot be married, that empirical research will never turn up a married bachelor. And he knows this because it is part of the logic of the word 'bachelor', part of its sense or meaning that, if one says that someone is a bachelor, he cannot also be married. The sentence in question exhibits this aspect of the meaning of the word 'bachelor' by specifying a necessary condition of its use, rather than making an empirical claim about the world.

Wittgenstein argued that genuine philosophy is concerned purely with the type of subject matter this sentence exhibits, with what can be known about language in advance of any empirical research, namely, the sense or meaning of the words, expressions and sentences it contains. Philosophy, therefore, has nothing of an empirical nature to discover about language, thus ruling out the natural scientific method of theory construction as an appropriate form of philosophical explanation. To conceive of the correct meaning of a word as an empirical phenomenon that needs to be discovered on the basis of an hypothesis is to conceive of language as an incomplete and defective guide to meaning, and hence to believe that meaning awaits empirical discovery. However, for Wittgenstein, this conception of meaning is radically misconceived. If someone is using language correctly then, by definition, his words already make sense, they already have meaning. Meaning is therefore not something that awaits approximation via an hypothesis, at least for those who can already use a language correctly. Rather, it awaits perspicuous characterization.

In his later philosophy, Wittgenstein puts the point this way:

> And we may not advance any kind of theory. There must not be anything hypothetical in our considerations. We must do away with all *explanation*, and description alone must take its place. And this description gets its light, that is to say its purpose, from the philo-sophical problems. These are, of course, not empirical problems; they are solved, rather, by looking into the workings of our language, and that in such a way as to make us recognize those workings: *in despite of* an urge to misunderstand them. These prob-lems are solved, not by giving new information...
>
> (PI §109)

5

Philosophy is concerned with 'the workings of our language', with what is already in place, not something unknown. The questions it asks are about sense and meaning, not about what is true and false; its problems result from the transgression of sense into nonsense, not from a deficit of empirical information; and its solutions consist of showing when and how such transgressions take place, not discovering new facts.

Thus, Wittgenstein wrote in the *Tractatus* that 'the word "philosophy" must mean something whose place is above or below the natural sciences not beside them' (TLP 4.111), (because philosophy is concerned with what can be known about language in advance of any empirical research) It is 'above or below' them because it is concerned with sense and nonsense, not what is true or false. Or, as he put it in the *Investigations*: 'One might also give the name "philosophy" to what is possible *before* all new discoveries and inventions' (PI §126).

Wittgenstein's rejection of theory as an appropriate form of explanation for philosophical enquiry therefore stems, in part, from a firm distinction he draws throughout his philosophical life between philosophy and the natural sciences. However, in his later philosophy, there is another rationale for this rejection, one which is intimately bound up with the fundamental shifts that occur in his thinking between the earlier philosophy of the *Tractatus* and the later philosophy of the *Investigations*. For although the *Tractatus*, in keeping with Wittgenstein's separation of philosophy and the natural sciences, does not propose a natural scientific theory of meaning, it does nevertheless propose a theory in the broader sense in which we defined the term at the beginning of this introduction. And it is largely in Wittgenstein's repudiation of the theoreticism of his earlier philosophy that the seeds of the later one lie.

In his contribution to this volume (Chapter 6), the philosopher John Hyman provides an elegant summary of the conception of meaning proposed by Wittgenstein in the *Tractatus*:

> Wittgenstein argues in the *Tractatus* that a language is a system of representation. Words are combined in sentences to form pictures or models of possible states of affairs in the world. Every meaningful sentence can be dissolved by analysis, until its only constituents are logical expressions (such as 'not' and 'and') and simple, unanalyzable names. Each of these names corresponds to an object [in reality], whose name it is. The syntax of a name, i.e. the ways in which it can and cannot be combined with other names to form a sentence, reflects the essential nature of the object which it names, i.e. the ways in which it can and cannot be combined with other objects to form a state of affairs. Hence, a meaningful combination of words corresponds to a possible combination of objects. If the arrangement of the simple names concealed in a sentence corresponds to the actual arrangement of the objects which they name, then the sentence is true. If not, it is false.

6

According to the *Tractatus*, the only meaningful use of language is to 'picture' or describe reality, and language is essentially a system for doing this. The task of philosophy is to lay bare this system, that is, the principles of logical syntax that govern the combination of unanalyzable names into 'pictures' of possible states of affairs.

Wittgenstein came to see that the conception of meaning proposed in the *Tractatus* is a theory of meaning because it possesses the two features of theories we describe above. First, it unifies the apparent diversity of meaningful uses of words, expressions and sentences in everyday language by reducing them to the same underlying principle: a system of basic entities (unanalyzable names) and their relations (the principles of logical syntax) that function in only one way as 'pictures' or descriptions of reality. This reduction of language to an underlying logical system is justified because the system putatively enables language to correspond to states of affairs in the world. Second, neither the system of language nor the reality to which this system supposedly corresponds are visible to the ordinary language user. They are something that must exist, a theoretical postulate, rather than something that is actually known and understood by the language user. Indeed, Wittgenstein himself was unable to analyze a single sentence into simple, unanalyzable names and their basic logical relations, or to identify the objects in reality to which these names correspond. This was something, he believed, that would be done by others in the future. The consequence is that, for Wittgenstein in the *Tractatus*, human beings use language correctly in ignorance of what meaning is, or what the real meaning of their words consists of (that is, the correspondence between unanalyzable names and their simple counterparts in the world):

externalist justification?

> Man has the ability to construct languages capable of expressing every sense, without having any idea how each word has meaning or what meaning is…It is not humanly possible to gather immediately from [everyday language] what the logic of language is.
>
> (TLP 4.002)

In many respects, Wittgenstein's later philosophy is the product of his rejection of both of these theoretical features of the *Tractatus*'s conception of meaning. First, Wittgenstein came to see that this conception is derived from a venerable, deeply rooted 'picture' of language, one that is so deeply rooted, in fact, that it is taken for granted and rarely explicitly articulated let alone interrogated by those who cleave to it (including the author of the *Tractatus*). This is what Wittgenstein came to call the Augustinian picture, which conceives of language as being made up of words whose meanings are the things they refer to or name, and which, when combined into sentences, describe how things are in the world. But why, Wittgenstein came to ask, must every sentence have the same essential function of describing a state of affairs, and every word have the same essential function of being a name? Why must all words or sentences have the same function at all?

In his later philosophy, Wittgenstein pointed to the huge variety of different ways in which words, expressions and sentences are used by human beings, famously comparing language to a 'toolbox' containing many different tools. Language is used to give and obey orders, report, speculate, sing, guess, joke, ask, thank, curse, greet, pray and many other things as well (PI §23). Why, therefore, should all language be reduced to the same essential function of describing something? Indeed, why not reduce it to another function, such as wishing? Wittgenstein therefore came to reject the idea that the apparent diversity of language use must be unified by reducing it to the same essential function as a totally unfounded prejudice.

Second, he came to reject as misconceived the other fundamental feature of the *Tractatus*'s theoretical conception of meaning, namely, that meaning is hidden from the human beings who use language and therefore needs to be laid bare by philosophy. As we have seen, Wittgenstein always contended that philosophical investigation is distinct from empirical investigation, and that the task of philosophy is the perspicuous characterization of meaning. However, in his early philosophy he believed that the way linguistic meaning is explained by the users of language themselves is deceiving, and that the task of the philosopher is to discern the hidden essence of meaning by logical analysis. In his later philosophy he came to reject the assumption that meaning is hidden, for how can a linguistic expression be used correctly by users who have no 'idea how each word has meaning or what meaning is'? An invisible system of representation of the sort postulated by the *Tractatus*, Wittgenstein came to realize, cannot account for how users of a language actually use language themselves. Rather, the meaning of an expression must be visible to its user if he is to be able to use it correctly. And the norms, standards or rules that define its correct use in a specific context must in principle be ones that its user can appeal to in justifying his usage, or in explaining how the expression is to be used correctly to others. If they were not, how could he himself ever use language correctly, or challenge the incorrect use of language on the part of another?

It is this *normative* dimension of language that the *Tractatus* fails to capture: that is, the way in which the meaning of a linguistic expression must be what is invoked by language users themselves in justifying or explaining the expression's correct use. And Wittgenstein's acknowledgment of it in his later work transformed his understanding of philosophy's exclusive concern with sense and meaning. In the *Investigations*, meaning is no longer something invisible that needs to be discovered by the philosopher through logical analysis, as it was in the *Tractatus*. Rather, philosophy now 'simply puts everything before us, and neither explains nor deduces anything - since everything lies open to view there is nothing to explain. For what is hidden is of no interest to us' (PI §126). Meaning is now 'open to view'. It is what is explained by the myriad quotidian ways in which language users themselves explain meaning: for example, by ostensive definition, explanations using examples or paraphrase, gestures, pointing to the context of an appropriate use of a word, and so on. These forms of explanation are in perfectly good order and are neither incomplete nor otherwise deficient, precisely because they enable human beings to use language meaningfully. Hence, formal definitions of the essential (or necessary and sufficient) conditions for the use of a word of the sort that philosophers have traditionally sought after – such as the example of bachelors invoked above – are not to be conceived of as better than everyday forms of explanation. Formal definitions are only 'better' in some specialized contexts where they serve a purpose, for example, in licensing rules of logical inference. In most contexts, human beings do not need them in order to use expressions correctly, and hence rarely employ them in teaching, justifying or explaining the meaning of an expression to others.

The non-theoretical conception of meaning that emerges in Wittgenstein's later philosophy is therefore one in which meaning cannot be explained by postulating something invisible to those who actually use language, something exterior to the practice of using language that determines meaning in advance of use. Instead, linguistic meaning in this sense is 'self-contained and autonomous' (PG §55). It is not determined by anything outside the use of a language in practice, such as the structure of thought or the world, or a pre-existing calculus (to invoke some traditional philosophical candidates). Rather, the meaning of a word is manifest in its correct use, and understanding the meaning of a word is manifest in mastery of the technique of using the word correctly, exemplified by the ability, when asked, to give an explanation of its meaning to others. What, then, determines the correct use of a word? Correct use is determined by received explanations of its use, which function as rules for the use of the word. But those rules do not fix meaning in advance of use. They only come into existence through the practice of using a word and explaining its meaning consistently. If there was no consistency to the use of a word or the explanation of its meaning, the rules for its use would be invisible rules, and rules that are invisible cannot play a normative role. Hence, Wittgenstein compares rules for using linguistic expressions to concrete signposts like a pointing finger (PI §85). How does a pointing finger function as a rule that determines the correct direction to be followed? Does it leave doubt about the way to go by, for example, creating indecision about whether to proceed in the direction of the finger or the opposite way? No, but not because the possibility of going the opposite way is ruled out in advance by being contained, as it were, in the sign. Doubt does not arise precisely because the sign is used in a certain way. It is embedded in a practice in which the accepted thing to do is to follow the pointing finger, rather than going the opposite way.

The consequences of these two fundamental shifts in Wittgenstein's thinking for theory as a form of explanation in philosophical enquiry must be obvious by now to the reader. For if meaning is visible, and if the assumption that meaning needs to be unified by being reduced to a single essential function such as describing has been rejected as mere prejudice, then theory of any kind (not just a theory that is explicitly scientific) must be an inappropriate methodology for philosophical investigations into sense and meaning. For there are no concealed, underlying principles of meaning to postulate, and no 'essence' to reduce meaning to, to unify it.

From this shift to a non-theoretical conception of meaning as autonomous stems much of Wittgenstein's later conception of philosophy. The philosopher's task, according to Wittgenstein now, is to describe the correct use of linguistic expressions in practice: 'Philosophy may in no way interfere with the actual use of language; it can in the end only describe it. For it cannot give it any foundation either. It leaves everything as it is' (PI §124). The philosopher elucidates the correct use – or 'grammar' – of linguistic expressions.

To those unfamiliar with the later Wittgenstein and the tradition of philosophy he spawned, this might seem like a thoroughly trivial conception of philosophy. Gone, for instance, is the grand enterprise of theory building in the image of science, or the construction of speculative systems. In their place is the apparently mundane activity of describing how linguistic expressions are used in practice. But when one realizes the consequences of failures to grasp the grammar (or correct use) of language, the importance of the philosopher's task as articulated by Wittgenstein becomes all too clear. For although as language users we come to master the grammar of our language and operate with ease within it, we typically lack the ability to give a clear survey of it, just as we follow rules when we speak and write – such as the rules that govern the position of adjectives before nouns – yet we typically lack the ability to state in a propositional form what these rules are (unless we have been taught how to do so). While as ordinary language-users we do not normally need to be able to survey our grammar, there are contexts in which the lack of such a survey can have major ramifications: for example, when doing philosophy, investigating the empirical world scientifically, or studying the arts. For without it, we can easily transgress our grammar, violating the accepted use of words, expressions and sentences, and straying beyond the bounds of sense into nonsense: 'A main source of our failure to understand is that we do not *command a clear view* of the use of our words – our grammar is lacking in this sort of perspicuity' (PI §122).

All problems of a properly philosophical nature, for Wittgenstein in his later philosophy, are the result of an inability to clearly survey relevant segments of grammar. Hence, the philosopher's task is to produce a 'perspicuous representation' of these segments (PI §122). Rather than discovering new facts or information, the philosopher draws our attention to aspects of our use of language in practice that we have overlooked, or not paid sufficient attention to, thereby 'assembling reminders' (PI §127). Many of the chapters in this volume are concerned with specific examples of precisely this inability on the part of theorists of literature, the arts and culture to 'command a clear view of the use of our words' in their theories, and the reader will be able to see in detail from these papers the consequences of this inability – the way in which theorists lapse into nonsense – and therefore the importance of the philosopher's role as conceived of by the later Wittgenstein.

However, this is not the only role that philosophy, as conceived of by the later Wittgenstein, has to play in humanistic disciplines that study the arts. As we suggested earlier, Wittgenstein's later philosophy also has far-reaching ramifications for the way human beings as social, historical and cultural beings are studied, for the forms of explanation that are logically appropriate for studying them. Now that Wittgenstein's later conception of philosophy and its rejection of theory has been spelled out, we can point to these ramifications. For if Wittgenstein is right to reject theory as an appropriate form of explanation for the uses of language in practice, then this has implications for theory as an appropriate form of explanation for the behaviour of those who use language in practice, namely, human beings, including the types of social, historical and cultural behaviour studied by the humanities. In Wittgenstein's own philosophy, these implications are most apparent in his investigations into the meaning of psychological concepts, and the distinctive logical character of explanations of human action that these concepts entail.

II

Wittgenstein's conception of the autonomy of linguistic meaning in his later philosophy, which emerges in the wake of his rejection of the theoreticism of his earlier philosophy, entails a distinctive understanding of the nature of psychological concepts, one which counters a deeply entrenched and pervasive view of the mind as something mysterious that requires theoretical explanation. Psychologists, Wittgenstein points out, often wish to treat the mental sphere in the same way that physics treats the physical world (PI §571). Psychological concepts, according to them, refer to states and processes in the mind that are just like external physical states and processes except for one important difference: unlike entities in the external world which can be directly observed, mental entities are internal and can therefore only be indirectly detected by being inferred from the observation of human behaviour. What another person is thinking, believing or feeling is inaccessible to us, such that we may be unsure what their thoughts, beliefs and feelings are; indeed, we may be unsure that they have thoughts, beliefs and feelings at all. Furthermore, while we know by introspection what our own thoughts, beliefs and feelings are, even in our own case what, say, a thought is exactly remains shrouded in obscurity, for we cannot literally observe the nature of our own psychological states and processes. Thus, what is required is a theory of the mind that can explain its inscrutable nature. This is just what Descartes provides by proposing that the mind is an immaterial substance the contents of which are known directly by first-person introspection and indirectly by third-person observation. The mind, for Descartes, is essentially invisible because it is literally immaterial:

> There are certain activities, which we call *corporeal*, e.g. magnitude, figure, motion, and all those that cannot be thought of apart from extension in space; and the substance in which they exist is called *body*...Further, there are other activities which we call *thinking* activities, e.g. understanding, willing, imagining, feeling, etc. which agree in falling under the description of thought, perception, or consciousness. The substance in which they reside we call a *thinking thing* or *the mind*, or any other name we care, provided only we do not confound it with corporeal substance.
>
> (Descartes 1910: 63)

Twentieth-century psychology has, of course, replaced this Cartesian mythology with properly scientific theories of the mind. In the first half of the twentieth century, behaviourists accepted the premise of Cartesianism that the mind cannot be directly observed, but repudiated the mythology of an immaterial substance with what seems to be a hard-nosed scientific response: mental states are at worst mere fictions (they are not observable, therefore they do not exist) and at best an indirect way of speaking about human behaviour, and should therefore be translated into a behavioural vocabulary. For the behaviourist, tears are not an expression of an invisible state of sadness; sadness is defined as being in a state of bodily excitation such as is likely to produce, or in fact does produce tears (to simplify the complex characterizations of human behaviour that behaviourism necessarily entails).

Some psychological theories developed in the second half of the twentieth century purport to avoid both the scylla of Cartesianism (the reduction of human psychology to an immaterial, inner substance) and the charybdis of behaviourism (the reduction of human psychology to mere behaviour) by arguing that advances in contemporary neuropsychology finally allow us to understand the relationship between mind and body in wholly materialist terms. Psychological states and processes, they argue, are states and processes of the brain. These psychological theories seem to their practitioners to provide a scientific solution to the problems of Cartesianism and behaviourism, for they propose a way of conceiving of the mind in a materialist fashion without reducing human psychology to mere behaviour.

However, from the perspective of Wittgenstein's later conception of the autonomy of linguistic meaning, both Cartesianism behaviourism and materialist theories of the mind exemplify the prejudices and illusions of theory that Wittgenstein identified in the theory of meaning proposed in the *Tractatus*.[1] Each of these theories attempts to arrive at the real meaning of psychological concepts by unifying them through reduction to an underlying principle that cannot be invoked by the language users who explain or justify to others the meaning of the psychological concepts they employ in the context of their everyday behaviour. In the case of Cartesianism, the underlying principle which mental concepts stand for or signify is the immaterial mind whose connection to everyday behaviour is fundamentally mysterious. In the case of behaviourism, it is human behaviour. Our psychological concepts are technical descriptions of human behaviour which are unavailable even to the most sophisticated language user to justify or explain the psychological concepts he or she employs.

Meanwhile, rather than representing the best of Cartesianism and behaviourism, contemporary materialist theories of the mind combine the worst. As Hanfling points out in this volume (Chapter 3), such theories in fact reproduce Cartesianism by replacing Descartes's immaterial substance of the mind with an inner, material substance: the brain. The difference is merely that since, for the materialist psychologist, the mind turns out to be the brain, psychological states and processes are not essentially invisible in the manner of an immaterial substance, but only contingently invisible: they await discovery like the gene or the atom. Furthermore, like behaviourism, such theories substitute complex technical definitions of our psychological concepts in place of the definitions we invoke in our everyday justifications and explanations of those concepts.

Let us be clear. Wittgenstein is neither a sceptic nor a romantic irrationalist who denies the success, legitimacy and explanatory power of science. Wittgenstein does not object to empirical psychology in general, nor to neuropsychology in particular. Human consciousness is only possible because we have brains. Furthermore, discoveries about the brain can also be discoveries about consciousness, for example, how we are able to stay awake and what causes us to fall asleep, how we are able to see, taste, hear and smell.

However, Wittgenstein is opposed to the assumption that the real meaning of our psychological concepts can be arrived at by reducing them to states or processes of the brain that cannot by invoked to justify their use by those who actually use them. For this assumption violates the autonomy of linguistic meaning. The meaning of psychological concepts, like the meaning of all the concepts we use, cannot be hidden awaiting discovery, otherwise language users would not be able to employ them in the first place. Nor can the correct meaning of such concepts be arrived at by unifying them through theoretical reduction. For their meaning is already given by their uses in practice, and there is no reason to assume that these uses have anything in common unless the commonality is manifested in the practice of using them.

Take, for example, the concept of intention. For Wittgenstein, it is pure theoretical prejudice to assume that it is possible to find the exact neural correlate or pattern of, say, an 'intention to paint the bathroom' (to use an example cited by Hanfling in Chapter 3) common to all occurrences of the intention. Even if such a discovery were made, it would not tell us what we mean when we say someone intends to paint the bathroom. What having an intention to paint the bathroom means is given by the way in which we justify and explain what having such an intention is in the context of our behaviour. Since a neural correlate is hidden from us, it cannot be part of the meaning of the concept of intention. At best, the discovery of a neural correlate would reveal the causal preconditions for having an intention to do something. Understanding what an intention is can only be grasped by surveying the uses of the concept of intention in the context of human behaviour, the way its meaning is defined in practice, in particular the relationship between intention, action and agency, the idea of having power do something and being (held) responsible for one's actions (PI §629–60; Hacker 1996: 619–39). The same is true of every one of our immense range of psychological concepts.

Wittgenstein's conception of the autonomy of linguistic meaning therefore has crucial ramifications for theory as a form of explanation of the mind. For if the meaning of psychological concepts must be visible, and if the assumption that their meaning needs to be unified by being reduced to a single principle has been rejected as mere prejudice, then a theory of the mind of any kind (not just a specific theory, such as Cartesianism) must be logically inappropriate for explaining the meanings of psychological concepts. Indeed, in order to avoid the lure of a theory of the mind, Wittgenstein counsels that it is best when clarifying our psychological concepts to imagine that we do not know at all whether the people we are acquainted with actually have nervous systems (RPP I §1063), or to imagine that their nervous systems are randomly scrambled (Z §608). Of course, Wittgenstein does not want to deny that human beings have nervous systems and that those nervous systems display consistently across our species. It is rather that the discovery of the nature and content of our nervous systems, which after all is a very recent discovery in the history of human culture, has no bearing on the use of our psychological concepts and our understanding of their use.

The illusions that result from the failure of psychological theories to respect the autonomy of linguistic meaning lead to further illusions in explaining human action, in particular the tendency to reduce one paradigm of explanation to another. The justification of human action, a form of explanation that involves the invocation of reasons for acting, is typically reduced by psychological theories to another type of explanation that is fundamentally different to it: causal explanation. The distinction between justificatory and causal explanation, between reasons and causes, lies at the heart of Wittgenstein's later thought, though it is, unfortunately, not a distinction that is subject to the same painstaking elaboration that he accords, say, psychological concepts. However, the outlines of the distinction are clear enough:

The proposition that your action has such and such a cause, is a hypothesis. The hypothesis is well-founded if one has had a number of experiences which, roughly speaking, agree in showing that your action is the regular sequel of certain conditions which we then call causes of the action. In order to know the reason which you had for making a certain statement, for acting in a particular way, etc. no number of agreeing experiences is necessary, and the statement of your reason is not a hypothesis.

(BB: 15)

A reason for an action is identified by the fact that it can potentially be cited by the agent to justify what he did. An agent's reason is typically authoritative and complete. That is, it is not a conjecture or hypothesis on the part of an agent or others observing the agent that further evidence might prove, disprove or qualify. Since the reason for an action is not an hypothesis, it is not something that is typically unknown or hidden. An agent does not usually discover his reason for doing something by deducing an hypothesis and testing it against the available evidence. The reason I send my mother flowers on Mother's Day is because she is my mother. This reason is one that is authoritative because I sincerely cite it as my reason. It is not a conjecture or hypothesis that I need more evidence to confirm (such as whether I send her flowers on Mother's Day next year). In most cases, my sincere avowal suffices to explain my actions, that is to justify them, or, as Hanfling puts it in Chapter 3, to make them seem reasonable or intelligible.

By contrast, in a causal explanation, the cause of an action is identified by a conjecture or hypothesis. Because it rests upon an hypothesis, the identification of a cause consists in the discovery of something unknown or hidden that is confirmed by experimentation but subject to revision in the light of further evidence. Causal explanation is open-ended. An hypothesis about the cause of my developing angina early in life is not one that is authoritative because I cite it. Rather, it is the best conjecture on the part of my doctor given the evidence available to him. It is one, furthermore, that may be modified or rejected given what he later finds out about my condition, or the condition of angina in general.

Psychological theories typically fail to respect this distinction because they fail to respect the autonomy of linguistic meaning. For instance, because he tends to believe that psychological concepts ultimately refer to states and processes in the brain awaiting discovery by science, the materialist psychologist will further believe that the reasons used to justify human action also ultimately refer to brain states and processes that have a causal connection to behaviour. Hence, the only thing that makes my belief that the bathroom needs a new coat of paint the reason for my action rather than just a reason must be that this reason is (or is in some way related to) a state or process in the brain that is causally connected to my act of painting the bathroom. But in so thinking, the theorist misconstrues the relation a reason bears to an agent's action by confusedly reducing it to a causal relation that is unknown or invisible to the agent in question. An agent's reason is one that he is typically able to cite in order to justify his action, and his avowal that this is his reason is typically authoritative. Furthermore, it is also usually self-sufficient in the sense that the agent does not have to find out any more information in order to better justify his action. Just as the meaning of a word cannot be unknown to the language user who uses it correctly – the meaning of a word must be what is invoked by the language-user when explaining or justifying his use of the word – the reason for an agent's action cannot be unknown to the agent in the way that a cause is. For if it were, it could not be his reason for acting in the way he did. In contrast to a reason, a cause is something unknown or hidden that is identified by an open-ended hypothesis, one that can be modified or even rejected in the light of future discoveries.

Although, as we have said, Wittgenstein did not systematically examine in his published writings the distinction between reasons and causes and the confusions to which it gives rise in any one domain, his students report in their notes from his lectures that the distinction lay at the core of the confusion he discerned in Freudian psychoanalytic theory. Freudian psychoanalysis, according to Wittgenstein, is founded on the conceptual confusion of a reason with a cause. In one of his lectures, Wittgenstein puts the confusion this way:

> When we laugh without knowing why, Freud claims that by psycho-analysis we can find out. I see a muddle here between a cause and a reason. Being clear why you laugh is not being clear about a cause. If it were, then agreement to the analysis given of the joke as explaining why you laugh would not be a means of detecting it. The success of the analysis is supposed to be shown by the person's agreement...Of course we can give causes for our laughter, but whether those are in fact the causes is not shown by the person's agreeing that they are. A cause is found experimentally...The difference between a reason and a cause is brought out as follows: the investigation of a reason entails as an essential part one's agreement with it, whereas the investigation of a cause is carried out experimentally.
>
> (AWL: 32–5)

Wittgenstein points out that for Freud, at least, psychoanalysis is a scientific theory whose method of verification lies in the procedure of free association. Free association affords proof, for Freud, of his hypothesis that there is an essential cause of human behaviour – the desire to fulfil a wish – that is hidden, as it were, beneath the manifold surface of conscious understanding and action. In this way, Freudian psychoanalysis aspires to the status of a natural scientific theory that attempts to discover the hidden cause of a visible physical phenomenon – say, the fact that the earth revolves around the sun – a cause that cannot be directly observed but is initially postulated via an hypothesis, and is then subject to verification in the light of future evidence. Furthermore, in answer to the question as to why this underlying cause is concealed from us, Freud offers another causal explanation: the mental 'mechanisms' of condensation and displacement. Thus, psychoanalysis purports to uncover the cause of human behaviour (the desire for wish-fulfilment) as well as the mechanisms that allow it to remain concealed (condensation and displacement).

However, according to Wittgenstein, the discovery of this cause is not actually one that issues from hypothetical approximation and experimental verification in Freudian psychoanalysis, because in order to confirm that the psychological material furnished by the patient in free association is evidence for the hidden, underlying cause of the patient's behaviour postulated by psychoanalysis, Freud relies on the assent of the analyzand. For Freud, psychoanalytic explanations of human behaviour are proven when the analyzand eventually admits in analysis that the cause postulated by Freudian psychoanalysis for human behaviour in general – the desire for wish fulfilment – is also the reason for his specific behaviour, thereby confusing reasons with causes. But reasons – the justifications an agent himself gives for his actions – have nothing to do with discovering the cause of a phenomenon. The earth, for example, has no reason for revolving around the sun, and I have no reason for developing angina early in life. Rather, any hypothesis about the causes of these phenomena will be accepted on the basis of their plausibility given the evidence. If the desire for wish fulfilment postulated by psychoanalysis really was a hypothesis about the cause of human behaviour, the patient's assent would be irrelevant to verifying it, in the same way that my assent is irrelevant to verifying the cause of my angina. Thus, Freud gets to have his cake and eat it too by conflating reasons and causes. Psychoanalysis is putatively proven to be true as a scientific theory, not by procedures of experimental verification of a causal hypothesis, as in science proper, but by the reason-giving assent of analyzands.

The ramifications of Wittgenstein's criticisms of psychoanalysis are not wholly negative, as Louis Sass makes clear in his contribution to this volume (Chapter 11). While psychoanalysis does not bring to light hidden causes, it does draw our attention to the complexity of human action. In particular, it draws attention to the way in which the authority we accord an agent in attesting to what his reasons are for acting can be defeated by circumstances in which unacknowledged motivations for acting are detected in an agent's pattern of behaviour. In other words, it points to the fact that there is a sense in which the ordinary explanations and justifications that we give for what we are doing may fall short.

However, it is the critical dimension of Wittgenstein's remarks that are important here. For while it is one thing to recognize the concept of unconscious motivation and to find a place for that concept within the overall tapestry of our psychological concepts, it is quite another to offer, as Freud does, a theoretical, causal explanation of what an unconscious motivation is and how it comes to be concealed. As with other psychological concepts, the meaning of the concept of an unconscious motivation cannot be hidden awaiting discovery by a scientist. To recognize that a motivation may remain hidden to an agent in the sense of being unacknowledged is therefore not to be confused with the discovery of a hidden cause, as if an unconscious motive were concealed behind a conscious motive like a painting which hides another (older) painting beneath it. If there is a sense to be given to the concept of a hidden motivation that remains to be discovered, it is akin to the sense in which our intentions are invisible to us or that we cannot hear colours. The fact that our ordinary justificatory explanations of why we do something may fall short in relationship to the overall context of our behaviour does not license a theoretical, causal explanation of why we act as we do.

Freud's account of unconscious motivation is deeply distorted because it is a theory *par excellence* according to the criteria we have been using to identify theories. It offers an extremely general way of characterizing human motivation as the desire to satisfy a wish, thereby reducing the multiplicity of types of reasons to act to a singular motivation; and it proposes an explanation for why the apparent diversity of human motivation can be reduced in this way: the singular motivation for human action is hidden from view. Within the context of the goals for this volume, Wittgenstein's criticisms of Freudian psychoanalysis are of particular interest. Psychoanalysis is often criticized by analytic philosophers for failing to meet the standards of science and is unfavourably compared with contemporary materialist psychological theories, which are perceived to possess a rigour that psychoanalysis lacks. As we have already stressed, Wittgenstein did not seek to deny the power and achievement of science, and philosophers and scientists are certainly right to point out the failings of psychoanalysis as a science. But while it is true that psychoanalysis is not a science, Wittgenstein's discussion of psychoanalysis shows how a non-scientific theory overtly and explicitly traffics in the same illusions of theory as scientific theories of the mind, such as behaviourism and contemporary materialist psychological theories. Given that most of the theories that currently populate humanistic scholarship on the arts are non-scientific ones like (and including) psychoanalysis, Wittgenstein's criticisms of Freudian psychoanalysis suggest that his conception of the autonomy of linguistic meaning has equal relevance for the evaluation of scientific and non-scientific theories of human behaviour and action alike. Both are equally confused if they run foul of the autonomy of linguistic meaning.

Wittgenstein's discussion of psychoanalysis is also of relevance to the concerns of this volume because it offers a diagnosis of the appeal of psychoanalysis that can be extended to other non-scientific theories, as well as (at least some of the time) scientific ones. In order to explain its appeal, Wittgenstein compares Freud's theory of human motivation to Goethe's *Urphänomen* or primary phenomenon, a preconceived idea that becomes a model or prototype to be used in the description of all phenomena: 'The primary phenomenon (*Urphänomen*) is, e.g., what Freud thought he recognized in simple wish-fulfilment dreams. The primary phenomenon is a preconceived idea that takes possession of us' (ROC 3, sec. 203). The appeal of psychoanalysis, Wittgenstein suggests, lies in its generalizing impulse. Like myth, it offers us a general framework for making sense of our lives. As Jacques Bouveresse writes, the *Urphänomen* is a method of description that:

is universally applicable, not because over time the facts have been shown to conform to the theory, but rather because of the initial decision to conceptualize them and describe them in this way. The counterexamples treated are in reality much less a threat to the contents of the theory itself than a challenge to interpretative ingenuity, and successfully raised each time by the theorist.

(Bouveresse 1995: 49–50)

The *Urphänomen* is characterized by its all-encompassing imperiousness, by the fact that it does not afford the possibility of disagreement. For adherents to the *Urphänomen*, the fact that it explains everything is precisely its strength.

On the one hand, Wittgenstein's characterization of psychoanalysis as an *Urphänomen* implies a contrast to scientific theory, for a scientific theory can be verified and, according to Wittgenstein, Freudian psychoanalysis cannot. In other words, what distinguishes science from myth is that myth is a projection upon the facts, whereas science issues in genuine empirical discoveries. An *Urphänomen* is therefore a theory whose scientific pretensions, or its claims to be grounded in fact, have been stripped away. Descartes's theory of the mind as an immaterial substance is just such an *Urphänomen*; so, too, is the Augustinian picture of meaning that, for Wittgenstein, informed his account of meaning in the *Tractatus*. 'I once said that a proposition is a picture of reality', Wittgenstein recalled. 'That might introduce a useful way of looking at it, but it is nothing else than saying, I want to look at it as a picture' (AWL: 32–5, 108; quoted in Bouveresse 1995: 50).

On the other hand, while psychoanalysis is not a scientific theory, it is presented by Freud as a scientific theory, and in this sense, Wittgenstein's comments on psychoanalysis imply that scientific theories, too, can possess the appeal of an *Urphänomen* or myth. This is confirmed in Wittgenstein's reported comments on Darwin's theory of evolution that occur alongside his comments on Freud. While Wittgenstein acknowledges that Darwin's theory may indeed be confirmed, he points out that widespread acceptance of Darwin's theory at the time it was formulated was not based upon the demonstration of its truth, but upon its appeal as an *Urphänomen*. 'People were *certain* of Darwin's theory on grounds that were extremely thin' (LA: 26). The possibility of scientific theory becoming myth is strikingly exemplified by many contemporary scientific theories of the mind. For while these theories are governed by a commitment to empirical methods of verification, they are also informed by the unshakeable conviction that, even though we cannot demonstrate it yet, the mind *must* be reducible to the brain or function like a computer.

Many of the theories – both scientific and non-scientific – of literature, the arts and culture that currently populate the humanities are, like Freudian psychoanalysis and Darwinism (at first), accepted on 'grounds that are extremely thin'. In other words, rarely, if ever, are they subjected to rigorous procedures of empirical investigation or verification. This suggests that their appeal for scholars of the arts lies in the fact that, like an *Urphänomen*, they explain everything. They are methods of description that seem to be universally applicable.

However, it is the overall ramifications of Wittgenstein's investigation into the meaning of psychological concepts for the methodology or forms of explanation employed in the study of humanistic phenomena that we are trying to elucidate here. For by showing how both scientific and non-scientific theories of the mind run equally foul of the autonomy of linguistic meaning, and by clarifying the distinction between a reason and a cause, this investigation establishes the philosophical foundations for elucidating the appropriate forms of explanation for intentional human behaviour and action in general, including the social, historical and cultural forms of behaviour studied by the humanities. Although Wittgenstein himself did not directly address these ramifications of his later philosophy, a number of philosophers have done so, in particular G.H. von Wright. The contributions to this volume by Oswald Hanfling (Chapter 3) and especially Peter Hacker (Chapter 2) spell them out in detail, and so we will only schematically rehearse them here.

III

First, some preliminaries. As Wittgenstein was keen to point out, language use is thoroughly interwoven with human behaviour. When a child learns a language, he or she does not just learn the meaning of a word but patterns of behaviour within which the use of the word makes sense. For instance, when a child learns how to use the word 'hello' correctly, he or she does not simply learn the word, but a surrounding pattern of behaviour within which the word is used meaningfully, namely, greeting other human beings. Similarly, when they learn to use the phrase 'it hurts' correctly, children learn surrounding patterns of behaviour within which the phrase is used meaning-fully, such as asking for help, being comforted, seeking relief from pain and so on. As von Wright puts it:

> To learn a first language is not to be given a catalogue of names of objects and perhaps some rules of correct speech. It is to grow up to take part in the life of a community, to learn 'how to do things with words'; calling persons, asking for objects and for help, reacting to commands and warnings, answering questions—at a later stage also describing things and events and speaking about what is not imme-diately at hand in space and time.
>
> (von Wright 1993: 166)

But language use – or linguistic behaviour – is not merely part of surrounding patterns of human behaviour. Rather, learning a language actually, in part, constitutes or gives rise to human behaviour. It trans-forms the brute nature human beings are born with, vastly extending and refining our cognitive and affective capacities and the acts and activities in which they are manifested. For instance, to use one of Charles Taylor's examples, the emotion of love and the various activities this emotion informs do not exist independently of the concepts provided by language to describe, express and enact love. Love is, in part, constituted by the acquisition of these concepts, as well as various other related concepts, forms of knowledge and beliefs that are acquired when mastering a language; for example, the distinction between what Taylor calls 'the passing and the permanent':

> I could not attribute...love to an agent who was incapable of having in any form whatever the sense of being bound to someone for life. That is why we cannot attribute many human emotions to animals. Some animals do in fact mate for life; but they cannot have the kind of love we are talking about, because this requires the sense that it is for life, and therefore the possibility of making a distinction between the passing and the permanent.
>
> Thus even before we are fully conscious of it, this emotion is characterized essentially by our self-understanding, by the sense we have of the meaning of its object to us.
>
> (Taylor 1985: 190)

Taylor's point is that the capacity to experience the emotion of love is, in part, dependent on the capacity, granted by language, to distinguish between 'the passing and the permanent'. And this is just one example of how language vastly enlarges our cognitive and affective horizons, thereby giving rise to new forms of human behaviour which are dependent on it.

In as much as human behaviour is thoroughly interwoven with and dependent on linguistic behaviour, it stands to reason that understanding and explaining human behaviour – including the forms of behaviour studied by the humanities – should be methodologically of a piece with understanding and explaining meaningful linguistic behaviour. And it stands to reason that, in as much as theories are methodologically inappropriate for explaining how human beings themselves use language meaningfully, they are also methodologically inappropriate for explaining the intentional forms of human behaviour and action which language informs, including the social, historical and cultural forms of behaviour studied by the humanities.

However, the real grounds for making this claim lie in the *fundamental kinship* between understanding intentional human behaviour and action, and understanding meaningful linguistic behaviour, a kinship which is due to the fact that linguistic behaviour is, of course, itself a form of intentional behaviour. Because of this kinship, what Wittgenstein has to teach us about the forms of understanding appropriate to the diversity and normativity of meaningful language use – and the inability of theory to capture this diversity and normativity – applies with equal force to the forms of understanding appropriate to intentional behaviour in general, including the forms of behaviour studied by the humanities.

As we have already demonstrated, according to Wittgenstein's conception of the autonomy of linguistic meaning, to use a linguistic expression meaningfully is to use it in accordance with accepted explanations of its correct use, which function as rules fixing its meaning in practice. These rules play a normative role in the use of the expression. They cannot be hidden or unknown to the language user who is using the linguistic expression correctly. They must in principle be ones he can cite in justifying the way he is using the linguistic expression, or in explaining its use to others. For a linguistic expression cannot be used correctly by those who do not know what the rules governing its meaning are, and therefore what its meaning consists of. Hence, if we want to understand the meaning of a language user's expressions, we must know and make reference to the rules that the language user himself is speaking in accordance with.

The same is true of understanding intentional human behaviour in general, not just linguistic behaviour. Just as in order to be able to understand the meaning of the linguistic behaviour of a human being we must know and make reference to the linguistic rules that define its meaning, so too in order to understand the meaning of a human being's actions, we must know and make reference to the huge variety of norms, standards and conventions, as well as the routines, practices and institutions in which they are embedded, with which the human being is acting in accordance. This is how von Wright puts it:

Both understanding *what* intentional phenomena mean and explaining *why* they occur makes reference to rules. Just as we cannot understand speech without mastering the rules of linguistic practice, we cannot grasp the significance of or the reasons for most human actions without knowing the conventions and regulations, say, for greeting people, honouring the dead, driving and parking cars, getting commodities against payment, transacting one's daily business in the role of official, employer or employee, teacher or student, child or parent, etc. Also most human wants and needs – with the partial exception of those which we share with other species of the animal kingdom – get articulated in the set frame of societal rules and institutionalized patterns of behavior.

(von Wright 1993: 166)

While the various types of 'societal rules' guiding intentional behaviour are not to be equated in any simplistic fashion with linguistic rules, they nevertheless play the same normative role in intentional behaviour as linguistic rules do in linguistic behaviour. In other words, they cannot be hidden or invisible to the human being who behaves in accordance with them, or to the person trying to understand his behaviour. For a human being cannot understand or follow a rule that he is not aware of, whether linguistic or not.

It is for this reason that theories are methodologically inappropriate for explaining the rule-governed dimension of intentional behaviour. Theories of language, such as the Augustinian picture or proto-theory, lapse into nonsense because they reduce meaning to something singular and hidden, something of which the actual users of language have no awareness. Hence, they cannot explain how language users themselves use language meaningfully. In the same vein, theories of rule-governed behaviour, in as much as they reduce that behaviour to something singular and hidden, similarly lapse into nonsense. For something hidden – such as an 'unconscious cause' or a 'cognitive process' – cannot explain why a human being himself acts in the way that he does. It cannot play a normative role in rule-governed behaviour. And it is pure theoretical prejudice to assume that the huge diversity of societal rules that human beings act in accordance with – just like the diversity of linguistic rules – can be reduced to something singular.

The methodological inadequacy of theories in relation to both linguistic and societal rules is equally true of understanding intentional action in general. As Hacker puts it in his contribution to this volume: 'Intentional action is action of which it always makes sense to ask for what reason the agent performed it' (Chapter 2). Unlike the blind movements of natural phenomena, human beings typically have reasons for their actions, and they are typically able to cite these reasons to justify their actions to others. The linguistic rules followed by language users, and the societal rules that human beings behave in accordance with, are merely one type of reason that a human being speaks or acts in the way that he does. And just like linguistic and societal rules, reasons in general play a normative role in human behaviour. As we have already laboured to show in elucidating Wittgenstein's distinction between reasons and causes, like the rules governing language and behaviour, the reasons for a human being's actions cannot be hidden from him. Reasons for intentional actions must be ones a human being can in principle cite in order to justify his actions, like the rules for the correct use of a linguistic expression. If they were not, they would not be his reasons for acting in the way that he does. Theories, in as much as they postulate singular, hidden causes for actions, cannot therefore explain intentional human behaviour. They cannot explain why a human being himself speaks and acts in the way that he does, for his reasons cannot be hidden from him. And, once again, it is pure theoretical prejudice to assume that the variety of types of reasons that human beings can offer for their actions can be reduced to a singular reason, such as the desire to fulfill a wish at the core of Freudian psychoanalysis.

If the later Wittgenstein is right, then his philosophy has far-reaching ramifications for humanistic disciplines, including those that study literature, art and culture. For in as much as the study of these phenomena is the study of intentional human behaviour – of practices governed by norms, standards, conventions, and various other types of 'rules' within which human beings make and consume cultural products and typically have reasons for making and consuming those products – then Wittgenstein's later philosophy, as we have laboured to demonstrate, provides compelling philosophical or logical grounds for concluding that theory-building is fundamentally inappropriate for explaining such behaviour. If we want to understand our practices with art – the various types of rules that govern them and the reasons that human beings participate in them – then theory cannot help us, according to Wittgenstein's later philosophy. Instead, we must employ forms of understanding that make reference to the rules, reasons, and concepts that are manifested within these practices, and that do not impose a false unity on their diversity. One such form of explanation – conceptual clarification – is on display in many of the essays in this volume.

Of course, this by no means rules out descriptive or explanatory generalizations about human behaviour from the realm of humanistic scholarship. The study of humans as social, historical and cultural beings necessarily involves generalizations, because human beings share languages, beliefs, values, forms of knowledge, practices, institutions and much else besides. They therefore often act in concert, in the same way, and for the same reasons. The key point is, however, that such generalizations should not be confused with *theoretical* generalizations, such as those found in the natural sciences, even though generalizations about human beings may sometimes seem like 'discoveries' of hidden 'laws' governing human behaviour. For if Wittgenstein's later philosophy is right, in order to have explanatory power, generalizations about human beings must always make reference to what in principle lies open to view in intentional human behaviour: namely, the reasons and motives informing the actions of human beings. Law-like regularities in human behaviour, in other words, are fundamentally unlike the nomothetic laws postulated by natural scientific theories. Von Wright provides a good example of this explanatory difference between a 'law' postulated by economics – Gresham's law, which states that 'when two kinds of money of unequal exchange value are available for payments, the one of inferior value tends to drive the one of higher value out of circulation' – and a law postulated by natural scientific theories.

> Suppose we explain – to paraphrase a famous example – the bursting of a water pipe during a frosty night by reference to the law that water expands when it freezes. If one is curious, one can ask why water expands when it freezes. But whether or not this question is raised and can be answered, one will understand why the pipe burst; and if one is incredulous one can make experiments and watch the result. One need only accept the law as fact in order to admit that it has explanatory force.
>
> It is different with Gresham's law. It has no explanatory power *of its own*. Unless we understand *why* 'bad' money should tend to drive 'good' money out of circulation, mere reference to the fact that it does so does not make what happened a whit more intelligible. If people fear that the paper money issued by the occupying power will be declared valueless once the occupation is over, whereas silver coins will at least retain their metal value, then it is clear that people are reluctant to give away what they have in silver and maybe even anxious to buy up coins in exchange for paper money at a nominal over-value.
>
> (von Wright 1993: 169)

Gresham's law, in other words, unlike a natural law, must still make reference to the reasons and motives of human agents if it is to have any explanatory value, reasons and motives which cannot be hidden to the human agents whose actions they inform. Thus, Gresham's law is not a theoretical generalization in the sense that we have defined theory throughout this introduction.

Another qualification is in order. Wittgenstein's later philosophy does not entail that theory has no role whatsoever to play in humanistic disciplines that study the arts. For without a doubt, some of the questions asked by humanistic scholars make reference to the natural constraints on our practices with art. And these natural constraints can only be explained, like natural phenomena in general, by theoretical enquiry. In the case of cinema, for example, certain basic stylistic features of the medium, such as movement, light and noise, are routinely used by film-makers across the world to draw the spectator's attention to parts of the filmic image. The fact that these stylistic features are so widely used for the same purpose can, in part, be explained by deducing hypotheses and building theories about the way human perceptual mechanisms work, and how they respond to movement, light and noise. However, in as much as the questions asked by scholars of the arts are about what makes artistic phenomena distinctively human, about what sets them apart from natural phenomena – namely, the rules that govern them, and the reasons for which human beings engage in them – then such questions can only be answered by forms of explanation that can make reference to these rules and reasons, if Wittgenstein's later philosophy is right. Theory, as we hope we have demonstrated, is not one of these forms of explanation.

Over the last twenty-five years or so, the prestige of theory within the study of the arts has grown exponentially. More and more scholars have come to believe that the most important questions about literature, art and culture can only be answered by theories, and theory has become a significant, if not the most important, way to introduce students to the study of the arts. (This is particularly true of the field which the authors of this introduction inhabit: the field of cinema studies.) These theories are often completely different in their methods and goals, but they share in common the assumption that human practices, such as our practices with art, can be explained from outside the framework of the norms, standards, conventions and various other types of normative 'rules' which govern them, the reasons human beings have for participating in them, and the linguistic concepts that inform them. This is not the place to essay a comprehensive critical history of the forms of theorization that have overtaken the study of the art in the last twenty-five years. It will suffice here to briefly isolate three diverse instances of theory from that history to illustrate the manner in which they succumb to Wittgenstein's diagnosis.

For a while, the structuralist programme promised to put the study of literature, film and other arts upon a scientific footing. This programme was predicated upon the adaptation of methods that had been developed for the analysis of language to the study of literature and narrative. Central to structuralist theory is the claim that the infinite number of individual works of literature or narrative are in fact discreet manifestations of an underlying structure that the theorist deduces as the source of all literary forms or narratives in the manner that theorists of language have claimed that the infinity of individual utterances can be generated from a shared, underlying linguistic structure. The structural theorist sets out to identify a lexicon of minimal units and then specifies the possible ways these units can be combined and transformed. He is motivated by the belief that our customary ways of understanding literature or narrative are rough and ready approximations of the real nature of the phenomena that can be superseded by definitions provided by the theorist. Thus one structural theorist, Roland Barthes, begins a structuralist analysis of narrative by observing that: 'In order to determine the initial narrative units', it is vital 'to recognize in advance that they will not necessarily coincide with the forms into which we traditionally cast the various parts of narrative discourse (actions, scenes...dialogues, interior monologues, etc.) still less with "psychological" divisions (modes of behaviour, feelings, intentions, motivations, rationalizations of characters)' (Barthes 1977: 90–1).

Barthes claims that the minimal units of narrative are 'functions' that broadly divide into distributional functions that specify a discrete narrative event such as making a telephone call, and integrational functions or indices that comprise everything that is not a discrete narrative event: 'psychological indices concerning the characters, data regarding their identity, notations of "atmosphere", and so on' (Barthes 1977: 92). Indices are integrational in the sense that they may be attributed to more than one functional unit. In order to understand what motivates the presence of an integrational function (indice) and explain the significance of a distributional function, functions are embedded in a higher 'level' that comprises a finite list of spheres of action (fraud, seduction, betrayal, struggle, contract etc.) attached to characters defined by their roles (helper, villain, seducer etc.).

To simplify the discussion, we shall focus only on the concept of a distributional function. Barthes divides distributional functions into two categories: cardinal functions are events that have narrative consequence, and catalysers are events that do not. A catalyser always implies the existence of a cardinal function to which it is attached. Distributional functions are not simply organized at the higher level of spheres of action, they are themselves nested hierarchically. Thus, Barthes notes, the narrative event, 'a telephone call', consists of 'some few cardinal functions (telephone ringing, picking up the receiver, speaking, putting down the receiver)' (Barthes 1977: 101). However, when examined closely, it becomes apparent that Barthes fails to provide a decision procedure that can determine what the list of functions belonging to the nested level consists in. For example, we might add 'hearing the telephone ring', 'intending to pick up the receiver', 'hesitating (or not) to pick it up', 'holding the receiver', and a potentially infinite range of more finely articulated specifications of the action. Furthermore, he fails to provide a clear procedure for discriminating catalysers from cardinals. Barthes writes that the space between 'a telephone rang' and 'Bond answered' is saturated with trivial incidents that are catalysers such as 'Bond moved toward his desk, picked up one of the receivers, put down his cigarette, etc.' (1977: 94). But why are these events catalysers rather than hierarchically nested cardinal functions? These problems of categorization are endemic to the theory. Neither the minimal units nor their rules of combination are accurately specifiable; the alleged deep structure of narrative is chimerical. But much more importantly, even if Barthes was successful in identifying a putative deep structure of narrative, the explanation he provides would not explain how it is that human beings actually make and understand narratives themselves. For the units and rules Barthes invokes are ones that human beings cannot in principle be aware of, precisely because they need to be 'discovered' by a theory. Hence, they cannot be the same, or would only accidentally be the same, as the normative 'rules' that do in fact guide the way we make and understand narratives.

Barthes justifies his theory in the following way: 'either a narrative is merely a rambling collection of events, in which case nothing can be said about it other than by referring back to the storyteller's (the author's) art, talent or genius – all mythical forms of chance – or else it shares with other narratives a common structure which is open to analysis' (Barthes 1977: 80). But this is a false dichotomy. Narratives are not merely a rambling connection of events mysteriously unified by an author, they are intentionally crafted artefacts based on convention. Neither must narratives have something in common if they are not to appear randomly concatenated. Narrative, as Barthes himself notes, is present in 'myth, legend, fable, tale, novella, epic, tragedy, drama, comedy, mime, painting, stained glass windows, cinema, comic, news item, conversation' (Barthes 1977: 79) and the list could be extended. What lies visibly in common between these forms of narrative is a network of overlapping similarities and differences that Wittgenstein analogized to the resemblance between family members rather than an essential element all narratives share. The point here is not to deny that there *is* something in common between different forms of narrative, but to deny the supposition that there *must* be something in common to what we call narratives in order for us to recognize, make and use them. If it is mistaken to suppose that we recognize and make use of narratives because they possess a common property, then it is also mistaken to propose that we conceive this common property as a structure that generates all instances of narrative.

Barthes wields 'science' as a challenge to the humanistic basis of arts criticism. He contests the idea that making and understanding art are normative practices. He uses 'science' as a yardstick to criticize the normative practices of making and understanding art from the outside, to make them appear irrational, mere epiphenomena of an underlying process revealed by science. What we take to be the work of an author is really the 'work' of an impersonal system of 'codes'; works of art are actually the products of impersonal, objective, pre-existing structures and elements. However, by using 'science' as a yardstick by which to measure our practices of making and understanding narratives, Barthes misconstrues the normative character of those practices. Making and understanding art is a perfectly rational activity without being explicable in scientific terms. It is rational for it is a purposive action, an action that is done for a reason or reasons. Barthes also misconstrues the nature of scientific theory. While structuralist theory superficially resembles the hypothetico-deductive procedures characteristic of science, it is not a genuine scientific theory because nothing can disconfirm the structuralist axiom that there must be an underlying structure that supports and makes possible the diverse forms taken by narrative in human cultures.

Structuralism is now out of fashion, and the later Barthes was partly responsible for this. One of the theories that has replaced structuralism in the study of the arts is Lacanian psychoanalysis. Once associated with a broadly structuralist analysis of culture, a new Lacanianism has risen in a more potent form in the writings of the prolific Slovenian theoretician Slavoj Žižek, one that is closer to Lacan's own surrealist roots. Lacan rewrites Freud's psychological theory of unconscious agency as a philosophical theory that describes the essential or constitutive paradox of self-representation. Lacanian theory has the aura of a scientific theory that makes empirical claims by borrowing the language of psychological and linguistic theories, but is actually immune from empirical confirmation and refutation. Žižek bases his interpretation of Lacan on the Hegelian dictum that the use of language that singles out human beings emerges against the background of an essential abyss of non-meaning, of the empty nothingness that is organic life. Human beings, when they begin to use language and strive to attain self-consciousness, negate or conceal this essential abyss of nothingness by entering into the pre-existing structure of language that is concrete, inorganic, inert and external. Human consciousness and its products, including culture, thus embody a subjection to an external and therefore alien authority. This subjection is at once essential to concealing the abyss of nothingness that is organic life and, at the same time, is only made possible and sustained by the existence of that concealed abyss and the 'pressure' exerted by it. This abyss of nothingness (called 'the Real') forms a traumatic core at the heart of human consciousness and culture that always threatens to disrupt the inert structure of human civilization that its concealment serves to make possible. For Žižek, the ego and its social and cultural analogues grow ever more rigid and paranoid in order to prevent the irruption of 'the Real', whose role in sustaining the social structure through a negative force or pressure is thereby only augmented and made more insistent. For Žižek, 'What we call "culture" is…in its very ontological status, the reign of the dead over life, i.e. the form in which the "death drive" assumes its positive existence' (Žižek 1992: 54).

Žižek (after Lacan), like Wittgenstein, proposes that what is distinctive about human beings is their capacity to use language. There the similarities abruptly end. For Wittgenstein, what defines language use, or activities such as making and responding to art, is once again that they are a species of intentional action. Žižek's metaphysical Freudianism involves stepping outside intentional human actions and the framework of 'rules', reasons and concepts that are woven into them in order to claim that all intentional behaviour has one and the same function: to express the death drive or the conversion of life into death. However, the only way in which the nature of human behaviour can be thus defined is by explaining it in terms of a single underlying condition or state, utterly invisible and essentially unknowable to the human agent, that determines the real nature of intentional action. Of course, some art may indeed allegorize this picture of the human condition, in particular, art influenced by Lacan and the influences upon Lacan such as Hegel and Freud. But the significance of such works are trivialized and misunderstood once they are mobilized as 'proof' of an all-encompassing theory of human behaviour. Indeed, this theory has precisely the compulsory, authoritarian qualities Žižek attributes to political institutions and culture: it is universal and inescapable. It is also irrefutable: therein lies its appeal.

Cognitive theories of art, by comparison with structuralist or psychoanalytic theories, seem like a breath of fresh (or cold) air. They predate contemporary critical theory, for example in the writings of E.H. Gombrich and Rudolf Arnheim, but they are becoming increasingly influential in fields of study such as film among those who are justifiably impatient with the flagrant logical and empirical inadequacies of theories such as structuralism and Lacanianism. However, the opposition of cognitivist theorists to structuralists and Lacanians lies not in the fact that structuralism and Lacanianism offer theoretical accounts of the practices of making and responding to art that seek to explain these practices from a position outside the framework in which the users of art understand and make sense of art. Rather, it lies in the fact that theories such as structuralism and Lacanianism provide an inadequate account of the data that they are supposed to describe: they do not give an adequate account of the facts. Such a criticism is scarcely telling against a theory such as Žižek's, which brashly pronounces its immunity from defeasibility as the source of its authority. Nonetheless, cognitive theorists have turned to contemporary psychology and the latest theories of the mind in order to place the theorization of art on a more scientific footing. Now, there are many questions of a causal nature that psychological theories of the arts have fruitfully addressed, such as colour perception, motion perception, depth perception, pattern recognition and so on. However, cognitive theorists of art go further and seek to explain the meaning of the psychological concepts we use when we engage with art, as if these concepts described an empirical process that can be explicated by a theory.

In Chapter 6 in this volume, Richard Allen describes two competing cognitive theories of narrative comprehension. David Bordwell (1985) seeks to explain narrative comprehension in film as the non-conscious deployment of a largely non-conscious body of beliefs or 'schemata' that the film spectator applies to the set of visual stimuli provided by the film. Understanding consists in a process of making inferences and hypotheses about what the visual cues actually refer to on the basis of testing out different schemata. Gregory Currie (1995), in contrast, argues that narrative comprehension, in large measure, does not involve the application of non-conscious bodies of belief, for such a theory fails to account for, amongst other things, the immediacy with which an ability, such as the ability to recognize and understand a simple narrative action, manifests itself. The ability to understand often seems not to involve thought of any kind. How then do we explain this ability? Currie proposes that a large part of our capacity to understand and respond to art is explicable by the existence of a special faculty in the mind, the faculty of imagination, that he defines in terms of mental simulation. This faculty allows us to comprehend an event from the point of view of others, without experiencing it ourselves. We simply simulate the process by which they acquire their beliefs in a manner that is detached from the 'perceptual causes and behavioural effects' (Currie 1995: 419) that characterize their response. Similarly, when I engage with a fiction, 'I simulate the process of acquiring beliefs – the beliefs I would acquire if I took the work I am engaged with for fact rather than fiction' (Currie 1995: 148).

From the point of view of the later philosophy of Wittgenstein, what lies in common between these theorists is far more significant than what divides them. Cognitive theory mistakenly conflates the elucidation of concepts which we use in the explication of our engagement with art, like imagination and understanding, with the formulation of hypotheses about causal processes that render our response to art possible. Wittgenstein does not dispute the validity of causal investigations into phenomena such as art. However, he alerts us to the confusions engendered when the cognitivist theorist of art seeks, in the case of Bordwell, to explain the normative ways in which understanding narrative film depends on formulating hypotheses. First, the theorist proposes a general theory of understanding or cognition as hypothesis formation which ignores the different ways we can go about understanding a work of art (and other things). Second, to support this general theory, the theorist postulates a hidden mechanism that underlies the apparent diversity of 'understanding': a theory of how all cognition is based upon the non-conscious application of hypotheses to visual data, even where hypothesis-making is not involved in cognition. Currie agrees that hypothesis-making is not involved in cognition, but then feels obliged to postulate the mechanism that is really involved in cognition by reducing the diverse, normative ways in which fictions enjoin us to use our imagination to a general theory of imagination as mental simulation, and by proposing that the mechanism of mental simulation is entirely invisible to us.

Cognitivism is light years away from the 'theoretical anti-humanism' that characterizes structuralist theory and Lacanain psychoanalysis. As we have seen, theoretical anti-humanist art scholars turn to theory as a way of attacking the assumption that making and responding to art is a normative activity. Cognitive theorists turn to theory because they want to elucidate more clearly the nature of this normative activity. Cognitivists are committed to the study of human beings as rational animals, and many have a great deal of respect for 'folk psychological' wisdom. Unfortunately, however, by turning to theory as a form of explanation for clarifying, expanding upon and modifying our folk psychological wisdom, they misconstrue that wisdom for something that consists in or can be understood as a proto-theory: sometimes the right explanation, sometimes not, but always capable of being improved upon. But if the later Wittgenstein is right, the idea that the psychological concepts we invoke in the practice of engaging with art are part of a primitive theory of responding to art profoundly misconstrues the nature of those concepts. The meaning of the concepts we use in engaging with art cannot be awaiting empirical discovery, according to Wittgenstein's conception of the autonomy of linguistic meaning. Rather, their meaning is 'open to view' in our practices with art.

This volume consists of essays that both directly and indirectly develop the themes we have outlined in this introduction. We have divided it into two parts. The chapters in Part I, 'Wittgenstein, the Humanities and Art', all directly address the relation of Wittgenstein's philosophy either to the humanities and/or art. The essays by Peter Hacker (Chapter 2) and Oswald Hanfling (Chapter 3) give relatively broad overviews of Wittgenstein's later philosophy and its relevance to humanistic scholarship. In 'Wittgenstein and the Autonomy of Humanistic Understanding', Hacker situates Wittgenstein's later philosophy within a historical survey of the relationship between scientific explanation and humanistic understanding from the Renaissance to the present. For Hacker, Wittgenstein's later philosophy, whose main features he expertly summarizes and elucidates, provides a bulwark against the encroachment of scientific explanation upon humanistic understanding that has proceeded apace through the nineteenth and twentieth centuries in spite of a few notable dissenting voices. Hanfling's essay, 'Wittgenstein on Language, Art and Humanity', further develops the argument that Wittgenstein's later philosophy defines and defends the autonomy of humanistic understanding. Hanfling shows how Wittgenstein clarifies what is 'distinctively human' about language, art, and therefore about human beings themselves. What is distinctively human about language, among other things, is that it is used in a wide variety of ways by human beings, and these ways of using language, which define the meaning of linguistic expressions, are 'open to view'. Scientific and other theories cannot, therefore, capture what is distinctively human about language because they are concerned with what is hidden. Similarly, argues Hanfling, theories cannot capture what is distinctively human about art – that aesthetics, in other words, cannot be a science – because it too is concerned with what is 'open to view'.

The remaining essays in the first section address other aspects of Wittgenstein's philosophy that are of relevance to humanistic scholars of literature, the arts and culture. Most of Wittgenstein's own views about art are preserved indirectly in the lecture notes of his diligent students. However, a number of informal comments about art written down by Wittgenstein in his notebooks have been published, and some of these form the basis for Graham McFee's detailed exegesis of Wittgenstein's approach to aesthetics in 'Wittgenstein, Performing Art and Action'

(Chapter 4). Wittgenstein, as McFee makes clear, does not offer a theory of understanding art. Instead, he explores the diverse criteria for aesthetic understanding that are manifest in human responses to art, and clarifies the meaning and significance of Wittgenstein's written comments about some of these criteria. Meanwhile, Malcolm Turvey (Chapter 5) takes issue with the interpretation of Wittgenstein best known to contemporary scholars of the arts, that of Stanly Cavell. This interpretation argues that Wittgenstein's later philosophy endorses a form of linguistic scepticism. Turvey, however, argues that this interpretation is misconceived. Scepticism, for Wittgenstein, is a species of nonsense, and his later, thoroughly humanized conception of linguistic meaning does not entail linguistic scepticism. John Hyman's contribution, 'The Urn and the Chamber Pot' (Chapter 6), explores the influence of Adolf Loos and artistic modernism upon Wittgenstein's early approach to philosophy and his only significant contribution to the arts, namely, the house that he built for his sister Margaret Stonborough Wittgenstein' between 1926 and 1928. Hyman argues that Loos's injunction to abstain from ornament in practical design is realized in the Stonborough house and informs, by analogy, the reductive, austere conception of language Wittgenstein propounded in the *Tractatus*.

The essays in Part II, 'Theory and the Arts', focus specifically on the propaedeutic value of Wittgenstein's later philosophical methodology by using it to extirpate the conceptual confusions prevalent in some of the most popular contemporary linguistic and psychological theories of the arts. In his essay 'Language and Painting, Border Wars and Pipe Dreams' (Chapter 7), Ben Tilghman undertakes a wide-ranging investigation into a notion that has become a mainstay of theoretical scholarship on the arts over the last thirty years, namely, that art, especially painting, is a form of language. Tilghman expertly shows how deeply confused this notion is by clarifying what our concept of language actually is. In the process, he proposes his own interpretation of the role of language in the work of one of the artists commonly used by theorists to endorse the notion that painting is a form of language, namely, René Magritte. In his essay 'Cognitive Film Theory' (Chapter 8), Richard Allen diagnoses the conceptual confusions that inform the effort of two cognitive theorists, David Bordwell and Gregory Currie, to develop a cognitive theory of narrative comprehension in film. Severin Schroeder's essay, 'The Coded Message Model of Literature' (Chapter 9), takes issues with an assumption pervasive in the theorization of literature, namely, that literary value lies in a work's message. More specifically, he challenges the most sophisticated form of this theory in literary structuralism where the message of a work is assumed to be hidden, written in a code that requires deciphering by the critic as theorist. He demonstrates the implausibility of this assumption in a series of case studies and diagnoses the conceptual confusion upon which it is premised; namely, a confusion between transitive and intransitive meaning. Charles Altieri's essay 'Wittgenstein on Consciousness and Language: A Challenge to Derridean Literary Theory' (Chapter 10) is the one essay in this volume that is being reprinted. Originally published in 1976, it represents a bold early attempt by a scholar of the arts to mount a Wittgensteinian defence of the autonomy of humanistic understanding against the encroachment of theory in the form of the work of Jacques Derrida. Altieri demonstrates how Wittgenstein's later philosophy provides the philosophical tools for diagnosing the conceptual confusions about language and mind that are rife in Derrida's work.

Finally, in a wide ranging essay, 'Wittgenstein, Freud and the Nature of Psychoanalytic Explanation' (Chapter 11), Louis Sass seeks to clarify the complex relationship between Wittgenstein's later philosophy, Freudian psychoanalysis and various influential Anglo-American interpretations of Freud. Sass pays close attention to Wittgenstein's criticisms of Freud, in particular, Freud's alleged confusion of reason and cause, but he also notes affinities between both thinkers with a view to developing an understanding of unconscious motivation that is informed by the later philosophy of Wittgenstein. While Sass is not directly concerned with the application of psychoanalytic theory to understanding the arts, his essay indirectly sheds light on the uncritical embrace of Freudian theory by scholars of the arts.

Together, these essays present the central tenets of Wittgenstein's later philosophy, locate and diagnose conceptual confusions in specific theories employed by theorists of the arts, and suggest that theory itself as a form of explanation (as we have defined it in this introduction) is in most cases logically inappropriate for understanding and explaining humanistic subject matter. They show that Wittgenstein's later philosophy is not another theory for scholars of the arts to apply to humanistic phenomena. On the contrary, the role it has to play in humanistic disciplines, they suggest, is a propaedeutic one. First, its methods can enable scholars of the arts to attain a perspicuous grasp of the distinctive concepts they use in studying artistic phenomena. Second, it provides a prophylaxis against theory, helping scholars of the arts to clarify the forms of understanding that are appropriate to the phenomena they study. They thereby show that an informed understanding of Wittgenstein's later philosophy is indispensable for scholars of the arts who wish to re-establish the humanistic foundations of their disciplines.

Notes

1 Of course Wittgenstein was not around to argue against contemporary materialist theories of the mind, but his diagnosis of the conceptual confusions that characterize gestalt psychology has ramifications for understanding the conceptual confusions within contemporary psychological theory, as P.M.S. Hacker makes clear in a number of essays, most notably 'Methodology in Philosophical Psychology' in (Hacker 1996: 401–45).

Bibliography

Arnheim, R. (1954) *Art and Visual Perception*, Berkeley and Los Angeles: University of California Press.

Barthes, R. (1977) 'Introduction to the Structuralist Study of Narrative', in R. Barthes, *Image - Music - Text*, ed. and trans. S. Heath, New York: Hill and Wang, 79–124.

Bordwell, D. (1985) *Narration in the Fiction Film*, Madison, WI: University of Wisconsin Press.

Bouveresse, J. (1995) *Wittgenstein Reads Freud: The Myth of the Unconscious*, Princeton, NJ: Princeton University Press.

Currie, G. (1995) *Image and Mind: Film, Philosophy, and Cognitive Science*, Cambridge: Cambridge University Press.

Descartes, R. (1910) *The Philosophical Works of Descartes*, vol. 2, trans. E.S. Haldane and G.R.T. Ross, Cambridge: Cambridge University Press.

Hacker, P.M.S. (1996) *Wittgenstein: Mind and Will: Volume 4 of an Analytical Commentary on the Philosophical Investigations*, Oxford: Basil Blackwell.

Russell, B. (1953) 'On Scientific Method in Philosophy', in B. Russell, *Mysticism and Logic*, Harmondsworth: Penguin.

Taylor, C. (1985) 'Cognitive Psychology', in C. Taylor, *Human Agency and Language: Philosophical Papers*, vol. 1, Cambridge: Cambridge University Press, 187–212.

von Wright, G.H. (1993) 'Humanism and the Humanities', in G.H. von Wright, *The Tree of Knowledge and Other Essays*, Leiden: E.J. Brill, 155–171.

Wittgenstein, L. (1958) *The Blue and Brown Books* (BB), Oxford: Blackwell.

—— (1958) *Philosophical Investgations* (PI), ed. G.E.M. Anscombe and R. Rhees, trans. G.E.M. Anscombe, 2nd Edition, Oxford: Blackwell.

—— (1961) *Tractatus Logico-Philosophicus* (TLP), trans. D.F. Pears and B.F. McGuinness, London: Routledge and Kegan Paul.

—— (1967) *Zettel* (Z), ed. G.E.M. Anscombe and G.H. von Wright, trans G.E.M. Anscombe, Oxford: Blackwell.

—— (1970) *Lectures and Conversations on Aesthetics, Psychology ans Religious Beliefs* (LA), ed. C. Barrett, Oxford: Blackwell.

—— (1974) *Philosophical Grammar* (PG), ed. R. Rhees, trans. A.J.P. Kenny, Oxford: Blackwell.

—— (1977) *Remarks on Color* (ROC), ed. G.E.M. Anscombe, Berkeley: University of California Press.

—— (1979) *Wittgenstein's Lectures, Cambridge 1932-35, from the notes od Alice Ambrose and Margaret Macdonald* (AWL), ed. Alice Ambrose, Oxford: Blackwell.

—— (1980) *Remarks on the Philosophy of Psychology*, Volume 1 (RPPI), ed. G.E.M. Anscombe and G.H. von Wright, trans. G.E.M. Anscombe, Oxford: Blackwell.

Žižek, S. (1992) *Enjoy Your Symptom*, New York and London: Routledge.

Part I

WITTGENSTEIN, THE HUMANITIES AND ART

2

WITTGENSTEIN AND THE AUTONOMY OF HUMANISTIC UNDERSTANDING

P.M.S. Hacker

Not merely destructive

Wittgenstein was a 'critical philosopher' in two more or less Kantian senses. First, he was concerned, early and late, with elucidating the limits of language. Where Kant had understood by 'Kritik' the delineation of the limits of a faculty, Wittgenstein gave a linguistic turn to a form of critical philosophy. Where Kant explored the limits of pure reason, Wittgenstein investigated the limits of language. Where Kant delimited knowledge in order to make room for faith, Wittgenstein, in the *Tractatus*, delimited language in order to make room for ineffable metaphysics, ethics, and religion. With the collapse of the *Tractatus* conception of the distinction between what can be said and what cannot be said but only shown, his later critical investigations into the bounds of sense led to the repudiation of metaphysics, effable or ineffable. Ethics and religion were conceived naturalistically or anthropologically as aspects of a form of life, ultimately beyond rational foundation or justification. The investigation into the limits of language no longer intimated a domain of ineffable truth beyond those limits, which nevertheless shows itself in the forms of language. There is nothing ineffable about ethics, aesthetics and religion, but a proper understanding of ethical, aesthetic or religious utterances requires an apprehension of their role within the distinctive form of life or culture to which they belong. The bounds of sense fence us in only from the void of nonsense. Philosophy as it were keeps the account books of grammar, and its task is to point out to us when we are drawing a draft on currency that does not exist.

The second sense in which Wittgenstein's philosophy is critical is complementary to the first. Critical philosophy is also concerned with what Kant called the 'critique of dialectical illusion', the systematic criticism of the 'logic of illusion'. Analogously to Kant, Wittgenstein was a remorseless critic of the philosophical illusions that result when the bounds of sense are inadvertently transgressed. He criticized behaviourism and dualism in the philosophy of psychology, savaged Platonism and intuitionism in the philosophy of mathematics, and undermined foundationalism in epistemology and in philosophy of language. He rejected the pretensions of metaphysics to give us insights into the allegedly language-independent essences of things, and repudiated the venerable belief that logic is a field of knowledge of the relations between abstract objects. He condemned as illusion the idea that the subjective and mental is essentially better known than the objective, and denied that the subject has privileged access to his own consciousness. In each such case, his criticisms are not haphazard, but, like Kant's dialectical critique, focus upon failures to accord with the conditions of sense and upon illicit extensions of the uses of expressions beyond their legitimate domains. Because the use of the first-person pronoun does not refer to the body and seems immune to misidentification and reference failure, we are prone to think of it as referring unerringly to a Cartesian ego with which we are intimately acquainted, inhabiting the body but distinct from it. Here we illegitimately extend the rules concerning reference and identification for the use of the other-personal pronouns to the first-person pronoun, failing to see that the use of 'I' standardly involves no identification at all and at best only a degenerate form of reference. We are inclined to think of the mind as a private domain of objects of subjective experience, which each person inalienably possesses, to which he has privileged access and of which he has privileged knowledge. Here we illegitimately extend the distinction between numerical and qualitative identity, which applies to material objects, to experiences – where there is no such distinction – and erroneously infer that two people cannot have the very same experience. And we mistakenly extrapolate from the use of the epistemic operator 'I know' upon such third-person, present tense, psychological propositions as 'he is in pain (believes such and such, thinks thus and so, expects, wants, etc.)' to the first-person case, and wrongly conclude that 'I know I am in pain' adds something more than emphasis to 'I am in pain'. We mistake the grammatical exclusion of doubt from a subclass of first-person psychological propositions such as 'I am in pain' for the satisfaction of criteria for certainty, and jump to the conclusion that such propositions are paradigms of certainty. And so forth.

It is easy to get the impression that Wittgenstein is the paradigmatically destructive philosopher, an impression to which he himself sometimes succumbed and indeed sometimes cultivated. In an apocalyptic passage in his diary of 1931, he wrote 'If my name survives, then only as the *terminus ad quem* of the great philosophy of the West. As the name of him who burnt the library of Alexandria, (Wittgenstein 1997: 37). Later that year we still find him saying to himself: 'I destroy, I destroy, I destroy' (CV: 21). This is understandable in view of the fact that the years 1929–31 were the period during which he dismantled the *Tractatus* and with it the understanding of metaphysics, ontology and logic[1] that had informed the great tradition of European philosophy. But despite the fact that over the next fifteen years he did a great deal of constructive elucidatory work in philosophy, much the same negative tinge is retained in his final masterpiece, the *Philosophical Investigations*. For he there queries:

> Where does our investigation get its importance from, since it seems only to destroy everything interesting, that is, all that is great and important? (As it were all the buildings, leaving behind only bits of stone and rubble.) What we are destroying is nothing but houses of cards and we are clearing up the ground of language on which they stand.
>
> (PI §118)

It is unsurprising that many of his readers concluded that his aim was wholly destructive, that what Moritz Schlick had hailed as 'the turning point of philosophy' (*die Wende der Philosophie*) was in effect 'the terminal point of philosophy' (*das Ende der Philosophie*).[2]

It is not difficult to defend Wittgenstein against this charge. Even if his philosophy were wholly negative and destructive, the critical task of philosophy can have no terminus as long as mankind is prone to fall into conceptual confusion, either in philosophical thought or in science, mathematics and the humanities. And since there can be no way of circumscribing the conceptual confusions which may distort human thinking or of predicting in advance fresh sources of conceptual entanglement which may emerge from a culture, there will be no end to the need for philosophical criticism.

However, despite his own pronouncements, Wittgenstein's philosophy also has a complementary constructive aspect to it, which he himself acknowledged. Side by side with his demolition of philosophical illusion in logic, mathematics and philosophy of psychology, he gives us numerous overviews of the logical grammar of problematic concepts, painstakingly tracing conceptual connections which we are all too prone to overlook. The conceptual geology of the *Tractatus* gave way to the conceptual topography of the *Investigations*. In place of the depth analysis envisaged by the *Tractatus*, he now described the uses of expressions, the various forms of their context dependence, the manner in which they are integrated in behaviour, the point and presuppositions of their use, and their relations of implication, compatibility or incompatibility with other expressions. Such a 'connective analysis'[3] of philosophically problematic concepts which give rise to philosophical perplexity aims to give us an overview of the use of our words. 'The concept of a perspicuous representation', he wrote, 'is of fundamental significance for us' (PI §122): it produces precisely that understanding which consists in seeing connections, and enables us to find our way through the web of language, entanglement in which is characteristic of conceptual confusion and philosophical perplexity. Providing such a perspicuous representation of some segment of our language, elucidating the conceptual forms and structures of some domain of human thought that is philosophically problematic is a positive, constructive achievement which is complementary to the critical and destructive task of shattering philosophical illusion, destroying philosophical mythology and dispelling conceptual confusion.

However, there is a further aspect to the philosophy of the later Wittgenstein which is in no sense destructive and negative. On the contrary, it betokens a trenchant attempt to protect and conserve a domain of knowledge and form of understanding from erosion and distortion by the scientific spirit of the age. For one may see Wittgenstein's philosophical endeavours as a defence of the autonomy of humanistic understanding against the illegitimate encroachment of the natural sciences. By 'humanistic studies' (*Geisteswissenschaften*) is to be understood the range of intellectual disciplines that study man as a cultural, social and historical being. This includes parts of psychology and linguistics, history, anthropology and the social sciences, as well as those disciplines that study the cultural products of man, such as the study of literature and the arts. I shall use the term 'humanistic understanding' to refer to the distinctive forms of explanation and understanding characteristic of humanistic studies. By 'scientism', I understand the *illicit* extension of the methods and forms of explanation of the natural sciences. Not all extensions of the methods and forms of explanation of the natural sciences to the study of man as a cultural, social and historical being are misconceived. But some are; and so too is the doctrine of the methodological homogeneity of scientific and humanistic understanding.

The doctrine of the Unity of Science, vigorously propounded by the logical positivists earlier this century with roots in nineteenth-century positivism and in earlier post-Cartesian mechanism, is a form of scientism. In its most extreme form it is reductive. The envisaged reduction may be logical or only ontological. The heyday of logical reduction in philosophy coincided with behaviourism in psychology and linguistics that flourished in the inter-war years of the last century. *Logical* behaviourism was a philosophical, not a psychological, doctrine. Where Watsonian eliminative behaviourism in psychology treated the mental as a fiction, logical behaviourism held that statements about the mental are *reducible* to statements about behaviour and dispositions to behave. The former treated the mental as if it were on a par with witches or dragons, the latter treated talk of the mental as if it were comparable to talk of the average man. Ontological reduction characterizes much contemporary philosophy of psychology. It is exhibited by the various forms of physicalism currently rife, which deny the translatability of psychological statements into non-psychological statements, but affirm the contingent identity of the psychological with the neural.

A non-reductive form of scientism is methodological. On that view, even

42

though social and psychological phenomena are not logically or ontologically reducible, even in principle, to physical phenomena, the logical structure of explanation in humanistic studies, in particular the explanation of human thought and action, is the same as that of typical explanations in the natural sciences. Accordingly, common or garden psychological explanation of thought and action is causal, and a fully scientific understanding of human behaviour requires knowledge of causes and of the underlying causal laws that determine it. These underlying causal laws may be conceived to be psychological or socio-historical (as in Hume, Mill or Comte) or physicalist, and hence taken to describe regularities of neural or abstract computational mechanisms. If so, then the whole field of the study of man as a cultural being, hence as a language using social and historical being, is methodologically of a piece with the study of nature. The physicalist version of this methodological thesis is currently common among philosophers.

Wittgenstein was not, by and large, directly concerned with the general question of the status of the study of man in the humanistic disciplines. His main preoccupation throughout his philosophical career was with the nature of representation, in particular linguistic representation – hence with meaning and intentionality. This general concern led him to investigations into psychological concepts and the logical character of explanations of human action. The results of these enquiries have, and have been seen to have, profound implications for the humanities.[4] In this sense it can be said that Wittgenstein provides guidelines for a kind of philosophical anthropology and hence the foundations for the philosophical understanding of humanistic studies. To this extent, his work constitutes a much needed bulwark against the illegitimate encroachment of science upon those disciplines which are concerned with understanding ourselves, our culture and society.

Since the achievements of Western science are among the intellectual glories of mankind, and since science is above all a vindication of the power of reason and observation to render the world we inhabit intelligible to us, it may seem atavistic to accuse science of trespassing upon territory inappropriate for it. How can there be any domain of experience which is not a subject for rational enquiry? And is not the spirit of scientific enquiry precisely that of rational investigation? If so, can it be limited within the sphere of the pursuit of knowledge and understanding? Does not the tradition of Western science spring from the very same sources as the tradition of Western humanism? And if so, how can there be conflict between them? I shall suggest answers to these questions in this chapter. In the second section, I shall give a synoptic view of the emergence of Renaissance humanism and the rise of modern science in the seventeenth century, of the manner in which the subsequent development of humanism, in the modern sense of the word, was initially allied with science in combatting irrationality and dogma. In the third section, I shall survey the development of the doctrine of the Unity of Science and the manner in which the methodology of the study of man became swamped by the model of scientific understanding. In the fourth section, I shall sketch some of the dissenting views in the eighteenth and nineteenth centuries, which insisted on the autonomy of humanistic understanding, views which were not heeded by mainstream reflection upon methodology. Thereafter, I shall adumbrate Wittgenstein's philosophy of language and philosophy of mind and action in order to show how his investigations give sound reasons for insistence upon the autonomy of humanistic understanding and repudiation of the doctrine of the unity of science. There are forms of rational enquiry that are not scientific, forms of understanding that are not modelled upon the scientific understanding of natural phenomena. Understanding man as a cultural and social being involves categories and forms of understanding and explanation alien to the natural sciences. There are other domains of enquiry of which that it is also true, for example, aesthetic understanding, understanding of myth and ritual, as well as philosophical understanding. These will not be discussed.

Humanism, science and the study of man

The term 'humanism' is of nineteenth-century origin, first in Germany (*Humanismus*) and later in Britain. It was used initially to refer to the spirit of the Renaissance humanists, who, beginning with Petrarch, revived classical learning and transformed the cultural self-consciousness of Europe. The *umanisti* revived the study of classical philosophy, literature, history and law. They advocated and practised the teaching of *studia humanitatis*, which was a course of classical studies consisting of grammar, poetry, rhetoric, ancient history and moral philosophy. The name was based on the Ciceronian educational, cultural and political ideal of *humanitas*, the development of the human excellences in all their forms, inspired by classical culture.

Renaissance humanism was not merely a scholarly movement of retrieval of ancient texts. Rather it pursued the rebirth of a cultural ideal of life, which would inform not only a distinctive *vita contemplativa* of literary and philosophical scholarship, but a *vita activa* informed by the ideals the *umanisti* discerned in the literary, and later also the artistic, remains of the classical world. It is no coincidence that the *umanisti* flourished not in the existing universities, but in Renaissance courts and academies set up for educational purposes at those courts. Nor is it a coincidence that the ideal of *humanitas*, of the classically educated man of civic virtue, was reborn in a republic (such as Florence) rather than a monarchy.

The retrieval, translation and editing of classical texts was due to the labours of the *umanisti* and the Byzantine scholars who fled to the West in the fifteenth century. Their work established standards of philological scholarship and a concern for studying original texts without the mediation of commentaries which was in due course to affect Biblical studies, encouraging the study of Hebrew and Greek in order to read the original texts rather than the Vulgate. Long-lost philosophical texts became available in the West for the first time since antiquity. The retrieval of the Platonic corpus is due to the labours of the humanists, as is the revival of ancient scepticism and of Stoic ethics. The writings of Roman poets, rhetoricians and historians not only stimulated Renaissance poetry and literature, as well as the writing of contemporary history, but provided models for them.

The endeavour was above all directed at a rebirth of, and application of, the wisdom of the ancients. Ancient history was studied not only for its own sake but also for the examples of virtue which it supplied in abundance and for the statecraft that could, it was thought, be learned from it and applied to the present. The study of Roman law revolutionized jurisprudence from the renaissance onwards. Ancient medical treatises, in particular Galen, were (on the whole unfortunately) influential, and anatomical research recommenced (for example, by Leonardo and Vesalius). Classical texts on mathematics were likewise stimuli to fruitful fresh endeavour, after a hiatus of almost a thousand years in the West. Alberti, who advanced applied mathematics in the art of projective perspective, in architectural engineering, in cartography and in cryptography, held mathematics to be the key to all sciences; Vittorino made it central to his pedagogical programme at Mantua; and, in the sixteenth century, Cardano advanced algebra.

Renaissance humanism contributed to the emergent individualism of the late fourteenth and fifteenth-century Italian city-states associated with the rise of the mercantile classes. The revival of the study of the intellectual heritage of the ancient world moulded the conception of humanity that informed the quickening intellectual life of the time. That reality is rational, that the power of human reason can render the world intelligible, that the pursuit of knowledge of the empirical world accords with the dignity of man, celebrated by Gianozzo Manetti and Pico della Mirandola, and is a constituent of the good life – these were important lessons the Renaissance learned from the culture of antiquity. The free intellect of man was glorified and its employment in enquiry into the natural world and into human society was conceived to be a requirement of cultivated man. Man was accorded a dignity, unique in nature, of moulding his destiny according to his choice. The Socratic ideal of self-knowledge and self-understanding was revived as a constituent of the life appropriate to the dignity of a morally autonomous being (see Petrarch, and, much later, Montaigne). It is no coincidence that autobiography was revived in the Renaissance (for example, by Alberti, Cardano, Cellini), and that the art of biography flourished as it had not done since antiquity. This humano-centrism marks a profound shift in sensibility relative to the Middle Ages. Nonetheless, it was not perceived to be at odds with, but complementary to, the ideals of Christianity. And it gave rise in subsequent centuries to a 'humanism' in a different sense of the term, signifying not only humano-centrism, but also an advocacy of the study of mankind, of the understanding of man and his works, which can be gained from knowledge of human history and the history of human institutions, and from the philosophical investigations (not distinguished from psychological investigations until the end of the nineteenth century) into human nature, the scope and limits of human understanding and the foundations of morality.

Despite the growing interest in the natural world in the fifteenth and sixteenth centuries, and despite great advances in technologically oriented and applied sciences, such as architecture, fortification, shipbuilding, navigation and cartography, the development of theoretical science lagged behind. The two theoretical sciences that were at the centre of Renaissance interests were astronomy, which was still inextricably interwoven with astrology, and alchemy, which only much later produced chemistry as a legitimate offspring. The conflation and confusion of magic and science were reinforced by Ficino's influential translation of the *Corpus Hermeticum*, mistakenly attributed to the mythological figure of Hermes Trismegistos, and revered by the neo-Platonists. The scientific revolution only gathered pace in the early seventeenth century, after the flowering of the Renaissance was over. With Kepler and Galileo, mathematical physics was advanced and physical astronomy was invented, replacing the merely mathematical astronomy which saved but did not explain appearances. *Laws* of nature, expressible in mathematical terms, were discovered, unifying and explaining disparate phenomena in supra- and sub-lunary nature alike. These advances, coupled with new astronomical observations, shattered Aristotelian cosmology. The classical teleological conception of the cosmos was displaced in favour of a mechanistic conception, and final causation discarded from scientific theory in favour of efficient causation. The laws of nature were no longer seen as constitutive of a cosmic *normative* order, of which humanity and human society were a part. Nature was now envisaged on the model of clockwork, intelligible in the language of mathematical and geometrical physics. It was, to be sure, still thought of as exhibiting design in its laws, but only in the sense that clockwork does (it was left to the philosophers of the Enlightenment, such as Hume, to reject this teleological residue). The order of nature, as studied and understood by the new science, is conceived to be a mechanical order, not a teleological and normative one. Solar centrism demoted man from the centre of the universe. This was in due course, after some appalling persecution (such as the immolation of Giordano Bruno and condemnation of Galileo), accommodated without excessive strain. For the insights of the new sciences into the machinery of the universe also glorified the power of human reason to fathom the handiwork of the Great Geometer, and indirectly confirmed man's favoured relation to God. Nonetheless, the shift to mechanistic science contained within itself the seeds of a new and irreligious answer to the question of man's place in nature, seeds which grew to fruition in the nineteenth century.

To be sure, mechanism was hotly disputed by vitalists. Some, such as the Cambridge Platonists, denied that mechanism could even explain the phenomena of physics, arguing instead that spirit alone explains *activity* in nature – matter being essentially inert and passive, and invoked the non-conscious spiritual substance of 'Plastick Nature' (Cudworth) or the 'Spirit of Nature' (Henry More). More lastingly, vitalists denied that mechanism could explain life, and rejected the Cartesian reduction of biology to physics. It was not until the twentieth century that vitalism was given its quietus by advances in biochemistry and molecular biology.

The scientific revolution had two great philosophical spokesmen: Bacon and Descartes. Both were concerned with demarcating the proper domain of science and elaborating its methodological foundations. Bacon was the ideological prophet of a scientific technology that would be put to use in the endeavour to ameliorate the human condition. His far-seeing prophecies were not fulfilled until the eighteenth century. For the early strides forward in technology were in the production of scientific instruments, pendulum clocks, telescopes, microscopes, barometers, thermometers – useful primarily in the pursuit of further knowledge (and navigation), rather than in easing man's estate. But from the eighteenth century until the present, Bacon's vision of productive technology has been confirmed beyond his wildest dreams, with destructive and disruptive consequences to both nature and society which he did *not* foresee. Knowledge, his famous slogan declared, is power – power to control and manipulate nature to human ends. The manipulative craving was ancient, and manifest in the magical and cabalistic doctrines of the Renaissance, in alchemy and astrology. What was novel, by contrast with the esotericism of Renaissance magi, was Bacon's recognition of the need for cooperative scientific research and the sharing of scientific knowledge (duly realized by the establishment of the Royal Society), and his insight into the relation between scientific (mechanical), rather than magical (animist), knowledge of nature and technological advance. For knowledge of laws of nature is also the foundation for knowledge of technical norms guiding the technological manipulation of nature. He was also the ideologist of experimental and inductive method. Descartes likewise envisaged a science that will make us 'the lords and masters of nature' (Descartes, 1911 Part vi: 119), but, by contrast with Bacon, he was the philosophical spokesman for rationalism in science. With hindsight, the conflict between them was only apparent. From our perspective (although not from theirs), each stressed different elements of science which we now recognize to be equally important. Inductivism and experimentalism on the one hand, and rationalist abstraction from the data of experience on the other, are complementary faces of theoretical science as it has developed in the West. Mere observation and correlation of phenomena without the abstraction requisite for mathematicization is blind to the underlying laws of nature, while rationalist, a priori abstraction is empty without observation and experiment aided by instrumentation and measurement.

Just as the Renaissance humanists did not see themselves as challenging the truths of Christianity but as complementing them, so too the heroic figures of seventeenth century science did not conceive of their discoveries or of the picture of the cosmos that they elaborated as challenging religion. On the contrary, they thought of themselves as reading the handiwork of God inscribed in the language of mathematics in the book of nature (see Galileo, 1623). The pursuit of knowledge of nature was a glorification of God, and so the fulfilment of human destiny as conceived by Christianity. Indeed, it has been argued that *Judaeo*-Christian monotheism, by contrast with Chinese Confucianism which eschewed reflection on transcendent reality and with Indian Hinduism which viewed the empirical world as mere *maya* (illusion), was the ideal seedbed for theoretical science (Quinton 1998). It accepted the reality and importance of the natural world while affirming the existence of a supernatural order. Behind the flux of experience, it envisaged a single omnipotent intelligence, Creator of the natural world in accordance with an intelligible design. That design is constituted by the laws of nature, which are mathematical. Scientific knowledge can be achieved by penetrating beneath mere appearances to disclose the hidden mathematical patterns of the Creator's design which determine the diversity and the dynamics of the perceptible world.

Nevertheless, the Renaissance humanists' outlook and the world view of the new science were, in due course, bound to generate conflict with the Christian vision of the day. The Renaissance humanists' classicizing interests were overwhelmingly secular, no matter how much they strove to reconcile the classical heritage with Christianity. Their philological scholarship inevitably endorsed challenges to the received interpretations of sacred texts. And their intellectual individualism encouraged the questioning of Catholic doctrine that was duly unleashed by the rise of Protestantism. Similarly, even though the new science did not arise with the intent of challenging religion, it was inevitable that it would clash with pre-scientific dogmas espoused by the church. It was unfair, but sapient, of Pascal to have observed:

> I cannot forgive Descartes. In all his philosophy he would have been quite willing to dispense with God. But he had to make him give a fillip to set the world in motion; beyond this, he has no further need of God.

> (Pascal 1669 §77)

The tensions were latent from an early stage. They became patent in the eighteenth-century age of Enlightenment, when deism seemed to the first generation of the *philosophes* the attractive alternative to a reactionary church and Christian doctrines. (The third and last generation of Enlightenment thinkers tended towards atheism, and, unlike their predecessors, inclined towards utilitarianism rather than natural law theory.) A far more fundamental challenge, not merely to Christianity but to religion in general, was presented in the nineteenth century with the advent of the theory of evolution. For Darwin's explanation of the evolution of species by natural selection gave a scientific, naturalist answer to the question of man's place in nature.

From the Enlightenment to the twentieth century, science and the forms of humanism (in the modern sense of the term) that evolved in the wake of the Renaissance humanists were allied against authoritarianism in doctrine, despotism in political practice, and irrationality as well as inhumanity in socio-political arrangements. By the twentieth century, the authority of religion on matters of fact had waned. The description and explanation of the natural world was the province of science. Religion still claimed authority from its adherents on matters of value and norm, while scientists were, on the whole, content to conceive of their disciplines as value free and of their discoveries as value neutral offerings to a society at liberty to use the resultant scientific knowledge and technology as it pleased.

As the twentieth century advanced, rifts opened between the spirit and methods of the natural sciences and the humanistic spirit with which they had hitherto been allied. These rifts are manifest today in various forms – in the erosion of humanistic values and the decline of high culture, in the transformation of conceptions of the value of education and its harnessing to the needs of post-industrial society, and in the devaluation of the role of the humanities in education – under pressure from economic forces released by advanced scientific technology. They are exhibited in the growing realization of the mortal danger of the power of knowledge unrestrained by understanding of humanity. They are also patent at the theoretical and intellectual level of the methodology of understanding human nature and the activities of mankind, in the view that the study of man is of a piece with the study of nature. Here too the fault lines are, with hindsight, visible from the inception of the transformation of Western culture by the Renaissance and scientific revolution.

Scientism and the doctrine of the unity of science

Descartes fostered the vision of the Unity of Science, with metaphysics as the root of all knowledge, physics the trunk, and medicine, mechanics and morals the branches. His invention of co-ordinate geometry encouraged him in his opposition to the Aristotelian conception of the methodological autonomy and irreducibility of different sciences (such as arithmetic and geometry). He denied Aristotle's claim that each science has standards of explanation and precision unique to itself, insisting instead upon the methodological unity of the sciences. His assimilation of the biological sciences to mechanics, and his conviction that micro phenomena wholly explain macro phenomena of the physical world, broke with Aristotelian anti-reductionist tradition. He denied that the soul is the form of the living body and rejected the Aristotelian conception of the vegetative and sensitive souls as necessary to explain vegetable and animal life. The limits of Cartesian mechanism lie at the portals of the mind. But Descartes redefined the mental in terms of consciousness and thought, the latter including subjective perception (seeming to perceive), sensation, pleasure and pain, mental images, emotion as well as intellectual activity and will. This contrasts with the Aristotelian and scholastic conception, which took the mind to be defined not in terms of consciousness but in terms of rationality, hence confined to the intellect and will. But three points are noteworthy. First, Descartes's mechanist successors in the eighteenth century (such as La Mettrie and d'Holbach) envisaged no such limitation to the proper domain of mechanist explanation, any more than did his contemporary, Hobbes. Second, Descartes had no philosophy of the historical and social sciences. His obliviousness to the latter is understandable in the context of his times, for the social sciences, as opposed to political theorizing and reflections on statecraft, did not yet exist. His contemptuous dismissal of history (Descartes, 1637, Part I: 84-85)) is more surprising, though intelligible in as much as the study of history is neither reducible to relations between simple natures nor explicable in terms of interaction of micro particles. Hence it lacks the explanatory forms of science and its mathematicization, and cannot hope to achieve the kind of certainty Descartes demanded of genuine scientific knowledge. Third, while he acknowledged freedom of the will, he envisaged the relation between volition and action as causal. By implication, the forms of explanation of human behaviour will be nomological, to the extent that causation is so conceived.

By the eighteenth century, the discovery of laws of nature had sufficiently advanced to make the idea of *laws of the operations of the mind* compelling. 'May we not hope', Hume wrote:

> that philosophy, if cultivated with care...may...discover, at least in some degree, the secret springs and principles, by which the human mind is actuated in its operations?...[Newton] seems, from the happiest of reasoning, to have also determined the laws and forces, by which the revolutions of the planets are governed and directed. The like has been performed with regard to other parts of nature. And there is no reason to despair of equal success in our enquiries concerning the mental powers and economy, if prosecuted with equal capacity and caution.
>
> (Hume 1748, section I: 14)

Hume's ambition was, indeed, to be a Newton of the mental sciences. In the first flush of youthful enthusiasm, he saw the operations of association of ideas as the psychological analogue of gravitation. Nomological regularity seemed as much a prerequisite of intelligibility in the domain of the psychological as in the domain of the physical. The laws of human nature are universal and trans-historical. 'It is universally acknowledged', he wrote:

> that there is a great uniformity among the actions of men, in all nations and ages, and that human nature remains still the same, in its principles and operations. The same motives always produce the same actions: the same events follow from the same causes...Mankind are so much the same, in all times and places, that history informs us of nothing new or strange in this particular. Its chief use is only to discover the constant and universal principles of human nature, by showing men in all varieties of circumstances and situations, and furnishing us with materials from which we may form our observations and become acquainted with the regular springs of human actions and behaviour.
>
> (Hume 1748, section viii, part I: 83)

The idea that there are laws of mental association seemed to hold out the promise of a genuine science of the human mind. That thought inspired a host of eighteenth and nineteenth-century thinkers, such as Hartley, Brown, the Mills and Bain. Indeed, it was this very vision that informed the rise of experimental psychology at the end of the nineteenth century with Wundt's introspectionist psychology. The conception of voluntary human action that had dominated thought from Hobbes and Descartes to the twentieth century was causal – a voluntary act is a bodily movement caused by a mental act of volition. How the mind could interact causally with the body was, to be sure, obscure – an obscurity hardly unveiled by the short lived Cartesian theory of interaction via the pineal gland. By the nineteenth century, the received explanation was in terms of kinaesthetic sensations, images of which guide the will in generating voluntary movements. Wundt, Bain, Helmholtz and Mach held that in addition to an image of the kinaesthetic sensation correlated in past experience with the desiderated movement, there must also be a feeling of innervation or impulse, an efferent sensation of volitional energy correlated with electrical currents directed to the appropriate muscles. Nascent neurophysiology was clumsily married to venerable, though misguided, philosophical analyses of voluntary action. The mental came to seem explanatorily redundant: the real explanations of behaviour must lie at the neurophysiological level. Hence if there are any *laws* of behaviour, they must be physiological, and ultimately physical, laws. It is, therefore, not surprising that the developments in neurophysiological psychology in the second half of the nineteenth century gave impetus to forms of epiphenomenalism (see, for example, T.H. Huxley). Advances in the neurosciences in the second half of the twentieth century similarly stimulated a corresponding marginalization of the mental, encouraging the thought that the true explanation of human behaviour is to be found at the neural level or at the level of non-conscious computational operations which have a neural realization.

The explosive growth of empirical psychology in the first decades of the twentieth century included the emergence of both radical (eliminative) and more moderate (methodological) behaviourism among psychologists reacting against the introspective psychology of the previous generation. Eliminative behaviourists, as noted, treated consciousness as a fiction. Methodological behaviourists eschewed subjective reports of mental states, under the misapprehension that such reports rest on introspection, conceived as subjective perception of inner states. Introspection, thus (mis)conceived, was held to fail the test of intersubjective verifiability, and hence to provide unreliable data for an objective science of psychology. Behaviourism dominated experimental psychology in the Anglophone world until the 1950s. It was displaced by the cognitivist revolution, which was intended to reinstate the psyche in psychology and the legitimacy of the empirical study of 'cognitive processes'. Ironically, this transformation coincided with the invention of the computer, the rise of computer sciences and the emergence of Chomsky's novel, eminently computerizable, theory of syntax, the rules of which the 'mind/brain' was supposed to 'cognize', even if the person did not. Hence the favoured conception of cognitive acts or activities became that of algorithmic information processing, and the study of the mind turned to the construction of models of unobserved but hypothesized cognitive processes in accordance with algorithmic transformations allegedly operated by the brain. Consequently, psychological theory was not so much humanized as computerized, a trend which cohered with neurophysiological developments on the one hand, in particular with the discovery of the functional architecture of the 'visual' striate cortex, and with engineering advances in information theory and artificial intelligence on the other.[5]

The social sciences were late advents upon the scene of Western culture. Just as the rise of the natural sciences in the seventeenth century had an ideologist in Bacon, the rise of the social sciences in the nineteenth century found its ideologist in Auguste Comte. His contribution to the social sciences was as negligible as Bacon's to the natural sciences. But his positivist vision of the character of the study of man as a social being was influential. Every science, he thought, must go through successive theological, metaphysical and positive phases. The several sciences are hierarchically related. The study of society is the last of the sciences to reach the maturity of a positive phase. 'Sociology', or 'social physics' as Quételet had called it, presupposes the antecedent sciences of mathematics, astronomy, physics, chemistry and biology. Its methodology is in essence no different from the inductive methodology of the other sciences. It studies the laws of the functioning of social wholes ('social statics'), just as biology studies the functioning of organic wholes, and it aims to discover the laws of social development ('social dynamics') as biology aims to discover the laws of biological development. The idea that there are 'iron laws' of social change, which it is the task of the social sciences to discover, informed nineteenth-century social theories, both Marxist and social Darwinist. Mill, who unlike Marx was a methodological individualist, likewise held the task of social science to discover general laws of social change. For 'if...the phenomena of human thought, feeling and action are subject to fixed laws, the phenomena of society cannot but conform to fixed laws, the consequence of the preceding' (Mill 1852, Book VI, ch. 6: 548-49). At the end of the century, Durkheim advocated the idea that:

> social life should be explained, not by the notions of those who participate in it, but by the more profound causes which are unperceived by consciousness...Only in this way, it seems, can history become a science, and sociology itself exist.
>
> (Durkheim 1897)

Internal incoherences were patent. Comte insisted upon invariable laws of social change, but also advocated the formation of a new religion of humanity and a new clergy of a scientific-industrial elite to guide history down the paths which he predicted it must inevitably follow. Marx insisted upon the historical inevitability of the law-governed transformation of society, while simultaneously advocating the need for determined participation in the class struggle. Social Darwinists insisted upon the iron laws of the survival of the fittest, while advocating social policies the adoption of which would ensure the dominance of the bourgeoisie. Freud preached a form of psychological determinism, while presenting psychoanalysis as a mode of liberation from the forces of the unconscious.

The transformation of Western consciousness, which commenced with the Renaissance, was deepened by the scientific revolution and swept triumphantly forward during the Enlightenment, was meant to liberate man from the shackles of dogma, moribund tradition and unreason, and to lead to the full realization of the capacities of humanity. Knowledge of nature and knowledge of human nature alike were envisaged as being within the powers of man. Achievement of the former would lead to mastery of the natural world, achievement of the latter to mastery of human nature. Mastery of the natural world would be manifest in control and manipulation of nature by technology. Mastery of human nature would be manifest not in control and manipulation of mankind, but in moral improvement through self-knowledge and self-understanding. However, the conception of what understanding of man consists in, of the character of knowledge and understanding in the study of man, of the distinctive nature of the forms of explanation in the humanistic studies, became obscured and then swamped by the forms of understanding and explanation characteristic of the natural sciences. The operations of the mind were first envisaged as subject to law in the same sense as the operations of nature. Psychological determinism, and subsequently neurophysiological determinism, were advocated. Behaviourism sought for laws of human behaviour which would explain and predict human action non-intentionalistically. And the demise of behaviourism led to a computationalist conception of the human mind which was modelled on the pattern of the machines invented by man. Paradoxically, the understanding of man in anthropomorphic terms was held to be illusory, or merely superficial.

Dissenting voices

There were dissenting voices in the eighteenth and nineteenth centuries. Vico had been a lone voice insisting upon the methodological distinctiveness of the study of man and combatting the Cartesian idea that *scientia* is possible only with regard to what is clearly and distinctly conceived, in particular with regard to mathematical descriptions of the mechanical workings of nature. On the contrary, Vico claimed boldly, although we can attain true knowledge in the domain of mathematics, that is because *we have made it*. But we cannot truly understand nature. Were we able to attain that true knowledge of nature which God alone possesses, we should be creating it – *Si physica demonstrare possemus, faceremus*. For *Verum et factum convertuntur* – 'the true and the made are convertible'. History, art, civil society and its institutions, unlike nature, are made by man and can be understood and known by man in a manner in which true knowledge of nature is inaccessible in principle to him. For the mode of investigation and consequent knowledge of the activities and products of man is altogether unlike the modes of investigation appropriate to the natural sciences. It involves *fantasia*, reconstructive imagination, the endeavour to enter into the minds of other peoples belonging to past times and earlier phases of culture, to see the world through their eyes and in terms of their categories of thought. This is to be done by studying their languages, their mythologies and poetry, their laws and customs, their monuments and rituals. However, Vico's revolutionary 'transvaluation of Cartesian values' went unheeded until he was rediscovered by Michelet in the nineteenth century.

Kant insisted upon a categorial difference between determination of events by causes and the 'determination' of human action by reasons, between the laws of causality and the laws of freedom. The concept of human agency, he argued, concepts of moral action and hence of moral responsibility, of autonomy and hence of doing and being good or evil, are essentially bound up with the form of freedom that is presupposed by behaviour that is 'self-determined' by reasons. That in turn implied a radical difference between the understanding and explanation of natural events in causal terms and the understanding and explanation of human behaviour in terms of reasons. But in the attempt to propound a form of compatibilism, to reconcile the inescapable conception of man as part of the order of nature with the equally necessary conception of man as a self-determining autonomous being, he wrapped these distinctions up in an incoherent dichotomy between a noumenal and phenomenal realm. Kant set the agenda for subsequent efforts to clarify what is distinctive about humanity that makes us both part of the natural order and yet also autonomous, a task with which we are still struggling.

Many of the ideas that are to be found, chaotically expressed and interwoven with wild speculation, in Vico's *The New Science* emerged again, apparently quite independently, in the writings of the post-Kantian German counter-Enlightenment. Like Vico, Herder repudiated the conception of human nature as static, trans-historical, fixed irrespective of time and place. This conception had informed the attempts of Renaissance historians such as Machiavelli to derive universal principles of statecraft from the study of the ancients; it was explicitly articulated in Hume's vision of a science of man; and it was shared by the *philosophes* of the Enlightenment. By contrast, Herder argued that human nature is essentially historically and culturally determined. The claim that man is essentially an historical being is to be understood as implying, *inter alia*, that human nature is plastic and changeable, moulded by socio-historical circumstances and national self-consciousness. Forms of thought and action, laws, social organizations and institutions which were appropriate in ancient Athens or Rome are neither possible nor appropriate for modern nations. Moreover, they are not to be understood in terms of the categories of modernity. The mentalities of the Jews of antiquity, of the ancient Greeks or of the Romans are not just phases in the linear unfolding of a trans-historical rationality, stages in the progress of mankind towards the Enlightenment and its ideals. Each nation has its own genius, its own forms of expression, its own conception of reality, which are not more or less primitive approximations to the rationalist world view of the Enlightenment. Hence to understand earlier or alien cultures, indeed, to understand human beings, their thought and works, human institutions, literature or art, requires *Einfühlung*, 'entering into', the subject in question in its social and cultural context.

The idea that there is a special 'Kunst des Verstehen' was elaborated by German theologians in the early nineteenth century, above all by Schleiermacher, whom Dilthey later characterized as the founder of systematic, methodologically self-conscious hermeneutics. His concern with the methodology of Biblical interpretation led him to much more general reflections on textual understanding. The nature of understanding, he thought, needs to be fathomed not only in cases of exegetically problematic passages, because contradictory or apparently nonsensical, but quite generally. For, he insisted, 'I understand nothing which I cannot apprehend as necessary and which I cannot construct myself' (the accidental echo of Vico's principle is striking). A text is the product of a particular individual, employing the symbolism of a language of a people, in specific historical circumstances, giving expression to his thoughts as formed within the context of the specific ways in which he views the world. The 'art of understanding' therefore recognizes a duality in all expression of thought, its relation to the totality of the language in which it is expressed and its relation to the totality of the thought of its author. Hence hermeneutics has two aspects, grammatical interpretation and psychological-technical interpretation. The former is concerned with the language of the text, with elucidating its syntax, meaning, style, genre, and their roots in the life and world view of a culture. The latter is concerned with the text as an expression of the individual mind of its author, the product of his individual world view. This requires a form of intuitive insight, an 'act of divination', a sensitivity to the movements of thought of another's mind, indeed a striving to understand an author better than he understood himself.

The self-conscious hermeneutical reflections of the German theologians provided stimulus for philosophers and philosophers of history later in the nineteenth century, such as Windelband, Rickerts and Dilthey. It was Dilthey above all who made familiar the distinction between the explanation (*Erklärung*) of scientific phenomena and the understanding (*Verstehen*) demanded by historical and social phenomena, and who advocated the principle that 'the methodology of the human studies is...different from that of the physical sciences'. We experience life as meaningful, see the actions of those around us as imbued with purpose and value, apprehend the past as significant, interpret life in terms of categories richer than the Kantian categories of sensible experience, for example in terms of the inner and outer (mental content and its expression), in terms of human powers to affect things, in terms of means and ends, of value, purpose and meaning. Understanding the phenomena of human life requires empathetic understanding, knowledge of the historical context and of the social and cultural systems in which they are embedded, and interpretation of the forms of thought of the participants. Dilthey's conception of understanding informed the sociological theories and methodology of Weber, who similarly insisted upon the autonomy of sociological understanding.

Nevertheless, such dissenting voices were a minority, and their insights, often confusedly and confusingly expressed, proved difficult to assimilate and to develop. Vico's claim that we have true knowledge only of what we (mankind) create, of history and culture, and not of nature, was preposterous. It masked what was true, namely that the two kinds of knowledge are radically different. His cyclical theory of historical development was patently false, and it obscured his genuine insights into the historically conditioned, variable nature of man. The counter-Enlightenment voices of the German romantics, with their emphasis on the uniqueness and creativity of the *Volksgeist*, *Volksseele* and *Nationalgeist* (terms originating in the writings of Herder) led less to a sustained development of a philosophy and methodology of humanistic studies than to the philosophical cultivation of irrationalism, nationalism and ultimately, in the hands of Heidegger and Gentile, of fascism. The terms in which such thinkers and their followers attempted inchoately to articulate the character of the form of knowledge and understanding which they thought distinctive of hermeneutics, 'fantasia', 'inner understanding', '*Einfühlung*', 'acts of divination', 'empathetic understanding' (and, in the twentieth century, 're-enactment' (Collingwood)), were obscure and their attempts to explain them were philosophically unilluminating. Small wonder, then, that they made little impression upon the realist, mathematically trained philosophers and their successors who displaced neo-Hegelian idealism in Britain and neo-Kantianism in Germany from the turn of the century.

The most distinctive philosophical movement of twentieth century thought was analytic philosophy, and in the first half of the century it paid scant heed to the hermeneutic tradition and its concerns. Logical positivism, the leading analytic school of the interwar years, advocated 'the scientific conception of the world'. Its leading members were trained mathematicians and physicists. They explicitly saw themselves and the 'scientific world view' which they advocated as heir to the ideals of the Enlightenment. The methodological goal of positivism was the unity of science. All science, the total domain of human knowledge, was held to be reducible to physicalist language: 'The physicalist language, *unified language*, is the Alpha and Omega of all science' (Neurath 1931/32: 293). Not only was the language of 'science' conceived to be unified, but the methods of science were held to be uniform: 'All states of affairs, are of one kind and are known by the same method' (Carnap 1934: 32). The 1929 Manifesto of the Vienna Circle declared that 'The attempt of behaviourist psychology to grasp the psychic through the behaviour of bodies, which is at a level accessible to perception, is, in its principled attitude, close to the scientific world-conception' (Vienna Circle 1929 §3.4).[8] Carnap (1931) contended that 'all sentences of psychology describe physical occurrences, namely the physical behaviour of humans and other animals'. Indeed, 'psychology is a branch of physics'. A similar view was taken of the social sciences. 'Sociology', Neurath declared, 'is not a "moral science" or "the study of man's spiritual life" … standing in fundamental opposition to some other sciences, called "natural sciences"; no, *as social behaviourism, sociology is part of unified science*' (Neurath 1931/32: 296). Brief forays into the philosophy of history (for example, by Hempel, Nagel and Popper) argued that historical explanation conforms to the hypothetico-deductive model of explanation which the positivists ascribed to the natural sciences.

The contribution of analytic philosophy in its early phases to the philosophy of psychology, the social sciences and the philosophy of history was superficial. The dominant interests of logical positivists and of Cambridge analysts were in the philosophy of physics, the foundations of mathematics, the philosophy of logic and epistemology. Eager to banish metaphysics to the dustheaps of history, and inspired by the ideals of the Enlightenment, they assumed that all rational explanation of any empirical phenomenon must have the same general logical form, exemplified by the forms of explanation in the natural sciences. Their vision of the unity of the sciences seemed to them to be a defence of rationality in the pursuit of knowledge and understanding in all domains, which, they thought, can be opposed only by dogmatism and metaphysics. The conceptual myopia of the Vienna Circle was, however, characteristic of the spirit of the age, and continued to dominate reflection on the methodology of the sciences of man long after the demise of logical positivism. It was encouraged by developments in neurophysiological psychology and by the development of computer sciences and artificial intelligence, which seemed to suggest that we are to be understood on the model of our machines.

However, there was a further reason for the impotence of the vision of understanding propounded by the hermeneutic tradition. The failure of its advocates to give a coherent and philosophically illuminating explanation of their several conceptions of empathy, *Einfühlung*, re-enactment, 'inner' understanding and so on, was in part a consequence of their lack of an adequate philosophy of language and philosophy of psychology.

Wittgenstein and the autonomy of meaning

The thought that man, though part of nature, is also unique in nature has preoccupied philosophers since antiquity. The characterization of what sets man apart from the rest of nature has varied. Some have thought it to be man's rationality, his capacity for reasoned thought, or his capacity for knowledge of eternal truths. Others have thought it to be our knowledge of good and evil, our possession of free will and of a moral conscience, or our capacity to act for reasons. Descartes thought that consciousness is unique to mankind. Others have shied at denying consciousness to animals, but have held self-consciousness, understood as knowledge of our own subjective states, to be uniquely human. Nineteenth-century historiography emphasized the uniqueness of man as a historical being: other animals have a natural history, but only man has a history and a historically determined nature.

It is striking that all these characterizations, most of which are true, are dependent upon a more fundamental feature, namely that mankind is unique in nature in possessing a developed language. The languages of mankind enable us to describe the world we experience, to identify and re-identify objects in a spatio-temporal framework and to distinguish the objects we experience from our experiences of those objects. Knowledge of truths of reason is knowledge of the norms of representation, and of the propositions of logic correlative to the inference rules, of the conceptual scheme constituted by a language. Only a language user can give articulate expression to his own thoughts, desires and feelings and ascribe thoughts, desires and feelings to others of his kind, can have and give expression to memories of the past, spatio-temporally locating the events experienced. Only such a being can form long-term intentions, guided by reasons and norms of behaviour, act on the basis of reflective reason and intentionally follow rules that determine the rightness or wrongness of conduct. What makes us the kinds of creatures we are is, to be sure, *also* our animal nature; but it is our animal nature transformed by our possession of a rich language, which expands our intellect, affections and will. It is not so much eating of the Tree of Knowledge of Good and Evil that expelled us from the Eden of animal innocence, but rather eating of the Tree of Language.[6]

The key to our nature is that we are language using animals. Our language conditions our nature, conditions our understanding of the world and of ourselves, and conditions the institutions we create that constitute the societies in which we live. The humanistic disciplines investigate mankind as cultural, social and historical beings. But we are such beings only in so far as we are also language users. Our animal nature is transformed by our acquisition of, and participation in the cultural institution of, a language. The phenomena that are the subject of humanistic studies are infused with language, intelligible only as properties and relations, actions and passions, practices and products, institutions and histories of language using creatures. The understanding of such phenomena therefore demands forms of understanding and explanation appropriate to and dependent upon the understanding of language and its uses in the stream of human life.

Wittgenstein was not directly concerned with the methodology of humanistic studies. Nevertheless, his philosophy of language and his philosophical psychology show why the subject matter of the humanistic studies is not in general amenable to the forms of explanation of the natural sciences and why the forms of explanation characteristic of the humanities are different in kind from and irreducible to that of the natural sciences. We shall first schematically survey his reflections on language.

A language, Wittgenstein argued, is essentially a public, rule-governed practice, partly constitutive of the form of life and culture of its speakers. Uses of language, and the words and sentences of language used, are bearers of meaning, objects of understanding that are subject to interpretation and misinterpretation, which are meant or intended by their user, and are embedded in the institutions and customs of their social life. The concept of the meaning of an expression is a holistic one; i.e. an expression has a meaning only in the context of the language to which it belongs. The meaning of an expression is a correlate of understanding, it is what one understands when one understands the expression and knows what it means. The criteria of understanding an expression fall into three broad kinds: correct use, or use in accord with the established rules for the use of the expression, giving correct explanations of the meaning of the expression in context, and responding appropriately to the use of the expression by others.

That a language must be 'public' means that there can be no such thing as a language which cannot in principle be understood by others. Every language is essentially shareable by creatures of a like constitution. Human languages are shared by members of human linguistic communities.[9] Human beings are not born with an innate ability to speak a language, but with an innate ability to acquire the ability to speak a language. They learn their languages in the communities in which they are born and bred. Learning one's first language is part of the process of acculturation. The child does not learn a list of names and rules of sentence formation; it learns forms of *behaviour*. 'Words', Wittgenstein emphasized, 'are deeds'. To learn a language is to learn to perform a wide variety of acts and activities that characterize the culture of a linguistic community: to give orders and obey them, to ask for reasons for action and to justify actions by reference to reasons, to describe objects or to construct objects from descriptions, to guess, to report events, to explain events and to explain human actions by reference to agential reasons, to listen to and to tell stories, to crack jokes, to ask, to thank, to curse, to greet, to pray, and so on. Hence a language relates to a way of living, to the form of life and culture of a human community.

Expressions of a language may be used correctly or incorrectly. They are correctly used if they are used in accordance with the received explanations of their meaning. The meaning of an expression is also a correlate of explanation – it is what is explained by an explanation of meaning. An explanation of meaning is a standard for the correct use of the expression – a rule for its use. Hence an explanation of the meaning of an expression is internally related to instances of its correct application. The internal relation between a rule for the use of an expression and its extension is fixed by the *practice* of applying the rule, of correcting misapplications of it, of explaining the meaning of the expression by reference to the rule, by the responses (of understanding, misunderstanding and not understanding) to the expression in use, which exhibit what counts *in practice* as correct and incorrect applications. Hence information processing, mechanistic models of language acquisition and linguistic understanding cannot be adequate. Mechanisms, both artificial and neural, may produce behaviour that accords with a rule, but cannot determine what counts as accordance. Nor can brains or computers follow rules, that is, intentionally act in accordance with a rule.

'Following according to a rule' is fundamental to the institution of language. To learn a language is to master the rule-governed techniques of the uses of its expressions. To understand the meaning of an expression is to be able to use it correctly. One cannot *follow* a rule which one does not know or understand. Hence the rules which determine and are constitutive of the meanings of expressions cannot be unknown, awaiting future discovery. Rather they are exhibited in the humdrum, common or garden explanations of meaning given in teaching, in correcting misuses of expressions, and in explaining what one meant by what one said. What an expression in use means and what the speaker meant by it normally coincide. Giving an acceptable explanation of meaning in context is a criterion of understanding. Someone who uses an expression in an utterance and cannot explain what he meant is judged not to have understood what he said.

Words have the meanings which they are given in the normative practice of their employment in the stream of human life. Their meaning is not determined by mental association or by any causal processes, and it is not answerable to the nature of the world which they may be used to describe. It is not determined by word–world connections, exemplified by linking words with things, names with nominata, but by conventions. It is not nominata and their language-independent nature which determine what names mean, but the rules for the use of names which determine their nominata and their defining nature. The meanings of words are neither 'in the head' nor outside the head, but are constituted by their use in the practice of their application. They are not *determined* by anything 'in the head' or by any object external to the head, but rather by received explanations of meaning which constitute rules for their correct use. Ostensive definition or explanation appears to connect language with entities in reality and to endow expressions with meaning by means of such connections. But that is an illusion. For an ostensive definition links words with samples that belong to the means of representation. It is a rule for the use of a word, akin to a familiar substitution rule, although the substitutable symbol in this case includes the sample ostended and ostensive gesture (e.g. instead of 'black' in the sentence 'the table is black', one may say 'this ☞ ■ colour'). There is no meaning endowing connection between the means of representation and what is represented. Rather, language is, in this sense, an autonomous, free-floating structure.

What the expressions of a language mean is not explicable by reference to behavioural stimuli and patterns of response. No attempt to explain the meanings of expressions in behaviouristic terms can explain the rule-governed connections within the network of language, for such connections are *internal* or logical, not causal, and correlation of stimuli and responses can at most establish external relations, not internal ones. A belief is internally related to the fact that makes it true, a desire is internally related to the occurrence of the event that fulfils it, an expectation to the occurrence of the event that satisfies it as an order is internally related to its compliance. There is no such thing as understanding an assertion without knowing what must be the case if it is true, or of understanding an expression of desire or of expectation, or an order *without* knowing what counts, respectively, as its fulfilment, satisfaction or as compliance with it. These are not extractable from a behaviouristic account of linguistic stimuli and responses. That the sign 'V!' is the expression of an order to V cannot be extracted from the fact that an animal is conditioned to act in a certain way on exposure to the stimulus of hearing the sign. For the animal may *mis*behave, it may react *wrongly* to the order. But that its behaviour *is* wrong is determined by reference to the meaning of the order, and does not determine it. The meaning of the order is determined by the conventions of meaning articulated in the conceptual truth that 'V!' is the order that is complied with by V-ing. It is precisely such patterns of internal relations that are constitutive of the meanings of words and sentences. There is no going *below* the level of rules and the normative practices of their application and invocation to determine what expressions of a language mean.

Understanding the expressions of a language is mastery of the rule-governed techniques of their use. The attempt to reduce understanding to stimulus-response correlations cannot account for what is understood, or for the ability that is acquired when the meaning of an expression is mastered. Equally, any attempt to reduce understanding to neurophysiological states is futile. For no neurophysiological story can capture the normative structure that is mastered or what counts as having mastered it. For the criteria of understanding cannot be located at the neurophysiological level, but only at the level of normative (rule-governed) behaviour. Similarly, cognitive scientists' attempt to explain the institution of language by reference to a 'language of thought' which the brain 'knows' and Chomskian theoretical linguists' attempt to explain language acquisition by reference to pre-linguistic 'cognizing' of a universal grammar of all humanly possible languages are equally incoherent. For a language of thought would indeed be a private language. Likewise, there could be no such thing as *following* the rules of a universal grammar (as opposed to exhibiting regularities) without understanding them. But neonate language learners cannot understand rules of any kind, and their brains can no more know or 'cognize', understand and follow rules, than their brains can hope or fear, fall in love, feel remorse or guilt, or undertake obligations. For these are properties of living creatures and not of their constituent parts.

Language, thought and action

Animals, *pace* Descartes, are conscious creatures. They can be perceptually conscious *of* features of their environment. For to be perceptually conscious of something is to have one's attention caught and held by it, and the capacity to have one's attention caught by items on the periphery of one's perceptual field is crucial for animal survival. They can learn and therefore come to know many things. They can remember and misremember things they have learnt. They can, in a rudimentary way, think or believe things to be thus and so. But their cognitive powers are strictly limited. A dog may now expect its master, if it hears and recognizes its master's footsteps, but it cannot now expect its master to return home next Sunday. It may now think that it is going to be taken for a walk, if it hears its leash being taken off the peg, but it cannot now think that it is going to be taken for a walk next month. It may remember where it left a bone in as much as it can go and dig it up, but not when it left it wherever it left it. For such capacities presuppose possession of a language.

The limits of thought and knowledge, Wittgenstein argued, are the limits of the possible expression of thought and knowledge. It only makes sense to ascribe to a creature such knowledge, memory, thought or belief as it can in principle express in its behaviour. For it is the behaviour of a creature that constitutes the criteria for such ascriptions. Hence the horizon of possible cognitive achievements of a creature is determined by the limits of its behavioural repertoire. But nothing in the behavioural repertoire of a dog could constitute criteria for ascribing to it knowledge or belief involving determinate temporal reference. But, to repeat, 'words are deeds', and the use of language is behaviour. It is *linguistic* behaviour, involving the use of a tensed language and of devices for temporal reference, that constitutes the primary criteria for ascribing to a creature knowledge, memory, thought and belief involving such reference to the past or future. And it is the *possibility* of such linguistic manifestations of knowledge, memory, thought and belief which makes intelligible the ascription of such cognitive achievements even when they are not exhibited.

The possession of a language therefore enlarges the intellect, makes it possible to think not only that things here and now are thus and so, but also that things – of an indefinite variety – are severally thus and so at indefinitely many other times and places. It is the availability of devices of generalization that makes it intelligible to ascribe to a creature knowledge, belief or conjecture of a universal kind. It is mastery of the use of general concept words, of count nouns, concrete mass nouns, and numerals, that renders accessible to a creature thought which goes beyond mere recognition, and knowledge, as opposed to mere recognition, of number and quantity. And it is the availability, in one's linguistic repertoire, of logical devices signifying negation, conjunction, implication and disjunction, that makes possible reasoning, and hence renders intelligible ascription of reasoning, that goes beyond the most rudimentary. We do ascribe to the higher animals rudimentary forms of thinking. We may even be willing to explain an animal's behaviour by attributing to it a reason for its thinking what it does. But we cannot go far down this road. For even if we are willing to say that the animal had a reason for thinking such and such, a large part of the essential role of reasons for thinking or believing cannot be fulfilled in the case of non-language using creatures. For a mere animal cannot *justify* its thinking by reference to a reason; it cannot *explain* its errors, as we can explain ours, by reference to the reasons it thought it had, for it cannot have *thought it had reasons*; and it cannot *reason* from one thought to another, even if it can perhaps be said to have a reason for an action.

The possession of a language extends the will and affections no less than the intellect. Animals, like us, do not only do things – as inanimate objects do things – they act. Like us they have, and exercise, two way powers, to act or refrain from acting as they please. That is a condition for having wants, as opposed to mere needs. Hence too, unlike plants, animals have wants and act in the pursuit of the objects of their desires. But the horizon of their desires is as limited as the horizon of their cognitive powers. A dog can want to go for a walk now, but it cannot now want to go for a walk tomorrow or next Sunday; it can want a bone now, but not now want a bone for Christmas. Animals have purposes, pursue goals, and choose among different possible ways of achieving their goals. But the trajectory of their will reaches no further than their behavioural repertoire can express, and the objects of their will are constrained by their limited preconceptual recognitional capacities. They can choose between patent alternatives, but not deliberate. There are reasons why an animal acts as it does, but only in the most tenuous sense can we say that they *have* reasons for acting as they do, and it is doubtful whether we can make sense of ascribing to an animal reasons for doing something which it did not do. Only a language-using creature can reason and deliberate, weigh the conflicting claims of the facts which it knows in the light of its desires, goals and values, and come to a decision in the light of reasons. In so far as animals can be said to decide, animal decision is not a matter of calling a halt to a process of reasoning, of weighing the pros and cons of a course of action in the light of reasons and coming to a reasoned conclusion, but only a matter of terminating a state of indecision. Similarly, even if we go beyond attributing purposes to mere animals and ascribe to them intentions, we can do so only in the most rudimentary sense. For without a language there can be no formation of intentions on the basis of reasons duly weighed and considered, no long term plans and projects, no beliefs based upon one's intentions, self-knowledge and assumptions about features of the world which may facilitate or hinder one's plans.

Being language users, we are also essentially intentional animals. Our uses of language are characteristically intentional. We mean something by what we say, and typically mean what we say. We intend to be understood in a certain way, and normally will correct misunderstandings in the light of the meanings of our words and what we meant by them. In saying what we say we perform a variety of speech acts, locutionary, illocutionary and perlocutionary. What we do is intentional in some respects, but may be unintentional in others. What acts we thus perform, intentionally or inadvertently, are determined in part by the words we utter in the context, and by our understanding of them. Hence our behavioural repertoire expands as we master the techniques of using words, and what we do is describable in terms which presuppose the concepts which we possess and exercise. However, it is not merely the speech acts we perform that are intelligible only in the light of the concepts we exercise, but also the vast range of our other intentional acts and activities, which presuppose forms of knowledge and belief available only to one who has mastered a language. The horizon of the intentions of a language user are limited only by the resources of his language, the historically conditioned institutions in which it is embedded, and the possibilities of action he knows or believes to be available in the social context of his life.

Intentional action is action of which it always makes sense to ask for what reason the agent performed it. To specify the agent's reason for his intentional action is to give one kind of explanation of his behaviour. When an agent gives his reason for doing what he did, he not only explains his action, but typically also purports to justify it. The factors which may be cited as reasons may be of different general types. Forward looking reasons may specify a further intent with which the action was performed, as when we V in order thereby to X or to attain G. In so doing, one may further specify the goal of the action in terms of some desirability characterizations which render the act intelligible, desirability characterizations that are intelligible in terms of the scheme of values of the culture of the agent. Backward-looking reasons cite past facts or events, and explain or justify the act by reference to them, as when we explain performance of an action as the fulfilment of a promise antecedently made, or as compliance with an order from someone with accepted authority or with a request, or as an expression of loyalty to someone to whom loyalty is owed. Description or redescription of the intended act may give a reason for performing it, if it is, for example, enjoyable, or just, or obligatory. One may also explain and justify one's action by specifying one's social role in the circumstances, given that the social conventions determining the role require or make appropriate such an action. The 'space of reasons', therefore, is also a cultural space.

Wittgenstein rejected the received account of voluntary action as movement caused by acts of volition, and repudiated both innervationist and non-innervationist (Jamesian) ideo-motor accounts of action in terms of mnemonic images of kinaesthetic sensations. To characterize a human movement as voluntary is not to specify the nature of its cause, but to *exclude* certain kinds of causes, namely, such causes as would rob it of the name of action. For a movement constitutes an action only if the agent could have done otherwise. To explain an action by specifying that its agent wanted to do it for its own sake, or wanted to do it for a further goal, is not to identify a mental cause of the action. For wants would be causes of actions only if the want were always a state or event identifiable independently of the action it allegedly produces. But this condition is patently not satisfiable in myriad cases of voluntary action, for example, in writing this very sentence, each word was voluntarily written, written because I wanted to write it and none other, but there was no independently identifiable want or volition corresponding to each word.

Contrary to the empiricist tradition, Wittgenstein did not think that either reasons for believing or reasons for acting are causes of believing or of acting. Nor did he think that explanation of intentional action in terms of the agent's reasons for acting is a form of causal explanation. Neither the grammar of 'a reason' nor the epistemology of reasons resembles that of 'a cause' and causes. We attribute reasons, but not causes, to people, as when we say that A *had* a reason for V-ing or that A's reason for V-ing was that R. Reasons, but not causes, may be good or poor, defensible or indefensible, persuasive or slight. There may be a reason, and A may have a reason, for V-ing, yet not V, and his failure to V does not intimate that there was no reason or that he had no reason for V-ing. Causes make things happen, reasons guide and justify agents' acting. Accordingly reasons, unlike causes, provide grounds for the evaluation of action as reasonable or foolish, right or wrong. An agent can do something for a reason only if he has the power to refrain from doing it. But if an agent is caused to do something in the sense in which the ice on the path may cause one to slip, he or it does not have the power to refrain from doing it. Knowledge of causes is generally (though not uniformly) inductive, but one's knowledge of the reasons one has or had for V-ing is generally not. One does not normally *find out* one's reason for thinking or doing something. In general, an agent's sincere avowal of his reason for V-ing is authoritative, even if defeasibly so. But an agent's sincere averral of causes is not. The concept of a reason is related to that of reasoning. Reasoning is a transition from one or more assertion or thought to another, the former purporting to *justify* the latter. A reason is characteristically a premise in reasoning, which may be the reasoning one actually went through or may be given *ex post actu* as the reasoning one could have gone through if challenged.

Explanation of an agent's action by reference to his reasons is not nomic. Specification of the agent's reason does not specify a sufficient condition for the performance of the action for which it is a reason. The agent's specification of his reason is not a hypothesis. Causal explanations, by contrast, are characteristically nomic (or generally so conceived by those who favour the methodological unity thesis), specify sufficient conditions, and are typically hypotheses. Explaining an action as done *for* a reason, or *for the sake of* a goal or *in order* to bring about a certain state of affairs is not giving a causal explanation. The explanatory link between reason and action is not forged by wants and beliefs (mis)conceived as causes, and does not instantiate a causal generalization. It is, in the most fundamental kind of case, what an agent *says* (or *would* say) is his reason that makes the connection between action and what is cited as his reason. Hence it is not normally independent of what the agent sees as the connection, that is of how *he understands his action himself*. His expressions of self-understanding in giving his reasons for his action may be defeated, as in cases of insincerity, disingenuousness, self-deception, and so on. But such circumstances of defeasibility are essentially exceptions to the rule. That is not because the agent normally has an unerring eye for the correct causal hypothesis which will explain his action. What he *says* was his reason *was* his reason, unless there are grounds for doubting the connection he makes between his action and the reasons he had for doing it. Such grounds are not typically afforded by alternative causal hypotheses which the agent has not taken into account, but by his having *other* reasons (often of a less laudable kind) for doing what he did, which fit his motivational history better than the reasons he avows.[8]

Consequences

The above conceptual observations describe but a small part of the web of concepts and conceptual relations which lie at the heart of the characterization of what is distinctively human. But Wittgenstein's connective analyses suffice to shed light upon the flaws in the thesis of the Unity of Science.[9] Stigmatizing the various forms of reductionism and the doctrine of the methodological uniformity of understanding as 'scientism' is not a form of anti-rationalism. It is not to deny to reason the power to understand both nature and man. Rather, it is to insist that the canons of understanding in the study of nature and in the study of man differ, that the forms of explanation appropriate for the one are typically inappropriate for the other. Although Wittgenstein did not concern himself with the nature of explanation and understanding in history and the social sciences, his philosophy of language and of psychology shed light upon the claims made by the hermeneutic tradition originating in Vico. Windelband's contention that history is idiographic, concerned only with the particular and unique, whereas science is nomothetic, concerned with general laws, is indefensible, but contains a grain of truth. Dilthey's distinction between the *Erklärung* (explanation) characteristic of the natural sciences and the *Verstehen* (understanding) characteristic of humanistic studies contains crucial insights, even if poorly expressed. Weber's contention that the objects of sociological investigation have a subjective *meaning* absent from merely natural phenomena indicates an important truth, masked by the obscurity of the notion of meaning invoked. And the hermeneuticians' insistence that understanding phenomena of man as a social, historical and cultural being requires 'divination', *Einfühlung*, *fantasia*, empathetic re-enactment of the thought of the past, similarly combines depth with obscurity and exaggeration.

The behaviour of man has to be *understood*, and sometimes *interpreted*, in a sense in which the behaviour of inanimate nature and much of animal behaviour do not. This is obvious in the case of human linguistic behaviour. The utterances of a human being have a *meaning*, which must be understood by reference to the rules of the language in question. Human discourse involves both speaker and hearer. The speaker may mean various things by what he says and what he means may be multi-layered and stand in need of an interpretation. The hearer may understand, misunderstand (misinterpret) or fail to understand what the speaker says or what he means. Hence both describing and explaining human discourse and its upshot, from case to case, requires minimally grasping how it was meant by the speaker and how it was understood or misunderstood by the hearer, and hence too how it is interwoven in the context, in the participants' understanding of that context, and in their motivational history. But the insistence upon the distinctive and irreducible forms of understanding and explanation in the humanistic studies reaches much farther than the understanding and interpretation of discourse. Dilthey held that human life can be understood only by reference to categories alien to the natural sciences, namely categories of meaning. Weber characterized the subject matter of sociology as 'social action', including in the category of 'action' those acts and activities to which the agent attaches 'subjective meaning'. It is doubtful whether the various human phenomena in question are usefully subsumed under the category of the meaningful, where that incorporates not only the notion of linguistic meaning, but also that of the intentional (what is meant), the purposive, that which is emotionally coloured, and what is, in one way or another, valued. Nevertheless, both were sensitive to important differences between the subject matter of the natural sciences and that of humanistic studies.

Since characteristic human behaviour, unlike the behaviour of inanimate nature, is not mere movement but action, its description requires reference to the manifold rule-governed practices and institutions within which human life is conducted. A man raises his hand and moves it back and forth: the movement can be described and explained physiologically and neurophysiologically. But such hand movements may be an act of greeting, or warning, or beckoning. It may be signalling that a run has been scored, it may be part of the activity of conducting an orchestra, or part of an explanation of what 'waving' means – and doubtless many other things too. Making a mark on a piece of paper can be described physically and neurophysiology, but whether making a mark on a piece of paper is writing one's name or something else, and whether the writing of one's name is signing a letter, a cheque, a contract or a will, inserting a name in a book one owns or dedicating to a friend a book one has written, all these and much else too requires reference to endless rules, conventions and institutions of social life, which are not reducible to anything sub-normative, and are products of social life at particular historical times.

The characterization of distinctively human behaviour and of the intentions that make it what it is can be said to be *context bound*, both 'locally' and 'globally' in a manner alien to scientific explanation. No matter what movements a person executes, they can only be constitutive of signalling a run in a game of cricket, conducting an orchestra, signing a cheque, contract or will if the appropriate cultural, social and legal institutions exist. An intention, Wittgenstein stressed, is embedded in human customs and institutions. Only if the techniques of chess exist can one intend to play the game and make a move as opposed to a mere movement; only if the institutions of contracts, wills, copyrights exist can one intend to make a contract or will, to sell or to violate copyrights. A medieval knight could not have intended to solve a differential equation, and a twentieth-century soldier could not intend to be knight-errant. The horizon of possible intentions is set by the historical context in which human beings find themselves. Were the situation to differ in such and such ways, nothing would *count* as having that intention, *no matter what went on in the mind or brain of the agent*. More locally, as it were, the description of a human being as hoping, expecting or fearing that things are thus and so requires an appropriate surrounding and antecedent history, as describing a human being as feeling pain or seeing something red do not. For these intentional descriptions, applicable on the grounds of behavioural criteria, demand an appropriate context for the criteria to constitute adequate grounds of ascription. An agent's utterance constitutes an intelligible expression of fear, hope, expectation, intention and so on, and hence a criterion for third-person ascription, only in the right setting and with the right kind of history. In the right context, such and such behaviour is a criterion for the agent's expecting a friend for tea, hoping to be able to repay a debt, fearing that there will be an explosion, and so forth. But if one could, as it were, cut a minute's worth of this behaviour out of its context and antecedent history, then what we would see would not *be* expecting, hoping, fearing thus (no matter what mental or neural events accompany it).

Consequently, the *description* of the phenomena that are the concern of humanistic studies requires concepts which are not needed by the natural sciences for the description of their subject matter. Although zoological sciences require psychological concepts for the description of animal behaviour, the range of concepts thus required is limited, and they are attenuated relative to their primary application to humanity because the relevant intentional contents are restricted to what is expressible in the animal's limited behavioural repertoire. The concepts needed by the animal behaviourist to describe rats would not go far for purposes of describing human behaviour, history and culture. For the manifold speech-acts of human beings, and the acts and activities involved in human discourse, including the understanding of the speech-acts of others and the responses to them, can only be rightly described by reference to linguistic rules internal to the rule-governed activities of speaking a language. Since linguistic meaning is, in the sense explained, autonomous and irreducible to non-normative behavioural or neurophysiological concepts, the description of such phenomena lies beyond the grasp of the concepts of the natural sciences. Equally, the identification of distinctively human behaviour presupposes conventions, systems of beliefs and values, and social institutions which are intrinsically related to the behaviour, and requires concepts associated with these conventions, value systems and institutions. The meaning or significance of such behaviour can therefore be grasped only historically and contextually.

The phenomena of nature do not, in the requisite sense, have a meaning, are not rule-governed or intentional, are not thus embedded in customs and institutions and in specific situations, and are not actions done for reasons. Once rightly identified, human behaviour often demands an explanation: we may correctly identify the behaviour as signing a cheque, a contract, a will or a death warrant, but still want to know why it was done. And for that we need recourse to explanations in terms of agential reasons and motives, and to social norms of conduct. Often the explanation will not only refer to the agent's knowledge and beliefs regarding the situation in which he finds himself, to his goals and values and consequent reasons, but also to his conception of himself and his role, and his conception of others' beliefs about himself. Often understanding his action requires not only an explanation of the agent's reasons, but also an explanation of why those reasons weighed with him, which can sometimes be given by reference to his self-understanding, or his conception of the expectations of others, or the values which he has imbibed in the context of the society of which he is a member. Such explanations are alien to the natural sciences. They are not reducible to causal, sub-normative explanations, and are not formally homogeneous with the nomological forms of explanation characteristic of the sciences.

Ramifications

To ward off misunderstandings, it should be emphasized that there is not a *single* form of explanation appropriate to understanding human behaviour. There are many different, though related, forms. To explain behaviour by reference to motives is not the same as explaining it by reference to reasons, and neither are the same as explaining behaviour in terms of tendency explanations. Although desires and wants feature in motive explanations, not all explanations by reference to wants involve motives, and the category of conative explanation is itself diverse. For explanation of behaviour in terms of felt desire, such as hunger, thirst or lust, is not the same as explanation in terms of purposes and goals. And these too are different from explanations in terms of tendencies. Tendency explanations are themselves diverse, since explaining behaviour by reference to custom is not the same as explaining it by reference to habit, and neither are the same as explanations by reference to dispositions of character. Explaining inaction or omission by reference to physical inability is not the same kind of explanation as explaining inaction by reference to normative inability, such as lack of legal power, and neither are the same as explaining omission by reference to ignorance, inattention, carelessness, inadvertence, mistake or accident, none of which are the same as explaining it by reference to intentions, and associated reasons or motives. Wittgenstein did not explore the complex relations between actions and omissions and the kinds of explanation and explanatory factors appropriate to them, nor did he examine the relations of compatibility and incompatibility between different types of explanation and explanatory factors. Others, since his death, have endeavoured to do so.[10]

What Wittgenstein's reflections show, if they are correct, is not that history, let alone psychology, sociology and economics, is *idiographic* (as Windelband suggested), concerned only with the particular and unique.[11] To be sure, much of history and historical explanation is, and so too are some of the concerns of the social sciences. It is also true that where the explanandum is thus specific, no matter whether it is as particular and individual an event as Elizabeth I's 'etceteration' or as complex, multiple-agent involving an event as the outbreak of the First World War, it is not explained by subsumption under general laws which apply to all events of a general kind, but by reference to the agents' reasons and motives, their understandings and misunderstandings of the situation that confronted them, their specific judgements, made in the light of their evaluations of the situation and of their values in that situation. Nevertheless, it would be wrong to deny to historians any *nomological*, i.e. generalizing, ambitions, and absurd to extend such a limitation to psychology and the social sciences. However, even nomological insights in the domain of the study of man as a social and cultural being are not *nomothetic*, i.e. do not specify strict, exceptionless laws. The valid generalizations that can be achieved through the study of history, economics and society are not akin to laws of nature, and their explanatory value is not akin to that of scientific laws. For what underlies the generalizations of the study of culture and society is not the blind movements of matter in space, but the actions and activities of man, sometimes intentional, often done for reasons, typically moved by motives and directed to ulterior goals, and only intelligible as such. Statistical correlations abound in the social sciences, as they do in the natural sciences, but no understanding of the phenomena described by such correlations in the social sciences, such as divorce rates or illegitimacy rates, is achieved in the absence of further investigations of the beliefs, motivations and values of the agents, which will render their behaviour intelligible. What Wittgenstein's elucidations show is that the relevant concepts are not reducible to the concepts of the natural sciences, are not eliminable, and that the relevant explanations are not logically homogeneous with explanations in the natural sciences.

Of course, experimental psychology aims to discover general laws of human nature. Its main successes have been, and could only be, at the level of the investigation of human capacities (for example, the capacities to perceive, recognize, remember, attend, calculate, reason inductively, draw inferences), the neurophysiological structures that underlie them, the dependence of these capacities and their exercise on innate dispositions, environmental circumstances, learning, and the order of their acquisition and development. Here there are generalizations to be discovered, perhaps even general laws. But they do not explain individual human behaviour save in so far as they disclose constraints on what a person can do or think in a given situation. For what is investigated are the conditions under which human capacities *can* be exercised, not why particular people under specific social and historical circumstances do what they do, the ways in which they understand the situation in which they act, and the reasons they have for doing what they do. To understand the latter requires attention to the specific agent and his unique life, to the way he views the world, to his beliefs and goals, to the reasons that weigh with him and to the values he embraces - which is why the greatest of psychologists are the great biographers and, above all, the great novelists (we understand more about Emma Bovary or Anna Karenina than about anyone we know).

Understanding the thought and action of other people does, to be sure, require sensitivity, imagination. 'What one acquires here', Wittgenstein noted, 'is not a technique; one learns correct judgements. There are also rules, but they do not form a system, and only experienced people can apply them right. Unlike calculating rules' (PI: p. 227). Only metaphorically speaking does it require one to 'enter into the mind of another'. It demands a grasp of the other's reasons for thinking or doing whatever they thought or did, understanding their fears and hopes, their purposes and values; and, in this sense, to see things from their 'point of view'. Many aspects of historical understanding are similar, save that such understanding also needs to be informed by scholarship, and not merely the sensitivity and judgement that is the product of life. It does not require the historian to 're-enact' the thought of the past in his mind, but to understand the thought and action of the past in terms of the beliefs, values, goals, reasons and motives available to the agents whose actions are being studied. For it requires a grasp of the mores and morals of the times, of the intellectual and volitional horizons set by the culture, of the social institutions and structures that obtained. These are not describable or explicable in terms available to the natural sciences. Nor are the terms in which they are describable and explicable reducible to the categories of the sciences.

It involves no denigration of science let alone of reason to insist that there are domains of enquiry which lie beyond the purview of science. Forms of rational understanding and explanation are diverse and logically heterogeneous. Science and humanism were indeed allied in their endeavours to combat unreason, moral and political dogma, and the myth-making power of religion. Science is a source of truth, and its achievements over the past four centuries are indeed remarkable. Every source of truth is also unavoidably a source of falsehood, from which its own canons of reasoning and confirmation attempt to protect it. But it can also become a source of conceptual confusion, and consequently of forms of intellectual myth-making, against which it is typically powerless. Scientism, the illicit extension of the methods and categories of science beyond their legitimate domain, is one such form, and the conception of the unity of the sciences and the methodological homogeneity of the natural sciences and of humanistic studies one such myth. It is the task of philosophy to defend us against such illusions of reason.

Notes

I am grateful to Professor Rom Harré, Dr John Hyman, Dr Stephen Mulhall, Professor O. Hanfling, Professor Herman Philipse and Professor G.H. von Wright for their comments on an earlier draft of this paper.

1   The task of dismantling the traditional conception of logic had already been undertaken in the *Tractatus*, in Wittgenstein's criticisms of Frege and Russell, who conceived of logic as a science (of the the the most general laws of thought or of the most general facts of the universe). But he then continued to cleave to the idea that logic is 'transcendental'. After 1930, this too was repudiated.

2   Schlick wrote an article with the title 'The Turning Point of Philosophy' in *Erkenntnis* I, 1929, in which he hailed Wittgenstein's *Tractatus* as the turning point of philosophy, putting an end to metaphysics and putting philosophy upon the proper path of the clarifier of sense.

3   This felicitous term is Strawson's (1992). Connective analysis is to be contrasted with depth analysis or reductive analysis.

4   For example, by Charles Taylor, Peter Winch, and G.H. von Wright. The following discussion is indebted to G.H. von Wright's illuminating essay 'Humanism and the Humanities' (von Wright 1993).

5   It is striking, but also encouraging, that one of the founders of the cognitive revolution in psychology, Jerome Bruner, is now 'decrying the Cognitive Revolution for abandoning "meaning making" as its central concern, opting for "information processing" and computation instead' (Bruner 1990: 137).

6   A point already sapiently made by Rousseau in his *Discourse on the Origin of Inequality*, First Part.

7   Save in aberrant cases, such as the last Mohican, or an as yet unshared, invented language. Much ink has been spilt over the question of whether Wittgenstein held language to be essentially shared or essentially shareable. For present purposes, this controversy is of no importance, since human languages are actually shared.

8   For further elaboration, see G.H. von Wright, 'Of Human Freedom' (von Wright 1998).

9   It should be noted that the thesis of the unity of science is doubly flawed. As argued above, it has no application to the study of man as a social, cultural and historical being. But it is also mistaken within the proper domain of the natural sciences. This theme will not be investigated here. For an illuminating discussion of the methodological disunity of the natural sciences themselves and the irreducibility of manifold scientific explanations to physics and its laws, see J. Dupré (1993).

10 For example, G.E.M. Anscombe, A.J.P. Kenny, B. Rundle, F. Stoutland, G.H. von Wright and A.R. White.

11 It would be equally mistaken to suppose that the natural sciences are never concerned with the particular and unique, with identifying the nature, causes and consequences of individual events in nature, such as the destruction of dinosaurs as a consequence of the impact of a large meteorite in the gulf of Mexico. But such 'idiographic' explanations in science do subsume the particular under general laws.

Bibliography

Ayer, A.J. (ed.) (1959) *Logical Positivism*, Glencoe, IL: Free Press.

Bruner, J. (1990) *Acts of Meaning*, Cambridge, MA: Harvard University Press.

Carnap R. (1931) 'Psychology in Physical Language' trans. George Schick in Ayer (1959), 165–98.

―――― (1934) *The Unity of Science*, London: Kegan Paul, Trench, Trubner and Co.

Descartes, R. (1637) *Discourse on Method, The Philosophical Writings of Descartes*, trans. John Cottingham, Robert Stoothoff and Dugald Murdoch, vol. 1, Cambridge: Cambridge University Press, 1985.

Dupré, J. (1993) *The Disorder of Things: Metaphysical Foundations of the Disunity of Science*, Cambridge MA.: Harvard University Press.

Durkheim, E. (1897) 'Review of A Labriola, Essais sur la conception materialiste de l'histoire', *Revue Philosophie*.

Galileo (1623) *The Assayer,* trans. Stillman Drake in *The Controversy on the Comets of 1618* Philadephia: University of Pennsylvania Press, 1960.

Hume, D. (1748) *Enquiry Concerning Human Understanding,* ed. L.A. Selby-Bigge, revised P.H. Nidditch, 3rd edn., Oxford: Clarendon Press, 1975.

Mill, J.S. (1852) *A System of Logic*, New York: Harper and Brothers.

Neurath, 0. (1931/32) 'Sociology and Physicalism', trans. George Schick in Ayer (1959), 282–317.

Pascal, B. (1669) *Pensées*, trans W.F.Trotter, New York: Random House, 1941.

Quinton, A. (1998) 'Religion and Science in the Three Great Civilizations', in A Quinton, *From Woodhouse to Wittgenstein*, Manchester: Carcanet, 3–22.

Rousseau, J.J (1754) *Discourse on the Origin of Inequality*, trans. G.D.H. Cole in *The Social Contract; and Discourses*, London: Everyman, 1993.

Strawson, P.F. (1992) *Analysis and Metaphysics: An Introduction to Philosophy*, Oxford: Oxford University Press.

Wittgenstein, L. (1953) *Philosophical Investigations*, trans. G.E.M. Anscombe, Oxford: Blackwell.

―――― (1980) *Culture and Value,* trans. P. Winch, Chicago: University of Chicago Press.

―――― (1997) *Denkbewegungen-Tagbücher 1930–1932/1936–1937*, ed. I Somavilla, Innsbruck: Haymon.

Vienna Circle (1929) *The Scientific Conception of the World.* trans., Reidel: Dordrecht, 1973.

von Wright, G.H. (1993) 'Humanism and the Humanities', in G.H. von Wright, *The Tree of Knowledge and Other Essays*, New York: Brill, Leiden.

―――― (1998) 'Of Human Freedom', in G.H. von Wright, *In the Shadow of Descartes: Essays in the Philosophy of Mind*, Dordrecht: Kluwer, 1–44.

3

WITTGENSTEIN ON LANGUAGE, ART AND HUMANITY

Oswald Hanfling

The later Wittgenstein may be described as a 'humanist' writer in a literal sense of the word. He displays what is distinctively human about language, about art and about human beings themselves; and also, of course, about philosophy itself. What is distinctively human, in this sense, may be contrasted with the realm of scientific research and theory. In this realm Hume's dictum is (with some reservations) appropriate: 'For all we know *a priori*, anything may be the cause of anything'. Scientific studies are largely concerned with what is 'hidden': there is room in them for theories in which unobservable entities or processes are posited, and also for surprising discoveries. But this is not to be so in the case of Wittgenstein's philosophical investigation. 'What is hidden', he wrote, 'is of no interest to us'.

> We may not advance any kind of theory...The problems are solved, not by giving new information, but by putting together [Zusammenstellung] what we have always known...Since everything lies open to view, there is nothing to explain. For what is hidden...is of no interest to us.
>
> (PI §109, §126)

In the case of scientific and other theories, it is common to posit some general law or principle by reference to which a variety of phenomena are to be explained; Wittgenstein, by contrast, directs our attention to 'the particular case' (BB: 18), as encountered in human life and language. We are not to suppose that there must be some general principle underlying the uses of language, the appreciation of art, etc.

Wittgenstein was interested primarily in questions of language, but the rejection of theory is present also in his discussions of art and of human beings. In each of these, he was concerned to do justice to the humanity of those things and activities.

Language

Between the early and later philosophies of Wittgenstein, there is continuity and discontinuity. His main concern throughout was about meaning: this is a continuity. An early expression of his later thought was the *Blue Book* of 1933–4, which opens with the question, 'What is the meaning of a word?', this being one of the main themes of the book; and this theme was also central to his early work, the *Tractatus*. The discontinuity lies in the answers he gave to that question. In the *Tractatus*, he had declared: 'A name means an object. The object is its meaning' (3.203); but in the later book he said: 'The use of [a] word in practice is its meaning' (BB: 69). In the later work he described the use and meaning of words in terms of their various functions in human life, but this aspect was absent from the earlier work.

Behind the *Tractatus* account of language there is a simple and plausible assumption: that there must be a one-to-one correspondence between items of language and items of reality. But which would be the items in question? If we think of words as the relevant items of language, we soon run into difficulties. Words are often used to refer to things that do not exist: things that have ceased to exist, or imaginary things that never existed at all. Yet a word does not lose its meaning when the thing corresponding to it ceases to exist, and neither is it devoid of meaning if there never was such a thing. The statement, 'My watch is on the table', would be perfectly intelligible even if there were no such thing as my watch. Again, such words as 'watch' and 'table' are only loosely related to their counterparts in reality. My watch, for example, is a concrete, particular thing, with various features that are peculiar to it; whereas the *word* 'watch' covers an infinite number and a great variety of things, all described as 'watches'.

In the *Tractatus* such difficulties were eliminated by resorting to the idea of *analysis*. Sentences such as 'My watch is on the table' were held to be analysable into 'elementary' sentences, consisting of what he called 'names' or 'primitive signs'; and corresponding to these there would *have* to be simple elements of reality (objects), for these would *be* the meanings of the names. (It is in this sense that the statement I quoted – 'A name means an object' – must be understood.) The analysis would proceed in accordance with the truth-functional system of logic, and it would show that underlying the apparent complexity and untidiness of ordinary language there is a realm of perfect order and simplicity. These qualities, he thought, were a sign that his account must be on the right lines.

Men have always had a presentiment that there must be a realm in which the answers to questions are symmetrically united – *a priori* – to form a self-contained, regular system. A realm subject to the law: *Simplex sigillum veri.*

(TLP 5.4541)

The *Tractatus* is a work of theory. The analysis proposed by Wittgenstein is not one that comes into play in actual human conversation; it could not do so, for it is a theoretical requirement and not something with which users of the language are acquainted. Nor did Wittgenstein produce examples of the relevant 'names' and 'objects': their existence was a 'requirement' or 'postulate' rather than an observed reality (TLP 3.23).[1] The problem that this postulate was supposed to answer was that of 'determinacy of sense'. How, given the imperfect correspondences between words and things, can the sense of what we say be determinate? The solution, according to the *Tractatus*, was to assume that behind the appearance of imperfection there must be ultimate constituents of language ('simple signs') that correspond perfectly with simple counterparts in the world. Thus 'the requirement that simple signs be possible is the requirement that sense be determinate' (TLP 3.23). But these 'solutions', together with the problems they are supposed to answer, were rejected in Wittgenstein's later works. The meanings of our words and sentences are usually evident from their use in a given situation, and when problems about meaning do arise, the remedy must be sought within that situation, as when we ask a person to explain what he means. There is no *general* problem, requiring a general (theoretical) solution, about determinacy of sense.

In the later work he drew attention to the great variety of uses of language (language games) (PI §23), including: giving orders, speculating about an event, making up a story, telling a joke, asking, thanking, cursing, greeting, praying and various others; while in the earlier work he apparently thought of this variety, and the human activities of which they are part, as a mere surface phenomenon. The *Tractatus* account of language was a de-humanized one. There is no place in it for the role of language in human behaviour, and the underlying structures postulated by Wittgenstein are hidden from us. 'Man possesses the ability', he wrote:

> to construct languages capable of expressing every sense, without having any idea how each word has meaning or what its meaning is...It is not humanly possible to gather immediately from [everyday language] what the logic of language is.
>
> (TLP 4.002)

Having rejected the *Tractatus* theory of meaning, what did the later Wittgenstein put in its place? As we saw, he now identified 'the use of a word in practice' with its meaning; and this is sometimes called 'the use theory' of meaning.[2] But Wittgenstein, as quoted earlier, renounced the quest for theories ('We may not advance any kind of theory', etc.). Was he not in fact advancing a theory in this case? No: in speaking of 'use', Wittgenstein was not positing some process or principle in the manner of a theory. 'Use' is not such a principle, for the fact that words are used is perfectly obvious. On the other hand, the reference to use would not serve to explain, say, how 'determinacy of sense is possible'. No such explanation is attempted in the later work, for none is regarded as necessary.

The point of Wittgenstein's identification of meaning with use is not to posit an alternative principle or type of analysis to replace the earlier one; it is that there is *no more* to the meaning of a word than its use in the language. In describing the word's use – which 'lies open to view' – we have said how it works; and to invoke some underlying principle to explain this is to seek explanations where none are needed (Z §314).

The craving for such explanations occurs also in relation to more specific questions about language that Wittgenstein discussed. Consider the question: 'How can we use the same word – say the word "game" – for a variety of objects?' An answer comes readily to mind: 'There must be something they all have in common'. This answer may properly be called 'a theory', because it offers to explain an apparently puzzling phenomenon, and it does so by reference to a principle that is posited rather than observed. Here, it seems, is something that needs explaining; and this, it seems, is the only way of explaining it: hence the 'must be' in the sentence 'there must be something', etc. But Wittgenstein rejects this 'must be' and the assumption behind it:

> Don't say: 'There *must* be something common, or they would not be called "games"' – but *look and see* whether there is anything common to all. – For if you look at them you will not see something that is common to *all*, but similarities, relationships, and a whole series of them at that.
>
> family resemblance
>
> (PI §66)

It is possible to misunderstand the point of Wittgenstein's argument here, and to underestimate the importance of it in his thinking. It is sometimes assumed that his position would be undermined if someone were able to meet the challenge, to produce a set of features that games, and only games, have in common; and various attempts have been made to this end. Now it must be admitted that Wittgenstein's review of candidates for that role is very sketchy and it might well be supposed that his invitation to 'look and see' would, in due course, produce a positive result. The essential point, however, is not that there is no such set of conditions, but that there *need* not be: that a word can function perfectly well without this support. 'Don't say: "There *must* be..."': this is the essential point, here and elsewhere.

On the other hand, if Wittgenstein is right about this, then it will be most unlikely that there is in fact a set of conditions that games, and only games, have in common. If no such set is *needed* for the use of the word, then its existence would be an inexplicable freak, rather like some freakish excrescence on the body of a animal which serves no purpose. What if some ingenious philosopher were to produce a hitherto unnoticed feature, or set of features, that games, and only games, have in common? This would not supply what the problem seems to demand, for it would not *explain* why we use words as we do. To do that, the feature would have to be familiar to speakers of the language, so that they could *refer* to it in explaining – justifying – their use of the word. A feature that needs to be discovered by an ingenious philosopher would not play this role.[3]

What *is* required of those who understand the word is to be able to recognize typical characteristics and examples of games. How, asks Wittgenstein, 'should we explain to someone what a game is?' An informal explanation would be sufficient: 'I imagine we should describe *games* to him, and we might add: "This *and similar things* are called 'games'". And do we know any more about it ourselves?' (PI §69). We can, if we like, 'draw a boundary', impose an artificial definition on the word; but, asks Wittgenstein, 'does it take that to make the concept usable?' Similarly, 'when I give the description: "The ground was quite covered with plants" – do you want to say I don't know what I am talking about until I can give a definition of a plant?' (PI §70). Here as elsewhere, Wittgenstein appeals to the use of language in ordinary human situations to illustrate what it is to explain and understand the meanings of particular words.[4]

In the section in which he warned the reader not to assume that 'there *must* be something common, or they would not be called "games"', Wittgenstein reviewed a number of features (skill, winning and losing, etc.) that might be proposed for this role, pointing out that none would be adequate. 'The result of this examination', he concluded, is that here 'we see a complicated network of similarities overlapping and criss-crossing', which he characterized as 'family resemblances' (PI §66–7). Now this again has led some readers to speak of a 'theory', the 'family resemblance theory' of meaning; as if, having rejected one theory ('there must be something common') Wittgenstein replaced it with another. But this is not right. Wittgenstein is not positing some explanatory pattern (a 'network of similarities') whose existence may or may not be confirmed; he is merely drawing attention to an obvious fact: that features associated with games appear in some games and not in others. His point is that there need be *nothing more* than that - nothing of a theoretical, 'hidden' kind to enable that word to perform its function.

The matter would be different if he had specified the contents and extent of a suitable 'network of similarities', but such an attempt would be contrary to the passage I quoted from PI §69 ('How should we explain to someone what a game is?'). Regarded as an explanatory theory, the 'family resemblance theory' would, in any case, suffer from an obvious weakness to which Wittgenstein himself drew attention. To such an 'explanation', he pointed out, 'it might be objected that a transition can be made from anything to anything' (PG §§5-6). Given any two items, there would always be some features or features that they shared.

'These and similar things are called games'. The person to whom this explanation is given would, of course, have to understand what was meant by 'similar' in this context; he would have to 'catch on' to how the word is used in practice – but not to some theoretical schema of overlapping similarities or anything else. In practice this requirement is usually satisfied, if not at the outset, then after a few more remarks of the same kind; and that is enough.

There is yet another aspect of Wittgenstein's 'humanization' of language as compared with what he had done in the earlier work, and what has often been done in the writings of philosophers. In the earlier work he had tried to define the 'essential nature of propositions' and for this purpose he used certain words in a technical sense; including 'name' and 'object', as noted earlier. But in the later work he would have none of this.

> When philosophers use a word – 'knowledge', 'being', 'object', 'I', 'proposition', 'name' – and try to grasp the *essence* of the thing, one must always ask oneself: is the word ever actually used in this way in the language in which it is at home?

[margin note: metaphysical expression vs experiential expression daily usage of the word]

What he proposed to do was 'to bring words back from their metaphysical to their everyday use' (PI §116). Thus, to the sceptic's claim that another person cannot 'know whether I am really in pain', he would reply: 'If we are using the word "know" as it is normally used (and how else are we to use it!), then other people very often know when I am in pain' (PI §246).

How else are we to use it? If the word 'know' is used in an abnormal way, then the statement containing it will not be addressing the question that was troubling us (whether another person can know, etc.); for this question was not meant in an abnormal sense. (If it were, then it would not be *troubling* us.)

It is, of course, no accident that the word 'know' has the meaning it has, as distinct from those given to it by certain philosophers. This word is deeply rooted in our form of life, and that is why questions about it are of philosophical interest. But that interest is undermined if artificial meanings, at variance with the ordinary use of the word, are introduced or assumed.

Language and mind

[margin note: that we can actually know the cause]

The distinction between what is hidden and what lies open to view is connected with a difference between two kinds of explanation. In the case of scientific explanation, there is, as pointed out earlier, a place for theory and discovery, and these can be surprising. Hence the appropriateness of Hume's dictum: 'For all we know *a priori*, anything may be the cause of anything'. This is not so, however, with another kind of explanation, and Hume's dictum would not make sense here. When a person gives reasons for what he says and does, his explanation is not a matter either of theory or of discovery. The point of such explanations is to make one's actions appear in a reasonable light – one that others can recognize as reasonable or at least intelligible; and the ability to provide such explanations is part of what we mean by 'a responsible agent'. Explanations of this kind have a justificatory role – the speaker tries to justify what he says or does – but there is no such role for the explanations of science.

To a large extent, Wittgenstein's later philosophy is an exploration of the justificatory kind of explanation and its limits; his main concern is to resist the temptation to push such explanations beyond their limits. Attempts to do so result, he argues, in a variety of spurious theories and confusions, including the confusion of one kind of explanation with the other. What happens in such cases is that when explanations of the 'manifest' kind run out, we try to make up the deficiency (as it seems to be) by resorting to explanations of the 'hidden', theoretical kind.

Section 1 of the *Investigations*, with its slogan, 'Explanations come to an end', contains the gist of much that is to follow. It begins with an account of language akin to that of the *Tractatus*, and this is followed by an everyday example in which someone goes shopping with a slip marked 'five red apples'. The shopkeeper, in accordance with this,

> opens the drawer marked 'apples', then he looks up the word 'red' in a table and finds a colour sample opposite it; then he says the series of cardinal numbers – I assume he knows them by heart – up to the word 'five' and for each number he takes an apple of the same colour as the sample out of the drawer.

Now the shopkeeper would be able to explain (justify) what he did by reference to the words on the slip and the recognized connections between them and his behaviour; but this presupposes that he would be aware of those connections – for example, the connection between the word 'five' and the procedure of counting. And in giving such an explanation he would assume that his listener, likewise, is aware of those connections. But now one might wonder how this awareness is itself to be explained. 'How does he know where and how he is to look up the word "red" and what he is to do with the word "five"?' This question is, however, resisted by Wittgenstein: 'Well, I assume he *acts* as I have described. Explanations come to an end somewhere'.[5]

Now one answer to the question 'How does he know…?' would be that he acquired this know-how in the course of learning his native language. It may be felt, however, that this is not good enough. Usually when we put the question 'How do you know?', we expect to be given reasons that a person *uses* in deciding how to act; and similarly when the question is put in response to some statement of fact. Thus, if we asked the shopkeeper how he knows that there are five apples in the bag, he might reply 'I counted them'; and here he would have *used* the procedure of counting to arrive at his conclusion, and the questioner would understand this.

But this satisfying kind of response is not available, if Wittgenstein is right, when we ask how the shopkeeper *knows how* to handle the words in the above example: 'what he is to do with' the words 'five' and 'red'. Here 'explanations come to an end'. Perhaps it will be thought that there must be something in the man's brain (some kind of 'wiring', as it is sometimes put) that would satisfy this demand for an explanation. But an item in the brain could not function in the desired way, for the man would not be aware of such an item; and even if he were, it could not serve as *his reason* for acting as he does.

More often, however, it is some entity or process in the mind, rather than the brain, that has been invoked to supply the desired explanation. Thus it has often been thought, both by philosophers and by ordinary people, that meaning and understanding are to be explained by reference to mental images or other mental occurrences; and this assumption is one of the main targets of the later Wittgenstein's philosophy of language. In combatting it, he uses a variety of examples from ordinary life.

> If I give someone the order, 'fetch me a red flower from the meadow', how is he to know what sort of flower to bring, as I have only given him a *word*?
> Now the answer one might suggest first is that he went to look for a red flower carrying a red image in his mind, and comparing it with the flowers to see which of them had the colour of the image.
>
> (BB: 3)

In other passages he is concerned with 'speaker's meaning' as distinct from 'word meaning'. 'I say "Come here" and point towards A. B, who is standing by him, takes a step towards me. I say "No; A is to come"' (Z §21). A was the person I meant; but what did my meaning A consist in? How is the difference between meaning A and meaning B to be explained? Again a 'mental' explanation suggests itself: I must have *thought* of A as I spoke (Z §13). Here, comments Wittgenstein, 'meaning is imagined as a kind of mental pointing, indicating' (Z §12). This 'mental pointing' would be more fundamental than the original pointing with one's finger, which, taken by itself, turned out to be ambiguous and hence insufficient.

Such 'mental' theories – of meaning, understanding, remembering, trying to 'find the right word', playing a piece of music thoughtfully – are discussed by Wittgenstein throughout his later writings. To do justice to the richness and depth of his discussions of these theories is beyond the scope of this essay; but it may be said that they are informed by three main concerns: to show that they are not as plausible as they may at first seem; that they are unnecessary; and that they could not, in any case, supply what seems to be required.

Let us return to the example of the red flower. In that discussion Wittgenstein immediately concedes that one *may* call up an image when obeying the request 'fetch me a red flower'. But must it be so? If we reflect on the great variety of things that one may be asked to do (or fetch), the idea that there must always be an appropriate image quickly loses its appeal. (Consider such requests as 'Fetch me a red or blue flower', or 'Fetch me the first flower you happen to see' or 'Fetch someone who knows about botany'.) But even in the original example, it is simply not true that people who are given that order would always form a mental image of what they are to fetch. This is a matter of personal psychology: some people are inclined to form mental images, others are not. (Here again, of course, the person advancing the theory may insist that it 'must be' so that an image must be present in every case, even when one is not conscious of it.)

But what, in any case, would be the explanatory force of such images where they do occur? An image, whether mental or physical, can always be interpreted in an indefinite number of ways.

> Imagine a picture representing a boxer in a particular stance. Now this picture can be used to tell someone how he should stand, should hold himself; or how he should not hold himself; or how a particular man did stand in such and such a place; and so on.
>
> (PI: p.11; cf. p.54; also Z §317)

To combat the assumption that we could not understand an order except by means of an image, Wittgenstein asks us to 'consider the order "*imagine* a red patch"'. One would not be 'tempted in this case to think that *before* obeying you must have imagined a red patch to serve you as a pattern for the red patch which you were ordered to imagine' (ibid). It would, of course, be useless to posit a *further* image, to enable one to 'imagine a red patch' correctly, for the same question would arise again about the further image, and so on.

Now the question 'How does he know how to obey the order to *imagine* a red patch?' may strike us as absurd. This, we might reply, is just something we are able to do, and no explanation for this is needed. But then, of course, we might just as well say the same about the original order, to fetch a red flower. The assumption that this *needed* explaining was unjustified. Suppose I were asked 'How did you know what you were to do?' The answer might be 'He told me'. This would be a perfectly good explanation. But suppose the questioner went on: 'How did you make the connection between a mere set of words and what you did?' The assumption that *this* needs explaining, and the resulting quest for a theory, are rejected by Wittgenstein.

How would we determine whether a person had *understood* the request to fetch a red flower from the meadow? Not by finding out what went on in his mind or brain, but by observing what he *did* in response to that request. In some cases this would consist simply in carrying out the request; in others it might be a matter of making a suitable reply, and so on. The appropriate response would vary according to circumstances. But the occurrence of an image in his mind would never settle the question.

In the mental theories of meaning and understanding we have another attempt to sever language from its human setting. Opposing such theories, Wittgenstein denies that what gives meaning to our words is something that 'takes place in a queer kind of medium, the mind...If we had to name anything which is the life of the sign, we should have to say that it was its *use*' (BB: 3, 4). Language is for communication between human beings, and not between minds or brains. This is the main point of Wittgenstein's discussion.

Human beings

The distinction between philosophy and science is one aspect of Wittgenstein's 'humanism'; another is the distinction between human beings and minds or brains. The Cartesian view, that a human being is essentially a mind, has its counterpart in recent writings, where a similar status is given to the brain. In contrast to both of these, Wittgenstein insists that the attributes that make us what we are are essentially tied to human behaviour in the world in which we live. It is human beings, and not their minds or brains, that think and feel, use language, understand and interact with one another, and so on.

Both of these aspects of Wittgenstein's thought – his rejection of theory and his position on human beings – are at odds with recent treatments of 'the problem of consciousness'. Here it is widely assumed that consciousness is a property of the brain, so that problems about it should be amenable to scientific theories and discoveries, just like problems about the properties of other bodily organs and, indeed, about the physical world in general. Why, it is asked, 'should consciousness be the one thing that can't be explained? Solids, liquids and gases can be explained', and so on (Dennett 1991: 455). Consciousness, it appears, is 'the largest outstanding obstacle [to] a scientific understanding of the universe' (Chalmers 1996: xi).

But is it right to assume that an understanding of consciousness is, or must be, part of 'a scientific understanding of the universe', to be acquired by scientific methods? This is certainly the way to gain understanding about the brain; and also of *some* aspects of consciousness. But are there not others about which it is 'true to say that our considerations could not be scientific ones' (PI §109)? Let us consider a remark about consciousness that occurs prominently in the *Investigations*.

> Only of a living human being and what resembles (behaves like) a living human being can one say: it has sensations; it sees; is blind; hears; is deaf; is conscious or unconscious.
>
> (PI §281; cf. §360)

This is not a scientific claim, but a statement about the use of language. Wittgenstein did not arrive at it by scientific methods, and the reader is not expected to subject it to scientific scrutiny; his own knowledge of the language should enable him to agree or disagree with it.[6]

Here is a typical example of philosophical thought as distinct from scientific research and theory; it also illustrates the way in which the former can be fundamental with respect to the latter. In the current science-oriented literature about consciousness we often find such questions as, 'How can brains be conscious?' But if the statement just quoted is true, then these questions embody a nonsensical presupposition, since the brain does not in the least resemble or behave like a living human being. It is true that the brain has an important causal role in connection with consciousness and its various modes (seeing, having sensations, and so on), but as far as resemblance to a living human being is concerned, it is no better than any other bodily organ.

The mere fact that it is possible to *question* whether consciousness can be ascribed to the brain – whether this makes sense – is sufficient proof of the distinction between scientific and philosophical enquiries, as pursued by Wittgenstein and others. That question about consciousness and the brain is not scientific and it cannot be treated by the methods of science. (Similarly, the question 'What is science?' calls for reflection on the concept of science and not for scientific research.)

What is the source of the assumption that consciousness is a property of the brain and that an understanding of it must belong to 'a scientific understanding of the universe'? Wittgenstein sometimes spoke of 'a craving for generality' (BB: 18) – a desire to treat a variety of items as if they were essentially of the same type, rather than doing justice to their variety. Such a craving is evident, and sometimes explicit, in the works of the writers I have mentioned. 'Somehow', declares Dennett, 'the mind must be the brain' (1991: 41). David Armstrong speaks of the 'attraction' that a 'materialist account of the mind' has for him: namely, that 'it provides a unifying account of the relation of mind to matter'. Given the example of a man who intends to paint the bathroom, he puts it to us: 'Must not the man continue in [a] certain definite state (a state of the brain, I would take it?)' (Armstrong and Malcolm 1984: 159). And this being assumed, 'it seems natural to go on and identify...the intention' with this state of the brain. Another writer, conceding that lack of scientific knowledge prevents us from identifying 'the exact neural substrate for the sudden thought that you are late with the rent', relies on a *'metaphysical commitment* to the primacy of the physical' to sustain him in his view that there must be such a substrate (Kim 1994: 581). Wittgenstein, in the passage about games quoted earlier, admonished the reader not to say, 'There must be...', but to 'look and see'. This advice was given in a discussion about language, but it is also appropriate for the 'commitments' and 'must be's' in the passages just quoted.

It has been claimed, however, that it is Wittgenstein, and not the scientifically minded philosopher, who is guilty of an irrational prejudice. According to John Searle, we need only open our minds to 'the contemporary scientific world view', to see that consciousness 'is part of the natural biological order..., falling into place naturally as an evolved pheno-typical trait of certain types of organisms...' (Searle 1992: 90). Some people, he continues, 'notably Wittgenstein', find the scientific world view repulsive; 'but like it or not, it is the world view we have'. There is, however, no reason to think that Wittgenstein would object to describing consciousness as a product of evolution or that he would find anything repulsive about this. The issue, in any case, is not about matters of taste or personal commitment; it is about the logical status of the claims and assumptions in question. Given a scientific question, the proper approach will be that of scientific methods; but *whether* a given question is scientific cannot itself be a scientific question: it calls for reflection on the logical status of that question, and not for scientific research. And similarly, the assumption, made by scientists or others, that a given question or claim makes sense, cannot itself be confirmed by scientific research.

Wittgenstein's statement ('Only of a human being...') undermines the excessive pretensions of theory in two ways. It is itself an example of non-theoretical reflection, and it challenges the assumption that questions about consciousness demand a theoretical response, involving the brain. Consciousness, it reminds us – sensation, thought, perception and the rest – is ascribed to human beings (and 'what resembles them', and so on), and not to parts of their bodies.

Art

In the last section I quoted Wittgenstein's warning about a 'craving for generality'. This craving, he suggested, has its source in a 'preoccupation with the method of science', of 'reducing the explanation of natural phenomena to the smallest possible number of primitive natural laws' (BB: 18). Philosophers, he warned, are 'irresistibly tempted to ask and answer questions in the way science does'; whereas, on his view, 'it can never be our job to reduce anything to anything'. These remarks are appropriate for the science-oriented treatment of consciousness, whereby the human being is reduced to a physical organ, the brain; and the multifarious behaviour of human being is reduced to the reactions of a physical organ in accordance with laws of physics and chemistry.

The remarks are also appropriate for the idea – the hope, perhaps – that aesthetics might be treated as a science; an idea that was considered by Wittgenstein in the 'Lectures on Aesthetics'. The science he had in mind was psychology: 'The idea is that once we are more advanced, everything – all the mysteries of Art – will be understood by psychological experiments' (LA: 17; cf. 11, 19). The expression 'once we are more advanced' is characteristic of such ideas. Thus the difficulties of physicalist treatments of consciousness, as discussed in the last section, are often regarded as merely temporary setbacks, to be overcome with the advancement of science, as if a logical incoherence could be resolved by scientific methods.

Why might aesthetics be regarded as a science? The contemplation of works of art produces certain feelings in us, and this is one reason why we value them. The situation is one of cause and effect, and this might lead us to try to establish 'laws of aesthetics', linking causes and effects in the same way as for natural phenomena. Such knowledge might be made available to creative artists who want their works to be *effective* in producing the desired feelings. (Aristotle seems to have held such a view: his aim was to present a recipe for the writing of effective tragedies, those that produce suitable feelings in the audience.) Such a 'science of aesthetics' would be akin to medical science where certain substances (drugs, etc.) are found, by experiment, to be effective in producing such and such desired results.

This view was, however, rejected by Wittgenstein. 'An aesthetic explanation', he said, 'is not a causal explanation' (LA: 18). Speaking of the 'justification for a feature in a work of art', he rejected the answer that 'Something else would produce the wrong effect'.[7] What we do in aesthetics, he said, is 'to *draw one's attention* to certain features, to place things side by side so as to exhibit these features'. To get someone to recognize that 'This is the climax' of a particular work or passage is like getting him to see that 'this is the man in the puzzle picture' (AWL: 38–9): 'Our attention is drawn to a certain feature, and from that point forward we see that feature'.

Wittgenstein did not say whom he had in mind in rejecting the causal, 'psychological' view of aesthetics, but the view that art is essentially about producing certain feelings in us had been vividly expressed by Clive Bell, for one. 'The starting point for all systems of aesthetics', he wrote,

> must be the personal experience of a peculiar emotion. The objects that provoke this emotion we call works of art...and if we can discover some quality common and peculiar to all the objects that provoke it, we shall have solved what I take to be the central problem of aesthetics.[8]

> (Bell 1915: 21–2)

This passage, with its 'common and peculiar', again expresses a craving for generality: the assumption that the relevant causal power must belong to a single kind of quality (which he went on to identify as 'significant form'). According to Bell, the expression 'work of art' can be defined in terms of this causal power, and 'we gibber' if we use it in the absence of such a definition (Bell 1915: 7).

Bell did not advocate a scientific treatment of aesthetics, but this would be a natural development of the view that art is essentially about the production of a particular emotion. Now Wittgenstein did not deny that, in aesthetics or elsewhere, science and theory may produce interesting results; what he resisted was the idea that they might *replace* the 'humanistic' approach. Thus, in the case of aesthetics, it might be found that positive and negative aesthetic judgements are correlated with 'particular kinds of mechanism in the brain' (LA: 20); and given a knowledge of such connections, we might be able to 'predict what a particular person would like and dislike. We could calculate these things'. The question was, however, 'whether this is the sort of explanation we should like to have' in aesthetics.

The difference between the two kinds of explanation is especially striking in the case of jokes. I recently heard it announced that 'scientists have discovered what makes people laugh'. What the scientists had discovered was that certain processes in the brain were correlated with the impulse to laugh, so that people could be got to laugh by stimulating that part of their brains. (The reaction was not merely automatic: the subjects rationalized it by reference to some object or text that had been placed before them.) But again, this is 'not the sort of explanation we should like to have' when we do aesthetics or explain a joke: such an explanation would not help us to see the point of the joke.

Another aspect of 'the sort of explanation we would want to have' is that, in appropriate cases, the person to whom the explanation is given should be able to *recognize* it as the right one. Thus, even if the explanation is put in causal terms, the causal relation would not be of the kind where 'anything may be the cause of anything'. An example used by Wittgenstein was that of 'someone [who] heard syncopated music of Brahms played and asked "What is the queer rhythm which makes me wobble?"'

> The answer might be 'It is the 3 against 4'. One could play certain phrases and he would say: 'Yes. It's this peculiar rhythm I meant'. On the other hand, if he didn't agree, this wouldn't be the explanation.
>
> (LA: 20–1)

Here we have a case of cause and effect (the effect being the 'wobble'), but not one that is akin to cause and effect in empirical science. What is important here is that the person receiving that explanation could hear for himself that it was right: he was able to *recognize* that rhythm as the one he meant. And his acceptance of this was not based on empirical evidence showing that such rhythms usually have that effect on people. (A similar point can be made about the connection between seeing the point of a joke and laughing.)

If causation in aesthetics *were* like that in the natural world, then it should not matter how the relevant feelings and other reactions were caused. Given the desired effects, one cause should be as good as another. But this is not so. Suppose I wanted to listen to a particular piece of music. Would my aim be merely 'to get this and that effect?' (LA: 29). 'Doesn't the minuet itself matter? – hearing *this*: would another have done as well?' And what if the same effect could be produced by some means other than music? 'Would a syringe which produces these effects...do just as well?' It is true, Wittgenstein points out, that 'you could play a minuet once and get a lot out of it, and play the same minuet another time and get nothing out of it'. And from this we might infer that what you get out of it, when you do, is 'independent of the minuet'. But this is not so: it is not as if you might get the desired effect without the minuet. Similarly, 'a man may sing a song with expression and without expression' (LA: 29), but it would be absurd to suppose that one might have the expression without the song. There *is* cause and effect in the enjoyment of art, but there is more to this than can be captured by the methods and descriptions of science.

Wittgenstein also discussed cases in which feelings are unlikely to play a role. A person trying on a suit at the tailor's might say no more than 'That's the right length' or 'that's too narrow'; and he would show his approval 'chiefly by wearing it often, liking it when it is seen', and so on (LA: 5). Again, in designing a door one might give such instructions as 'Higher, higher... and yes, that's right' (LA: 13). In discussing such cases he contrasted what he called 'discontent' with 'discomfort', by which he meant a feeling. The person designing a door or trying on a suit would be *discontented* until their proportions had been got right, but this would not mean that he was experiencing a feeling (of discomfort). We are not to suppose that a statement such as, 'This door is too low', is 'something like an expression of discomfort *plus* knowing the cause of the discomfort and asking for it to be removed' (LA: 13). Such statements are not expressions of feeling, and the relevant relation between speaker and object is not one of cause and effect.[9]

Art and philosophy

Wittgenstein, as quoted earlier, saw his philosophical investigation as being of things that 'lie open to view', so that 'what is hidden is of no interest to us'. Now this may seem a paradoxical attitude. What, it may be asked, can be the point of an investigation that promises neither 'new information' nor 'any kind of theory' (PI §109, §126)?

Wittgenstein was not the first to characterize philosophy in this way. In a famous passage in Plato's *Meno*, Socrates and his interlocutor address the question 'What is virtue?', and after some attempts to produce a satisfactory answer, Meno draws attention to the apparently paradoxical nature of their enterprise. Either they already know what virtue is, in which case there is no need for the enquiry; or they do not, in which case they will not be able to recognize the object of their search even if they come upon it (80D–E). In response to this, Socrates (using a rather implausible mathematical analogy) argues that there is a place for enquiries in which, in a certain sense, the answer we are looking for is already known to us. Although one may not be able to say what virtue is, one should be able to recognize a correct account of it, if and when it were given.

In this respect philosophical progress, as conceived both by Wittgenstein and by Socrates in the *Meno*, is analogous to progress in aesthetic appreciation. A skillful critic can enhance our appreciation of a work of art by pointing out features that lie open before us – aspects of the work to which we had not paid due attention, or the right kind of attention. He 'opens our eyes', we say; even though, of course, our eyes were open already. And here, as in philosophy, it is essential that we come to see for ourselves the significance of what has been pointed out to us.

There is also an analogy between philosophy and the art of fiction. It is sometimes said that such works can communicate important truths about the human condition, and this is held to be one of the main reasons for valuing them. But how can this be? If the putative communication is of things of which we are ignorant, why should we trust it, given that we are dealing with a work of fiction? If, on the other hand, we can recognize the account as true ('true to life', as we might say), how can we *learn* from it? The way out of the dilemma is to acknowledge that learning is not always a matter of acquiring new information. A work of art, like a work of philosophy, can provide *insight* into the human condition without informing us of facts of which we had been ignorant.

These analogies must not, of course, be pressed too far. The differences between understanding a philosophical argument and appreciating a work of art are obvious enough; and so are the differences between the insights provided by philosophy and those to be found in works of fiction. But there are, at least, some family resemblances here.

Notes

1 'Requirement', in the Pears and McGuinness version, seems the better translation of 'Forderung'; but the Ogden version, which uses 'postulate', was done with Wittgenstein's collaboration.

2 'For a *large* class of cases...', he writes in PI §43, '"meaning" can be explained thus: the meaning of a word is its use in the language'. What he meant by this formulation has been a matter of debate, which I shall not go into here. (I discuss the matter in Hanfling 1999.)

3 An interesting example here is the word 'art', which has long been subject to attempts at definition. Following the publication of Wittgenstein's work, it was suggested that the word might be definable by reference to some feature not visible in the work itself, a 'non-exhibited property' (Mandelbaum 1965); and this led to George Dickie's definition of 'work of art' in terms of what had been done with it, as distinct from any property apparent in it (the 'institutional theory'). According to this, what makes something a work of art is (roughly) the fact that it has been offered as 'a candidate for appreciation' by someone acting on behalf of 'the artworld' (Dickie 1974). (For critical discussion, see Hanfling, 1999.)

4 It might be thought that in speaking of *explaining* 'what a game is', Wittgenstein is not conforming to his resolve to 'do away with all explanation'; but this is not really so. Of course we can, in various ways, explain the meanings of particular words. What Wittgenstein is opposing is the idea of a *general* explanation – a theory – of meaning.

5 The example is marred by the choice of 'red' as the colour in question, since it is hardly likely that a normal speaker of the language would need a colour chart for this colour. But it would be easy to invent an example with a less familiar colour, where this would be necessary.

6 The remark is qualified by Wittgenstein in the next section (PI §282) but this does not affect the issue.

7 AWL: 38. As with the 'Lectures on Aesthetics', this text is compiled from notes taken by those who attended, and not from material written down by Wittgenstein himself.

8 Herbert Read, writing in the 1930s, put forward a causal explanation of *beauty*. 'Certain arrangements in the proportion of the shape and surface of the mass of things', he wrote, 'result in a pleasurable sensation, whilst the lack of such arrangement leads to indifference or even to positive discomfort and revulsion' (Read 1972: 18). According to Peter Lewis, Wittgenstein may have had in mind I.A. Richards's *The Principles of Literary Criticism*. Richards treated his topic in connection with what he called 'a psychological theory of value'. (Lewis 1998).

9 Some of Wittgenstein's examples were probably taken from his experiences in designing the 'Wittgenstein house' in Vienna. This is the house he designed in partnership with the architect Paul Engelmann for his sister Margarete. The final plan

was drawn in 1926 and the house completed in 1928. In later years another sister, Hermine, described how unyielding Wittgenstein had been in getting the measurements of internal features absolutely right. Thus the ceiling of a particular room had to be raised by three centimetres after the house was almost completed. 'His feeling', she adds, 'was absolutely right, and this feeling had to be obeyed' (Nedo 1983: 208). She also spoke of 'a great longing to see those noble doors [of the house] again, from which, even if all the rest of the house fell down, one could recognize the spirit of its creator' (Nedo 1983: 218). It may be worth adding an illustration of another aspect of Wittgenstein's spirit. In a letter of 1946 he expressed the hope that some of his sisters would return to live in the house rather than let it stand 'meaningless'. If the house was not to their taste, he added, this would at least be a *'family* non-resemblance [*Familien* unahnlichkeit]' (Nedo 1983: 219).

Bibliography

Bell, C. (1915) *Art*, London: Chatto & Windus.

Armstrong, D.M. and Malcolm, N. (1984) *Consciousness and Causality*, Oxford: Basil Blackwell.

Chalmers, D.J. (1996) *The Conscious Mind*, Oxford: Oxford University Press.

Dennett, D.C. (1991) *Consciousness Explained*, London: Penguin.

Dickie, G. (1974) *Art and the Aesthetic: An Institutional Analysis*, Ithaca, NY: Cornell University Press.

Hanfling, O. (1989) *Wittgensteins Later Philosophy,* London: Macmillan.

—— (1999) 'The Institutional Theory: A Candidate for Appreciation', *British Journal of Aesthetics* 39(2): 189–94.

Kim, J. (1994) 'Supervinience', in S. D. Guttenplan (ed.), *Companion to the Philosophy of Mind*, Oxford: Basil Blackwell, 575–83.

Lewis, P. (1998) 'Wittgenstein's Aesthetic Misunderstandings', in K.S. Johannesson (ed.), *Wittgenstein and Aesthetics,* Bergen: University of Bergen Press.

Mandelbaum, M. (1965) 'Family Resemblances', *American Philosophical Quarterly* 12(3): 219–28.

Nedo, M. (ed.) (1983) *Wittgenstein*, Frankfurt: Suhrkamp.

Read, H. (1972) *The Meaning of Art*, London: Faber.

Searle, J. (1992) *The Rediscovery of the Mind*, Cambridge, MA: MIT Press.

Wittgenstein, L. (1958) *Philosophical Investigations* (PI), ed. G.E.M. Anscombe, Oxford: Blackwell.

—— (1958) *The Blue and Brown Books* (BB), Oxford: Blackwell.

—— (1961) *Tractatus Logico-Philosophicus* (TLP), trans. D.F. Pears and B.F. McGuinness, London: Routledge and Kegan Paul.

—— (1967) *Zettel* (Z), ed. G.E.M. Anscombe and G.H. von Wright, trans G.E.M. Anscombe, Oxford: Blackwell.

—— (1970) *Lectures and Conversations on Aesthetics, Psychology and Religious Beliefs,* (LA) ed. C. Barrett, Oxford: Blackwell.

—— (1974) *Philosophical Grammar* (PG), ed. R. Rhees, trans. A.J.P. Kenny, Oxford: Blackwell.

—— (1979) *Wittgenstein's Lectures, Cambridge* (AWL) *1932–5*, ed. A. Ambrose, Oxford: Basil Blackwell.

4

WITTGENSTEIN, PERFORMING ART AND ACTION

Graham McFee

Introduction

This chapter explores some central ideas for aesthetics that might be found within Wittgenstein's writing; in particular, themes for (or from) the performing arts. For good reasons, Wittgenstein's writings offer no general account of art or of the aesthetic. We can reconstruct (from his hints) what Wittgenstein could have said about the nature of, for example, art and our understanding of art, especially for the performing arts: why was he right not to say more himself? Following him here engages with both the nature of philosophical generality, as Wittgenstein (rightly) conceived it, and the place of generality in aesthetics.

Ludwig Wittgenstein might be expected to have written extensively about art. Such an aesthetics both represents one of the standard elements of philosophy, as in (for example) Schopenhauer, and reflects a particular interest. His friends report Wittgenstein's admiration for music and for (at least) the dance of Fred Astaire (Rhees 1984: 120); students' notes from his lectures on aesthetics of summer 1938 providing the text for the *Lectures and Conversations* volume.[1] Yet Wittgenstein wrote very little on the arts, to go by what has come down to us in the *Nachlass*. This in contrast to most of the topics on which he thought in the last twenty years of his life, where the norm was a re-working of large stretches of argument (although aspects of Wittgenstein's style, together with some editorial practices, have prevented some observers noticing the sustained discussions characteristically produced). Even a remark with an explicitly artistic theme is often directed at some concern in the philosophy of mind or the philosophy of understanding. As we shall see, performing arts provide *examples* because they suit Wittgenstein's other purposes (in the philosophy of psychology) and because they point *away* from rationalistic conceptions of human behaviour in general on which one can (in principle) always *say*, if asked, what one is doing, and *how* – that is, provide one's (relevant) beliefs, desires, etc. (although the subtlety and contextual character of some of Wittgenstein's remarks will be lost if we consider students' notes for his lectures, rather than his own meticulous writings).

So, this chapter briefly (and rather sketchily) addresses a passage from Wittgenstein's writings in which he develops his insight that philosophers should investigate understanding of (in this case) *music* by considering *explaining* music; which leads to a succinct discussion of the presuppositions and context of such explanation. Consideration of the place of competent judges offers morals for aesthetics from Wittgenstein's remarks and procedures, before a brief conclusion (of a more general kind) on the picture of philosophy thereby subtended. As we shall see, Wittgenstein's insights should not be thought to constitute a theory; at least, not in any strong sense of that term. For they do not combine in any comprehensive way to yield a positive and (fairly) universal account of, for instance, *action* (his case) or *art* (our case). That is, we should see Wittgenstein's remarks as slogans, rather than theses.

The text

In his notebook for 15 February 1948 (MS 137: 20ff), Wittgenstein wrote a longish remark – his one comment of the day – ostensibly about understanding music, now largely published,[2] and here identified by paragraph number.[3] This passage reflects one moment in Wittgenstein's thought (he drew no sub-dividing lines round part of it, for example, as he often did). Taking it as a whole, we may glean insights different from those found in students' notes of lectures, where both their status as *notes* and as *from lectures* might be stressed by those who regard Wittgenstein as a meticulous writer.

Although a sustained argument of Wittgenstein's, not all its features (or argumentative directions) need concern us here: some are directed to identifying the philosophical cul-de-sac. So I highlight the argument from just five of these paragraphs ([a], [b], [f], [h], [m]), to draw on some themes specific to our concerns here; but, of course, I both chose them as importantly linked and present them in that way.[4]

Wittgenstein begins by asking about how 'explaining a music phrase' (para [a]) is related to *understanding* that phrase. As he notes, 'sometimes the simplest explanation is a gesture; on another occasion, it might be a dance step' (para [a]). But why might this common sense way of explaining one's understanding be rejected? The answer lies in (mistaken) assumptions about how 'explanation' here must be understood; what form it must take – in particular, the completeness of any satisfactory explanations of understanding.

In illustration, Wittgenstein considers the suggestion that understanding the musical phrase involves 'experiencing something whilst we hear it'. On this view, such an experience would just occur at the same time as one's hearing of the music. But then, how could reference to such an experience be genuinely explanatory: 'what part does the explanation play' (para [a]) if that experience is just a concomitant of hearing the music? Clearly, there could be no role for such explanations, were this the right answer. Mere concomitance gives us no possibility of offering the one as a reason for our understanding of the other.

Elsewhere, Wittgenstein assumes this conclusion about musical understanding to make a point about understanding language: 'Speech with and without thought is to be compared with the playing of a piece of music with and without thought' (PI §341). In this remark, Wittgenstein's argumentative point is that the difference between a passage of music played with thought and that passage played without thought cannot lie simply in what the performer is thinking. On the contrary, it must be apparent in the playing, in how the tones are sounded: and if we sometimes describe such differences in playing as 'imperceptible', they are precisely not that. For we did recognize the two pieces of playing as different. So, whatever the difficulty of this point for speech, Wittgenstein assumes it will be obvious for music.

In our passage, though, Wittgenstein sketches an argument for that conclusion. Consider, for example, the dance step imagined here accompanying my hearing of the music as a way of explaining the music: if the imagined dance step is so important, 'it would be better to perform *that* rather than the music' (para [a]) – the music (our original concern) drops out of consideration. Rather, the dance step *alone* would be sufficient. Yet, if so, how could the dance step *explain* the musical phrase? Thus, to conceive of explanation in this way sets up an unbridgeable gap between the proffered explanation – the dance step, say – and the artwork (the music). Wittgenstein concludes, and rightly, 'that is all *mis*understanding' of how appreciating music really works, for we cannot see how the content of the explanation relates either to 'the content of the music' or to the content of the understanding: or rather – were this the right account – there could be no connection. In trying to 'rate' the dance-step in contrast to the music, we would separate explanation from what is explained. For such objects as artworks, this is a confusion: the understanding in this case must be *of the music*. And we can see what explanatory roles that understanding might play just in case we can imagine others failing to understand the musical work – then our explanation might help them (as stressing the metre helped Wittgenstein understand Klopstock (LA: 4) – though it would not necessarily help another person nor necessarily help Wittgenstein understand another poet).

So identifying such a view as 'all *mis*understanding' recognizes that one danger here is the separation of explanation from what is to be explained. But what account of understanding *does* this recognition subtend?

In answer, Wittgenstein rehearses a successful explanation: 'I...tell him "It's as though..."; then he says, "Yes, now I understand" or "Yes, now I see how it's to be played..."'(para [b]) (note that playing and listening are treated together: CV: 51). Explanation of the *relevant* sort would indeed yield understanding, but at the level of one's perception of the artwork, hearing the music in this case: the insight achieved through the explanation must be an experienced insight – he comes either to hear the work differently as a result of my explanation, or to recognize for himself the character of his own experience of the work through my explanation of it. Without this, the explanation does not engage with his listening to that music. So my explanation does not simply offer detached information about the work – only what informs perception of the work is a contribution to understanding of the work, even when that more general understanding is inflected by knowing what, say, Schoenberg intended (if this differs from what he achieved). So any account of the relation of explanation of a work to its understanding will also be 'all *mis*understanding' when it assumes that such an explanation can provide more of a guarantee than is implicit in our usual practices of explaining, describing, teaching, and the like; at least, if these are treated reflectively.

For philosophical purposes, it is often misleading to treat understanding in terms of images and so on: but is it always wrong? Certainly, Wittgenstein is not here railing against *all* explanations of this sort (although that is how some theorists read him: a point to return to). Instead, he asks what perplexity such an answer addresses: what might one realistically be asking, if a satisfactory answer is in terms of mental images or kinaesthetic sensations? Perhaps such an account would be useful in getting a particular pianist to produce a certain tonal quality. If this answer works in such a case, it does all that I (its utterer) need. More usually, though, concern with the understanding of particular musical works will not be profitably answered by focusing on the experience of listener or player: rather, we must turn to something public. Here, we should consider someone taught to understand music, 'for that is the only sort of teaching that could be called explaining music' (para [f]). And explaining must be more than causing to understand; explanation is neither brainwashing nor 'beating sense into'. Further, explanation is connected to content: when I have taught a person to understand a piece of music, I have explained that piece to him.

Yet what are the presuppositions of such understanding or appreciation? Wittgenstein answers figuratively by urging that 'appreciating music is a manifestation of the life of mankind' (para [h]). So, describing that appreciation to someone would involve describing music to him, as well as saying 'how human beings react to it'. Wittgenstein makes a connection through to the later idea of a 'special conceptual world' (para [m]: Z §165), but also to the powers and capacities of humans: making appropriate artistic judgements (that is, judging artworks as artworks) involves recognizing both the art-status of those works and their artistic value. In this sense, then, seeing artistic value requires beings of appropriate capabilities.

But acknowledging that such-and-such a movement sequence is *in fact* a dance (an artwork) should be seen as a transforming of the movement sequence into dance, such that anyone who misses, or cannot make sense of, that transformation misperceives the movement sequence. Hence, following Danto (1981), we might speak of 'the transfigurational character' of art-status, where such transfiguration is a condition of there being art, with its distinctive value. Furthermore, the person must be taught to understand this musical work for himself: that is, not just given information, but so that the information/knowledge is mobilized in experience.[5] He must find the work (for example) expressive for himself: and this is fragile. For each generation must come to see particular key works as expressive for itself: the artistic centrality of those works must be retrieved if they are to continue to be understood (and hence valued) as previously with a particular cultural community (see McFee 1992b). But, relatedly, there is a (potential) contribution of his general knowledge of, for instance, poetry or painting, so that one might (also?) teach him these (para [h]): and this speaks to justifying the use of one expression, *art*, here.

Moreover, the connection between such understanding and the performance of the work is clear enough; as Wittgenstein asks elsewhere: 'Would it make sense to ask a composer whether one should hear a figure like *this* or like *this*; if that didn't also mean: whether one should *play* it this way or that?' (RPPI §1130). As this rhetorical question urges, both hearing the figure a certain way and playing it that way are implicated in the nature of the work.

Despite the fact that we readily say, 'I *experienced* that passage quite differently' to describe our understanding that musical passage differently, too much weight must not be given to the term 'experience'. This form of words – with its apparent reference to *experience* – is only misleading to those not 'at home in the special conceptual world that belongs to these situations' (para [m]): that is, to the world of music. Wittgenstein offers an informative analogy, obscured in the translation: the German text literally says, 'I have won the party'. It is a useful analogy here because this way of describing victory is used only for matches at chess (and other serious board games),[7] and so is accurately rendered into English (as the translation has it), 'I won the match'. Someone who understood the German *words* but knew nothing of how serious board games such as chess are discussed (in German) would/could take this as some oblique remark about parties. So the analogy is that, in the cases of both music and this remark about (say) chess, one needs more than just an understanding of individual elements. Then those not part of 'the special conceptual world' of chess will typically fail to make sense of that remark, taking it as about parties or failing to make sense of it at all. These remarks show Wittgenstein stressing the powers and capacities of knowledgeable individuals, against the backdrop of 'the life of [hu]mankind' (para [h]); and recognizing that explanation of a particular artwork takes place against a background of art-making, art-understanding and art-valuing.

Central here is a rejection of any hard-and-fast contrast between (neutral) understanding of art and its valuing (see Dickie 2000: 232; and compare McFee 1989), although seeming to import such contrast. Understanding music is affective – emotion-involving, one might think – in ways some other kinds of understanding (say, understanding of physics) are not for most people. Indeed, although typically lost when thinking from other cases, the (affective?) connection between understanding and appreciative valuing is central for art. To recognize that the object is an artwork is, other things being equal, to recognize its (artistic) value: anything else is not *you* recognizing that value. So personal 'impact' is clearly important: 'taking someone's word' for artistic merit cannot replace direct engagement, as is shown by our reaction to (a) 'head in catalogue' tours of an art gallery; (b) taking the 'advice' of a dance critic writing in a newspaper. In both these cases, lack of perceptual engagement and lack of (possible) affective engagement go hand in hand. Relatedly, one has reasons to doubt that someone understands a particular artwork if he/she is entirely unmoved by it: similarly, for those who cannot value that work (once art-status is granted) – for are they really seeing its features and its connections to the past (value) of art if they fail to recognize its value? Wittgenstein questions whether such people are locating the artwork in the context of artistic understanding (para [g]), since appreciating a work is here both appreciating (recognizing) what its features are and what is good about them. So we might doubt that so-and-so really understood music if he/she had no appreciation (no affect) in respect of it, at least for great music. Even Tibby (in Forster's *Howard's End*)[8] 'who is profoundly versed in counterpoint, and holds the full score open on his knee' (pp. 44–5) responds: he may follow the score, but he (also?) follows the music. Thus, as the transition passage for the drum approached, he 'raised his finger' (p. 46) – about as emotional a gesture as that young man manages![8]

As an example of merely apparent understanding of art (or understanding only adequate for limited purposes), consider the conclusion to Tom Wolfe's discussion of Abstract Expressionism:

> in that moment of absolutely dispassionate abdication, of insouciant withering away [of art's traditional concerns and practices], Art made its final flight, climbed higher and higher in an ever-decreasing tighter turning spiral until, with one last erg of freedom, one last dendritic synapse, it disappeared up its own fundamental aperture...and came out the other side as Art Theory!
>
> (Wolfe 1975: 109)

This may sound like a way of understanding the artworks without valuing them: instead, Wolfe implies that the objects he discusses have no intrinsic worth (or no worth open to direct scrutiny); they have no place within art's traditional concerns and practices. It is a way of denying them a place in 'the special conceptual world' (para [m]: Z §165) of art. So, far from 'understanding but not valuing' these artworks, this view disputes their art status.

Of course, a work might be recognized as of little value; as a minor artwork. Thus talk of valuing here should not be overstressed. Further, one might, exceptionally, recognize bad artworks or artworks of no value: here, the 'exceptional' nature of the case reiterates the original point, for this will be the exception (McFee 1989: 230–1). Moreover, one might, on some occasions, be content with a very low-level understanding of an artwork: here, its artistic value need not be moot, and hence need not be mentioned. In such a case, judgements of someone who, unbeknownst to us, could not value the work might be quite satisfactory. But, typically, if the kind of 'understanding' such a respondent manifests will answer the questions raised about an object, the worries were not about what is central to art; at best, you were perhaps interested in what is called (by others) art. Perhaps he has understood something, but not *art*: these represent understanding in 'different senses' (para [h]).

As we will see, recognition of the role of competent judges (which Wittgenstein acknowledges elsewhere: see PI: p. 227 [h]) permits wide ranges of competence, but locates such competence within the powers and capacities of individuals, regarding it as a competence relative to ideas, issues or questions. Thus the two parts of this passage from Wittgenstein (the CV part and the Z part) augment as well as complement one another: for the 'life of [hu]mankind' (para [h]) provides a background of preconditions for the 'special conceptual world' (para [m]) of music. Therefore the range of Wittgenstein's comments here will be obscured for those who read only one of the parts, or do not connect them.

Some morals from the text

If we looked in detail at these passages, we would notice how – contrary to what one finds in students' notes and to what some critics assert – Wittgenstein is both careful and tentative. So, first, Wittgenstein's remarks are recognized as precise and contextual. For example, he is not the shrill critic of explanations in terms of images that one might have been led to expect: we would 'more likely' (para [f]) say something different – with the implication that we would sometimes, and with justification, say *this*. Moreover, the 'warrant' here could amount to its being true, genuinely descriptive or explanatory. So, anyone trying to understand Wittgenstein's own view should at least begin from what he writes himself, rather than assuming his real view to be something different.

The point here might seem to warrant extensive commentary, since Wittgenstein is generally taken to oppose explanation in terms of mental images. And if Wittgenstein were required to have a single view, applicable at all times and places and in all circumstances, such a view would have to reject this kind of explanation. But why should only a single, exceptionless view be permitted? As this passage indicates, Wittgenstein makes no such assumption.[9] Thus, the upshot of these remarks is highly circumscribed: we might say this, 'in some circumstances' (para [d]). Even if explanation in terms of images is not always what is needed, Wittgenstein does not dismiss it out of hand. Instead, he recognizes that no one need necessarily be misled by this remark: we find the remark necessarily problematic only once philosophers have taught us both a way to read it and the falsity of the remark so 'read'.

Such a point highlights a contextualism or particularism in Wittgenstein's thought often missed by commentators: we need not assume that what is true here is true exceptionlessly (compare Travis 1989: 311–24). Moreover, the point connects with one of Wittgenstein's own explanations of the project of philosophy: 'What *we* do is to bring words back from their meta-physical to their everyday use' (PI §116 [b]). For Wittgenstein does not just say that words should be brought back to their 'everyday use', as though there were an identifiable everyday use. Rather, he clarifies the term that wears the trousers, 'metaphysical use': the 'ordinary use' is basically anything else![10]

Moreover, in an earlier context, Wittgenstein goes on to exemplify his point: 'The man who said that one cannot step into the same river twice said something wrong; one can step into the same river twice' (TS: 213; PO: 167). And the mistake, of course, comes from offering a metaphysical use of 'same river', a use that would be misleading to me if, say, I found a concep-tual impossibility in your suggestion to swim today in the river we swam in yesterday. Here we begin to see why: 'our answers, if they are correct, must be ordinary and trivial. But look at them in the proper spirit, and then it doesn't matter' (PO 167–8). So, philosophical puzzlement comes from meta-physical uses of expressions. But which are these? No brief answer can be given. Instead, we find which utterances to dispute by looking at the conse-quences of them: that is why I can 'say what...[I]...choose' (PI §79 [d]) here – as long as I respect key distinctions! And which distinctions are key is both a matter for reasoned dispute and one where there is a knowledgeable consensus (in most cases).

A second gain from considering the passage from MS 137 recognizes the precision of the purpose or target of the remarks: faced with a particular puzzlement of yours, I might say this to you or do that for you; and the procedure be effective in explaining matters *to you* – there is no implication that this would always, and to everyone, be the thing to say or do, nor that it would always be effective against puzzlement. In fact, not only might *I* be unable to explain the particular musical work to you (despite numerous strategies), and hence lead you to understand it, but no one might be able to do this, in your case, for this piece of music.

Third, the text is rich with modal suggestions (both 'external' and 'internal' modals (Morris 1994: 295)). Wittgenstein just tells us that there are circumstances where one *might* say this, where doing so might be radically revisionary of our understanding in a positive way. But he is simply offering sets of cases against the thought that such-and-such is normal or that this is the only way this phenomenon could be understood: he might say this, but equally he might not. For instance, Wittgenstein treats understanding (roughly equivalent to appreciating) music in terms of listening and playing; but 'at other times too' (para [g]). So two main concerns are identified here: the *combination* of cases from listening and playing musical works in those circumstances; and the *other* cases, for instance, talk of musical works or of musical structure, and of other (artistic?) structure (para [h]).

Learning to see and to value

Wittgenstein's emphasis on teaching here (in para [a] and following) – although not child psychology[11] – suggests the strategy of characterizing understanding or appreciation in terms of what is needed in order to understand or appreciate (in our case) art objects, arriving at that analysis (as we will see) partly from explanation of failures of understanding or appreciation. As we saw earlier, rejection of a hard and fast contrast between understanding and valuing might still usefully offer roles for the explanation of failures of understanding in terms of failing to recognize and/or failing to appreciate. Moreover, Wittgenstein's route to making public our musical understanding concentrated on the teaching of such musical understanding. Following this trajectory of Wittgenstein's thought will emphasize a person's becoming a competent judge in respect of matters artistic (sometimes in relation to some particular artform, sometimes more generally). For here, too, I would urge, one learns correct judgements. There are also rules, but they do not form a system (i.e. *not* a 'calculus [operating] according to definite rules': PI §81), and only 'experienced people can apply them right' (PI: p. 227 [h]). Thus, one does not learn 'what correct judgements *are*'; rather, one learns to *make* correct judgements. Still, there remain different explanatory structures, considerations to be met (say, through education) in different ways. So learning to be a competent judge in this sense might be characterized, via two slogans, as *learning to see* and *learning to value*.

Such 'learning to see' is best understood by a comparison with a similar 'problem' facing someone looking for the first time at X-ray photographs (say, of the chest). Radiologists can distinguish the condition of the internal organs, when the untrained barely make out the ribs.[12] Differences in cognitive stock (Wollheim 1993: 135) between radiologist and beginner reflect the mobilization of different concepts in our perception of the same patterns of light and shade in the X-ray plate. But one can come to see the X-ray plates in that way for oneself: and the process closely parallels that in respect of a multiple-figure – one is encouraged to view the characteristics of the X-ray plate in a certain fashion. In this way, one learns to see X-ray photographs appropriately: one learns to 'read' them or to understand them, although this is just a matter of looking at them.

This is the situation when one learns to understand artworks: one learns to see their characteristics (that is, their characteristics once transfigured to art), and certain ways are appropriate to doing so (not one only, but not 'anything goes'). So the first slogan (learning to see) identifies the perceptual base of artistic understanding, recognizing the possibility of misperception: that is, of failure of artistic appreciation resulting from inability to perceive an artwork in ways appropriate to it.

Central here is the contrast between artistic judgement and (merely) aesthetic judgement: that is, between judgements, appreciations and so on of those objects appropriately taken as artworks (and taking them as artworks) in contrast to the judgements made of all those other objects where we admire grace, beauty, and so on (or their opposites). The details of this contrast are highly contentious (UD: 38–44, 165–93).[13] At its centre, though, is the thought of both a kind of understanding and a kind of value appropriate to artworks and not appropriate to other aesthetic objects. To deny this contrast is to confuse our interest in the great painting with our interest in the wallpaper on the wall it hangs on; or to deny any difference between these interests.[14]

So works in a particular artform must be understood as part of a complex tradition of art-making and art-understanding. Someone who does not know dominant narratives of art history cannot see or judge works as part of those narratives (Carroll 1993). But there are many different ways of knowing the narratives, typified by different ways of learning about them; as artist, art historian, theorist of aesthetics (etc.), and not all learning should be reduced to 'book learning' or the propositional.

Appreciation then takes the form of perceiving the work (looking at the painting, hearing the music) in the light of such understanding. As Wollheim (1993: 142) puts it, 'perception of the arts is…the process of understanding the work of art': given suitable conditions and knowledge, people have the capacity for such understanding of art because they have the capacity to perceive artworks. But, of course, this is merely a precondition for such understanding, since neither the requisite sensitivity nor the informedness is guaranteed.

Moreover, some consensus around judgements follows from our being competent to discuss a certain topic: if your list of composers of classical music does not include *any* of Mozart, Beethoven, Bach, Mahler, Stravinsky, Schoenberg, it will be hard for a conversation on classical music to start – your taste in it is just too eclectic (see Cavell 1969: 193).

In line with the second slogan, artistic value is recognized in perception. So learning to *see* the work of art in question appropriately is learning what to see as valuable in it (or how to see it as valuable), and hence learning to value it; although I may rebel against what I have learned. Thus someone who claimed merely to understand what a particular group valued in an artwork (without finding it valuable himself/herself) would, for that reason, be failing to view the object as an artwork, to make artistic judgements of it. As earlier, this account (if true) would, in typical cases, ground our argument that this person did not understand this particular artwork: after all, this person can see no artistic value in it. So how is it more important or interesting than, say, wallpaper?

At the least, artistic appreciation is appreciation of that object (painting, dance, etc.), and artistic value is value inhering in the artwork: so such appreciation minimally requires perceptual engagement with those works. For appreciation is demeaned if considered as a kind of elaborated daydream stimulated by the artwork. Of course, such daydreaming is entirely possible. Yet the person engaged in it is not really appreciating that artwork, because not engaging with its properties; and hence, not really doing artistic appreciation (although of course such a perceptual engagement is, at most, just necessary for such appreciation, rather than guaranteeing it).

Since artistic appreciation makes the possibility of misperception of an artwork central to our defence against subjectivism (it is not 'anything goes'), this notion of misperception is crucial for the first slogan (learning to see): I misperceive a work (a) if I take for an artwork something that is not (misapplying artistic judgement where aesthetic judgement was appropriate); (b) if I consider an artwork from one category as though it were in another, or (c) as though it were not art at all.

But when errors in understanding artworks are explained in terms of the misperception of those works, there can be failures both to understand the work appropriately and to appreciate it appropriately. Treating music by Messiaen as though it were genuine birdsong (no doubt pleasing, but meaningless), I misperceive it by applying the wrong category; but I also misvalue it, since the normativity that follows from recognizing it as art (rather than as merely aesthetic) would be inappropriate to birdsong. Treating it, instead, as though it were tonal music, I import a normativity all right, but my judgements will be inappropriate to Messiaen. And hence my valuing of it will also be inappropriate.

So learning to see the value of artworks (and to see certain features of the works as reasons for my judgements) is engaging with the narrative of art history in respect of that artform. If my judgement of that artwork is to be explained or justified to others, reference must be made to the history and development of the artform in question, perhaps referring to a revolution against traditional ways of working in that form. For this connects my claims for this work to what is acknowledged as valuable from other works – and hence to artistic value.

Suppose (for instance) that a discussion of whether or not Milton Avery was 'a minor precursor of Rothko or a great master' (Carrier 1987: 39) led to 'a major debate about how to write the history of modernism...[amounting to]...whether Avery's work belongs in every major museum' (Carrier 1987: 39) – on the assumption that Rothko's does! But how to write the history is, in effect, also how to judge other works by drawing on that history, which includes knowledge of other artworks (and perhaps other works by the artist under consideration).

In addressing what is good about *this* artwork, I may refer to characteristics which – even when explanatory of the value of other works (which is not always) – may there amount to something different. Perhaps unity provides the clearest example. Unity is a virtue of a great many works, but amounts to something different in different cases; the unity of a short poem, of a symphony, of atonal music, of a Graham-technique dance work, of a novel driven by narrative, of an epistolary novel and so on. There seems no easy way to move onwards from the recognition that unity is important in all of these, since in each the character of the unity relates to the character of the work.

Still, such engagement may usefully be supplemented by discussion, drawing parallels and so on, as I might help you to see a multiple-figure design (say, by pointing this out as such-and-such a feature, that as so-and-so, etc.). I suggest that a sequence near the beginning of Christopher Bruce's *Ghost Dances* (1981) should be seen, structurally, as exemplifying canon, on the assumption that your knowledge of canon in other works (of music or dance) permits you to see the implications of this concession; or urge that the chosen sequence is a rejection of this or that general 'principle' from past dance construction, principles you have seen exemplified in such-and-such a work and (perhaps) rejected in so-and-so a work. At the centre of both strategies is the suggestion that *this* be seen in a way one already sees *that*: so either strategy may be augmented by looking at *other* works too. But in the last analysis, you either see it or you do not. This is a crucial characteristic of artistic judgement too: I can bring you to the artwork, but I can't make you drink it in. So, although appreciation is centrally perceptual, the spectator's perceptual judgements (and taste) can be 'influenced'; just as well for arts educators!

Moreover, one's ability to learn to see (and hence to learn to value) – to the degree one can – may be limited. Since it is 'one step at a time', there may be some concepts I either cannot acquire or cannot mobilize in my experience of this work of art (perhaps of art generally). Try as I might, I may be unable to see a certain artwork in the appropriate way, just as I may be unable to see such-and-such in the X-ray plate. For me, that artwork will be a closed book. If I cannot see that a particular artwork has a certain property, despite your best efforts, nothing you can do will guarantee my coming either to see the work as you suggest or to value the work in that way.

One explanation might lie, for instance, in other knowledge or other valuing of mine. For example, as an admirer of the minimal (say, Rothko), with no time for the sentimental (say, Holman Hunt), we might expect the transition from my understanding of the dances of Martha Graham to those of Merce Cunningham to be an easy one; and explain its facility in terms of my avowed admiration for the minimal, viewing Merce as more minimal than Martha (and a converse explanation for my difficulties in coming to grips with sentimental choreographers).

As we have seen, competent judges (compare Travis 1989: 47–8, 56–67) have a conceptual role in the understanding of art (and hence in learning to understand art) in two ways. First, what one learns is not what correct judgement (in its varieties) is but rather how to make it (PI: p. 227 [h]). Second, that art is meaning-bearing (or has a 'cognitive dimension') depends on the possibility of creatures able to recognize such meaning, just as it is the possibility of persons following them that transforms posts by a roadside into signposts (Baker 1981: 55). The possibility of competent judges, therefore, is a conceptual requirement for any artistic judgement at all. But how should such judges be conceptualized?

Competent judges?

Humans (typically) have the potential to find artworks valuable, although on the basis of education. This is what it means to locate artworks both in 'the life of [hu]mankind' (para [h]) and as requiring entry into a 'special conceptual world' (para [m]: Z §165). Here, a useful comparison is with, say, colour: its colour is a public, shareable property of a red object, and yet requires a world with beings of suitable discriminatory powers. Thus we recognize the relation of that property to human powers and capacities – and even to human concerns.[15]

Moreover, Wittgenstein recognizes a reciprocal relation between value and structure (although for a different purpose), so that, although *major* and *minor* (applied to artworks) 'can also be used purely to describe a perceived structure', these terms 'certainly have emotional value' (PI: p. 209 [c]).[16] And so value, like structure, is amenable to recognition (by the suitably sensitive) in ways not dissimilar to the recognition of colour – is, in that sense, objective (McDowell 1998: 134). Thus, the possession of the artistic properties (by artworks) relates to the powers and capacities of the audience for those works, while leaving the properties as clearly properties of the artworks. For musical appreciation – and, by extension, dance appreciation – draws on powers and capacities consequent on, roughly, *this* anatomy and physiology: a set of potentialities open to humankind, although actualizable in a variety of different ways in different contexts (including 'not at all').

While general powers and capacities may be guaranteed (in a typical case) by anatomy and physiology, Wittgenstein rightly stresses (para [f]) that the capacity to actually *make* artistic judgements, or to engage in the appreciation, is not. Rather, it must be learned, if possible. And even that is not guaranteed. For having the concepts (demonstrated one way) is not equivalent to being able to mobilize those concepts – itself characterizable in terms of one's sensitivity to art and, then, to works in this form, (perhaps) this genre, and so on.

Our suitably knowledgeable audience has not merely learned to see – that is, to recognize the artistic, and to apply (some) categories of art – but also, first, has learned to mobilize those concepts in the experience of artworks (where this contributes to being 'suitably sensitive') and, second, has learned to value; to see artworks as valuable.[17] So, we are acknowledging the contribution of what the audience has learned. Crucial here is the conceptual structure of the artform at issue: thus, one's entry into that 'special conceptual world' (para [m]) might draw on one's understanding both of genre- or tradition-specific concepts and of the concept of art itself. And such conceptions are not obviously shared with, say, the Lascaux cave painters or the American Ghost Dancers (UD: 286). For any identification of a concept as *art* would be defeated if, for example (and respectively), it included works made when the authors lacked that concept, or when they took their activity as suitable to rid the plains (of the USA) of the White Man. As such cases suggest, the sense in which the value of art is *there* in the artworks at least resembles the sense in which objects are coloured: both require a (learnable) conceptual background for recognition, and both require beings of sufficient recognitional abilities.

Further, as Wittgenstein recognizes, explanation should not begin prior to the behaviour of judgement (at least in typical cases). So we should not seek to ground artistic judgement in terms of, say, feelings of disgust, even if we recognize that the human potentiality for such feelings as a presumption of such judgements. This is the upshot of Wittgenstein's slogan, 'in the beginning was the deed' (OC §402; CV: 31; PO: 395). The imperative here is that one should not (typically) begin explaining human behaviour from anything (logically?) prior to the action itself. Here, I simply assume this point, from Wittgenstein. Applied to a particular deed of artistic judgement, this might mean, roughly, that we should not ask how one's perception of, in the simplest case, the painting in question is achieved, nor how it is related to one's judgement (or appreciation) of that painting. One simply sees, and appreciates: there is no gap here between seeing the Picasso a certain way (understanding it a certain way) and judging it that way. For learning to see (Slogan 1) and learning to value (Slogan 2) come together in *learning to judge*.

Wittgenstein's insight is that the idea of a competent judge does not require concretization by itemizing the knowledge and understanding required of such judges. So that, when the powers and capacities of such judges operate smoothly, there is nothing more to be said: they are marked out as competent judges (in respect of art, in that form, etc.) by this role in the explanation of art (in that form, etc.). So we do not say how they do it; nor (exactly) what they do – although we would of course explain failures of judgement as, say, failures to recognize or failures to value. Thus, nothing separable can be stated here that would be both comprehensive and true of all. Instead, the thought is that one does not do something else in order to do artistic appreciation; that is, to understand (in this case) a musical work.

Given who I am, and what I know, that dance (today) will look such-and-such a way, and have so-and-so valuable features, etc. And I might refer to these characteristics to justify my judgement, if challenged. Similarly, one can readily explain failures of judgement in terms of failures of knowledge or failures of sensitivity (this is sometimes cashed out in terms of a failure to mobilize certain concepts in one's experience of the artwork in question). For instance, we might explain my difficulties with the dance of Martha Graham via my huge experience of works in the Classical Ballet repertoire, and my ignorance of modern dance: now, the flexed feet can look ugly, perhaps even suggesting poor technique in the dancers. Where are the pointed toes and the pointe-work? But then I might be taught to recognize the virtues of modern dance, a contribution to my cognitive stock. Or perhaps I know a lot about modern dance but cannot see the dance that way, as many who (having been taught a critical vocabulary for poetry) cannot 'find' that vocabulary in the appreciation of poems: and then, suddenly, they can! Here, we might say, the cognitive stock has not changed; but it can now be mobilized in experience of the poem (McFee 1997: 35).

Equally, we do not require an explicit contribution from knowledge here: there are many ways to acquire the requisite knowledge and understanding, other than through (say) art history classes. I imagine most dancers, for instance, acquire them *en passant*, in training and performing. But they do know: and, if pressed, they might even explain what they knew (although this ability is not required). Still, such dancers can perhaps then draw on the knowledge and understanding, perhaps as choreographers.

More generally, explanations are required only when there is some specific reason to want them in that case – so, not in the usual or uncomplicated cases ('no modification without aberration': see Cavell 1969: 13). When we have reason to say more, we therefore have reason to treat the case as non-typical, and vice versa. Thus, if we know a case is non-typical (as, say, the formulated intentions of some artist might suggest to us), we therefore have reason to say more. So, if John Cage explicitly asserts his attempt in some musical piece to subvert previous artistic structures – or if Merce Cunningham tells us this (for dance studies) – and when the resultant works are uncontentiously art, we may articulate enough of the narrative of art history to justify our conclusion: say, by quoting Cage's remark that 'the twelve-tone system has no zero in it'. Further, explanation of action is typically 'after the fact': I just do such-and-such, and then am called for (roughly) an explanation by way of justification. Thus, asked to elaborate my understanding of Mats Ek's *Swan Lake*, I then comment on what is striking about *it*, recognizing that these features are not valuable in *all* the works in which they occur; and that they depend on both 'life of [hu]mankind' (para [h]) and 'special conceptual world' (para [m]).

So I use these ideas to explain my judgement to you (and partly justify it to you); as Wittgenstein suggests, there is no implication here that I explicitly thought through this chain of connections. Rather that, knowing as much about ballet (and about the work of Mats Ek) as I do, the appreciation is obvious for me: I just see the work that way. This emphasis on judging as an activity highlights one reason why the presentation given thus far may seem excessively rationalistic: what I learn through art education is not to think something and/or to value something, but to do something: namely, to judge competently, based on a clear view of the art object and the ability to explain (after the fact?) my judgement of it, where both of these are ways my judging might go wrong. So talk of 'two processes' (learning to see and learning to value) really does no more than highlight two ways in which one's judgement might go awry.

Of course, the (appreciative) perception of artworks is mutable under changes in what is thought or known: what concepts are mobilized in that perception. Changes here might be voluntary, as when I endeavour to expand my knowledge of, say, Martha Graham's dance or my sensitivity to it – this last both by watching it and from critical discussion. Equally, (some) artistic judgement is relatively 'fixed': given who I am, knowing what I know, etc., I may be extremely unlikely to change my judgement. For instance, my appreciation of Martha Graham's work may be so central to my view of dance that revising it substantially would thoroughly overthrow many of my other judgements of dance works – revising my whole 'narrative' of dance history, say, or the range of categories and critical concepts I deploy. While not strictly impossible, this is highly improbable. So perception of art is not as fixed, nor judgement of it as mutable, as one might have thought.[18]

On a particular day, I may not see particular works as I normally would: I may be tired, or not in the mood for this kind of material. Equally, my perception of a particular artwork (say, piano music by Scriabin) may be affected by recent, sustained experiences of a very different art-genre (say, piano music by Schoenberg): my usual appreciation of the first is affected by that sustained attention to the second, so that, for instance, the Scriabin now sounds inflated rather than rococo. Again, the (relative) inexorability of artistic judgement reflects the fact that, in my imagined example, no new learning has taken place: I simply mobilized (in my experience of the artworks) the concepts I then already had.

Of course, I can regard differently a work previously seen a certain way; or an 'insight' of yesterday can seem insubstantial or misconceived today. Here there is a difference in how I take the work: my mobilizing different concepts in my appreciation of that work would be explicable to some degree – for example, 'explained' by my acquiring new concepts or becoming able to mobilize different concepts in my experience of the work. And the first of these might involve my bringing to bear concepts not previously brought to bear, other narratives I'd found relevant; perhaps because, say, of the re-hanging of a familiar picture.

Naturally, some of the force of that judgement might reflect temporary features of my condition (or my temporary condition), if I have not engaged in the kind of focus Wollheim (1987: 8) describes, designed to ensure my detachment from my immediacies. But that is a practical limitation here: conceptually, artistic judgements are suitably detached from what I have called 'association' (UD: 86). So the basis of artistic judgement is general in that it ultimately depends on nothing special about my particular situation. Hence, any failures to understand will be explicable in ways highlighted before: in terms of differences of cognitive stock, mobilization of concepts, and sensitivity (at least once we have recognized art's 'historical character'; McFee (1992b)).

Yet mere change of my judgement or appreciation might not seem crucial. Rather, motivated change is needed; in particular, motivated revision of previous judgements. So how is self-criticism possible? *That* it is possible is, of course, granted; but how is the activity understood? In the clearest case here (a) I change my view of such-and-such a painting, and (b) I explain my change of view. The view to be resisted is that what I offer under (b) must be the basis on which I change my view: that is, the basis of (a). Instead, perhaps I move from vague disquiets with the judgement or appreciation I had been voicing – it does not quite fit (the colour *too* brittle; the dance step *too* angular) – to a reconsideration of how my judgement of this work coheres with my judgements of other works (do those judgements – or those works – now seem odd too?); and on to my coming to another judgement, but one I can (now) justify, in terms of the cognitive stock I now have, as now mobilized in my experience of this artwork. In telling 'the tale' to you, perhaps I come to see its narrative structure for myself; and for the first time. There seems no reason to suppose that what constructs a plausible chain of reasoning for you – a chain I accept and recognize – will be unacceptable unless it reconstructs a chain of thought actually present in my psychology. This would just reify the psychological in a contentious fashion. So my ability to be self-critical (itself something I have learned, both as a principle and a practical method) is compatible with the picture of judgement (or action) Wittgenstein endorses.

Action and judgement

To call judgement an action is simply to stress that it is something people do, that it is intentional and explicable. Wittgenstein's acknowledgment of (for example) hearing with understanding emphasizes both that the appreciative judgement might be implicit in the behaviour which goes with the hearing (the beating time, or the rapt expression) *and* that the action of appreciating the music might be best characterized via teaching and learning to understand and to appreciate – that no separate account of one's reasoning need be sought. In this way, emphasis on action works against misguidedly rationalistic accounts of artistic judgement: I simply see the artwork in a certain way and, in doing so, value it a certain way.

Of course, performing with understanding and listening with understanding are hugely different, especially in the competencies required of the typical performer. Yet the logic of the two situations does not diverge so completely, as Wittgenstein explicitly addresses (RPPI §1130): both are actions, requiring competencies of agents. And nothing more may need explanation: in another slogan (mentioned previously), 'in the beginning was the deed' (OC §402). Here Wittgenstein invites us to recognize the fundamental character of ourselves as agents, thereby working against any conception of, say, thought, meaning and understanding which plots them as (necessarily) involving chains of prior planning.

If judgements here were rooted in both knowledge and motivation (separably), we could explain why one person admired a work while another did not, although both knew the same things about it ('had the same beliefs about it') by saying that the first additionally had, and the second lacked, the motivating attitude or desire in respect of the work. But this does not tally with our account of artistic judgement as perceptual and as guiding to action: seeing the work that way is judging it that way.

A major insight of Wittgenstein is that persons are first and foremost agents, capable of doing certain things, where the explanation of that doing should be seen as typically 'after the fact'. If Wittgenstein's point is granted, reason or knowledge are not 'motivationally inert' (Price 1988: 87), at least in all contexts. First, what principally needs explanation is behaviour different from the norm, or from what is expected: what Wittgenstein (PO: 379) calls 'reasons for leaving a familiar track'. When we deviate from the path, an explanation is needed in ways it is not when we stick to the path. (This goes for figurative as well as for real paths.) Second, and relatedly, these are cases where we simply do something. Following signposts is a normative activity, in that we can do it badly or wrongly; but that explanation will only be invoked when my behaviour stands in need of explanation, when it is not transparent; I do not have to give such explanations to myself. (What could that mean, in typical cases, except being a roundabout way of talking about my deliberating?) As Wittgenstein (PI §217) puts it, 'it is about the justification for my following the rule in the way I do'. And the explanatory application of rules must stop somewhere; if not, we have the vicious regress with a rule needed for the application of that rule, and another rule needed for the application of the new rule, and so on. So there are actions whose explanation is rarely required: but, when it is, it should not be expected to retrieve some explicit (and prior) thought process of the agent. And, if this is sometimes true, it removes the need for a general account of agent motivation.

Applied to artistic judgement, this model for coming to understand artworks draws on what we know: we are assuming the requisite powers and capacities. Only then can, say, stressing the work a certain way for someone (see Klopstock discussion, LA: 4) help her to understand a certain work. The appreciation then takes the form of perceiving the work (looking at the painting, hearing the music, etc.) in the light of one's understanding, including one's understanding of the narratives and categories of art. But the central thought here is that the presumptions for artistic judgement noted earlier – cognitive stock, sensitivity, mobilization – should not be thought actions, or operations of our psyche, at least in typical cases. For 'in the beginning was the deed': that is where we start explanation of such typical cases. But when there *is* reason to dispute the judgement, that dispute can readily begin by citing failures in one (or more) of these three features. (And we should remind ourselves of the injunction 'to begin at the beginning. And not try to go further back' (OC §471). That is, to explain failures in this way; and likewise the demands of education (to prevent or remedy failures) without locating a positive 'faculty', beyond simply referring to human powers and capacities.) So, substantially, we have located the conceptual centrality of competent judges, have seen how failures of this role might be understood (as failures to see or failures to value), and hence how education into the role might be roughly characterized. Further, we have located this account within a more general sketch of human agency.

Place of slogans?

Thus far, I have explored three lines of discussion:

1   A conception of understanding art thereby suggested, on which coming to understand and appreciate music – or art more generally – can be modelled as learning to see artworks correctly or appropriately.[19]
2   Relatedly, a primary conception of humans as agents; or, to put it less grandiloquently, that people *do things* – and where some of those 'things' include art criticism, both formal and informal. For we can and do understand artworks.[20]
3   The role of the conceptual background for art understanding and appreciation: how, as Wittgenstein put it, 'appreciating music is a manifestation of the life of mankind' (para [h]). But also how the 'special

conceptual world' (para [m]) of music is implicit in the judgements we make of musical works.

But Wittgenstein explicitly denies that philosophy should 'advance any kind of theory' (PI §109). Yet the picture just offered might seem to amount to an aesthetic theory: how is this possible (given that I am not mistaken)? My reply associates theory of the rejected sort with exceptionless *theses* (compare PI §128). So I claim that Wittgenstein is right to deny that there are *theses* here – how can that be? For have I not just identified a number of theses of his?

As an example, recognize that expressive playing is not merely a *sign* of something: to be playing (genuinely) expressively is a guarantee of understanding (para [j]: Z §163) – partly, a failure to understand would *defeat* any claim of the playing to be genuinely expressive (it is a 'recognized head of exception'; UD: 61–5), rather as we would disallow as *chess* moves which, while legal, were entirely accidental. Here, Wittgenstein is stressing both the theme of 'in the beginning...' and the yet more general idea of what stands in need of explanation ('to begin at the beginning...': OC §471). To understand why these are not theses, we must turn to the next consideration:

4 The place of slogans: or, if this is different, the difference between slogans and theses.

For there are two quite different ways of offering what might be mistaken for remarks of equal generality: the contrast is between theses and slogans. Throughout, I have been at pains to characterize Wittgenstein's remarks as the second. For he is (rightly) denying the kind of generality and determinacy the term 'thesis' might be thought to imply.

To explore briefly the contrasts here, consider three related features implicated in those contrasts. First, notice the different situations in which theses and slogans might be rejected: offered a *thesis*, I can reasonably reject it faced with a counter-example. For the thesis was implicitly that all so-and-so's are such and such (or equally that 70 per cent are). So finding one that was not (or one such in the 69th percentile) would make us reject the thesis. And this is especially clear for theses in philosophy, which are thereby reckoned conceptual truths (when true) – at least on many conceptions of philosophy (compare Scruton 1994: 11–12), where such truths are (necessarily) exceptionless, univocal, determinate (Baker and Hacker 1980: 367–85).

In denying theses to philosophy, Wittgenstein is attacking just this conception. For there remains a point in, say, asserting that cheetahs can run faster than men, a slogan judged on its usefulness in this context. That slogan is not refuted by recognizing cheetahs with broken legs and world sprint champions. And not rejecting the claim when faced with such cases is not irrational: that was not what the slogan meant. To think otherwise is to treat the slogan here as a thesis, and to do so would be to find it false. Yet Wittgenstein's claims (say, about meaning or agency) are not required to be exceptionless.

Also (our second point) understanding does not necessarily require a single 'reading'. Our model here draws on contextual consideration: although there are cases where the hearer of a slogan may not know how to take it, in fact it is clear once the context is taken into account. Thus, while it might have misled me, it is not misleading. For a simpler case (UD: 121), suppose I work as assistant to both a marine biologist and a cook. Both are interested in red fish, the cook in a surface swimming red fish, the biologist in a deep swimming one. Now the instruction, 'Bring me a red fish', is clear once I know which of my masters uttered it. We can readily see both how I might end up confused (I don't know who said it) and how it is not confusing. So I might be unable to fulfil the task but – in this case – what I am being asked is perfectly clear (Travis 1989: 18–21). And scope of this sort is implicit in slogans.

Moreover, contextualizing the slogans allows ways of explaining why they fail to be compelling in such-and-such a case. Thus, I point out the defeasible (UD: 62–3) nature of the judgement: then any 'burden of proof' will be on the objector, once certain conditions are fulfilled. And – while the judgement is generally justified once those 'certain conditions' are fulfilled – this implication will be defeated if an objector raises one of several 'recognized heads of exception' (as a contract would be defeated if it were not 'true, full and free' Baker (1977: 33)). So specific conditions for defeat are implicitly recognized, without undermining the certainty of undefeated judgements. And to enter into the 'special conceptual world' (para [m]) of the relevant artform is to learn such conditions.

The third feature addresses the point of having a slogan. Since slogans are not 'all or nothing', they more readily accommodate apparent counter-cases. But why should slogans be wanted? What is their primary argumentative purpose? Since, as we have seen, they are necessarily not exceptionless, their primary purpose cannot be to explicate *all* cases. Nevertheless, there is an implication towards all cases. Yet, as just noted, contextualizing a slogan typically identifies 'heads of exception' by highlighting places where the slogan (appropriately 'read') does not apply. And this feature of slogans is visible in the use made (for example, here) of the major claims. In treating them as slogans, we recognize that they will deal with uncontentious cases, and 'explain' what is uncontentious about them; namely, they follow the slogan. So, rather than trying to explain cases where all goes well, we need say no more here. Instead the 'heads of exception' are invoked when the slogan is not applying (or not useful), as a way of characterizing why not: *this* or *that* has gone wrong; and, again, in *this* context, not in all.

Three related worries (apart from technical ones) seem to arise here. Slogans will be false (in their full generality) without ceasing to be useful. But, first, how are we to avoid being misled? Second, how is the scope of a particular slogan to be recognized? And, third, how can slogans be the business of philosophers?

An example may help. Consider my suggestion that we meet at sunrise (McFee 1999: 13; compare Squires 1995: 83). Now, none of us believe in sunrises: we recognize heliocentricity. So talk of sunrises might seem inherently misleading. But this just reflects a philosophical thesis (much beloved of sceptics) that what is misleading *in principle* thereby misleads. In contrast, we are typically quite capable of recognizing the limitations on what follows from talk of sunrises; and, when we accidentally transgress those limits, in recognizing appropriate correction. Thus, for example, nothing follows about (say) the possibility of the sun standing still. So, while we cannot readily say how, we are typically capable managers of slogans, accommodating both their scope and their lack of (full) generality.

The remaining matter is more perplexing, and has two dimensions. First, as contextualism acknowledged, there can be problems for philosophy (McFee 2000: 141–7; Stroud 1984: 128–69) which are only problems for philosophy: where, as we saw, the only misconceptions a slogan generates is a misconception among philosophers and, typically, *only* given certain ways of 'reading' the slogan. For example, a spectre of 'dualism' might lead to an unwarranted hesitancy about, say, explanations appealing to images or sensations (para [f]). But if the explanations are not for a philosophical audience, nothing here need mislead. Second, and relatedly, we recognize that to draw inappropriate consequences from a slogan is both to be misled by it and for that misconception to be a troubling one: indeed, it is the conjunction of these as (recognized) misconceptions and yet following – apparently – from our other commitments that makes them troubling at all. The recipe here (Wittgenstein's, although I have not the space to explore it; see Wrigley (1980: 475–6)) is to acknowledge that the potentially problematic need not be genuinely so – that a 'contradiction' through which our thought does not pass on a particular occasion need not be a relevant 'contradiction'. One feature of Wittgenstein's thought made explicit here is rejection of (necessary) 'chains of prior reasoning'.

So our discussion has suggested how much that might have generated such (apparent) 'contradictions' is actually an explanatory structure, 'after the fact', of action: hence, not really a suitable basis – in typical cases – for misconceptions troubling for us; for they could be 'troubling misconceptions' only because what makes them count as misconceptions here also renders them troubling. Thus, to mistake the scope of a slogan might suggest a 'metaphysical use' of the term 'art' (say, as implying beauty) which seems to raise issues about key danceworks (is Bruce's *Ghost Dances* not art because not beautiful, or is it *really* beautiful, despite.... Neither seems right). Our 'metaphysical use' combines with a conception of (required) generality here to make the case seem problematic: what am I to make of this dance? In fact, I need simply to remind myself of the work's features and of its art-status. But that means not being drawn into the philosopher's discussion.

113

Notes

1 Lest this volume be taken to offer precise details of Wittgenstein's positions, we recall the crucial role in philosophical discussion played by issues of consistency between remarks, when a parallel project (LPP) cannot reconstruct uncontentiously even the number of lectures, let alone their content.

2 The sections of the passage were published: (i) in CV pp. 79[d]–81[a], here referred to as paragraphs [a] to [h]; (ii) in Z §§162–5, here referred to as paragraphs [i] to [j] and [l] to [m]. The remaining section, paragraph [k], is presently unpublished. In my translation, it reads: [k] 'I can therefore say, "Now I have understood it for the first time" – but not what that consists of: as an explanation I can say, "I followed it", or that these elements have made an inpression on me for the first time'. (My thanks to my colleague Udo Merkel for advice on this translation.) NB translations of the 1st edition of CV are used throughout.

3 As was his practice, Wittgenstein annotated the notebook, dividing it into passages for dictation/typing, passages to keep (but not [yet] dictate), and passages to ignore. The second half of the 15 February entry was marked for dictation/typing, and typed in TS 232; a typescript Wittgenstein subsequently cut up, including this passage in the box of fragments that became *Zettel*. (For its history, see Z iv–v.)

TS 232 was later published as RPPII (the relevant passage is 466–9): is the passage's location there revealing? The Cornell microfilm describes TS 232 as 'A typescript rearrangement of Bande Q & R' (that is, MSS 136 and 137). The editors' decision to publish indicates that they took TS 232 to be a relatively finished object. In contrast, I conjecture that Wittgenstein intended TS 232 as raw material for the (literal) 'cut-and-paste' he used to compose later typescripts. It simply types up remarks from the manuscripts, following almost exactly the ordering of the original notes (except for a few minor changes [for instance, the transposition of 561 and 562]), as though merely copy-typed from the notebook. It seems unlikely that Wittgenstein re-ordered at this stage. First, issues Wittgenstein would have been able to resolve remain: one word from the last remark, difficult to read in the manuscript, is queried in the typescript (and ultimately changed: I do not know how, or by whom – the editors' 'Preface' to RPPII gives no indication of such changes). Had Wittgenstein meant to change the word (say, during dictation), he would have done so (or indicated alternatives – a common practice of his). Second, the last passage is enclosed within double lines, as though meant to be moved: this replicates the manuscript's double lines – Wittgenstein could have moved the passage. Although not more than suggestive, together these features suggest that this location is not revealing. (Clearly, the editors of RPPII took a different view.)

4 Some paragraphs – in modified form – are recycled from McFee (forthcoming).

5 This expression of Wollheim's is discussed briefly in McFee (1997: 35).

6 For help with this, and with the translation generally, my thanks to my native German-speaking colleague, Udo Merkel.

7 Page references are to the Penguin edition.

8 NB the 2nd edition of CV translates the key word [*Verständnis*] here as 'appreciation... in a different sense' (CV: 81), rather than 'understanding'.

9 If the reading here is not, in this way, exceptionless, that might give pause to traditional ways of reading PI.

10 This point is especially clear if one looks to an earlier appearance of (basically) this sentence, in TS 213 (PO: 167), where Wittgenstein fluctuates between 'normal use' and 'correct use'.

11 Wittgenstein shows no interest in how so-and-so is learned, but only in the implications of its being learned: compare PI §257, where he happily grants to a
'genius' child a personal solution to the problem of other minds – and then investigates its implications for knowledge of one's own mind.

12 A personal experience of mine: see also Polanyi (1973: 101).

13 McFee (1992a) is cited throughout as UD.

14 On my version of the artistic/aesthetic contrast, therefore, it is less misleading to
think of artworks as not sharing (not having) aesthetic properties: of the beauty
of an artwork as different from the beauty of a painted surface.

15 Putnam (1999: 5 ff) is good on ways of connecting our powers and our concerns.

16 Compare also MS 132: 59; CV; 9 [f]. Moreover, those who heard Wittgenstein for
example, Rhees (1969: 136); LA I: (17–23)) explicitly attribute this to him.

17 Compare (a) McFee (1999), and (b) the sense in which this 'as' has nothing to do
with aspect-perception, as discussed in McIntyre (1999: 44–6).

18 The following two paragraphs are reworked from McFee (forthcoming).

19 UD: 138–47 suggests a stronger thesis: a central issue concerns perception of
linguistic arts, where there is (a) no sensory modality for sense/meaning, and (b)
variety of potential modalities – for example, read to oneself, heard read aloud,
perhaps read in Braille.

20 This might be denied: but the context of this chapter begins from Wittgenstein's
assertion that we do understand music (even if we lack a clear understanding of
what that might amount to).

Bibliography

Baker, G.P. (1977) 'Defeasibility and Meaning', in P. Hacker and J. Raz (eds), *Law,
Morality and Society*, Oxford: Clarendon, 26–57.

—— (1981) 'Following Wittgenstein: Some Signposts for PI §§143–242', in S.
Holtzman and C. Leich (eds), *Wittgenstein: To Follow a Rule*, London: Routledge
and Kegan Paul, 31–71.

Baker, G.P. and Hacker, P.M.S. (1980) *Wittgenstein: Understanding and Meaning*,
Oxford: Blackwell.

Carrier, D. (1987) *Artwriting*, Amhurst, MA: University of Massachusetts Press.

Carroll, N. (1993) 'Essence, Expression and History', in M. Rollins (ed.), *Danto and
his Critics*, Oxford: Blackwell, 79–106.

Cavell, S. (1969) *Must We Mean What We Say?*, New York: Scribner's.

Danto, A. (1981) *The Transfiguration of the Commonplace*, Cambridge, MA:
Harvard University Press.

Dickie, G. (2000) 'Art and Value', *British Journal of Aesthetics* 40(2): 228–41.

McDowell, J. (1998) *Mind, Value and Reality*, Cambridge, MA: Harvard University
Press.

McFee, G. (1989) 'The Logic of Appreciation with the Republic of Art', *British
Journal of Aesthetics* 29(3): 230–8.

—— (1992a) *Understanding Dance* (UD), London: Routledge.

—— (1992b) 'The Historical Character of Art: A Re-Appraisal', *British Journal of
Aesthetics* 32(4): 307–19.

—— (1997) 'Meaning and the Art-Status of *Music Alone*', *British Journal of
Aesthetics* 37(1): 31–46.

—— (1998) 'Are there Philosophical Issues in Respect of Sport?', in M. McNamee
and S.J. Parry (eds), *Ethics and Sport*, London: Routledge, 3–18.

—— (1999) 'Wittgenstein on Art and Aspects', *Philosophical Investigations* 22(3): 262–84.

—— (2000) *Free Will*, Teddington: Acumen.

—— (forthcoming) 'Wittgenstein and the Arts: Understanding and Performing', in P. Lewis (ed.), *Wittgenstein and the Arts*, Aldershot: Ashgate.

McIntyre, A. (1999) *Dependent Rational Animals*, Chicago: Open Court.

Morris, K. (1994) 'The "Context Principle" in the Later Wittgenstein', *Philosophical Quarterly* 44(176): 294–310.

Polanyi, M. (1973) *Personal Knowledge*, London: Routledge and Kegan Paul.

Price, H. (1988) *Facts and the Function of Truth*, Oxford: Blackwell.

Putnam, H. (1999) *The Threefold Cord: Mind, Body and World*, New York: Columbia University Press.

Rhees, R. (1969) *Without Answers*, London: Routledge and Kegan Paul.

—— (ed.) (1984) *Recollections of Wittgenstein*, Oxford: Oxford University Press.

Scruton, R. (1994) *Modern Philosophy*, London: Sinclair-Stevenson.

Squires, R. (1995) 'Dream Time', *Proceeding of the Aristotelian Society* 95: 83–91.

Stroud, B. (1984) *The Significance of Philosophical Scepticism*, Oxford: Clarendon.

Travis, C. (1989) *The Uses of Sense*, Oxford: Blackwell.

Wittgenstein, L. (1953) *Philosophical Investigations* (PI), trans. G.E.M. Anscombe, Oxford: Basil Blackwell.

—— (1967) *Zettel* (Z), trans. G.E.M. Anscombe, Oxford: Blackwell.

—— (1969) *On Certainty* (OC), trans. D. Paul and G.E.M. Anscombe, Oxford: Blackwell.

—— (1970) *Lectures and Conversations on Aesthetics, Psychology and Religious Belief* (LA), Oxford: Blackwell.

—— (1980a) *Remarks on the Philosophy of Psychology*, vol. 1 (RPPI), trans. G.E.M. Anscombe, Oxford: Blackwell.

—— (1980b) *Remarks on the Philosophy of Psychology*, vol. 2 (RPPII), trans. C.G. Luckhardt and M.A.E. Aue, Oxford: Blackwell.

—— (1980c) *Culture and Value* (CV), trans. P. Winch, 2nd edn, Oxford: Blackwell, 1988.

—— (1988) *Wittgenstein's Lectures on Philosophical Psychology 1946–47* (LPP), ed. P.T. Geach, London: Harvester.

—— (1993) *Philosophical Occasions 1912–1951* (PO), ed. J. Klagge and A. Nordmann, Indianapolis: Hackett.

Wolfe, T. (1975) *The Painted Word*, New York: Farrar, Straus and Giroux.

Wollheim, R. (1987) *Painting as an Art*, London: Thames & Hudson.

—— (1993) *The Mind and Its Depths*, Cambridge, MA: Harvard University Press.

Wrigley, M. (1980) 'Wittgenstein and Inconsistency', *Philosophy* 55(214): 471–84.

5

IS SCEPTICISM A 'NATURAL POSSIBILITY' OF LANGUAGE?

Reasons to be sceptical of Cavell's Wittgenstein

Malcolm Turvey

The primary goal of this volume is to demonstrate to its readers the properly philosophical role that Wittgenstein's later philosophy can play in humanistic disciplines that study the arts. To start with, several contributions outline the later Wittgenstein's humanized conception of meaning, language and intentional behaviour. A major ramification of this conception, these contributions argue, is that it provides the philosophical grounds for clarifying the logically appropriate methods and forms of explanation for explaining intentional behaviour, including the forms of behaviour studied by the humanities. Meanwhile, other contributions exemplify Wittgenstein's later conception of philosophy as conceptual clarification, by identifying and diagnosing conceptual confusions in prominent theories of the arts. They thereby demonstrate that elucidating the meaning of the distinctive concepts that scholars of the arts employ is crucial to preventing lapses into nonsense.

Taken together, these contributions suggest that the philosophical role Wittgenstein's later philosophy has to play in humanistic disciplines can best be characterized as a propaedeutic one. Its methods enable a perspicuous grasp of the distinctive concepts scholars of arts employ in their studies; its overall tenets provide the foundations for a philosophy of the humanities, one that elucidates the logically appropriate forms of explanation for studying humanistic phenomena.

The propaedeutic role that Wittgenstein's later philosophy can play in their disciplines is, it seems fair to say, almost totally unknown to contemporary scholars of the arts, and this volume is designed to help rectify this situation. However, this does not mean that Wittgenstein's later philosophy has no visibility at all in contemporary scholarship on the arts. Indeed, for a few scholars, it is of paramount importance in studying art. However, it is employed by such scholars for a very different end than the propaedeutic one envisioned by this volume. Instead of drawing on Wittgenstein's later writings to answer properly philosophical questions about sense and meaning that pertain to but antecede the practice of humanistic inquiry into the arts, they employ it *in* that practice itself, or at least one aspect of that practice, namely, interpreting art works. In other words, rather than drawing on its methods and tenets to clarify concepts and appropriate forms of explanation in a propaedeutic fashion prior to the interpretation of art works, they use Wittgenstein's later philosophy in the actual act of interpretation itself, or at least in the interpretation of art works that seem to bear some relation to philosophical arguments that Wittgenstein putatively makes in his later philosophy, or the style in which he makes them. In the work of such scholars, Wittgenstein's later philosophy plays an interpretive role, not a propaedeutic one.

While there are a number of contemporary scholars of the arts who employ Wittgenstein's later philosophy in this manner,[1] the most prominent is undoubtedly Stanley Cavell.[2] Although Cavell is a philosopher, his work has become increasingly influential among scholars of the arts, in part because of the central role that interpretations of art works play in it. According to Cavell, Wittgenstein's later philosophy acknowledges what Cavell calls 'the truth of scepticism', and this acknowledgment has many profound ramifications. One such ramification is that many art works can be interpreted as acknowledging 'the truth of scepticism' in the same way that Wittgenstein's later philosophy does, and Cavell's writings contain a large number of interpretations of a wide range of art works that are implicitly or explicitly predicated on this affinity.[3]

There are, I think, very good reasons to be sceptical of Cavell's claim that Wittgenstein's later philosophy acknowledges 'the truth of scepticism', and in this chapter I spell out these reasons. But before doing so, I want to suggest why it is important to challenge this claim within the context of the goal of this volume. For Cavell's reading of the later Wittgenstein is incompatible in at least one fundamental way with the propaedeutic role for Wittgenstein's later philosophy that this volume envisions. Cavell's 'truth of scepticism' has all the hallmarks of what Wittgenstein, borrowing from Goethe, called an *Urphänomen*, exemplified for Wittgenstein by Freud's theory of dreams as fulfilling wishes.[4] An *Urphänomen*, according to Wittgenstein, is a 'preconceived idea that takes possession of' the person employing it, who uses it to describe any and all phenomena, whether or not such phenomena are suitable candidates for such a description (ROC 3, sec. 203). An *Urphänomen* is a method of description that becomes applicable to phenomena in general for the person 'possessed' by it, regardless of whether these phenomena – like many of the dreams Freud analyzed – exemplify the *Urphänomen*. According to Jacques Bouveresse, this is 'not because over time the facts have been shown to conform to' the *Urphänomen*, but rather because of an 'initial decision to conceptualize [phenomena] and describe them' according to it (Bouveresse 1995: 49–50). (A list of *Urphänomen* that currently populate humanistic disciplines that study the arts might include Žižek's 'the Real', Foucault's 'power', Derrida's 'differance', and Freud's unconscious.)

That 'the truth of scepticism' is, in Cavell's work, an *Urphänomen* is in part evident in the role he believes that it plays in Wittgenstein's later philosophy. Rather than scepticism being *one* philosophical topic among many others that Wittgenstein addresses, according to Cavell 'Wittgenstein's teaching is *everywhere* controlled by a response to scepticism' (CR: 7; my emphasis); 'In Wittgenstein's work, as in skepticism, the human disappointment with human knowledge seems to take over the *whole* subject' (CR: 44; my emphasis). This is so even though large stretches of Wittgenstein's later writings, including his major work the *Investigations*, make little or no mention of sceptical topics at all. Scepticism, in other words, is an underlying principle of *all* of Wittgenstein's later philosophy, according to Cavell, regardless of whether Wittgenstein is addressing it.

But it is also evident in the fact that, in Cavell's work, 'the truth of scepticism' is an underlying principle of just about every human phenomenon imaginable, not just Wittgenstein's later philosophy, however unconnected with scepticism such phenomena are. As Stephen Mulhall puts it in his meticulous exegesis of Cavell's writings:

> Cavell's work grows out of the tradition of ordinary language philosophy; and although it began by focusing on issues in aesthetics, ethics, politics, and philosophical methodology, the specific conclusions it generated led him to explore themes in literary criticism and literary theory, film studies, psychoanalysis, and the writings of Emerson and Thoreau. The overarching concern of this diverse body of work is scepticism; on Cavell's understanding of its nature, the sceptical impulse is to be understood not only as that with which and against which modern philosophy distinctively struggles, but also as a central presence in other projects, disciplines, and bodies of work...
>
> (Mulhall 1994: viii)

The introduction to this volume makes clear that Wittgenstein was highly critical of the *Urphänomen*, exemplified for him by Freud's theory of dreams as fulfilling wishes, and that his criticisms were a corollary of his humanized conception of meaning, language and intentional behaviour. For a central feature of this conception is that, as Oswald Hanfling puts it in Chapter 3 of this volume, 'Wittgenstein...directs our attention to "the particular case" (BB: 18), as encountered in human life and language. We are not to suppose that there must be some general principle underlying the uses of language, the appreciation of art, etc'. This, of course, does not mean that Wittgenstein never advances generalizations in his later philosophy. His distinction between reasons and causes, outlined in the introduction, is a good example of just such a generalization. However, the difference between such generalizations and an *Urphänomen* is that they are about what lies 'open to view' in a given human practice (PI §126), and they are arrived at on the basis of looking and seeing whether any commonalities are manifest in the practice in question (PI

§66). They are not methods of description that are decided upon in advance of looking and seeing, and then applied to human practices regardless of whether they manifest the principle or not, as is the *Urphänomen*.

If it is true, as Cavell argues, that 'the truth of scepticism' is the underlying principle of not only Wittgenstein's later philosophy in its entirety but almost every human phenomenon imaginable, then this volume's presentation of Wittgenstein's humanized conception of meaning, language and intentional behaviour, as well as the propaedeutic ramifications of this conception for humanistic disciplines that study the arts, is thrown into doubt. If Cavell is right, then Wittgenstein – despite his oft-stated intention to attend only to what lies 'open to view' and to 'the particular case' in human practices, and his repeated criticisms of attempts to reduce such practices to general, underlying principles as nonsensical – is in fact acknowledging 'the truth of' just such a principle in his later philosophy: the *Urphänomen* of scepticism. He is thereby violating his stated conception of what is, as Hanfling puts it, 'distinctively human about language, about art and about human beings themselves'. Hence, some kind of challenge to Cavell's reading of Wittgenstein is in order in this volume, if its goal is to be achieved convincingly.

I

First, a preliminary. Cavell's writing is notoriously opaque and, according to some, 'self-indulgent', something which even his defenders acknowledge.[5] While there may be important reasons for this opacity that are internal to Cavell's philosophical project, it nevertheless often makes for difficulty in identifying precisely what Cavell is arguing. I must therefore warn in advance of the arguments that I attribute to Cavell that they are ones Cavell *seems* – given the obscurity of his prose – to be making about Wittgenstein, in the full knowledge that some of his defenders and interpreters may dispute whether Cavell is actually making such arguments. However, I will also do my best to provide as clear-cut textual evidence for these arguments as possible.

According to Cavell, scepticism is the modern or 'secular' form of something intrinsically human, which Cavell refers to as 'the human wish to deny the condition of human existence' (IQO: 5). By this, Cavell seems to mean that human beings possess a basic, almost natural impulse to view the conditions of their existence, such as mortality, as limitations, and hence to want to escape those conditions. This impulse, he argues, 'is essential to what we think of as the human' (IQO: 5). Scepticism – the familiar philosophical argument that 'we can never know with certainty of the existence of something or other; call it the external world, and call it other minds' (CR: 37) – is one form of 'deny[ing] the condition of human existence', because it views the human capacity to know as limited. Certainty about the existence of the external world and other minds is impossible. As the modern form of the intrinsically human impulse to 'deny the condition of human existence', scepticism, in turn, 'cannot, or must not, be denied' (IQO: 5). It is a manifestation of a fundamental feature of human existence, the symptom of an existential impulse. In his writings, Cavell therefore routinely refers to it as 'the truth of skepticism' (CR: 7; IQO: 5).

However, for Cavell, scepticism is not simply the symptom of an existential impulse. Rather, there is a legitimate philosophical motivation behind sceptical doubt, and this motivation has to do with the nature of human language. It is Wittgenstein's later philosophy that, for Cavell, contains the clearest acknowledgment of this motivation, much to its credit.

According to Cavell, Wittgenstein:

> does not negate the concluding thesis of skepticism, that we do not know with certainty of the existence of the external world (or of other minds). On the contrary, Wittgenstein, as I read him, rather affirms that thesis, or rather takes it as *undeniable*, and so shifts its weight.
>
> (CR: 45)

For Cavell, the philosophical motivation behind Wittgenstein's affirmation of the 'concluding thesis of scepticism' is to be found in a single concept that occurs in his later writings: the concept of a 'criterion'. According to Cavell, Wittgenstein argues that 'any concept we use in speaking about anything at all...call for criteria' (CR: 14). Criteria are the means by which human language-users 'regulate our application of concepts' to the world (IQO: 5) in that they are, in part, what enable human beings to agree about what objects to apply what concepts to. By this, Cavell means that in order to be able to apply the concept of, for example, a cat to the same objects that other English speakers do, one must learn the various criteria that define what objects are counted as cats in English: that a cat is a small animal with fur, a tail, four legs, that meows and so on. These are criteria that English-speakers share by virtue of having learned how to use the concept of a cat, and they facilitate widespread agreement among English-speakers about what objects count as cats in the practice of applying the concept. Criteria, therefore, are logically or grammatically related to the concepts and linguistic expressions for the use of which they are criteria. In other words, they in part determine the meaning of concepts and linguistic expressions. That certain criteria in part determine the meaning of the concept of a cat is not a consequence of empirical experience or inductive correlation on the part of the English-speaker, but rather is laid down a priori by the rules governing the use of the word cat in English. Thus, criteria constitute non-inductive logical grounds for applying a concept to an object or justifying a judgement or proposition about an object, such as, 'That is a cat'.

For Cavell, the legitimate philosophical motivation behind sceptical doubt is to be found in Wittgenstein's concept of a criterion:

the explanatory power of Wittgenstein's idea [of a criterion] depends on recognizing that criteria, for all their necessity, are open to our repudiation, or dissatisfaction (hence they lead to, as well as lead from, skepticism); that our capacity for disappointment by them is essential to the way we possess language...

(IQO: 5)

Sceptical doubt can arise, according to Cavell's reading of Wittgenstein, because criteria – which are an essential condition of human language-use because 'any concept we use in speaking about anything at all...call for criteria' (CR: 14) – can be viewed by human beings as limited. However, this is not simply because of the intrinsically human impulse to view any condition of human existence as limited. Rather, it is because of the nature of criteria. They are by definition, according to Cavell's reading of Wittgenstein's concept of a criterion, 'open to our repudiation', 'dissatisfaction, and 'disappointment'. Hence, sceptical doubt is always a potential product of human language-use for Wittgenstein, because in order to communicate with language, human beings must employ criteria, and criteria by their very nature are 'open to our repudiation'.

If the fact that we share, or have established, criteria is the condition under which we can think and communicate in language, then skepticism is a *natural* possibility of that condition; it reveals most perfectly the standing threat to thought and communication, that they are only human, nothing more than natural to us.

(CR: 47)

It is because sceptical doubt is always a '*natural* possibility' of human language-use that scepticism is the underlying principle of Wittgenstein's later philosophy *in toto*, that 'Wittgenstein's teaching is *everywhere* controlled by a response to skepticism' (CR: 7; my emphasis). Or as Cavell puts it elsewhere:

Wittgenstein's teaching is...that skepticism is (not exactly true, but not exactly false either; it is) a standing threat to the human mind, that our ordinary language and its representation of the world *can* be philosophically repudiated and that it is essential to our inheritance and mutual possession of language, as well as to what inspires philosophy, that this should be so.[6]

II

Before going on to examine Cavell's reading of Wittgenstein's concept of a criterion, it is perhaps worthwhile pausing to raise an obvious objection to what Cavell has said so far. For anyone familiar with Wittgenstein's later writings would, I suspect, find Cavell's claim that Wittgenstein affirms the 'concluding thesis of scepticism', or at least 'takes it as undeniable', a highly implausible one regardless of what he says about the nature of criteria. Cavell's choice of words here (and elsewhere) makes it seem as though Wittgenstein is making a substantive philosophical argument about scepticism, namely, that it is true, or, if 'not exactly true', it is 'not exactly false either'. However, it is very hard to find anywhere in Wittgenstein's later writings – and certainly in the *Investigations* – where Wittgenstein argues that scepticism is either 'true' or 'false' (or a combination of the two). And the reason why it is so hard, I suspect, is because Wittgenstein's overwhelming and repeatedly stated (and enacted) concern in his later writings is with questions of sense and meaning, *not* with making arguments about what is true or false. Given this concern, in as much as Wittgenstein might address sceptical topics in his later philosophy, one would expect him to do so by investigating whether the sceptic's use of words such as doubt, certainty, knowledge and so on to advance his arguments makes sense or not, and not whether the arguments themselves are true or false. Unsurprisingly, this is precisely the way in which Wittgenstein does tackle sceptical topics in those later writings that explicitly address them, which have been collected together in the volume *On Certainty*. In these writings, Wittgenstein investigates how the sceptic uses (or more appropriately 'misuses' (OC §6)) words such as doubt and certainty in order to see if the sceptic's arguments make sense. Thus, it seems highly unlikely that Wittgenstein would be affirming the 'concluding thesis' of anything, let alone scepticism, given his general concern with questions of sense and meaning, the way he explicitly addresses sceptical topics in his later writings, and the lack of textual evidence to the contrary.

What makes Cavell's claim even more implausible is, of course, that far from affirming that scepticism is 'true' or 'undeniable', when he does explicitly address sceptical topics in his later writings Wittgenstein is clearly attempting to show that scepticism is a species of *nonsense*, that the sceptic's use of words is *meaningless*. To take just one of many instances from *On Certainty*, Wittgenstein investigates uses of the concept of doubt in a variety of practices to show that the concept is only employed intelligibly against a background of certainty: 'The game of doubting itself presupposes certainty' (OC §115). Here are some of the examples he comes up with: 'If the shopkeeper wanted to investigate each of his apples without any reason, for the sake of being certain about everything, why doesn't he have to investigate the investigation?' (OC §459). The shopkeeper, in other words, has to rely on the investigation in order to investigate his fruit, otherwise he will be forced into the senseless procedure of investigating his investigation of his investigation of.... Similarly, in the empirical sciences: 'If I make an experiment I do not doubt the existence of the apparatus before my eyes. I have plenty of doubts, but not *that*' (OC §337). Or in mathematics: 'If I do a calculation I believe, without any doubts, that the figures on the paper aren't switching of their own accord' (OC §337). These examples seem to show that in order to doubt intelligibly in practices such as investigations, experiments and calculations, doubt must take place against a background of certainty. Indeed, Wittgenstein suggests, even the most radical sceptic must be certain about something, namely, the meaning of the words he uses to express his scepticism. For if he doubts the meaning of his words, then surely the sceptic cannot rely on getting the meaning of the word 'doubt' right, and therefore should not even attempt to express his or her scepticism linguistically: 'If you are not certain of any fact, you cannot be certain of the meaning of your words either' (OC §114).

Although the writings collected together in *On Certainty* are in various ways unfinished and lack the authority of the *Investigations*, they clearly suggest that the later Wittgenstein thought that the general, systematic or universal way in which the sceptic employs the concept of doubt is unintelligible: 'A doubt that doubted everything would not be a doubt' (OC §450). Scepticism, it seems from these writings, is neither true nor false for Wittgenstein, but senseless. Nor does this view of scepticism only emerge in the later philosophy. The following passage is from the notebooks Wittgenstein wrote in between 1914 and 1916:

> Scepticism is *not* irrefutable, but *obvious nonsense* if it tries to doubt where no question can be asked.
>
> For doubt can only exist where a question exists; a question can only exist where an answer exists, and this can only exist where something *can* be *said*.[7]

Thus, as G.P. Baker and P.M.S. Hacker have observed in their critique of sceptical readings of Wittgenstein on rule-following: 'It would be very surprising to discover that someone who throughout his life found philosophical scepticism *nonsensical*, a subtle violation of the bounds of sense, should actually make a sceptical problem the pivotal point of his work' (Baker and Hacker 1984: 5).

Surprising, but not of course impossible. For it could be the case that scepticism is, as Cavell argues, the 'pivotal point' or underlying principle of Wittgenstein's later philosophy, even though there is much evidence to suggest that he thought it was a species of nonsense. This possibility is rendered less implausible by the fact that, for Cavell, the precise sense in which Wittgenstein affirms the 'concluding thesis of scepticism' is more complex than my presentation of his reading has acknowledged so far, and in fact approximates Wittgenstein's explicitly articulated view of scepticism as a species of nonsense, despite Cavell's confusing use of words such as 'true' and 'false' to articulate it. In order to understand exactly what it is about the sceptic's 'concluding thesis' that is 'true' or 'undeniable' for Cavell's Wittgenstein, we must turn to the philosophical motivation behind this thesis, which, according to Cavell, is to be found in Wittgenstein's concept of a criterion.

III

The point of departure for Cavell's reading of Wittgenstein's concept of a criterion is what he refers to as the 'official' view of this concept among Wittgenstein's interpreters at the time of writing the first drafts of the early chapters of *The Claim of Reason* in the late 1950s. According to this 'official' view, the concept of a criterion was intended by Wittgenstein to constitute a philosophical refutation of scepticism, because for Wittgenstein criteria guarantee the existence of something with certainty (CR 6; 37). They do so because of the logical relation that obtains between criteria and the concepts and linguistic expressions the use of which they are criteria for. Cavell quotes the philosopher Norman Malcolm as a representative of this view from an article published in 1950:

> the satisfaction of the criterion of *y* establishes the existence of *y* beyond question...It will not make sense for one to suppose that another person is not in pain if one's criterion of his being in pain is satisfied.[8]

(CR: 38)

However, as Cavell rightly points out, although the relation between a judgement about whether a person is in pain and the criteria upon which such a judgement is made is a logical one for Wittgenstein, this relation cannot be one of straightforward logical entailment, as Malcolm implies in the above quotation. Criteria for the presence of pain do not constitute necessary and sufficient conditions for its presence. They do not *logically* exclude the possibility that the person about whom the judgement is made is not in pain. This is because such a judgement may be defeated by later discoveries, even though all the criteria for the person's being in pain are satisfied at the time of making the judgement. For example, it may turn out that a person judged to be in pain is in fact feigning his pain: that a soccer player who satisfies all the criteria for being in pain after being fouled (by rolling around on the ground, screaming in agony, etc.) is in fact feigning his pain in order to be awarded a penalty kick, as revealed later by slow-motion television footage. And if this is so – if judgements about the presence of pain made on the basis of the satisfaction of the criteria for pain can be defeated and are therefore not logically entailed by the satisfaction of those criteria – then 'what kind of certainty', asks Cavell, do Wittgensteinian criteria guarantee about the presence of pain (CR: 38–39)?

The 'official' view of Malcolm and others is that the certainty they believe Wittgensteinian criteria guarantee can be preserved against defeasibility by arguing that in cases such as the soccer player who feigns his pain, the criteria for pain only *seem* to be satisfied. They are not *really* satisfied. If they were *really* satisfied, then the soccer player would certainly be in pain. However, Cavell insists that this answer does not preserve certainty. For it does not provide any way of differentiating between the actual and apparent satisfaction of criteria for the presence of pain at the time of making a judgement. In the case of the soccer player, it does not provide a way of determining whether he is really satisfying the criteria for the presence of pain or merely seeming to. For in both cases, the criteria are the same, and they are equally well satisfied by his behaviour.

> For 'He's rehearsing' or 'feigning', or 'It's a hoax', etc. to satisfy us as explanations for his *not* being in pain (for it to 'turn out' that he is not in pain) *what* he is feigning must be precisely *pain*, what he is rehearsing must be the part of a man *in pain*, the hoax depends on his simulating *pain*, etc. These circumstances are ones in appealing to which, in describing which, we *retain the concept* (here, of pain) whose application these criteria determine. And this means to me: In all such circumstances he has satisfied the criteria we use for applying the concept of pain to others.
>
> (CR: 45)

Cavell therefore concludes that the satisfaction of the criteria for pain cannot guarantee the presence of pain with certainty in the way that the 'official' view of Wittgensteinian criteria wants to argue.

Cavell's challenge to this 'official' view points to a distinctive feature of Wittgenstein's employment of the concept of a criterion in his investigations into psychological concepts, one that has caused his interpreters many problems. For on the one hand, the relation between a criterion and what it is a criterion of is a logical or grammatical one. But on the other, a criterion – at least in the examples of the ascription of pain to others that Cavell addresses – is defeasible. Thus, as P.M.S. Hacker puts it, Wittgenstein:

> allocates to a grammatical (conceptual) relationship a property usually associated only with empirical (inductive) evidence. If p logically implies q, then no matter what other propositions are true, it still implies q. In this sense it is indefeasible. Inductive evidence is different, for however good the correlation between p and q may have been discovered to be...an additional piece of evidence may undermine the support p gives to q.
>
> (Hacker 1990: 251)

Although a criterion has a non-inductive logical relation to what it is a criterion of, it nevertheless is in at least some cases defeasible by future discoveries, much like inductive evidence.

However, while Cavell is right to point to the defeasibility of Wittgensteinian criteria in at least some cases of the ascription of psychological states such as pain to others, this does not mean that the conclusions that he draws from doing so are correct. For it is on the basis of this *single* example of the defeasibility of Wittgensteinian criteria that his claim that, for Wittgenstein, scepticism is a '*natural* possibility' of human language-use rests. This claim consists of five interconnected arguments that Cavell makes in quick succession following his discussion of the failure of the 'official' view of Wittgensteinian criteria to preserve certainty against defeasibility.

First, Cavell in effect accepts that the only possible account of Wittgensteinian criteria guaranteeing the presence of pain is the one provided by the 'official' view. Because this view fails to provide a way of differentiating between the actual and apparent satisfaction of the criteria for pain, he therefore concludes that criteria *never* guarantee the existence of pain for Wittgenstein. Knowledge of the criteria for pain only allows the language user to identify the presence of the criteria for pain in a person's behaviour, not 'pain itself': 'There are [no criteria for the presence of pain] that go essentially beyond the criteria for the behavior's being pain-behaviour' (CR: 44).

Second, Cavell in effect assumes that he can draw a conclusion about all Wittgensteinian criteria from the single example of their defeasibility that he examines. For he concludes on the basis of this one example that criteria *never* guarantee the existence of anything for Wittgenstein, not just pain, presumably because he thinks that all criteria are defeasible. The role of criteria in human language for Wittgenstein, according to Cavell, is simply to determine in part the meaning of concepts and linguistic expressions, thereby allowing language users to identify phenomena. Their role is not to enable the language user to know with certainty whether the phenomena he identifies actually exist or not.

> Criteria are 'criteria for something's being so', not in the sense that they tell us of a thing's existence, but of something like its identity, not of its *being* so, but of its being *so*. Criteria do not determine the certainty of statements, but the application of the concepts employed in statements.
>
> (CR: 45)

Criteria in general only 'settle questions of identity rather than existence' (Mulhall 1994: 84) for Cavell's Wittgenstein.

Third, Cavell concludes that Wittgenstein's concept of a criterion affirms the 'concluding thesis of skepticism' (CR: 45). For if the role of criteria in human language is to settle questions of identity rather than existence, then appeals to criteria cannot refute the sceptic's claim that we do not know with certainty the existence of the external world and other minds. The sceptic is right, according to Wittgenstein's concept of a criterion: human beings never know with certainty the existence of anything on the basis of criteria. Thus, this concept could not have been intended by Wittgenstein as a refutation of the sceptic's conclusions, as it was according to the 'official' view. Quite to the contrary, it affirms those conclusions (CR: 45).

Fourth, while Wittgenstein's concept of a criterion shows that the sceptic is right, it also shows why scepticism is wrong or unintelligible. For the fact that the role of criteria in human language is to settle questions of identity rather than existence means that criteria cannot intelligibly be accused of *failing* to settle questions of existence, which is precisely what the sceptic accuses criteria of doing. For the sceptic argues that human knowledge is limited, that it is a disappointment, because human beings fail to know with certainty the existence of the external world and other minds on the basis of criteria. However, it only makes sense to say that something fails if success is a logical possibility. And in the case of criteria, success in settling questions of existence is not a logical possibility because the role of criteria is to settle questions of identity. Hence, accusing criteria of failing to guarantee the existence of something is akin to accusing human beings of failing to see sounds or hear colours. Failing to see sounds is not an empirical failing on the part of human perception, but is logically excluded by the concepts of sight, sound and so on. Similarly, failing to guarantee existence is not an empirical failing on the part of criteria, but is logically excluded by the concept of a criterion. Scepticism is therefore also 'false' or nonsensical for Cavell's Wittgenstein: that criteria only guarantee identity, not existence, is only a failing on the part of criteria from the sceptic's ultimately unintelligible point of view, which wrongly assumes that criteria should be able to guarantee existence.

Fifth, because criteria cannot intelligibly be said to either fail or succeed at guaranteeing the existence of anything with certainty, then the relation of human beings to the world via criteria and the concepts and linguistic expressions they in part define cannot be one of certain knowledge. As Cavell puts it: 'Our relation to the world as a whole, or to others in general, is not one of knowing, where knowing construes itself as being certain' (CR: 45). For according to Cavell's reading of Wittgenstein's concept of a criterion, it is senseless or unintelligible to claim on the basis of criteria that I know with certainty that the world and other minds exist, or that I do not know with certainty that the world and other minds exist. Both claims are equally nonsensical, because criteria neither fail nor succeed in guaranteeing the existence of anything with certainty.

Thus, the legitimate philosophical motivation behind scepticism, according to Cavell's Wittgenstein, is the role that criteria play in human language. While scepticism itself is ultimately 'false' or unintelligible, it nevertheless gets off the ground, so to speak, for a legitimate philosophical reason, namely, that criteria only settle questions of identity, not existence.

Scepticism is therefore always a *'natural* possibility' of human language use. Where the sceptic errs is in misrecognizing the fact that criteria only settle questions of identity, not existence as a failing on the part of criteria, and Cavell's own philosophy is in large part an attempt to explain why it is the sceptic does fall prey to this misrecognition.

<h1 style="text-align:center">IV</h1>

On a charitable interpretation of Cavell, even though Cavell never examines Wittgenstein's writings that explicitly address sceptical topics, and even though he confusingly uses words such as 'true' and 'false' to describe Wittgenstein's view of scepticism, his reading nevertheless concludes by approximating Wittgenstein's explicitly articulated view of scepticism as a species of nonsense. For Cavell's Wittgenstein, scepticism is ultimately unintelligible.

But in the process of arriving at this conclusion, a great deal is ceded to the sceptic on Wittgenstein's part. For even though ultimately unintelligible, for Cavell's Wittgenstein scepticism is 'true' in the sense that its 'concluding thesis' elucidates one crucial aspect of the role that criteria putatively play in human language. The 'cannot' of the sceptic's claim that criteria cannot guarantee existence, if understood as a logical 'cannot', is 'true' in the sense that criteria only guarantee identity, not existence, thereby showing that, 'Our relation to the world as a whole, or to others in general, is not one of knowing' (CR: 45). The sceptic's conception of the nature of criteria and their role in human language is in part correct, according to Cavell's Wittgenstein.

However, in my view, this conception of criteria is nowhere to be found in Wittgenstein's later philosophy, for two basic reasons. First, examinations of Wittgenstein's use of the concept of a criterion undertaken since the 1950s have shown that it plays a much more varied role in his later philosophy than Cavell's one example suggests, including the role of conferring certainty on judgements about the psychological states of others made upon the basis of defeasible criteria. Wittgenstein's concept of a criterion licenses neither the conception of criteria as guaranteeing identity, not existence; nor the corollary of this conception: that, 'Our relation to the world as a whole, or to others in general, is not one of knowing' (CR: 45). Second, this conception of criteria in effect entails that claims such as, 'I am certain he is in pain', made on the basis of the satisfaction of criteria for pain, are unintelligible, because criteria only guarantee identity, not existence. But given that it makes perfect sense to make such claims, this conception of criteria and its corollary, that, 'Our relation to the world...is not one of knowing', constitute a philosophical interference with meaning of the first order. They stipulate that the way we standardly use concepts of knowledge, certainty and doubt in the ascription of psychological states to others upon the basis of criteria – such as when we say 'I know for a fact he is in pain', or, 'I am not quite sure whether he is really sad' – is senseless. In that a fundamental tenet of Wittgenstein's later philosophy is that it is unintelligible for the philosopher to interfere with meaning because meaning is autonomous and can only be described (PI §124), Wittgenstein would not have endorsed the conception of criteria motivating such an interference.

While this may seem like nit-picking over precisely what Wittgenstein meant by the concept of a criterion, it should be remembered that, if correct, Cavell's reading of this concept has major ramifications for this volume. For it is on the basis of this reading that Cavell concludes that scepticism is, for Wittgenstein, a *natural* possibility' of human language use in general. And it is because scepticism is just such a *natural* possibility' that leads Cavell to conceive of scepticism as an *Urphänomen*, an underlying principle of Wittgenstein's entire later philosophy. As I suggested in the introductory paragraphs of this chapter, if Wittgenstein's later philosophy is acknowledging 'the truth of' the *Urphänomen* of scepticism, then this volume's presentation of the later Wittgenstein's humanized conception of meaning, language and intentional behaviour is thrown into doubt. But if Cavell's reading of Wittgenstein's concept of a criterion can be shown to be wrong, as I think it can be, then there is no reason to conclude that Wittgenstein violated his stated philosophical method of describing what lies 'open to view' in 'the particular case', by acknowledging 'the truth of' a general, underlying principle which he explicitly viewed as a species of nonsense.

Cavell's claim that, for Wittgenstein, scepticism is a *natural* possibility' of human language-use is premised on (1) his argument that, according to Wittgenstein, 'any concept we use in speaking about anything at all...call for criteria' (CR: 14); (2) his assumption that, for Wittgenstein, all criteria are defeasible just like the criteria for pain in the single example that he looks at; and (3) his argument that the defeasibility of criteria means that criteria for Wittgenstein do not confer certainty. They settle questions of identity, not existence, meaning that 'Our relation to the world...is not one of knowing'. However, an examination of Wittgenstein's employment of the concept of a criterion quickly shows that none of these is the case for him.

First, it is not the case for Wittgenstein that 'any concept we use in speaking about anything at all...call for criteria'. For instance, certain first-person expressions (avowals) constitute an important example of the use of psychological concepts in which criteria play no role at all. Exclamations such as 'Ow', 'That hurts', and 'I'm in pain', uttered in certain circumstances, are linguistic expressions of pain on the part of a speaker, not descriptions of an internal state of pain made on the basis of the satisfaction of criteria. In this way, such exclamations are like screams, cries, groans and other instinctual forms of behaviour. I do not cry out in agony on stubbing my toe because I have first determined through introspection that my toe satisfies the criteria for being in pain. Rather, my cry is a natural manifestation of my pain. The same is true if I exclaim, 'Ow, that hurts!', instead of simply crying out. Indeed, for Wittgenstein, it is crucial for all sorts of reasons to recognize that avowals are learned extensions of criterionless instinctual expressions of pain and are themselves forms of behaviour: 'words are connected with the primitive, the natural, expressions of their sensation and used in their place. A child has hurt himself and he cries; and then adults talk to him and teach him exclamations and, later, sentences. They teach the child new pain-behaviour' (PI §244). A child is not taught to use avowals of pain by first teaching him to determine through introspection whether the criteria for the presence of an internal state of pain have been satisfied (something that according to Wittgenstein's private language 'argument' would be a logical impossibility anyway). Rather, the child learns to 'replace' and extend instinctual manifestations of pain with avowals.

Thus, criteria are by no means a universal feature of language-use for Wittgenstein. And because it is the nature of criteria that constitutes the legitimate philosophical motivation behind sceptical doubt, according to Cavell, it cannot be the case for Wittgenstein that scepticism is a *'natural* possibility' of human language use in general. At the very most, it can only be a *'natural* possibility' of those regions of language use in which criteria play a role.

Second, even in such regions where they do play a role, it is not the case that criteria are always defeasible for Wittgenstein. In some cases, according to Wittgenstein, criteria do constitute necessary and sufficient conditions that logically entail that something is the case. For example, a certain condition can be used by medical science as a necessary and sufficient condition for the presence of a disease: if a patient has the condition, then he necessarily has the disease:

> If medical science calls angina an inflammation caused by a particular bacillus, and we ask in a particular case 'why do you say this man has got angina?' then the answer 'I have found the bacillus so-and-so in his blood' gives us the criterion, or what we may call the defining criterion of angina.
>
> (BB: 25)

Similarly, in mathematics, that a figure is a triangle is a necessary and sufficient condition for it having three sides (LFM: 164). And there are various other similar examples in Wittgenstein's later writings.

Thus, for Wittgenstein, criteria are not always defeasible, as they can be in the ascription of psychological states to others. And because it is the *defeasible* nature of criteria that constitutes the legitimate philosophical motivation behind sceptical doubt according to Cavell, it cannot be the case for Wittgenstein that scepticism is a *'natural* possibility' of those regions of language use in which criteria play a role. At the very most, it can only be a possibility of those regions of language use in which *defeasible* criteria play a role, such as in the ascription of psychological states to others.

Third, it is not the case that, for Wittgenstein, the defeasibility of criteria means that they do not confer certainty. For when we examine Wittgenstein's investigations into those regions of language use in which defeasible criteria play a role, such as his investigations into psychological concepts, we find that he clearly acknowledges that criteria can and do confer certainty. 'I can be as *certain* of someone else's sensations as of any fact', he claimed, including the 'fact' that 'twice two is four' (although the type of certainty in the case of a mathematical calculation is logically different from the type involved in the ascription of psychological states to others) (PI: p. 224). And again: 'If we are using the word "to know" as it is normally used (and how else are we to use it?), then other people very often know when I am in pain' (PI §246). Thus, for Wittgenstein, criteria do not necessarily leave the language user bereft of certainty in his judgements about the psychological states of others. It cannot be the case for Wittgenstein, therefore, that scepticism is a '*natural* possibility' of those regions of language use in which defeasible criteria play a role. For even in these regions criteria can confer certainty.

Why would Wittgenstein have thought that criteria can and do confer certainty on judgements about the psychological states of others? First, and most obviously, he would have thought so because judgements such as 'I know for sure that he is in pain' made upon the basis of criteria are perfectly intelligible. A fundamental tenet of Wittgenstein's later philosophy is that meaning is autonomous and can therefore only be described. This tenet would have been seriously violated if – as Cavell in effect argues he does – Wittgenstein had suddenly departed from his descriptive method in his philosophy of psychology and interfered with meaning by stipulating that we do not know with certainty whether another person is in pain upon the basis of criteria, even though it is perfectly intelligible to say that we do.

Second, it is not at all clear that the defeat of criteria by future discoveries in the ascription of psychological states such as pain to others is always a logical possibility. If I am walking down a street with my two-year-old son and he falls down and cracks open his head on the sidewalk, screaming in pain as the blood pours out, it would be nonsensical for me to stand and think, 'Perhaps he is not in pain, but just feigning his bloodied broken head', instead of rushing to comfort him and take him to the nearest hospital.

But third, even in less extreme cases involving clearly defeasible criteria, Wittgenstein demonstrably rejected as nonsensical the sort of sceptical argument Cavell makes to the effect that defeasible criteria do not confer certainty on judgements about the psychological states of others. Cavell, it might be remembered, argues that we do not know with certainty whether another person is in pain upon the basis of criteria because those criteria may be defeated by future discoveries, because we may find out that the person in question, for example, is not really in pain but is only pretending to be so. But if this is the case in the present, then it is also the case in the future. If the fact that criteria are defeasible constitutes grounds for doubting or withholding a judgement about whether a person is in pain in the present, then it will also do so in the future, meaning that we will never be able to know with certainty whether the person in question is in pain or only pretending to be so. But this is unintelligible. It makes no sense to argue that we can never know with certainty whether another person is in pain because we may discover in the future that he is pretending to be in pain if such a discovery is impossible. I cannot discover in the future that a person is pretending to be in pain and therefore defeat criteria in the present if it is impossible for me to ever know with certainty whether someone is in pain or only pretending to be so.

Cavell's sceptical argument commits the same logical error that Wittgenstein sought to expose in sceptical arguments in general: it employs concepts, such as the concept of pretence, unintelligibly by robbing them of the criteria for their meaningful use. Its outcome, as Wittgenstein pointed out, is *not* that we cannot know with certainty whether another person is in pain because he may be pretending to be in pain, but that the concept of pretence (and pain for that matter) becomes 'unusable' because it is robbed of the criteria for its meaningful use.

> But what does it mean to say that all behaviour *might* always be pretence? Has experience taught us this? How else can we be instructed about pretence? No, it is a remark about the concept 'pretence'. But then this concept would be unusable, for pretending would have no criteria in behaviour.
>
> (Z §571)

The logical possibility of being certain about whether a person is pretending to be in pain is part of the grammar or meaningful use of the concept of pretence.[9] Cavell's sceptical argument is unintelligible because it rules out this possibility. Wittgenstein would have thought that defeasible criteria can and do confer certainty on judgements about the psychological states of others in part because he showed that sceptical arguments to the contrary, such as Cavell's, are nonsensical.

One of the problems with Cavell's sceptical argument about the defeasibility of criteria is that, like many sceptical arguments, it mistakes the logical possibility of doubting that p for a legitimate ground for doubting that p. Cavell assumes that the logical possibility of the defeasibility of criteria constitutes a legitimate ground for doubting or withholding judgements about the psychological states of others. However, as Wittgenstein pointed out in his writings on scepticism, that it *makes sense* to doubt that p is not necessarily a legitimate ground for doubting that p: 'But what about such a proposition as "I know I have a brain"? Can I doubt it? Grounds for *doubt* are lacking! Everything speaks in its favour, nothing against it. Nevertheless it is imaginable that my skull should turn out empty when it was operated on' (OC §4).

One of the reasons Cavell makes this mistake, I suspect, is that he focuses too exclusively on the role of criteria in conferring certainty on judgements about the psychological states of others. He thereby overlooks the role played by what Wittgenstein sometimes called the 'framework' or 'form of life' (PI §240-2) within which such judgements are made. The 'framework' presupposed by the psychological concepts we use, argued Wittgenstein, includes elementary regularities in human behaviour that are bequeathed to us by our biology, such as primitive instinctual reactions, just as other language games, such as those involving measuring or weighing, presuppose certain regularities in the natural world. It is these stable regularities that give our language games their point.

> It is only in normal cases that the use of a word is clearly prescribed; we know, are in no doubt, what to say in this or that case. The more abnormal the case, the more doubtful it becomes what we are to say. And if things were quite different from what they actually are – if there were for instance no characteristic expression of pain, of fear, of joy; if rule became exception and exception rule; or if both became phenomena of roughly equal frequency – this would make our normal language-games lose their point. – The procedure of putting a lump of cheese on a balance and fixing the price by the turn of the scale would lose its point if it frequently happened for such lumps to suddenly grow or shrink for no obvious reason.
>
> (PI §142)

Our use of the concept of weighing presupposes certain natural regularities, such as the fact that the weight of an object does not fluctuate while it is being weighed. Although this regularity is not part of the grammar or meaning of the concept of weighing, it is one of the normal circumstances within which we learn and use this concept. As Wittgenstein points out in the above quotation, the more such normal circumstances break down, the less we are able to use the concepts that presuppose them. If all of a sudden the weight of objects did fluctuate wildly while they were being weighed, then the language game within which we employ the concept of weighing would lose its point, and we would be uncertain how to play it with the concept that we have.

Similarly, our use of psychological concepts such as pain presupposes certain regularities, such as the fact that human beings instinctively express themselves in 'characteristic' ways when they are in pain due to their biological nature. Usually, human beings wince, groan, cry out or scream when they are in pain (rather than smile or sing), and usually they go on to seek comfort and alleviation from their pain (rather than more pain). While this regularity is not part of the meaning of the concept of pain – it does not constitute a criterion for ascribing it to others – it is nevertheless part of the normal circumstances within which we learn and use the concept. If all of a sudden the instinctual behaviour of human beings in pain lost this regularity and became wildly unpredictable – if all of a sudden 'rule became exception and exception rule' and some human beings laughed when they were in pain while others sang – then the concept of pain we possess would lose its point and we would be unsure how to use it. While the regularity of the behaviour of human beings in pain has a degree of flexibility – and the defeasibility of the criteria for applying the concept reflects this flexibility – nevertheless this regularity ensures in part that the times when 'we know, are in no doubt' that another person is in pain but turn out to be wrong remain the 'exception', not the 'rule'. By considering criteria in isolation from the 'framework' of such regularities that surrounds our use of psychological concepts, Cavell, I suspect, is unable to see how it is possible for human beings to be certain about the psychological states of others upon the basis of defeasible criteria alone. He therefore makes a sceptical argument about defeasible criteria, which he also attributes to Wittgenstein.

Whether or not this is in fact one of the reasons Cavell makes his sceptical argument about defeasible criteria, it should by now be clear that this argument is not Wittgenstein's. Wittgenstein does not argue that the defeasibility of criteria means that criteria do not confer certainty, that they only settle questions of identity, not existence, and that consequently, 'Our relation to the world...is not one of knowing'. For even in those regions of language use in which defeasible criteria play a role, as in our judgements about the psychological states of others, certainty is possible: for it is perfectly intelligible to say 'I am certain he is in pain' upon the basis of criteria; it is by no means clear that all criteria for the ascription of pain to others are defeasible; and even when they are defeasible, the sceptical argument that they do not confer certainty turns out to transgress the bounds of sense in a way that Wittgenstein himself pointed to in his attempts to show that scepticism is a species of nonsense.

Thus, if it is not the case that criteria are a universal feature of language use for Wittgenstein; or that all criteria are defeasible for Wittgenstein; or that, even when they are defeasible, they fail to confer certainty for Wittgenstein; then Cavell's reading of Wittgenstein's concept of a criterion cannot be right. And if this is so, then there is no reason to agree with the argument that this reading gives rise to, namely, that for Wittgenstein scepticism is a *'natural* possibility' of human language use. There is no reason, in other words, to think that Wittgenstein violated his stated philosophical method of describing what lies 'open to view' in 'the particular case', by acknowledging 'the truth of' a general, underlying principle which he explicitly viewed as a species of nonsense: the *Urphänomen* of scepticism.

Notes

1 See, for example, Perloff (1996).
2 I use the following abbreviations throughout: CR for Cavell (1979); IQO for Cavell (1988).
3 He also sometimes suggests that there are other affinities between Wittgenstein's later philosophy and art works. For example: '*Philosophical Investigations*, like the major modernist works of the past century at least, is logically speaking, esoteric' (CR: xx).
4 See the introduction to this volume pp. 19–20.
5 See Mulhall (1994: xii).
6 Quoted in Mulhall (1994: 103).
7 Quoted in Baker and Hacker (1984: 5).
8 In order to avoid needless complication, I will not assess whether Cavell's reading of Malcolm's argument is correct.
9 Another way of saying this is that defeasibility is itself dependent on the logical possibility of certainty, of discovering in the future that something is the case. For without the possibility of such a discovery, it makes no sense to say that criteria can be defeated.

Bibliography

Baker, G.P. and Hacker, P.M.S. (1994) *Scepticism, Rules and Language*, Oxford: Basil Blackwell.

Bouveresse, J. (1995) *Wittgenstein Reads Freud: The Myth of the Unconscious*, Princeton, NJ: Princeton University Press.

Cavell, S. (1979) *The Claim of Reason: Wittgenstein, Skepticism, Morality, and Tragedy* (CR), New York: Oxford University Press.

—— (1988) *In Quest of the Ordinary: Lines of Skepticism and Romanticism* (IQO), Chicago: University of Chicago Press.

Hacker, P.M.S. (1993) *Wittgenstein: Meaning and Mind, Volume 3 of an Analytical Commentary on the Philosophical Investigations, Part 1: Essays*, Oxford: Basil Blackwell.

Mulhall, S. (1994) *Stanley Cavell: Philosophy's Recounting of the Ordinary*, Oxford: Clarendon Press.

Perloff, M. (1996) *Wittgenstein's Ladder: Poetic Language and the Strangeness of the Ordinary*, Chicago: University of Chicago Press.

Wittgenstein, L. (1958) *The Blue and Brown Books* (BB), Oxford: Blackwell.

—— (1967) *Zettel* (Z), ed. G.E.M. Anscombe and G.H. von Wright, trans G.E.M. Anscombe, Oxford: Blackwell.

—— (1969) *On Certainty* (OC), ed. G.E.M. Anscombe and G.H. von Wright, trans. D. Paul and G.E.M. Anscombe, Oxford: Blackwell.

—— (1976) *Wittgenstein's Lectures on the Foundations of Mathematics* (LFM), ed. C. Diamond, Sussex: Harvester Press.

—— (1977) *Remarks on Color* (ROC), ed. G.E.M. Anscombe, Berkeley: University of California Press.

6

THE URN AND THE CHAMBER POT

John Hyman

In 1931, Wittgenstein listed ten influences on his intellectual development. 'I don't believe I have ever *invented* a line of thinking', he wrote. 'I have always taken one over from someone else. I have simply straightway seized upon it with enthusiasm for my work of clarification. That is how Boltzmann, Hertz, Schopenhauer, Frege, Russell, Kraus, Loos, Weininger, Spengler, Sraffa have influenced me' (CV: 19).[1] The order in which these names occurs is probably the order in which Wittgenstein encountered them, or their ideas. As we shall see, the title of this article derives from Kraus. But its subject is Loos's influence on Wittgenstein.

Loos is unique among the influences Wittgenstein acknowledged. He is the only one who made a major contribution to the arts, as an architect, and as a pioneer of modernism. He was not merely a critical and prophetic voice, as Kraus and Weininger and Spengler were, but a seminal force in the principal artistic movement of the twentieth century. Moreover, his influence on Wittgenstein is an especially interesting one, given this book's theme, because it involves both Wittgenstein's philosophical writings and the only other significant contribution he made to the arts, namely, the house which he built for his sister Margarete Stonborough-Wittgenstein between 1926 and 1928. As we shall see, Wittgenstein's early conception of the nature and purpose of philosophy, which unfolded between 1914 and 1919, was influenced by Loos's cultural criticism and theory of design. And the design of the house in Kundmanngasse would have been inconceivable without the example of Loos's work, and the influence of his ideas.

Accordingly, I shall divide this article into three parts. I shall begin by describing Loos's principal ideas. Then I shall consider the house which Wittgenstein built for his sister. Finally, I shall comment on Loos's influence on Wittgenstein's philosophy.

Adolf Loos

Adolf Loos was born in Brno, Moravia in 1870, and died in Kalksburg in 1933. He is buried in Vienna's main cemetery. In 1956, the municipality erected a tombstone based on Loos's own drawing: a cube of granite on a flat slab. Loos studied architecture at the Technical College in Dresden from 1890 to 1893. After completing his studies he travelled to Philadelphia, where an uncle worked as a watchmaker, and visited Chicago, St Louis and New York. He returned to Vienna in 1896, and began his career as an architect and writer. Much of the practical work on which his reputation rests, and to which his influence is due, is in Vienna. It includes shops and cafés, such as the Café Museum (1899); the Looshaus in Michaelerplatz (1911); a number of projects for municipal housing, conceived between 1920 and 1932; and several villas and mansions for private clients, including the Steiner House (1910), the Scheu House (1912), the Moller House (1928) and the Müller House in Prague (1930). The domestic architecture is the most important. Its principal marks are, first, the absence of ornament; second, on the exterior, the lucid geometry of cubic forms, elegant and sometimes scattered fenestration, and the stepped terrace; third, on the interior, the *Raumplan* of connected volumes and split levels, and the use of fine materials, including various kinds of wood, coloured and veined marble, glass and mirrored glass.

Loos's writings are discussed below. Most of his articles appeared in pages of the *Neue Freie Presse*. In 1921, he published *Ins Leere Gesprochen*, a collection of articles originally published between 1897 and 1900. His later articles were published under the title *Trotzdem* in 1931.

The immediate influences on Loos's architecture and theory of design were Louis Sullivan, Otto Wagner and, in a more reciprocal manner, Karl Kraus.

Sullivan and Wagner were among the earliest architects to conceive of the machine as the source of a modern style, and not as a means to reproduce forms originally produced by hand. Hence, unlike John Ruskin and William Morris, they did not deplore the increasing pre-eminence of engineering design, or associate it with the decline of craftsmanship and pleasurable work. Sullivan belonged to the group of architects which rebuilt Chicago, after the fire of 1871. In a series of skyscrapers, from 1887 to 1895, he gradually freed the design of buildings with a steel structure from the forms inherited from masonry. And although he developed an extravagant and individual style of decoration, he anticipated Loos's proscription of ornament in his essay *Ornament in Architecture*, which was published in 1892: 'It would be greatly for our aesthetic good', he wrote, 'if we should refrain entirely from the use of ornament for a period of years, in order that our thought might concentrate acutely upon the production of buildings well formed and comely in the nude' (Sullivan 1947: 187).

Wagner shared Loos's admiration for English and American design. He advocated, and in the Vienna Post Office Savings Bank (1904) he eventually achieved, an architecture which was explicitly adapted to the use of modern materials and methods of construction. A block of flats, he said, should display 'a smooth surface subdivided by many equivalent windows' (Wagner

1898: 83). And in his Inaugural Lecture at the Art Academy, delivered in 1894, he anticipated a style of architecture guided by the practical requirements of modern living: 'horizontal lines such as were prevalent in Antiquity, table-like roofs, great simplicity and an energetic exhibition of construction and materials' (Wagner 1898: 99).

Kraus's influence on Loos was of a different kind. Kraus published his satirical fortnightly *Die Fackel* from 1899, when he was twenty-four, until 1936, the year he died. From 1911, he wrote it entirely. Both Loos and Kraus were brilliant polemicists, and both were convinced that questions of style are essentially ethical. Kraus dissected the language of the Viennese liberal press and found, reflected in its evasions and falsifications, and in its very stylistic infelicities, the inhumanity and the hypocrisy of Vienna's political, social and artistic life. For his part, Loos could detect depravity in the cut of a jacket or the colour of a bathtub:

> Instead of being enamelled in white, the only suitable colour, tin bath tubs are also covered in dark enamel. Then there are tin baths which try to look as if they were made of marble. Even those good folk are catered for with the same level of taste as the Red Indians, who decorate everything within reach. You can buy Rococo flush valves, Rococo faucets and even Rococo wash stands.[2]

Clean lines, clean baths, clean bodies and clear minds: all are combined in Loos's imagination to form a picture of civilized life. And when Kraus explained the connection between his own ideas and Loos's, many years later, good design was still allied with sanitation:

> Adolf Loos and I – he literally and I grammatically – have done nothing more than show that there is a distinction between an urn and a chamber pot and that it is this distinction above all that provides culture with elbow room. The others, those who fail to make this distinction, are divided into those who use the urn as a chamber pot and those who use the chamber pot as an urn.[3]
> (Kraus 1913: 389–90)

Like Loos, Kraus insists on separating art from practical design. And while it goes without saying that Kakania needs good chamber pots, Kraus argues that it needs a press whose language is equally hygienic, and free from artifice.[4]

I shall turn now to Loos's writings. Loos attacked historicism and the Sezession, the Viennese art nouveau style, with equal vehemence. The Ringstrasse, the great boulevard which runs between Vienna and its suburbs, was an obvious target. 'Those who pretend to be more than they are', he wrote, are confidence-tricksters and universally despised. And if someone tries to produce this effect by faked stone and other imitations? There are countries where such a man would be treated in the same way. Vienna has not progressed that far...If I stroll along the Ring, I always have the impression that a modern Potemkin wants us to believe that Vienna is a city of *nobili* only.

(Loos 1982a: 95)

But he did not confine his attack on historicism to architecture: 'Down with the telephone!...Let us encase it in Rococo ornament. Or Gothic. Or Baroque. Whatever the customer desires'.[5]

His attack on the Sezession was trenchant and personal. He satirized its self-conscious artiness; he deplored its infiltration of traditional crafts; and he excoriated the idea that a decorative programme could be the style of the time. 'Cutlery for people who can eat, after the English fashion, and for people who cannot eat from designs by Olbrich' (Loos 1982b: 288). Alongside the English, as a source of modern style, he set the engineers: 'Behold the bicycle! Does not the spirit of Periclean Athens permeate its forms?'.[6] 'Are there still people who work in the same way as the Greeks? Oh yes! The English as a people, the engineers as a profession. The English and the Engineers are our Hellenes'.[7]

The various themes which recur in Loos's writings – his campaign against historicism and art nouveau, and his advocacy of truth to materials, the comfort and ease of an idealized English style, classicism and engineering design – are coordinated by two fundamental ideas: first, the idea that Kraus drew attention to, namely, the separation of art and practical design; and second, the rejection of ornament. Both of these ideas are proclaimed repeatedly in Loos's published writings. I shall look at two of his most influential articles: 'Ornament and Crime' (1908), and 'Architecture' (1910).[8]

The principal claim of 'Ornament and Crime' is that the evolution of culture is commensurate with the removal of ornament from objects of daily use. Decoration, Loos claims, is the origin of fine art,

the babble of painting. The first ornament that came into being, the cross, had an erotic origin...A horizontal line: the reclining woman. A vertical line: the man who penetrates her. The man who created it felt the same urge as Beethoven, he experienced the same joy that Beethoven felt when he created the ninth symphony.

But what is natural to a primitive or a child is a sign of degeneracy in modern man. The Papuan can be expected to eat his enemies and tattoo his skin. But the modern man who does either of these things is a criminal or a degenerate; and so is the modern man who daubs the walls with erotic symbols: 'one can measure the level of culture in a country by the number of graffiti on its lavatory walls'.

Every period has its style. In the past, 'style' meant ornament. But the mark of modernity is that new ornament is impossible: 'We have outgrown ornament, we have struggled through to a state without ornament'. Unfortunately, neither the State nor the Professoriate has acknowledged this yet. There is an epidemic of ornament, promoted by the luminaries of art nouveau and subsidized with government money. The supporters of ornament believe that the urge for simplicity is a kind of self-denial. On the contrary. 'To me, it tastes better this way. The dishes of past centuries which used decoration to make the peacocks, pheasants and lobsters appear more appetizing produce the opposite effect on me. I look on such a culinary display with disgust when I think of having to eat these stuffed animal corpses. I eat roast beef'.

The revival of ornament is both aesthetically and economically harmful. 'Ornament is not merely produced by criminals, it commits a crime itself by damaging a nation's economy and thereby its cultural development... Ornament is wasted manpower and therefore wasted health. It has always been like this. But today it also means wasted material, and both mean wasted capital'. It tyrannizes the worker, who is forced to work long hours for inadequate pay. Since ornament is no longer organically connected with our culture, the fashion in ornament is constantly changing. Decorated objects are rapidly discarded, and the labour involved in making them is correspondingly devalued.

'I preach to the aristocrats', Loos concludes:

> We have our culture which has taken over from ornament. After a day's trouble and pain, we go to hear Beethoven or Wagner. My cobbler cannot do that. I must not rob him of his pleasures as I have nothing else to replace them with. But he who goes to listen to the Ninth Symphony and who then sits down to draw up a wallpaper pattern is either a rogue or a degenerate.

Several of the ideas expressed in 'Ornament and Crime', and several of the examples which illustrate these ideas, also appear in earlier and later articles, including 'Architecture'. But the main theme of the latter is that architecture is not among the arts. 'Only a very small part of architecture belongs to art: the tomb and the monument. Everything else that fulfils a function is to be excluded from the domain of art'.

Art, Loos claims, is an expression of will and a transcendent utterance, passionate, personal and prophetic; craft work is mundane, traditional, and governed by the practical requirements of living. 'Only when the deceitful catch-phrase "applied art" has disappeared from the vocabulary of the people, only then will we have an architecture of our time'. Loos's own work, he says, has drawn on the work of craftsmen who have not been 'placed under the supervision of those who wish to distort our culture'. He has based a modern corner solution on the design of boxes for silver cutlery, and found locks and ironmongery in the workshops of luggage-makers and piano-makers.

Loos argues that a house must be as practical as a suit of clothing:

> A house must please everyone, in contrast to a work of art, which need not please anybody. The work of art is a private matter for the artist. The house is not. A work of art is born without there being a need for it. A house meets a need...The work of art wants to tear you out of your comfortable existence. The house is to serve comfort. The work of art is revolutionary; the house is conservative.

There are tasteful and tasteless buildings. But if we infer that architecture is an art, we confuse art with culture. Taste in architecture is simply good manners. 'It is no feat to build tastefully just as it is no feat to avoid putting a knife into one's mouth or to brush one's teeth in the morning'.

The great tradition to which great architecture belongs derives from Rome. 'It is no coincidence that the Romans were incapable of inventing a new column order, or a new ornament...The Greeks could hardly administer their cities; the Romans administered the globe. The Greeks exhausted their inventiveness on the orders; the Romans expended theirs on the plan. And he who can solve the great plan does not think of new mouldings'. While minor architects who use ornament divert the course of architecture, a great architect guides them back to antiquity. 'At the threshold of the nineteenth century stood Schinkel. We have forgotten him. May the light of this towering figure shine upon our forthcoming generation of architects'.

Let me summarize. In 'Ornament and Education' (1924), Loos defines an architect as a mason who has learned Latin. He may be thinking especially of Vitruvius; and he may also have in mind the Attic style of oratory which Cicero commends: limpid and straight, aiming always at propriety, and dispensing with the charm of ornament. In any event, the remark is a personal one, since Loos was the son of a sculptor and mason, and he trained as a mason himself, before studying architecture; and it epitomizes several themes in Loos's writings. It identifies architecture as a practical skill; it expresses his adherence to the classical tradition; and it encapsulates the restrained and unornamented style at which he aimed.

Loos's principal ambition, as a cultural critic, and not merely as a theorist of architecture, is to effect a clear separation between art and practical design. The purpose of the separation is twofold. First, it will purify our daily lives. 'I want neutral things in my room', Loos writes. 'It is un-Greek to express one's individuality with the things one has around for daily use'.[9] Second, it will liberate and renew the arts, which are crippled and defiled by their place in contemporary life. The real purpose of art, Loos argues, is to grant man an intimation of transcendence: 'to make him more like a God'.

But humanity no longer knows what art is. An exhibition was recently held in Munich, with the title *Art for the Businessman*: 'No hand was there', Loos writes, 'to chastize the author of this presumptuous phrase!' (Safran and Wang 1987: 108).

Finally, the means by which this separation can be achieved is the abolition of superfluous ornament: 'I have liberated mankind from superfluous ornament', Loos writes, in the preface to *Trotzdem*. 'Ornament was once the epithet for the beautiful. Now, thanks to my life's work, it is the epithet for the mediocre. But the echo which reverberates thinks it is the voice'.[10]

Ludwig Wittgenstein, Architekt

Wittgenstein knew Loos personally, but there is no doubt that he also read Loos's writings and knew many of Loos's buildings in Vienna. The two men were introduced by Ludwig Ficker on 27 July 1914, at the Café Imperial. Wittgenstein enlisted in the army just a few days later, but he continued to meet Loos occasionally during the war, when he was on leave in Vienna. When they met for the first time after the war had ended, in August 1919, Wittgenstein was appalled by Loos, who seemed to Wittgenstein to have compromised his intellectual integrity (Engelmann 1967: 17). But their friendship appears to have survived.

Wittgenstein's lectures on aesthetics, which were delivered in 1938, as well as his occasional remarks on taste and culture, recall Loos's writings at several points. His description of the arts and crafts movement as 'an enormous wart' and a disease is one obvious example. (The hyperbole itself is reminiscent of some of Loos's essays, and uncharacteristic of Wittgenstein.) A disparaging reference to 'imitations' in architecture is another. And a reminder that modern dress is relatively simple, and 'adapted to certain violent activities, such as bicycling' is a third (LA: 7, 10).

More generally, the emphasis Wittgenstein places on technical correctness in design and his readiness to talk about clothing, hairdressing and architecture in the same breath are surely due, at least in part, to Loos's influence. But there is no evidence that Wittgenstein ever shared Loos's view about the position of architecture in relation to the arts, either in 1926–8, or later. On the contrary, in a remark he wrote in a gloomy mood in 1940, he described the Stonborough house as 'the product of a definitely refined hearing, of *good* manners' and as 'the expression of a deep *understanding* (of a culture, etc.)', but as lacking 'the *primordial* life, the *wild* life that strives to be given free rein' (CV: 38). If Wittgenstein associated passion striving for expression with the arts, as Loos did, and good manners with practical design, this remark places architecture among the arts.

Thus several traces of Loos's influence are discernible in the *Lectures on Aesthetics*. But there are two more important places where we can look for Loos's influence on Wittgenstein: first, in the design of the Stonborough house; and second, in the main body of his philosophical writings. I shall discuss these in turn.

In 1926, Margarete Stonborough-Wittgenstein commissioned Paul Engelmann to design and build a mansion for her family on a plot of land in Vienna. She was an independent woman, extremely wealthy and a patron of the arts. It is difficult to imagine a more important commission for a private client. Engelmann had been a pupil of Loos, and later his assistant. He had met Wittgenstein ten years earlier, through an introduction by Loos, and had become an intimate friend of Wittgenstein's and a family friend as well.

Engelmann produced a series of drawings for the Stonborough house in April and May 1926. But Wittgenstein was interested by the project, and it appears that Engelmann invited him to collaborate in the design. Wittgenstein soon took the project over completely. Since he had not been trained as an architect, Jacques Groag, also a student of Loos's, was employed to produce the blueprints and technical specifications for the building. The plans were approved by the municipality in November 1926, and the building was completed two years later.

It is hard to say exactly how much the eventual design still owes to Engelmann.[11] The volumetric composition of the building, the floor plan of the beletage and the design of the hallway evidently derive from Engelmann's drawings. But they were altered by Wittgenstein in many ways and he appears to have been wholly responsible for the choice of materials, and for the design of the lift, doors, windows and radiators. The final appearance of the building, exterior and interior, is due to Wittgenstein. The cover of this book shows the front elevation of the building, in 1992.

It is easier to say how far the building reflects the influence of Loos. On the exterior, the flat roof, the terraces, the asymmetric cubic form and the absence of ornament – the various elements which Loos said could be as pleasant in Vienna as in Algiers – recall a number of Loos's houses, especially the Scheu house, which was built in 1912. But the building's massive form, its symmetrical fenestration and the tall windows with their narrow vertical panes produce a more austere and less domestic impression than any of Loos's houses.

The interior owes less to Loos: little more, in fact, than the absence of ornament. The principal aim of Loos's architecture was to combine a lucid and unornamented geometry with the comfort and informality he admired in English houses. The two parts of his solution were his original treatment of space and the use of fine materials, adapted where necessary to the function of a room. Wittgenstein rejected both of these devices, and preferred geometry to comfort.

When ornament has been eliminated, materials, proportions and the play of light are all-important. Wittgenstein's choice of materials is severe throughout. The floor of the beletage is made of an artificial stone, the colour of anthracite, laid in squares. Elsewhere there are parquet and tiled floors. The walls and ceilings are plastered, off-white and white, without skirtings or mouldings of any sort. The door-frames and window-frames are metal, painted grey-green, and panelled either with metal or with clear or milky or mirrored glass, with the effect that much of the space is lit from more than one direction. The light fittings are bare bulbs. The proportions and the disposition of the principal rooms are palatial. The hallway recalls the *Galerie* of the Alleegasse, the *palais* which Wittgenstein's father had bought in 1890 and which his eldest sister still occupied. The plan is conceived entirely in separate floors, without the fluid and informal use of space which Loos invented.

Two aspects of the house deserve particular comment: the choice of proportions, and the engineering design which it involved. In her memoir of Wittgenstein, his sister Hermine records that he decided to have the ceiling of the salon raised by three centimetres just as the cleaning of the completed house was about to begin. The height of the ceiling is almost four metres. This was, she comments, 'the strongest proof of Ludwig's relentlessness with regard to precise measurements'. And she adds, with evident conviction, 'His instinct was absolutely right and his instinct had to be followed'. As this remark suggests, Wittgenstein did not rely on any system of proportions. Various arithmetical and geometrical ratios occur in parts of the design, and the exterior proportions appear to have been decided intuitively. There is a curious passage in one of Wittgenstein's lectures on aesthetics, from 1938:

> You design a door and look at it and say: 'Higher, higher, higher...oh, all right'...Perhaps the most important thing in connection with aesthetics is what may be called aesthetic reactions, e.g. discontent, disgust, discomfort. The expression of discontent is not the same as the expression of discomfort. The expression of discontent says: 'Make it higher... too low!...do something to this'.
>
> (LA: 13)

If an architect is meant to be talking to a craftsman about a door, it is difficult to see what can be happening. But the passage plainly suggests that an architect must keep his compasses in his eye, and it may contain an echo of Wittgenstein's expensive reaction to the original ceiling in the salon.

The mechanical parts of the house are designed with the same relentless precision. Wittgenstein was a trained engineer, and the house contains abundant evidence of his passion for machinery and his skilful engineering. He added a lift to Engelmann's design. The windows have roller blinds whose mechanical parts are concealed in the walls, and the glass doors in the outer walls of the beletage have metal curtains which can be drawn up from the floor. The metal doors and window frames are simple in appearance and ingenious in construction. The dumb-waiter and the complex plumbing and electrical systems were also designed by Wittgenstein.

The Stonborough house is a remarkable achievement, but an eccentric and expensive one, especially because of Wittgenstein's enthusiasm for mechanical engineering, and because of the minute tolerances entailed by several aspects of the design. Its cubic geometry and unornamented style are inconceivable without the precedent of Loos. But it could not have been built by Loos. In various ways, and above all in the conception of domestic life which it embodies, it is an aristocratic *palais*. There is nothing congenial or inviting about it, on any scale, from the design of door handles, which are simply brass bars bent at a right angle, to the elevations and the fenestration. 'My ideal', Wittgenstein wrote in 1929, 'is a certain coolness. A temple providing a setting for the passions without meddling with them' (CV: 2). Of course the Stonborough house is not a temple. But its design aspires to a certain kind of unperturbable decorum.

It is not entirely successful. With Loos, simplicity is a mark of discretion. But if we compare the Stonborough house with Loos's domestic architecture, its austerity and refinement appear a little overwrought. Having said that, it is touching to read Engelmann's generous praise of Wittgenstein's achievement. Had he built the house himself, he wrote, it would have paled by comparison. For her part, Margarete had happily allowed an engineer with an idealized conception of grammar to take over from a mason who had learned Latin, and she was delighted with the result. Even Wittgenstein himself appears to have been pleased with the house, except for the staircase window on the north-west façade. He sent some photographs to Keynes, with the cheerful remark: 'Enclosed you will find a few photos of my house and [I] hope you won't be too much disgusted by its simplicity'.[12]

Loos and the *Tractatus*

Where is Loos's influence on Wittgenstein's philosophy to be found? The answer is that nothing in Loos's writings appears to have stimulated any particular doctrine or argument expounded by Wittgenstein; but there is clearly an analogy between the conception of philosophy advanced in the *Tractatus* and Loos's theory of design. If Wittgenstein seized on a line of thinking which he found in Loos, this is where the evidence of it appears.

Wittgenstein argues in the *Tractatus* that a language is a system of representation. Words are combined in sentences to form pictures or models of possible states of affairs in the world. Every meaningful sentence can be dissolved by analysis, until its only constituents are logical expressions (such as 'not' and 'and') and simple, unanalyzable names. Each of these names corresponds to an object, whose name it is. The syntax of a name, the ways in which it can and cannot be combined with other names to form a sentence, reflects the essential nature of the object which it names, the ways in which it can and cannot be combined with other objects to form a state of affairs. Hence, a meaningful combination of words corresponds to a possible combination of objects. If the arrangement of the simple names concealed in a sentence represents the *actual* arrangement of the objects which they name, then the sentence is true. If not, it is false.

It follows from these doctrines that the only licit use to which words can be put is to state the facts. For a fact is the existence of a state of affairs, and a state of affairs is a combination of objects. Any attempt to describe the essential nature of an object or the syntax of a name, and any attempt to expound a theory of representation, is bound to result in nonsense. The propositions of the *Tractatus*, Wittgenstein claims, are themselves nonsensical. What they attempt to say is made evident by the well-formed sentences of a language, since a meaningful combination of names cannot fail to show that *these* names can be combined in *this* way, without transgressing the rules of logical syntax. But 'what expresses *itself* in language, *we* cannot express by means of language' (TLP 4.121). For the same reason, the traditional aim of metaphysics, namely, to set down the essential nature of the world in a body of necessary propositions, is unattainable. For the only statement of a necessary truth which the syntax of a language will permit is a tautology: for example, 'Either it is raining or it is not raining'. But a tautology *says* nothing, and it *shows* that it says nothing (TLP 4.461).

In addition to the logical and linguistic doctrines expounded in the larger part of the *Tractatus*, the book includes a small number of remarks concerned with ethics, aesthetics and what can be roughly described as spiritual or existential problems, which are subsumed under the term 'the mystical'. The principal theme of these remarks is that like metaphysics and logic, all of these matters are sublime but ineffable. 'Ethics is transcendental' (TLP: 6.421), Wittgenstein claims, echoing the earlier remark that logic is transcendental (TLP: 6.13). And he adds, in parenthesis: '(Ethics and aesthetics are one and the same.)' 'There are, indeed', he insists, 'things that cannot be put into words. They *make themselves manifest*. They are what is mystical' (TLP: 6.522). But since a sentence can only be used to state a contingent matter of fact, 'it is clear that ethics cannot be put into words' (TLP: 6.421). 'Our words', he wrote in 1929, 'will only express facts; as a teacup will only hold a teacup full of water even if I were to pour out a gallon over it' (PO: 40).

I shall not attempt to explain Wittgenstein's views about ethics, aesthetics and the mystical.[13] What I should like to emphasize is this. As Wittgenstein struggled to clarify his ideas about these matters, his conception of philosophy, and hence of the purpose of the *Tractatus* itself, was substantially altered.

In the *Notes on Logic*, which Wittgenstein dictated to Russell in 1913, he already distinguished sharply between philosophy and science. While natural science provides us with pictures of reality, he claimed, philosophy does not. Philosophy cannot confirm or disconfirm any part of science. It is 'the doctrine of the logical form of scientific propositions' (NB: 106). By logical form, Wittgenstein means the form which logical analysis is meant to reveal, and which a proposition must have in common with the situation which it represents, in order to be capable of representing it at all. For example, a musical score or transcription is a spatial arrangement of marks, whereas the corresponding piece of music is a temporal arrangement of sounds. Hence they do not share either a spatial or a temporal form. What they *must* share, if one represents the other, is a logical form.

Thus Wittgenstein initially believed that philosophy has its own field of enquiry: not the natural world itself, which is the province of natural science, but the form which the world and a logical picture of it – for example, a scientific model – must have in common. But as his conception of logical form unfolded, he abandoned this idea of philosophy. And as we have seen, this really was inevitable. For if every proposition represents a state of affairs, it follows that propositions cannot represent logical forms. This is how Wittgenstein puts it in the *Tractatus* (TLP: 4.12):

> Propositions can represent the whole of reality, but they cannot represent what they must have in common with reality in order to be able to represent it – logical form.
> In order to be able to represent logical form, we should have to be able to station ourselves with propositions somewhere outside logic, that is to say outside the world.

Wittgenstein arrived at the conclusion that logical form cannot be described in 1914 (NB: 108). By the time he wrote the *Tractatus*, this thought had gradually led to a novel conception of philosophy, which he began to formulate as follows:

> The correct method in philosophy would really be to say nothing except what can be said, i.e. what belongs to natural science, i.e. something that has nothing to do with philosophy, and then whenever someone else tried to say something metaphysical to show him that he had not given any reference to certain signs in his sentences.[14]
>
> (NB: 91)

This remark, which first appears as a notebook entry made in December 1916, is immediately preceded by a remark which is omitted in the *Tractatus* and which records a misuse of a sign purporting to express the concept of identity: 'We could introduce the arguments also in such a way that they only occurred on one side of the sign of identity, i.e. always on the analogy of "$(Ex).\Phi x.x = a$" instead of "Φa" [i.e. "Something is both Φ and identical with a" instead of "a is Φ"]' (NB: 91). In this way, we could convey the false impression that 'Socrates is wise' says that something which is related to Socrates in a particular way – viz. the way expressed by the sign '=' – is wise; whereas in fact the sentence only says that Socrates is wise.

The philosophical method which Wittgenstein recommends here, like the conception of language which underlies it, is an austere one. But there are several remarks in the *Tractatus* which present a more expansive picture of what Wittgenstein believes the purpose of philosophy must be, if it cannot expound 'the doctrine of the logical form of scientific propositions'. 'Philosophy', he urges, 'aims at the logical clarification of thoughts'. It is not a body of doctrine, and it does not result in 'philosophical propositions'. It is an activity which aims to make the propositions of science, i.e. empirical propositions, clear and to give them sharp boundaries (TLP: 4.112):

It must set limits to what can be thought; and, in doing so, to what cannot be thought.
It must set limits to what cannot be thought by working outwards through what can be thought (TLP: 4.114).
It will signify what cannot be said, by presenting clearly what can be said
(TLP: 4.115).

What is remarkable about this sequence of remarks is the gradual transition they make, in the space of half a dozen lines, from the claim that philosophy is merely a critical discipline, to the thought – however tactfully expressed – that it can reveal the very essence of the world. Philosophy, it seems, merely aims to eradicate the confusions and unclarities which are present in scientific – i.e. empirical – propositions, by disclosing the logical structures which are hidden by their superficial grammar. But once this has been done, the logical form of reality itself will be displayed in the lucid forms of factual speech. It will be there for us to see, just as long as we do not try to describe it; like a gift which is promised to us, as long as we do not ask for it by name. But there is one more twist. For as we have seen, what cannot be said includes both ethics and aesthetics, as well as the logical form of reality. Hence, if philosophy sets limits to what cannot be thought, if it demarcates the ineffable, it can also reveal the correct attitude for us to take towards absolute values. In matters of value, Wittgenstein holds, we must be reverent, but mute. And this is something which philosophy can teach us.

The evidence of Wittgenstein's *Notebooks*, the earlier *Notes on Logic* and the notes Wittgenstein dictated to Moore in 1914 prove that his early philosophy, from its inception, was directed towards the solution of philosophical problems generated by the study of formal logic. But Wittgenstein's own view of the *Tractatus* was gradually transformed between 1916 and 1919. As it happens, the transformation is precisely analogous to a visual phenomenon which he describes in the *Tractatus* (TLP: 4.063; 5.5423) and which later obsessed him. He came to regard the exterior limits of thought as the interior limits of the inexpressible in the same way as a black mark on a sheet of white paper might at first be seen as a black shape on a white ground, and then as a white shape extending outwards from the line surrounding a shadowy hole at its centre. In a letter Wittgenstein wrote to Ficker in 1919, he said of the *Tractatus*:

> The book's point is an ethical one...my work consists of two parts: of that which is under consideration here and of all that I have *not* written. And it is precisely this second part that is the important one.
>
> (Luckhardt 1979: 94)

Both Loos and Wittgenstein were struck by the affinity between their ideas. Indeed, Loos was sufficiently impressed to exclaim to Wittgenstein, with characteristic hyperbole, 'You are me!' (Engelmann 1967: 127). The literature contains less pardonable exaggerations. Engelmann, who recorded this remark, and whose memoir of Wittgenstein contains the earliest discussion of his relationship with Loos, comments nicely that both men were 'creative separators' (Engelmann 1967: 131); but he exaggerates their similarity, and makes Loos appear to waffle, by dressing his ideas in Tractarian phrases:

> Loos counters the ever-renewed attempts of the architects of his time either to revive new forms or invent new and supposedly modern ones with *his* demand: to be silent where one cannot speak; to do no more than design a building with technical correctness, guided by the right human approach, and leave the right and truly modern form to emerge *spontaneously*. This form should not be proclaimed explicitly and purposefully in the architect's design of an article of daily use or a building, but should be *manifest* in it.
>
> (Engelmann 1967: 127)

In conclusion, I would say this. There is a striking analogy between Loos's clarification of practical design and Wittgenstein's clarification of the language of science. Sentences and houses are like chamber pots and jackets. They are all artefacts. They are designed for daily use, and their use constrains their form. Both Loos and Wittgenstein wanted to strip bare the construction of these practical devices, and to confine them in the mundane sphere of *Sachlichkeit*, both for the sake of moral candour and to safeguard the sublime. But it remains unclear how much Wittgenstein owed to Loos. At the very least, the influence of Loos's ideas reinforced a tendency in Wittgenstein's thinking, in particular, at the point at which Wittgenstein found a connection between the substance of his philosophy and the ethical purpose which it seemed capable of serving. But there is too little evidence to say more. If this uncertain conclusion seems disappointing, the feeling may be mitigated by recalling a remark Wittgenstein made in the same year as the remark with which I began:

> The historical explanation, the explanation as an hypothesis of development, is only *one* way of assembling the data – of their synopsis. It is just as possible to see the data in their relation to one another and to embrace them in a general picture without putting it in the form of an hypothesis about temporal development.[15]

Notes

Where possible, references are to English translations of Loos's writings, but I have not always followed these translations. Quotations from Wittgenstein's *Tractatus Logico-Philosophicus* follow the translation by D.F. Pears and B.F. McGuinness.

1 The remark is one of several in which Wittgenstein expressed doubts about his originality as a thinker. It would be a mistake to assume that all of the names listed mark an important intellectual debt. But each records an influence.
2 'Plumbers', (Loos 1998: 87).
3 The urns Kraus has in mind are the ornamental urns which appear on the façades of many eighteenth and nineteenth century buildings in Vienna, including St Michael's church, on the Michaelerplatz, across the road from Loos's most controversial building.
4 'Kakania' is the name Robert Musil gave to the Austro-Hungarian empire in *Der Mann ohne Eigenschaften*.
5 'The English Schools in the Austrian Museum', (Loos 1998: 145).
6 'A Review of Applied Arts I', in (Loos 1998: 134).
7 'Glass and China', (Loos 1998: 69).
8 I have generally followed the translations which appear in Safran and Wang (1987: 100–09) 'Ornament and Crime' can also be found in Loos (1998: 167–76).
9 'A Review of Applied Arts I', (Loos 1998: 135).
10 Loos's classicism led him to qualify his opposition to the use of ornament, e.g. in the following remark from 1924: 'Classical ornament brings discipline into the shaping of objects of daily use...It brings order into our lives' (1998: 188). For this reason, Loos's classicism has been described as a failure of nerve. But an aesthetic programme is not a philosophical system, and in the final analysis, its consistency is an aesthetic matter, not a logical one. 'Less is more' will not pass muster in a logic class; but we understand it perfectly, because we recognize its application.
11 A careful analysis appears in Wijdeveld (1994), to which I am indebted.
12 I interpret this as an expression of confidence and pleasure, not apprehension. Wittgenstein, who distinguished carefully between disgust, discomfort and discontent, knew that simplicity does not arouse disgust.
13 On this topic, see Hacker (1986: ch. 4).
14 see also TLP 6.53.
15 'Remarks on Frazer's Golden Bough' (PO: 131)

Bibliography

Engelmann, P. (1967) *Letters from Ludwig Wittgenstein, With a Memoir*, ed. B. McGuinness, trans. L. Furtmüller, Oxford: Basil Blackwell.

Hacker, P.M.S. (1986) *Insight and Illusion*, revised edn, Oxford: Oxford University Press.

Kraus, K. (1913) *Die Fackel*.

Loos, A. (1982a) 'Potemkin City', in A. Loos, *Spoken into the Void: Essays 1897–1900*, trans. J.O. Newman and J.H. Smith, Cambridge, MA: MIT Press.

—— (1982b) *Trotzdem*, ed. A. Opel, Vienna: G. Prachner.

—— (1998) *Ornament and Crime*, ed. A. Opel, trans. M. Mitchell, Riverside, CA: Ariadne Press.

Luckhardt, C.G. (ed.) (1979) *Wittgenstein: Sources and Perspectives*, Hassocks: Harvester.

Safran, Y. and Wang, W. (eds) (1987) *The Architecture of Adolf Loos*, 2nd edn, London: Arts Council of Great Britain.

Sullivan, L. (1947) *Kindergarten Chats and Other Writings*, revised edn, New York: Wittenborn Schultz.

Wagner, O. (1898) *Moderne Architektur*, Vienna: A. Schroll.

Wijdeveld, P. (1994) *Ludwig Wittgenstein, Architect*, London: Thames & Hudson.

Wittgenstein, L. (1961) *Tractatus Logico-Philosophicus* (TLP), trans. D.F. Pears and B.F. McGuinness, London: Routledge & Kegan Paul.

—— (1978) *Lectures and Conversations on Aesthetics, Psychology and Religious Belief* (LA), ed. C. Barrett, Oxford: Basil Blackwell.

—— (1979) *Notebooks: 1914–1916* (NB), 2nd edn, ed. G.H. von Wright and G.E.M. Anscombe, trans. G.E.M. Anscombe, Oxford: Basil Blackwell.

—— (1980) *Culture and Value* (CV), 2nd edn, ed. G.H. von Wright, trans. P. Winch, Oxford: Basil Blackwell.

—— (1993) *Philosophical Occasions: 1912–1951* (PO), ed. J. Klagge and A. Nordmann, Indianapolis: Hackett.

Part II

THEORY AND THE ARTS

7

LANGUAGE AND PAINTING, BORDER WARS AND PIPE DREAMS

Ben R. Tilghman

I

Philosophers of art as well as art critics and art historians, not to mention artists themselves, are wont to construct theories about art or, in some cases, to borrow other peoples'. These theories, even when advanced by those who are not professional philosophers, nevertheless tend to be philosophical in character. While philosophers usually construct theories of art in general, the side of criticism has been inclined to theories of the particular arts, literature, painting and so on. In recent decades theories about language have been given pride of place in critical and art historical inquiries under the assumption that the arts themselves are forms of language or closely related to language. It is then assumed that a proper theory of language will take us some distance toward an understanding of the nature of the arts. The influences in this direction have largely derived from Ferdinand de Saussure, and to some extent C.S. Peirce, as filtered through structuralism and deconstruction. Interestingly enough, it is language that has been the primary focus of twentieth century Anglo-American 'analytic' philosophy to which one would have to add the powerful influences of Frege and the Viennese positivists. It was thought by this latter movement that only through a proper understanding of language and the distinction between sense and nonsense could a proper understanding of the traditional problems of philosophy be reached. It would have been inconceivable to these philosophers to think of art as a language, although they were sometimes much concerned with the logical nature of the language used in aesthetic judgements and descriptions.[1] The roots of most critical theory, however, have been in the continental tradition of de Saussure and his posterity, rather than in analytical philosophy which by and large has been opposed to that tradition.

I want to do three things in this chapter: provide a critical examination of the idea that art, especially painting, is a form of language; look at some of the things that have been said about supposed relations between words and images that depend upon thinking of images (paintings) as language; and end by considering certain discussions of paintings of René Magritte where some of the consequences of thinking of art as language can be seen at work. Throughout all this, my discussion will be informed by Ludwig Wittgenstein's conception of philosophy and what he has to tell us about language.

Before examining theories of art as language it will be well to begin with some general considerations about theories. The contention that art is a kind of language has been given a veneer of plausibility because its proponents have bought into a kind of theory about language in general. Theory, after all, is the philosopher's stock in trade. When the philosopher seeks to understand some field of interest, be it knowledge, ethics, science, mathematics, politics or whatever, he most often supposes that a proper understanding of that field can only be provided by a theory of it. This is certainly true when philosophers come to look at art. Philosophers of art, especially in the twentieth century, have often argued that a theory of the arts is required to identify works of art and to distinguish them from other things, to explain our responses to art and the nature of our aesthetic judgements and, in addition, have sometimes argued that a satisfactory theory of art should provide criteria and standards of artistic value as well.[2]

There are a great many things we are prepared to call theories, and it is by no means certain that there is a common thread that unites them all. For all that, I think that our notion of theory seems most at home in the natural sciences and it is by looking at some aspects of scientific theories that we can get a basis for a better understanding of what has been wanted by theorists of the arts. Classical Newtonian mechanics may be taken as a paradigm of a scientific theory. One of the great accomplishments of this theory was to show that a number of apparently disparate phenomena of motion could be understood as essentially connected. The motions of falling bodies, of pendulums, projectiles and planets, can be shown to be so connected because they can be explained by the same general laws. Newtonian mechanics is completely general, that is, it purports to apply to all objects (masses) whatsoever. Consider the second law: $f = ma$. The law states a functional relation between force, mass and acceleration. For this law to be anything more than a universally quantified statement containing variables whose values remain unspecified, certain things have to be done. Acceleration is defined as change in velocity with respect to time (dv/dt) and velocity is defined as change in space with respect to time (ds/dt). In order to give the quantified variables values, then, there must be ways of measuring s, t and m. One learns these various techniques of measurement in learning physics. The theories of science are clearly tied to scientific practice and can mean nothing in abstraction from their use in that practice. It happens to be the case that classical mechanics applies to an extraordinarily wide range of objects and although one is tempted to say it applies to all masses whatsoever, that is not quite right. Classical mechanics begins to break down at the sub-atomic level, and also goes awry at velocities approaching the speed of light and in the presence of large gravitational masses. Learning physics is in part a matter of learning the limitations of particular theories and the range of phenomena to which they can properly be applied.

The point of these remarks is to stress the importance of practice in understanding science. Scientific theories are not simply abstract formulations – although some of them can be formulated abstractly – but get their sense and importance within a particular region of human activity. To know science is not simply to know that there is such a functional relation between force and acceleration, but is also to know how to use that function to describe and explain particular phenomena. There may be a moral to be drawn from these observations about the various theories that historians and critics of the arts have offered about their subjects.

If we are to understand and explain the physical behaviour of objects, be they gears and connecting rods or the planets of our solar system, theory is required. We could not design machinery or build bridges without the theory of mechanics. We have to pause to ask whether or not theory is required to understand an art such as painting and, more specifically, whether a theory of language is required to understand and explain art.

Now on to the theory that art is a language. A recent text gets underway with this idea:

> A picture is worth a lot more than a thousand words. No amount of words can describe an image or an object exactly, whether it is a picture, a sculpture, or a work of architecture. This is because words constitute one kind of language and imagery another, thereby creating a need for translation.
>
> (Adams 1996: xiii)

So it is said that the visual arts constitute a language and because it is a different kind of language it is supposed to follow that words cannot describe works of visual art exactly. Let us look at the two contentions in this passage, that words cannot describe art exactly and that art is a kind of language. It is often a useful tactic in a philosophical investigation when faced with the thesis that something is not the case to ask for a detailed statement of what is being denied. Therefore with respect to the first contention, we have to ask what it is that words cannot do. To economize I will speak only of pictures. What would it be like to describe a picture exactly? We must imagine some uses of 'exactly'. It is quite possible to place a sufficiently fine grid over a picture so that the contents, the colour, say, of each square of the grid can be specified and we might say that in this way we could provide an exact description of the picture. The binary code for a computer image does much this sort of thing, and might be described as a symbolic equivalent of a picture. I tell a friend that there is a painting in the museum that he must see because it is so bad. He is to look for the picture of the Virgin as a child who is shown praying, but her pious expression is so obviously phoney that she can only be trying to work the nuns at the convent school.[3] Later he says that I described the picture exactly.

Theorists would doubtless reject these examples as not at all what they had in mind. What, then, do they have in mind? Since they have specified no criterion of exactitude we do not know what would count for them as an 'exact description' and, since we do not know that, we cannot understand the contention that words cannot describe a picture exactly. It sheds no light at all on how we do in fact talk about and describe pictures nor on the point of doing so.

Perhaps the claim is in part a reflection of the fact that there are times when we want the real thing and not merely a description of it. Extant examples of ancient Greek painting are almost non-existent and although Pliny has left us a host of descriptions, it is not the same as being able to see, appreciate and study them for ourselves. Painting is by no means the only thing of which this is true. You tell me how hilarious it was when Aunt Mabel slipped on the banana peel, guffawing all the while, but I cannot appreciate the recital as I would have appreciated the event itself. In neither of these cases is the shortcoming of the description a function of its belonging to a different 'language' than the thing described. I suggest this is partly a matter of our reactions to things. We may find the account of Aunt Mabel's embarrassment amusing, but this is not to find the event amusing. Likewise we may have many responses to and views about Pliny's descriptions, but these are about the descriptions and not the paintings. Let us suppose we could produce a notational equivalent of a painting of the sort suggested earlier which, for the sake of argument, we can call a 'translation' from the 'language' of painting into another system. In such a case our responses to the notational representation will not be the same, could not be the same, as our responses to the painting itself. It would make no sense to speak of the description as visually balanced, as cubist in style or garish in colour. Perhaps the best that could be hoped for here is that by some new and improved technology an exact facsimile of the painting could be produced from the description which we could then talk about and appreciate as we do the original.

The second contention is that words and imagery constitute two different kinds of language. At first glance there is something wildly implausible about describing art as a language at all despite such familiar, and borrowed, language-describing expressions as, 'This artist has something to say', 'He made a statement with that painting', and 'She exploited the vocabulary of cubism in her work'. The things that artists are doing under these descriptions do not seem much like what we are doing when we have something to say in the departmental meeting, make a statement to the police or employ the vocabulary of the gutter. In response to someone's contention that art (painting, etc.) is a language one obvious reductio is to ask that person to say something in art. How do you say 'Where is the toilet?' in art? Like as not the response will be that art is not that kind of language. But what kind is it? And what is meant by a kind of language? Are there different kinds of language? There are several different ways of classifying languages, such as Indo-European/Altaic, inflected/uninflected, and so on. Those distinctions, however, do not seem to be what is wanted, but it is by no means clear what is wanted.

When it is said that art is a language we must bring to this claim our understanding of what a language is, otherwise we could not understand what is being claimed. A language is such a thing as English, French or German, therefore if we are to say that art is a language, we must suggest that art is something like English, French or German. I suppose it must follow from that that a particular work of art is like a sentence within the language of art. To add to the implausibility of thinking of art as a language we must note that art has neither a syntax nor a semantics, two features that seem essential to language. Syntax is required to distinguish meaningful expressions from mere sequences of words, that is, sense from syntactic nonsense, and a semantics is required to provide a notion of truth and to distinguish true statements from false ones and thereby make one kind of connection between language and the world.

It may seem that there are painterly analogues of the true/false and sense/nonsense distinctions in language. We can speak of a painting as a true likeness of a person or accurate portrayal of some thing or event. The ability to lie is characteristic of a language speaker. It might be said that a painting can lie to the extent that it purports to be an accurate portrayal when in fact it is not. A Spanish courtly painter of centuries past could have described his work as a lie when self-interest dictated that he portray his royal subjects as rather more attractive than the ugly creatures actually were. If we think of painting as documentation, then there are circumstances where it makes sense to describe a painting as true, false or a lie. Some times accuracy of portrayal is relevant to the appreciation of a painting and sometimes it is not.

Can a painting also be nonsensical? Syntactical nonsense occurs when a string of words is not properly ordered, but the question is whether there could be an analogous breakdown of pictorial ordering. There are times, however, when surprising sense can be made of what seems utter nonsense, if only one can exercise enough ingenuity. Wittgenstein once offered 'Milk me sugar' as an example of syntactical nonsense,[4] but one wag imagined being accosted by a cow who said, doubtless in a sultry voice, 'Milk me, Sugar'. It is instructive that the result of this ingenuity is a joke. It is difficult to imagine unequivocal examples of paintings that are nonsense. There can certainly be unusual juxtapositions of objects in paintings that could never be found in reality such as the miniature steam locomotive emerging from an ordinary parlour fireplace in Magritte's *Time Transfixed*. Surreal juxtapositions can be intriguing, amusing, suggestive, but not necessarily nonsensical. Like as not some story could be devised to account for it. Perhaps we can call a painting nonsense in which a number of unrelated figures are scattered about the canvas randomly with no coherent organization or design, but then we should never underestimate the ingenuity of some latter day critics. Wittgenstein has a remark that does suggest the possibility of one kind of pictorial nonsense.

> It looks as if we could say: 'Word-language allows of senseless combinations of words, but the language of imaging does not allow us to imagine anything senseless'. – Hence, too, the language of drawing doesn't allow of senseless drawings? Suppose there were drawings from which bodies were supposed to be modeled. In this case some drawings make sense, some not. – What if I imagine senseless combinations of words?
>
> (PI §512)

Some of Escher's drawings with their impossible perspective are obvious examples of drawings from which nothing could be constructed and in that respect would be nonsense.[5] The nonsense here is a function of 'that respect'. I am given what purports to be the technical drawing for a piece of machinery and I remark, 'This makes no sense; nothing could go together like this'. In this case the sense of the picture is a function of the use to which we wish to put it. We intend to use such drawings in the construction of machines, but this one cannot be so used. Other drawings cannot be so used either, but that may be because they show only a single elevation or are insufficiently detailed and not because they make no sense; they are simply incomplete. Wittgenstein has given us here one specific example of where the sense/nonsense distinction can intelligibly be applied to pictures. It is only by a metaphorical extension that we might speak here of syntax in a diagram and, once more, it need not have any artistic relevance.

A theory must provide a completely general account of its subject matter, and thus a theory of painting as language must provide a general account of its language-making features including semantics and syntax. The application of these notions to pictures where we have seen that they are intelligible, however, are to particular cases in this and that respect and by no means can be made to apply across the board. These particular cases, we have noted, may or may not have relevance for the artistic value and appreciation of painting. We should be suspicious of any attempt to insist upon general accounts of the distinctions in abstraction from particular circumstances and to suppose that there are such things as principles of semantics and syntax for pictures and images analogous to those for natural languages.

II

The primary force behind the thesis that art is a kind of language derives from Ferdinand de Saussure. De Saussure thought of language as a code for expressing thoughts (de Saussure 1959: 16). Language itself is said to be a system of signs and a sign is defined as a union of meanings (concepts) and what he calls sound-images; both of which are said to be psychological entities. In the familiar jargon the concept is the signified while the sound-image is the signifier. With this goes a picture of what happens when two people talk with one another. In the brain of one a concept is associated with a sound-image. A spoken word, which is an instantiation of a sound-image, is then produced that is heard by the other and which triggers in the hearer the reverse process whereby a sound-image is created that is associated with the same or a very similar concept. De Saussure is sanguine about the general success of this process of communication for he says that, 'Among all the individuals that are linked together by speech, some sort of average will be set up: all will reproduce – not exactly of course, but approximately – the same signs united with the same concepts' (de Saussure 1959: 13).

He envisaged semiology as a general science of signs. Customs and rites, for example, are listed as systems of signs along with language. This science 'would show what constitutes signs, what laws govern them' (de Saussure 1959: 16). Just as Newton's mechanics explained a disparate range of phenomena by bringing them under a common set of laws so presumably the imagined science of semiology will show that a range of phenomena that apparently have nothing in common really do have significant common features by subsuming them under the single genus of signs. The assumption that sets this web of notions into play is clearly the idea that thoughts exist in logical independence of any particular expression of them. It follows that anything whatsoever could become associated with a thought and thereby be an expression, that is, a sign, of that thought and thus the way is opened to suppose that works of art as well as what we say in our natural languages belong to systems of signs. In this respect painting is not essentially different from English and we might as well say that painting is just as much a language as is the tongue of Chaucer and Donne.

There is more than one confusion in all of this. De Saussure's picture of human communication taken on its own terms commits us to complete scepticism about what anyone is saying. Since signs (concepts and associated sound-images) are internal psychological entities there is no way that I can know what signs are present in the brain (mind?) of another and de Saussure can have no grounds whatsoever for his contention that 'all will reproduce...the same signs united with the same concepts'. The theory grounds the words of our language in presumed psychological events which are private to the one who has them. Meanings are thus necessarily private and language turns out to be 'private language'. De Saussure has fallen victim to the hoary other-minds problem. The essential objection to de Saussure, however, is not simply that his theory leads to complete scepticism, but that the picture of thoughts and communication upon which it is based is incoherent.[6]

I have been following Wittgenstein in describing de Saussure's view as a 'picture'. A philosophical picture is basically a misleading analogy. It takes as a model a use of language that is perfectly intelligible and then seeks to transfer it to a situation where it has no application. De Saussure pictures communication as like sending a telegram. A message, such as, 'Arriving on the six o'clock train', is encoded into the dots and dashes of Morse code and then decoded at the other end to retrieve the original message. The thought plays the role of the message and language plays the role of the Morse code. It has to be shown that the model of telegraphic communication has no application to conversation.

There is only a contingent connection between the messages we send over the wires and the code in which they are sent. That is to say, we can easily imagine using other electronic codes. There is, nevertheless, serious confusion in the idea that the connection between thoughts and the language that is supposed to be an expression or encoding of them is only a contingent one. The telegraph clicks express the message that I am arriving on the six o'clock train. To push the matter into de Saussure's domain we have to ask what the thought is that is expressed by the message. This thought has to exist apart from any expression of it, so it will not do to say that the thought is that I am arriving at six, for 'I am arriving at six' is only another expression of the thought. No matter how we try to get at the thought we arrive only at expressions of it, but this should not be taken as a failure to come up with the thought itself. The word 'thought' does not function as the name of an object or event, not even a mysterious private one. Its use always involves an expression of what is thought. Thoughts, unlike objects, are individuated and identified by their expressions. We can put this by saying that the connection between a thought and its expression is a necessary and internal one rather than a contingent and external one.

An interesting consequence of this is that many thoughts can be had only by language users. I intend to catch that train and want to be met. To have these thoughts, intentions and desires, I must be able to use the telegraph, have a wife at the other end, not to mention participate in all the other human practices that surround railroads and their schedules, family life and so on. Wittgenstein has an intriguing passage that speaks to this:

> A dog believes his master is at the door. But can he also believe his master will come the day after tomorrow? – And what can he not do here? – How do I do it? – How am I supposed to answer this?
>
> Can only those hope who can talk? Only those who have mastered the use of a language. That is to say, the phenomena of hope are modes of this complicated form of life. (If a concept refers to a character of human handwriting, it has no application to beings who do not write.)
>
> (PI §174)

Note that to believe his master will come the day after tomorrow the dog would have to have some knowledge of the calendar and days of the week.

De Saussure's picture[7] of how words get their meanings and how communication takes place has some of the appearance of a genuine scientific theory. Unlike a genuine scientific theory, however, the terms of the theory have no application. Nothing can count as an example of either a signifier or a signified and these notions can play no role in our understanding of language. The problem here is deeper than mere lack of verifiability for its assumptions about thoughts and their expressions makes the fact that we can talk to one another unintelligible. Faced with de Saussure's non-starter, we have to look elsewhere to understand language and communication, not to mention painting.

III

Stripped of all the psychological baggage that makes nonsense of the signifier/signified notions, de Saussure's view of how words get their meanings seems to come down to something like this. The meaning of a word is what it is associated with, that is, what it refers to, regardless of what the referent might be. The important thing is that a word gets its meaning by standing for something. In this theory, words are thought of as signs and we must suppose that they are thus one with billboards, stop lights, darkening clouds and a host of other things. Now apply that idea to paintings. Paintings represent things, and it is tempting to say that in that way they refer to them. Given that temptation we may as well say that in that respect pictures are like the words of our language, not to mention advertising hoardings, traffic lights and all the rest. They are presumed to acquire their 'meaning' in just the same way. It is the implications of this that I want to pursue.

If a general theory of signs is to have explanatory value, it must show that there is a unity among the range of apparently disparate things it is willing to call signs. That unity must be found in the relation between the 'sign' and what it means, refers to or stands for. That relation must be the same for all 'signs'. The assumption that there is such a unity must be challenged, and I propose to do it by making use of some of the things that Wittgenstein says about language.

Wittgenstein wants us to realize that the words and expressions of our language have many different uses. Early on in *Philosophical Investigations*, he calls our attention to the fact of those many uses and stresses the point that speaking a language is a human practice and part of what he calls a form of life. In a series of remarks from §11 on, he compares language to a set of tools and reminds us that just as the tools in a toolbox have different uses, so do words. In another analogy, they are said to be like the handles in a locomotive cabin which are manipulated in different ways to different ends

(PI §12). He adds 'When we say that "Every word in language signifies something" we have so far said *nothing whatever*; unless we have explained exactly what distinction we want to make' (PI §13). Think of the distinction between genuine words and jabberwocky ('tove' doesn't mean – refer to – anything) or nouns and, say, prepositions. In §23 he gives us some examples of the many different uses language has: giving orders and obeying them; describing the appearance of an object; constructing an object from a description (a drawing); reporting an event; speculating about an event; forming and testing an hypothesis; presenting the results of an experiment in a diagram; making up a story; play-acting; singing catches; guessing riddles; telling a joke, solving a problem in practical arithmetic, translating from one language to another; asking, thanking, cursing, greeting, praying. He compares the myriad aspects of language to games and speaks of 'language games'. The game analogy calls attention to two things. Just as the moves in a game are governed by rules so there are rules and regularities in our use of language. Secondly, playing a game is an activity and using language is an activity – a series of activities – embedded in human life.

He then gets to the philosophical meat of what he has been suggesting to us about language.

> Here we come up against the great question that lies behind all these considerations. – For someone might object against me: 'You have taken the easy way out! You talk about all sorts of language-games, but have nowhere said what the essence of a language-game, and hence of language, is: what is common to all these activities, and what makes them into language or parts of language...'.
>
> And this is true. – Instead of producing something common to all that we call language, I am saying that these phenomena have no one thing in common which makes us use the same word for all, – but that they are *related* to one another in many different ways. And it is because of these relationships, that we call them all 'language'.
>
> (PI §65)

Let us follow Wittgenstein's lead and look for elements common to different language games. What, for example, do telling jokes and saying prayers have in common? It is not at all clear what would serve as an answer. These are activities embedded in very different facets of our lives. Wittgenstein has given us every reason to believe that a general theory of language and what words mean or, by implication, a general theory of signs that encompasses language – not to mention art – is a fantasy. The assumption on which a general theory of language would have to be constructed is that all human activities and practices have something in common. There is no reason to believe that there is any such common feature or features – nor have we any idea of what might be a candidate for such a feature – and consequentially that there is any set of general laws that will make clear what is common to all the human practices in which language figures and in which what we are willing to call signs play a role. It is difficult to see how any envisioned theory would contribute to a better understanding of human life with its myriad activities and practices.

What is true of language is also true of what we ordinarily think of as signs – when we are not in the grip of semiotic theory. To understand this we need to remind ourselves of the many different roles that signs play in the activities of our lives. The red traffic light is a signal to stop backed up by the traffic laws. The bent arrow warns of a curve ahead. The darkening clouds are signs, evidence, that a storm is likely. The roadside billboard touting THE WORLD'S LARGEST BALL OF TWINE bespeaks no legal penalty for not stopping and neither warns of nor is evidence for anything, but rather seeks to persuade you to stop and pay your money. None of these signs have anything in common, but work in many different ways. We do, of course, say that these signs all mean something or signify something, but recall Wittgenstein's remark that 'When we say that "Every word in language signifies something" we have so far said *nothing whatever*; unless we have explained exactly what distinction we want to make', and see how it can also apply to signs. It is important to keep in mind that the words 'mean' and 'signify' themselves have different uses. To break the hold of the idea that when we say that all signs have signification, that we have said something important, we must remember the many different roles that signs play in our lives and activities. Then we may realize the pointlessness of insisting on a common denominator as well as the emptiness of saying that they all mean something.

Just as a theory of mechanics establishes connections between apparently disparate physical phenomena so a general theory of signs seeks to do the same thing with the phenomena of language, signs, art, and so on. Against Wittgenstein's reminder that the meaning of words and signs is embedded in human activities and practices, a theory of signs would have to show that there are elements common to all the vast multitude of human practices. To put that in particular terms, one would have to show that saying a prayer is at bottom like both telling a joke and obeying the speed limit, not to mention understanding a painting. We should conclude from this that the thesis that art is a kind of language – a thesis connected with a general theory of signs – tells us nothing about art in general or painting in particular.

IV

The view that painting is a kind of language and its corollary that it is a different kind of language has introduced considerable obscurity into the discussion of particular works of art. This is certainly true in the case of René Magritte's intriguing painting, *The Betrayal of Images*, a realistic painting of a pipe which has beneath it the legend, 'Ceci n'est pas un pipe'.

This painting, as well as some other Magrittes, has been thought to raise puzzling questions about the relation between language and painting, words and images. For some, Michel Foucault is a key figure in this alleged puzzlement. Gary Shapiro, in his account of *ekphrasis*, speaks of Foucault:

> noting the different registers of the linguistic and the visual; neither can be reduced to the other…This becomes clear in Foucault's essay on René Magritte, *This is Not a Pipe*, in which he argues that painting has overcome the code, traditional, at least since the fourteenth century, that prohibited interchanges between the linguistic and the visual. There he complicates the genre of ekphrasis, the verbal description of a visual work, by writing of a painting that, on his reading, has already entered into the linguistic realm.
>
> (Shapiro 1998: 235)

This, however, is not quite what Foucault says. His clearest statement seems to be this:

> Separation between linguistic signs and plastic elements; equivalence of resemblance and affirmation. These two principles constituted the tension in classical painting, because the second reintroduced discourse…into an art from which the linguistic element was rigorously excluded.
>
> (Foucault 1982: 53)

As near as can be made out, this seems to tells us that in some unspecified way verbal descriptions and painting were not supposed to mix, but traditional representational art usually presents us with scenes that we can identify and describe; for example, here is Abraham getting ready to sacrifice Isaac, or this is the swan about to get it on with Leda, and so pictures and words really have been mixing all along. Perhaps the point is that Magritte's work is supposed to bring this issue, if it is one, to a head.

James W. Hefferman, after defining *ekphrasis* as '*the verbal representation of visual representation*' (Hefferman 1993: 3) goes on to add in the spirit of Shapiro's remark about Foucault, 'because it verbally represents visual art, *ekphrasis* stages a contest between rival modes of representation: between the driving force of the narrating word and the stubborn resistance of the fixed image' (Hefferman 1993: 6). In this view, words and visual art are both modes of representation; one might as well say both are languages. Not only are they thought to be languages, but they are also thought to be rivals in some sort of competition. We may suppose that the competition is to see which does the best job of representation.

In 1927 Magritte published an essay entitled 'Les Mots et Les Images',[8] in which he points out by means of little sketches a number of relations that words and pictures may have. A word may serve to identify the object pictured, a picture may replace a word as in a rebus and so on. In each instance the assumption seems to be that just as words name things so pictures represent things. It has been noted that there are striking similarities between what Magritte says about words and de Saussure's theory of language, although there is no reason to think that Magritte was aware of the latter's work. Frederik Leen, however, reminds us that 'it is significant to know that his word paintings were conceived in an intellectual context which was becoming increasingly aware that our knowledge of the world is subject to the idiosyncratic character of language' (Ollinger-Zinque and Leen 1998: 27). This intellectual context includes Peirce, Frege and the Wittgenstein of the *Tractatus Logico-Philosophicus* as well as de Saussure. Leen goes on:

> In his word paintings, Magritte shows that the contents of works of art cannot be determined by the actual limitations of word and image as conventional sign-systems, nor by their dependence on an object...Artists are not obliged to focus on the usual dependencies between these systems as this would simply be to affirm the existing order. That is why Magritte was so keen to foment border disputes between word, image and reality.
>
> (Ollinger-Zinque and Leen 1998: 25)

Here again, the theory that art is a kind of language comes into play with its corollary assumption that the two are rivals and engaged in 'border disputes'. There are, to be sure, circumstances in which it is intelligible to consider the relative merits of words and pictures in doing certain jobs. A picture, plan or diagram is essential for, say, assembly instructions (place tab A in slot B) where a verbal description would be lengthy, complex and confusing. Another circumstance is propaganda where a picture of the atrocity may be more effective in arousing passions than a description of the event. Neither of these cases, however, have anything to do with art, and it is by no means clear what the rivalry is when it is a matter of the art of painting nor what is the traditional code that prohibits interchanges between the linguistic and the visual that presumably makes a border dispute possible. Is it simply the conventional Renaissance practice of not painting words into pictures like the banners common in medieval painting?

Perhaps the assumptions at work have something to do with Renaissance and early modern disputes about the relative merits of poetry and painting. Such disputes can arise only on the assumption that painting and poetry are trying to do essentially the same thing, and then it is a matter of which one does it better. What they both were thought to do, of course, is to imitate nature. Leonardo says this:

> Painting serves a nobler sense [sight] than poetry and represents the works of nature with more truth than poetry...And if you, poet, wish to confine yourself exclusively to your own profession in describing the works of nature, representing diverse places and form of various objects, you will be out-distanced by the painter's infinitely greater power.
>
> (Leonardo da Vinci 1949: 53, §22)

Apart from the fact that the old theory of the arts as imitation inherited from antiquity was still very much alive and well in Leonardo's thinking, what is important to note is the assumption at work in all of this that both poetry and painting have something important in common, but it is not the common element assumed by a general theory of signs.

In a later century, Lessing would suggest a different way of getting at this common element that may seem closer to the posterity of de Saussure:

> If it be true that painting employs wholly different signs or means of imitations from poetry, – the one using forms and colors in space, the other articulate sounds in time, – and if signs must stand in convenient relation with the thing signified, then signs arranged side by side can represent only objects existing side by side...while consecutive signs can express only objects which succeed each other ...
>
> (Lessing 1957: XVI, 91)

Lessing classifies signs as either arbitrary, such as the letters and words of our language, or natural, such as pictures.[9] Pictures are said to be natural signs because they are supposed to look like what they are pictures of. Generally speaking and in most familiar circumstances, anyone can tell what a picture is of, such as a man, a dog, a horse or, in an essentially Christian culture, the Virgin Mary. On the other hand, not everyone (non-English speakers, for example) can tell what the word 'man' means. Note that when we come to describe the difference between the two kinds of 'signs' it seems natural for the vocabulary to change. The painted image is a 'picture of' while the word 'means'. The use of the word 'sign' to cover both words and pictures suggests that 'picture of' and 'means' refer to the same relation. And, as we have seen, that is not the case.

To add to what has been said earlier, it is useful to remind ourselves of the different ways that 'to mean' can be employed and the different ways the meaning of a word is explained. Sometimes we explain the meaning of a word by a synonym, sometimes by a description, by an illustration or example and sometimes by the grammatical role it plays in sentences. It is tempting to suppose that the relation between a word and its meaning on the one hand and a picture and what it pictures on the other must be different because pictures resemble what they are pictures of while words do not resemble the things they refer to. We should fight temptation here by asking what it is that words do not do. That is, what would it be like if a word did resemble what it means? In concrete and calligraphic poetry words can be printed in shapes that picture objects, but the thesis demands that we imagine all words in all cases resembling their referents. We have no idea what that would be like.

In view of the many different ways the word 'sign' is used, it has to strike us as odd, if not downright crazy, to think that in the painting of the Holy Family before us this figure is a 'sign' of the Virgin Mary in the same way that the familiar female outline is a sign for one side of the public toilets in the airport. Let yourself be struck by the oddness of thinking of the figure in the painting as a 'sign' of the Virgin as if we had a relation like that of the other sign and the ladies' room: here the sign, there the facility. The painting is not a 'sign' of the Virgin Mary, in the painting it is the Virgin Mary. Her picture can, of course, be used as a sign, pointing the way, say, to the shrine, but that is not how the painting works.

Lessing's concern in *Laocoon* – and this is also true of Leonardo – is with how a painter is to draw on a story for his subject. He thinks of paintings largely as illustrations of episodes in stories and painters then have the task of which episodes to select, what details to include, how best to render the expression of the figures and the like. His own views about how painters should carry out that task and whether he got it right are not here to the point. What does want noting is that he seems to start out with something like an incipient 'theory of signs' that presumably is to give theoretical underpinning to his view of the proper work of painters as opposed to poets. When we look at what Lessing actually does, however, we see that the arbitrary/natural sign business is so much baggage and plays no role in his strictures about how painters should or should not draw on the subjects of poetry. Everything he says about the two arts can be said without that theoretical baggage. Lessing's incipient 'theory of signs' works no mischief in what he actually does. This may not be the case, however, for more recent work in art theory; some of the accounts of Magritte are my case in point.

V

I want to go back to the sentence 'Ceci n'est pas un pipe'. What is it doing in Magritte's painting? Foucault was sufficiently puzzled by this to write an essay about it. Foucault says 'The statement is perfectly true, since it is quite apparent that the drawing representing the pipe is not the pipe itself' (Foucault 1982: 19). And again:

> The drawn form of the pipe is so easily recognized that it excludes any explanatory or descriptive text. Its academic schematicism says very explicitly, 'You see me so clearly that it would be ridiculous for

me to arrange myself so as to write: This is a pipe. To be sure words would draw me less adequately than I re-present myself'.

(Foucault 1982: 25)

We may also be inclined to agree with Foucault that what the painted legend says is too obvious to need saying; of course the thing is not a pipe, it is only a picture of one. We must challenge that inclination. Wittgenstein will be our guide in this.

It is well known that Wittgenstein spoke often of meaning as use. He said that for a great many cases the meaning of a word is its use in the language (PI §43). There are disputes about how this is to be understood. Our question, however, concerns not the meaning of the single word 'pipe', but rather the sense of the whole sentence, 'This is not a pipe'. To illustrate the kind of thing that Wittgenstein is talking about with respect to use consider the following passage:

> 'After he had said this, he left her as he did the day before'. – Do I understand this sentence? Do I understand it just as I should if I heard it in the course of a narrative? If it were set down in isolation I should say, I don't know what it is about. But all the same I should know how this sentence might perhaps be used; I could myself invent a context for it.
>
> (PI §525)

To understand the importance of use we must realize the importance of the context in which a sentence is used. Imagine Wittgenstein's sentence occurring in different works of literature, a story, novel or play with different characters in different situations. Perhaps the story is about Tarzan and Jane, Willy Loman and his wife or Bluebeard and his latest wife. Alternatively, imagine different things the speaker might be doing with the sentence: telling a tale for our amusement, reporting the latest neighbourhood gossip or providing a sample sentence for grammatical analysis. The context also includes such things as the tone of voice in which it is spoken as well as accompanying gestures which help to establish the remark as serious, joking, ironic or the like.

Another passage is especially to my point:

> Just as the words 'I am here' have a meaning only in certain contexts, and not when I say them to someone who is sitting in front of me and sees me clearly, – and not because they are superfluous, but because their meaning is not determined by the situation, yet stands in need of such determination.
>
> (OC §348)

We may be inclined to say that those words are superfluous, that is, it is only too obvious that I am here and so it does not need saying. To suppose this, however, is to treat the expression as if its meaning is perfectly clear. Wittgenstein's point, by contrast, is that its meaning is not clear at all, but stands in need of some determination. In this respect it is like the sentence from the previous passage; we understand it to the extent that we know how it can be used and we can invent contexts for it. Here are two such possible contexts that can determine a sense. The boss has called me to his office. I sit down and say, 'You wanted to talk to me. I am here'. After a long and arduous journey I sit down before my true love's fireside and say, 'At last, I am here'.

Discussions of Magritte's paintings that include words seem to assume that these words have a definite sense. Frederik Leen describes the words as 'captions' but then points out that the captions and images cannot be connected by any associations. 'Nor', he says, 'is it the case that the labels have been mixed up – no matter how you rearrange them, the puzzle never falls into place' (Leen 1998: 20). It would appear that we have to go on a hunt armed with theories about words and images to discover what it all means. Let us apply what we have learned from Wittgenstein and note that in the absence of any clear contextual determination we simply do not know how the expressions are being used, if they are being used at all and not simply idling or 'on holiday'. Perhaps this is what Foucault is getting at when he speaks of 'the impossibility of defining a perspective that would let us say that the assertion is true, false or contradictory' (Foucault 1982: 20). Contrary to Foucault, however, we have seen that we can easily imagine 'perspectives', or contexts, that would give the sentence a use although we must keep in mind that whatever we imagine is in no sense a 'discovery' of what Magritte was really about.[10]

Leen's assumption that there is a puzzle comes from supposing that Magritte was engaged in breaking down the borders between words and images. That Magritte was breaking down borders may mean no more than the fact that he wanted to paint words into his pictures. Critical theorists, however, cannot have in mind anything that simple. For them the very idea of there being borders between words and images depends upon theories about 'signs' that tumble language, art and everything else into the same hopper. We have every reason to believe, however, that these are only philosophical confusions. We have no notion of what such a border is nor where the two are supposed to come into competition. This talk of borders obscures the relations that actually obtain between painting and language. I have in mind such things as how a title can make clear what a painting is about, how information can serve to put a painting in an appropriate art historical context and how certain descriptions can help us to see what is in a painting. Although Leen says that Magritte was raising questions about the 'borders' between words and images, he would have been wiser to say that he thought he was raising these questions. He cannot be described as actually doing that since no sense has so far been given to talk of such borders.

I have tried to point out several objections to the idea that art is a language, albeit a different kind of language that is thought to be incommensurate with what we ordinarily think of as language yet is in some kind of competition with it. The assumption that it is a language derives ultimately from de Saussure's semiotic theory. In the first place that theory is based on an incoherent philosophical psychology. In the second place, unlike language, paintings have neither syntax nor semantics. Lastly, its notion of signs confuses and confounds a multitude of diverse human practices and the attempts to apply it to the understanding of particular works of art leads to thinking of painters as engaged in projects to which no sense has been given.

Philosophical theories about art and language are of no help in understanding Magritte, or anything else, as I am inclined to believe. To understand and appreciate painting we must rely on our own sensitivity and experience with art rather than theories. What, then, are we to make of Magritte? Perhaps some remarks that he made in a letter to Foucault contain a suggestion. After some unclear assertions about thought being invisible and resembling 'by being what it sees, hears, or knows; it becomes what the world offers it', he says 'What does not "lack" importance is the mystery evoked in fact by the visible and the invisible, and which can be evoked in principle by the thought that unites "things" in an order that evokes mystery' (Magritte, in Foucault 1982: 57). The key here is the word 'mystery'. Let us understand mystery, not in the detective story sense where there is always an answer to whodunit, but in that other sense of the word in which we encounter something inexplicable and in the face of which we can only wonder. In a Magritte painting the connection between the image and whatever words are found there may be just such a mystery, a mystery to which a solution is not to be sought. It is quite enough that it intrigue us. We should not, however, rule out the alternative that Magritte is simply having his fun with us.[11]

Notes

1   One exception to this may be Nelson Goodman who says that paintings, along with the words of language, musical notations, architectural drawings, etc., have denotations. He makes clear, however, that what he calls the 'allographic' nature of pictures makes them very different from language (Goodman 1968). Sorting all that out is a task for another occasion. Other aspects of analytical philosophy and its relation to aesthetics are discussed in Tilghman (1991).
2   I have discussed some of these theories and their problems in Tilghman (1994).
3   The painting I have in mind is Zurbaran's *The Virgin as a Child*.
4   PI §498
5   Samuel Y. Edgerton (Edgerton 1991: ch. 8) has shown several seventeenth-century Chinese woodcuts illustrating translations of Western mechanical treatises. The Chinese artists did not understand the Western conventions of technical drawing and their versions of the drawings are thoroughly impossible.

6 The incoherence of the picture of mental events as 'private objects' and the attendant idea that our language is therefore a 'private' language is made clear in PI §§253ff.

7 Interestingly enough, de Saussure has an actual picture, a simple drawing, of two heads with lines connecting the two brains (de Saussure 1959: 11). One cannot help but see these as two telegraph offices and the wires between them.

8 A translation of this article is in Ollinger-Zinque and Leen (1998).

9 Our language is arbitrary in that it is a matter of history that we have the alphabet, grammar and vocabulary that we do; these could have been different. Our use of this language, however, is not arbitrary. To be understood we have to make use of its resources as it is. That is glory for you.

10 As a possible circumstance suppose that the blowdown valve activated by the Escape key on the new steam powered computer bears more than a passing resemblance to the vicar's old briar. The article in *Popular Science* teases us with an illustration telling us that it is not a pipe.

11 I am indebted to James Hamilton, Malcolm Turvey and Richard Allen for helpful comments and discussion.

Bibliography

Adams, L.S. (1996) *The Methodologies of Art: An Introduction*, New York: Westview Press.

de Saussure, F. (1959) *Course in General Linguistics*, ed. C. Bally and A. Sechehaye, trans. W. Baskin, New York: Philosophical Library.

Edgerton, S.Y. (1991) *The Heritage of Giotto's Geometry*, Ithaca, NY: Cornell University Press.

Foucault, M. (1982) *This Is Not A Pipe*, ed. and trans. J. Harkness, Berkeley, CA: University of California Press.

Goodman, N. (1968) *Languages of Art*, Indianapolis, IN: Bobbs-Merrill Company.

Hefferman, J.A.W. (1993) *Museum of Words: The Poetics of Ekphrasis from Homer to Ashberry*, Chicago: University of Chicago Press.

Leen, F. (1998) 'A Razor is a Razor', in G. Ollinger-Zinque and F. Leen (eds), *Magritte: 1898–1967*, Ghent: Ludion Press; 25–36.

Leonardo da Vinci (1949) *Paragones*, trans. I.A. Richter, London: Oxford University Press.

Lessing, G.E. (1957) *Laocoon*, trans. E. Frothingham, New York: Noonday Press.

Magritte, R. (1998) 'Words and Images', in G. Ollinger-Zinque and F. Leen (eds), *Magritte: 1898–1967*, Ghent: Ludion Press.

Shapiro, G. (1998) 'French Aesthetics: Contemporary Painting Theory', in M. Kelly (ed.), *Encyclopedia of Aesthetics*, vol. 2, Oxford: Oxford University Press; 235–40.

Tilghman, B.R. (1984) *But is it Art?*, Oxford: Basil Blackwell.

—— (1991) *Wittgenstein, Ethics and Aesthetics: The View From Eternity*, Basingstoke: Macmillan.

Wittgenstein, L. (1958) *Philosophical Investigations* (PI), 2nd edn, trans. G.E.M. Anscombe, Oxford: Basil Blackwell.

—— (1969) *On Certainty* (OC), ed. G.E.M. Anscombe and G.H. von Wright, trans. D. Paul and G.E.M. Anscombe, Oxford: Basil Blackwell.

8

COGNITIVE FILM THEORY

Richard Allen

Cognitive film theory emerged as a distinctive research paradigm in film studies in the mid-1980s. This emergence can be explained against the background of two intellectual contexts which I shall briefly sketch. The relationship between film and human psychology has always been a source of fascination for film theorists, and many writings in film theory are informed by the belief that film has a special relationship to human psychology. Historically, film theory has been preoccupied with the thought that the film camera is, in some sense, like the human eye, or that ways of juxtaposing images are like forms of thought. Film theorists have differed in the kind of mental processes they emphasize and whether or not the mimicked processes are rational or irrational. Furthermore, film theorists have differed in their understanding of what exactly mimesis consists in. Does film simply replicate human perception or does it augment it and transform it? A particular version of the mind-film analogy, influential in the recent past, likens film to the irrational mental processes that psychoanalysis purports to illuminate. The camera is not simply like a perceiver, it is voyeuristic. Films are like dreams or fantasies rather than simply like thoughts. In the context of this long and rich tradition of psychological theorization, cognitive film theory emerged in the 1980s on the basis of rejecting the reasoning by analogy that was central to it.[1] For the cognitivist, films are not like mental processes, they actually engage mental processes. The cognitive theorist seeks to understand how films engage our minds 'with the best available theory'. As philosopher and film theorist Gregory Currie has written, the cognitive theorist emphasizes the

> ways in which our experience of cinematic images and cinematic narrative resemble our experiences of seeing and comprehending events and processes in reality...This leading idea suggests a method as well as a doctrine: in seeking to understand our responses to film, apply the best available theories of perception, information processing, hypothesis-building, and interpretation.
>
> (Currie 1999: 106)

The second context for understanding the emergence of cognitive film theory is as a reaction to the dominance of psychoanalytic theory in film theory of the recent past. In the postwar period, the psychology of film received a new inflection from the study of film as mass culture. Reacting to their experience of fascism, Marxist cultural critics of the Frankfurt School saw film as a medium that had the power to influence and shape the beliefs of the population and diagnozed its power using the tools of psychoanalysis. In the 1970s, a new generation of Marxist-oriented film theorists and critics developed a psychoanalytically-informed theory of film spectatorship that was distilled from an intoxicating mix of French thought: the Marxism of Louis Althusser, the psychoanalysis of Jacques Lacan, and the semiotics of Roland Barthes and Julia Kristeva (Heath 1981; Rosen 1985; Silverman 1983). Considered as a psychological theory of film, the theory developed by psycho-semiotic Marxists was characterized by the assumption that the resemblance films bear to everyday perception confounds the spectator: cinema is a system of signification that produces an illusion of reality. Whereas psychoanalytic-semioticians conceived film spectatorship as an essentially irrational activity in which the spectator is duped by what she sees, her responses passively tutored by the unfolding images and sounds on the movie screen, cognitive film theorists insist that film spectatorship is a rationally motivated and informed action. Again, the motivation of the cognitive theorist is to apply the best available theory to understanding film spectatorship, and the cognitive theorist assumes that this theory is not one in which film spectatorship is considered to be essentially irrational.

Put this way, the assumptions underlying cognitive film theory – looking at films is like looking at other things, watching movies is not an essentially irrational act – sound like common sense. However, cognitivism becomes a theory only when the theory is produced: what kind of understanding of 'rational action' does the cognitivist propose? How does the cognitivist explain the way that 'we see and comprehend events and processes in reality'? What kind of 'fit' does the theorist seek between the general theory and an explanation of motion picture perception and cognition? Cognitive film theorists pose different kinds of answers to these questions, and these answers must be examined at the level at which they are proposed. In this chapter, I undertake a conceptual investigation, following Wittgenstein, of the work of two of the most important and influential cognitive film theorists. The primary focus of my investigation is the cognitive theory of narrative film proposed by the distinguished film scholar, David Bordwell, who founded the cognitive study of cinema. I argue that Bordwell's cognitive theory of film exemplifies the conceptual confusion that inheres in the cognitive psychology upon which he draws. I go on to discuss aspects of the cognitive film theory of philosopher Gregory Currie, and examine key respects in which it contradicts and challenges Bordwell's theory of film from within the framework of cognitivism. I suggest that, despite the apparent contrast in theoretical assumptions,

Bordwell and Currie share the same underlying, and mistaken, picture of the mind. Furthermore, cognitive theory, in Currie's hands, fails to support the kind of concrete investigation and analysis of the ways in which we consciously engage with narrative film that redeems Bordwell's discussion of film from the theoretical framework it inhabits.

Bordwell's theory of narrative comprehension: a preliminary sketch

Bordwell's analysis of hypothesis formation and inference-making in film viewing in *Narration in the Fiction Film* is motivated by a theory which it is taken to exemplify. This theory is 'constructivist' cognitive psychology, in particular a cognitive psychological theory of perception. The sources of this theory lie in the perceptual psychology of von Helmholtz, the founding father of modern optics, and its influence can be traced through the writings of Karl Popper to contemporary perceptual psychologists such as R.L. Gregory and Irvin Rock. According to this psychology of perception: 'Sensory stimuli alone cannot determine a precept, since they are incomplete and ambiguous. The organism constructs a perceptual judgement on the basis of nonconscious inferences' (Bordwell 1985: 31). One of Bordwell's authorities, Irvin Rock, writes that:

> perceptual processing is guided by the effort or search to interpret the proximal stimulus, i.e. the stimulus impinging on the sense organ, in terms of what object or event in the world it represents, what others have referred to as the 'effort after meaning'. In other words, the goal of processing is to arrive at a description of the outer object or event.
>
> (Rock 1983: 16)

Here is Bordwell's own summary of Rock's theory:

> Rock shows that the distal stimulus, say a tree, is registered initially on the retina as a proximal stimulus. From this raw material the visual system starts to generate formal descriptions of the stimulus in terms of part/whole relations, regions, and figure/ground relations. Eventually there emerges a 'preferred precept', a mental description of the tree as a three dimensional object. The cognitivist tint of this account comes largely from Rock's insistence that perceiving anything involves description, problem solving, and inference – all constructive processes we would normally associate with higher-level activities. The senses are engaged in an 'effort after meaning' that is both structurally analogous to more abstract thought and intimately bound up with it.
>
> (Bordwell 1989: 18)

176

Another perceptual psychologist cited by Bordwell, R.L. Gregory, writes:

> perception involves going beyond the immediately given evidence of the senses... the senses do not give us a picture of the world directly; rather, they provide evidence for the checking of hypotheses about what lies before us. Indeed, we may say that the perception of the object is an hypothesis, suggested and tested by the sensory data.
>
> (Gregory 1990: 21–2)

The constructivist theory of perception plays a central role in Bordwell's theory of narrative comprehension for several reasons. First, film is a visual medium and therefore narrative comprehension presupposes the activity of visual inference. Second, 'visual perception has furnished the classic illustrations of Constructivist psychological theory' (Bordwell 1985: 31) and thus provides a model for thinking about cognitive processes that are less immediately perceptual in character. Third, there is 'no easy separation' between perception and cognition. 'In some cases', Bordwell writes,

> the inference proceeds principally 'from the bottom up', in which conclusions are drawn on the basis of the perceptual input. Color perception is a good example. Other processes, such as the recognition of a familiar face, operate 'from the top down'. Here the organization of sensory data is primarily determined by expectation, background knowledge, problem-solving processes, and other cognitive operations. Both bottom-up and top-down processing are inferential in that perceptual 'conclusions' about the stimulus are drawn, often inductively, on the basis of 'premises' furnished by the data, by internalized rules, or by prior knowledge.
>
> (Bordwell 1985: 31)

Following this statement, Bordwell contrasts bottom-up and top-down processing on the grounds that bottom-up perceptual processing operates in a fast, involuntary way, whereas top-down processes 'are more overtly based on assumptions, expectations and hypotheses' (Bordwell 1985: 31). Thus, for Bordwell, in practice, all cognitive processes are linked to perception because they involve 'the organization of sensory data', and all perceptual processes are cognitive because perception is a form of inference, albeit unconscious inference.

Bordwell's conception of constructivist psychology is unified through his use of the term 'schemata'. One of Bordwell's authorities quotes the following definition:　模式 ：

A schema is a naive theory of some stimulus domain and the individual using it a 'naive scientist'...When we apply a particular schema for thinking about some stimulus object it does two things. First, it tells us about what to attend to. Like a scientific theory, it makes some attributes relevant, that is salient, while allowing others to be ignored. Second, a schema contains the network of associations that is believed to hold among the attributes of the stimulus and thereby provides rules for thinking about the stimulus. Thus, if information conveying some relevant attribute is unavailable from the stimulus itself or is ambiguous or is unavailable from memory, the schema allows for the 'filling in' of such information with 'default options'.

(quoted in Hastie 1981: 40)

Bordwell defines a schema as 'organized clusters of knowledge' that 'guide hypothesis making': 'The mental image of a bird is a schema for visual recognition, and the concept of a well-formed sentence functions as a schema in speech perception' (Bordwell 1985: 31).[2] Following Reid Hastie, Bordwell distinguishes between different schemata: 'Schemata may be of various kinds – prototypes (the bird image, for instance), or templates (like filing systems), or procedural patterns (a skilled behavior, such as knowing how to ride a bicycle)' (Bordwell 1985: 31).

How then do schema enter into narrative comprehension? 'Generally', Bordwell writes,

the spectator comes to the film already tuned, prepared to focus energies toward story construction and to apply sets of schemata derived from context and prior experience. This effort toward meaning involves an effort toward unity. Comprehending a narrative requires assigning it some coherence. At a local level, the viewer must grasp character relations, lines of dialogue, relations between shots, and so on. More broadly, the viewer must test the narrative information for consistency: does it hang together in a way we can identify? For instance, does a series of gestures, words, and manipulations of objects add up to the action sequence we know as 'buying a loaf of bread'? The viewer also finds unity by looking for relevance, testing each event for its pertinence to the action...Such general criteria direct perceptual activity through anticipations and hypotheses, and they are in turn modified by the data supplied by the film.

(Bordwell 1985: 34)

But why should the student and scholar of film be interested in the inferential processes that are deployed in the activity of perceiving and comprehending motion pictures if they are not essentially different from the inferences that govern other practices of everyday life? Bordwell offers at least three reasons why it is important to reveal these patterns of inference. First, there are processes of inference-making solicited by narrative film that are particular to it and other kindred forms of narration such as prototypical expectations that frame what kind of elements and relationships we assume to be a part of a story. For example, Bordwell argues that narrative comprehension in general is guided by what he terms 'the canonical story format'. Second, the presence of inference-making demonstrates that the spectator is an active spectator in contrast to the passive spectator proposed by psychoanalytic film theorists. Bordwell writes: 'Seeing is thus not a passive absorption of stimuli. It is a constructive activity' (Bordwell 1985: 32). Third, Bordwell claims that what distinguishes aesthetic perception from everyday perception is that we deploy our cognitive-perceptual skills for non-practical ends:

> in experiencing art, instead of focusing on the pragmatic results of perception, we turn our attention to the very process itself. What is nonconscious in everyday mental life becomes consciously attended to. Our schemata get shaped, stretched, and transgressed; a delay in hypothesis-confirmation can be prolonged for its own sake, and like all psychological activities, aesthetic activity has long-range effects. Art may reinforce, or modify, or even assault our normal perceptual-cognitive repertoire.
>
> (Bordwell 1985: 32)

It is not immediately clear how 'constructive activity' contrasts with passivity in Bordwell's second claim, since the inference-making procedures identified by constructivist perceptual psychology are, according to the theory, unconscious or non-conscious procedures. Their salience to narrative comprehension would not make the spectator active. A constructivist psychology of perception does not necessarily entail an active percipient, one who is consciously seeking out cues, for it is possible for a spectator who engages in all the requisite inference-making procedures to remain entirely unaware of them. Bordwell does claim that top-down processes are more overtly based upon expectations, and speaks in the paragraph quoted above of an 'effort toward meaning'. This may support the idea of an active spectator. But to justify the concept of the active spectator this way requires drawing a sharp distinction between bottom-up and top-down processes, a sharp distinction that Bordwell rejects. Either Bordwell owes us an explanation of how it is that the presence of unconscious inferences makes the spectator an active seeker out of meaning as opposed to the passive recipient of the message of the text, or else we have to accept that it is only where inference is explicit in aesthetic activity that the spectator becomes active. However, if it is the case that spectators are made active only where they are explicitly called upon to make an inference or form an hypothesis by a film, then the role of constructivist psychological theory in his account of narrative comprehension is already called into question. For why should these hypotheses or inferences be considered visual inferences made on the basis of sensory data since perceptual inferences are supposed to be non-conscious, and ·what relevance have non-conscious inferences in general to understanding narrative comprehension?

The thesis of the active spectator does make sense if it is considered in relationship to the third motivation for Bordwell's account. It is not, it seems, the presence of inference-making *per se* that makes the spectator an active spectator; rather it is the way in which responses that are distinctively aesthetic in character require the spectator to engage in the formulation of hypotheses and the making of inferences for their own sake, as an end in themselves rather than as a means to an end. Rather than passively following practised routines of cognition as a means to an end, as we do in riding a bike or driving a car, the pursuit of these routines becomes the explicit goal of the spectator viewing a film. However, if it is aesthetic activity rather than 'perceptual processing' that makes the spectator an active spectator, then Bordwell still owes us an explanation of what role is played by non-conscious as opposed to conscious inference in his theory.

One way of restoring the salience of perceptual-cognitive psychology to Bordwell's theory of narrative comprehension is to adopt a more neutral formulation of the importance of non-conscious inferences in narrative comprehension that remains consistent with Bordwell's intention to contest psychoanalytic theories of spectatorship. Non-conscious inferences do not imply an active spectator but define the rationality of the film spectator. The active spectator results from the fact that the rational psychological processes underlying perception and understanding are made explicit in film viewing. In other words, Bordwell's conception of the active spectator is a product not (or not simply) of a cognitive psychology of film viewing, but is part of a separate theory of 'aesthetic perception' in which art is defined as an activity that makes explicit cognitive and perceptual processes we do not otherwise attend to. In the light of this theory, if conscious inferences in film are to be aesthetically significant, they must be making explicit processes that we routinely engage in but do not otherwise attend to. I shall not contest Bordwell's neoformalist definition of aesthetic activity here. Instead, I shall argue that the constructivist theory of perception and understanding is conceptually incoherent and that therefore the conscious inference-making procedures he discerns in film cannot be coherently construed as making manifest non-conscious inferential processes.

Constructivist cognitive psychology: perception as inference

Bordwell does not offer a great deal of argument for his view that we should construe perceptions as inferences from hypotheses other than to claim that this view was at the time of writing a prevalent view of perception in the psychological literature. I will thus turn to that literature to unpack the claim that 'sensory stimuli are ambiguous and incomplete', and that it is for this reason that 'the organism constructs a perceptual judgement on the basis of non-conscious inferences'. According to Rock:

> Logically, a given local stimulus is only an ambiguous indicator of the relevant property of the object producing it. For example, an image of a given size, measured by the visual angle that an object subtends at the eye, will be produced by a whole family of objects of varying sizes each at a different distance. Thus the perceptual system could never determine from an image's visual angle alone what the size of the object that produced it is...Yet perception of such properties is generally not ambiguous. We tend to perceive objects of definite size, shape, and the like.
>
> (Rock 1983: 22)

Thus he concludes that the perception of size constancy is a result of inference. The 'visual system' infers object constancy by applying information about object distance to the 'extent' that is 'perceived on the basis of the visual angle' (Rock 1983: 274). The reason the perceptual system sees a constant object of a particular size is because it 'interprets' the 'extent' that it perceives on the basis of visual angle in the light of information available that the object producing that visual angle is at a certain distance.

What exactly are the sensory stimuli that are supposed to be 'logically' incomplete, and are they something of a character whose ambiguity with respect to what it is we report that we perceive licenses the conclusion that our perceptual reports are hypotheses? The clearest candidate to function as the ambiguous sensory stimuli is the retinal image that Rock repeatedly refers to in his book. It is certainly true that if we were to arrive at a description of an object upon the basis of our perception of the retinal image cast by that object alone, then we would be led to misconstrue the nature of the object, for retinal images are very small, upside down, and left–right inverted! We might also, in the absence of countervailing visual cues, construe a square moving quickly towards our eye as an expanding square rather than as a square of constant size that is getting closer, if we were to look only at the retinal image of a fast-approaching square. But, of course, when we perceive an object we do not perceive a retinal image of the object, we perceive the object. Since we cannot perceive a retinal image, the retinal image cannot be the stimuli that provide us with ambiguous information about the object producing it.

Rock knows that we do not perceive the retinal image, but he insists on the importance of the fact that we can perceive something that is like the retinal image. When Rock states that a particular 'extent' can be perceived based on the visual angle, he means that we may with some effort perceive the square that moves before us just with respect to its two-dimensional properties, its looming size. Rock refers to this kind of perception as perception in the 'proximal mode', which differs from literal perception by being 'subjective'. The relevant contrast here is with the kind of shape perceptions characteristic of certain kinds of ambiguous figures such as the fact that we can see the picture of a three-dimensional wire cube as a two-dimensional arrangement of lines. This kind of perception is closely related to perception in the 'proximal' mode because both are two-dimensional. But whereas perception in the proximal mode is subjective, our perception of the cube as two-dimensional is objective. Having isolated the 'proximal mode of perception', Rock argues that 'instructions to match in accord with the "projected shape" rather than the objective shape will result in matches that are closer to the shape of the retinal image than to the object shape' (Rock 1983: 256). By this, he presumably means that if we were to look at our retinal image, our report on what we see would be like our reports on what we see if we attend only to the 'projected shape' of an object. It is this subjective perception, rather than a perception of the retinal image that it is like, that functions to accompany the objective or 'world mode' perception. Since the 'projected shape' is something that is perceived, it is fit to function as the ambiguous stimuli that prompt us to resort to inference in order to determine what it is we actually see.

The reason that Rock claims that what we perceive in the proximal mode is subjective is presumably that he wants to isolate something that we perceive that can enter into all circumstances where we make perceptual reports, something that is neither unseen like the retinal image, nor objectively available to perception in the manner that an arrangement of two-dimensional lines can be seen as an alternative to perceiving a three-dimensional cube. But what exactly is it that is subjective about perceiving an approaching object as if it were increasing in size? In the case of looking at a cube drawing as an arrangement of two-dimensional lines, no appearance or illusion is involved, for the figure may be seen one way or another. On the other hand, in the case of the approaching object, the object appears to increase in size when it does not. But this distinction does not single out the experience of the looming object as a subjective experience in contrast to literal perception. Perception of the size increase of the looming object is a kind of visual illusion. When we perceive an illusion such as the Müller–Lyer illusion, we see lines that appear to be of unequal length even though they are equal. There is nothing subjective about what we see when we see the Müller–Lyer lines as unequal in length. The illusion is objective: the lines appear unequal when they are not, that is what makes it an illusion. Perception is the size increase of the looming object is equally objective: the object appears to increase in size when it does not. The looming object is distinguished from the Müller–Lyer illusion only by the circumstance dependence of the perception: the object has to be approaching the eye and approaching at speed in such a way that we ignore depth cues. We do not have to see the object in this way. This is the only feature of the experience in virtue of which it might be called subjective, but it is precisely the feature of the experience that entails that perception in the proximal mode does not invariably accompany object perception.

Rock's concept of subjective perception in the proximal mode is a misguided attempt to discover a perceptual correlate for the retinal image. So what then is the ambiguous stimuli that grounds inference in perception? Why cannot the retinal image function as the ambiguous sensory stimuli, without assuming that the retinal image or its analogue is something that is perceived? Surely that is precisely what is needed. After all, Rock is trying to account for the complex causal process connecting the proximal input to the visual cortex that makes perception possible. Unfortunately, as John Hyman (1989) has pointed out, the retinal image plays no essential part in this causal story. What occurs at the 'input' end of the causal process underlying perception is the irradiation of the retina. The retina could be irradiated and a signal passed to the visual cortex without a retinal image being formed, if, for example, the surface upon which the retinal image were projected were to render it invisible. Once the retinal image drops out of the causal story, there is no concept of internal representation available upon which to hook the concept of interpretation or inference. But Rock remains wedded to the idea that perception is based upon the retinal image as an internal analogue of the external object. It is something unseen therefore internal, yet something that is in principle perceivable. The retinal image can thus seem to function both in the causal account of perception and as the grounds for an inference about what we see and thus allow the psychologist to cast the causal account in inferential terms. But the retinal image plays no essential role in the causal account, and nor is a retinal image (or its putative analogue) something from which we infer what is perceived. For though a retinal image invariably accompanies perception, we cannot see it, and while, under certain circumstances, we may see an object in the 'proximal mode' of perception, this way of seeing an object does not invariably accompany our perception of it.

Underlying Rock's theory of perception is a misconception about the nature of psychological verbs that is pervasive in psychology. Dubbed by Anthony Kenny 'the homunculus fallacy', this misconception involves 'the application of human-being predicates to insufficiently human-like objects' (Kenny 1991: 155). As Wittgenstein writes in the *Philosophical Investigations*, 'Only of a human being and what resembles (behaves like) a living human being can one say: it has sensations; it sees; is blind; hears; is deaf; is conscious or unconscious' (PI §281). Kenny points out that Descartes was one of the first philosophers to draw attention to the fallacy in his *Optics*. Descartes argues that while a retinal image 'retains some degree of its resemblance to the objects from which it originates', nonetheless, 'we must not think that it is by means of this resemblance that the picture makes us aware of objects – as though we had another pair of eyes to see it, inside our head' (Kenny 1991: 156). While Rock, like other modern psychologists, is quick to reject the notion that the retinal image is something we see, the role assigned to the retinal image in his account of perception is one which leads him to posit an 'executive agency' in the brain which interprets, makes inferences and forms hypotheses on the basis of the visual or sensory information that is registered in the visual image. When Rock claims that the reason the perceptual system sees a constant object of a particular size is because it 'interprets' the 'extent' that it perceives on the basis of visual angle in the light of its knowledge of the distance of the object and in the light of its knowledge of the rule that perceived extensity is inversely proportional to distance, he is either appealing to the incoherent idea of the proximal stimulus (qua subjective perception) as a ground for inference, or else he is ascribing personal agency and the capacity to follow rules of inference or to act normatively to the brain or parts of the brain. The first explanation can be construed as a failed attempt to avoid the incoherence of the second. For a rule to act as a rule, for it to function normatively, it must be capable of being followed and being broken and be invoked by the agency that is following the rule to justify the inference or interpretation being made. Causal processes are mechanisms and mechanisms are not normative in character. Brains cannot infer, they cannot justify their inferences by invoking rules, and nor can they make mistakes.

It is tempting for the psychologist faced with this kind of criticism to retreat back from talk of brain processes to more everyday considerations in order to grasp the manner in which perceptions are based upon inference. Thus for example, R.L. Gregory writes:

> If the light is dim, or if there are confusing shadows, then I am quite likely to mistake even my own desk for another object or a shadow. This decrease in reliability of recognition proceeds gradually and continuously as sensory data are removed, or become unavailable. There seems to be no sudden break between perceiving an object and guessing an object. If all perceiving of objects requires some guessing, we may think of sensory stimulation as providing data for hypotheses concerning the state of the external world. The selected hypotheses, following this view, are perceptions.
>
> (Gregory 1973: 61)

This passage, and Gregory's version of the theory of perceptions as hypotheses, has been subject to systematic criticism by P.M.S. Hacker (1991). I will restrict myself to a few summary remarks.

It may be difficult to discern an object in a darkened room, and it is certainly more difficult the more darkened the room becomes. In these circumstances, we may be unable to see what is in the corner of the room and guess or infer that what we see only indistinctly must be a table lamp (say by a process of elimination of the other likely candidates). Furthermore, the conditions under which we lapse into guesswork are not sharply different from those where we do not. However, it does not follow from the fact that conditions are not sharply different that we never escape guesswork, for they do nonetheless become different. Familiar with table lamps, I do not guess that it is a table lamp I see in the corner of the room when the room is adequately lit, I simply perceive it. Furthermore, where I do see something indistinctly, the 'data' on which I base my inference are features I *can* see such as the outline of a table corner that need not involve guesswork or inference. Nor do I confirm my inference when I switch on the light with another inference. I simply perceive the table.

Even cursory reflection on the concept of perception reveals that the idea that perceptions are inferences is nonsensical. The concept of perceiving something and making an inference are fundamentally distinct. An inference is a form of thought, but a perception, that is, a glance, a glimpse, a gaze or a look, is not a thought. An inference may conclude with a judgement that *p*. We also make perceptual judgements when we report that we saw *p*. Furthermore, a perceptual judgement may be the result of an inference. I may be uncertain about what I am seeing and come to a judgement about what it is I am seeing by inference based on visual and other sensory 'cues' and past experience of the environment I am in. However inference is not required to form a perceptual judgement, that is a report, about what we see. The 'basis' on which I make the report 'I see a table' is nothing other than the fact that I see a table. It is only in particular circumstances, circumstances, we might say, that require detective work, that hypothesis formation and inference-making intervene.

The psychologist's conception of perception as the interpretation of sensory stimuli in the light of prior rules of inference or cognitive schemata (to use Bordwell's preferred vocabulary), rests upon a misunderstanding of the relationship between 'inner' and 'outer'. Perception is erroneously conceived as a process that takes place inside the mind like other psychological capacities and abilities such as understanding a film. However, perception is discriminated from these other putatively 'inner' psychological processes in a way that allows the connection between 'inner' and 'outer' to be forged. Perception is conceived as an inner, mental process which involves the interpretation of raw stimuli – conceived in terms of abstract material properties such as shape, texture and light – as perceived objects. But if Wittgenstein is correct, there is no such thing as an inner world that contains psychological processes in the manner that the outer world contains things. The brain is no more a candidate as the container for these processes than is

Descartes's immaterial substance. There is one world of material things, some of which, sentient creatures, are possessed with the capacity to see material things. One of these sentient creatures, human beings, equipped with the tools of language, have refined and broadened that capacity to an extraordinary degree; they possess, as it were, perceptual self-consciousness, that allows them to describe what they see. Perception is a mental or psychological capacity, and like all such capacities it is dependent upon material (causal) processes. But the capacity to perceive is not itself a material process, it is an ability, and abilities are characterized by the way they manifest themselves in behaviour. As humans, we manifest our ability to see in linguistic behaviour, in perceptual reports that state what it is that we see (although we could use a different tool to report on what we see, for example a drawing or a physical sample). The psychologist confuses the characterization of our ability to perceive that is manifest in our use of perceptual verbs with the investigation and elucidation of inner, mental processes.[3]

Constructivist psychology and narrative comprehension

I shall now turn to Bordwell's application of a constructivist psychology of perception and cognition to understanding film. To repeat the summary I gave earlier of his argument:

> Generally, the spectator comes to the film already tuned, prepared to focus energies toward story construction and to apply sets of schemata derived from context and prior experience. This effort toward meaning involves an effort toward unity. Comprehending a narrative requires assigning it some coherence. At a local level, the viewer must grasp character relations, lines of dialogue, relations between shots, and so on. More broadly, the viewer must test the narrative information for consistency: does it hang together in a way we can identify? For instance, does a series of gestures, words, and manipulations of objects add up to the action sequence we know as 'buying a loaf of bread'? The viewer also finds unity by looking for relevance, testing each event for its pertinence to the action... Such general criteria direct perceptual activity through anticipations and hypotheses, and they are in turn modified by the data supplied by the film.[4]

(Bordwell 1985: 34)

I will focus on four aspects of his account in the context of the criticisms I have already made about constructivist psychology and in the course of amplifying Bordwell's views: first, the relationship the putative mental processes underlying narrative comprehension are supposed to have to conscious behaviour; second, the role Bordwell assigns to visual inferences (inferences made from perceptual data) in his understanding of the role of inferences in narrative comprehension; third, Bordwell's understanding of the role of narrative conventions in narrative comprehension; and finally, Bordwell's overall claim that spectators 'construct' the narratives they comprehend.

The theory of perception and cognition I have outlined prescribes that the kinds of inferential processes involved in recognizing, say, a 'proximal stimulus' as 'buying a loaf of bread' are unconscious; we are not aware of making these inferences, nor could we be aware of making them. However, as we have seen, the vocabulary that Bordwell uses to describe 'narrative comprehension' is one of conscious agency: the spectator comes to the narrative 'prepared to focus energies', 'the viewer must grasp character relations'. If the procedures Bordwell describes are supposed to be conscious, then his characterization of narrative comprehension is ill-conceived. We do not have to think in order to decide whether the actions that we see are buying a loaf of bread, still less do we infer that a sequence is buying a loaf of bread on the basis of processing a set of perceptual cues in the light of hypotheses. We must of course possess a certain level of cognitive development (including some linguistic mastery) in order to manifest the ability to recognize an action as buying a loaf of bread. However, the possession of this ability is not indicated by our skill in deploying hypotheses. Rather, it is manifest in our appropriate reactions to what we see. A child, we might note, can recognize that her mother is buying a loaf of bread long before she can formulate an hypothesis! We don't typically 'test each event for its pertinence to the action' as if we were unsure about the relationship that the event had to what comes before. Of course we can imagine a work that did enjoin this mode of spectatorship – the experimental narratives of Jean-Luc Godard come to mind – but these kinds of work are exceptions that prove the rule. An attitude of uncertainty about how the bits of narrative relate to one another at the local level is not typically engendered by a narrative film precisely because the typical narrative film is one whose conventions we are familiar with. Understanding a film may require a conscious 'effort toward meaning', if that means an effort to understand what it is that we see and hear, but different films require a different level of effort, and some films require of the average adult spectator, reasonably familiar with fiction film conventions, no effort at all (compare, for example, the works of Ingmar Bergman and Sylvester Stallone).

It might be claimed that I have misconstrued the nature of these processes by suggesting that they are conscious. On the contrary, as we would expect from cognitive theory, they are essentially unconscious; narrative comprehension is often effortless. We can 'become conscious' of these processes only in the sense that we can, armed with the right theory, grasp the nature of the processes that make understanding possible – its causal preconditions. Bordwell writes: 'For the viewer, constructing the story takes precedence; the effects of the text are registered, but its causes go unremarked' (Bordwell 1985: 48). But what is the nature of the processes that are supposed to causally enable the spectator to 'construct' the story? 'Focusing', 'assigning', 'grasping', 'looking', and 'testing' are verbs of agency characterizing conscious mental activities which have a normative import, that is, they are activities undertaken in the light of achieving certain goals and against the background of knowledge about how to attain and how not to attain them. These are not the kind of activities that can be attributed to a causal mechanism, as I have already argued. If these processes are not predicated of the conscious agent in the sense that it is not the agent who actually infers, tests and forms hypotheses, then it must be the activities of something or someone else who is the object of knowledge, of an homunculus whose psychological processes mimic our own but are explicable in terms of material processes. But, as we have seen, the homuncular conception of the mind is incoherent, it involves predicating psychological capacities to a brain that can only rightfully be predicated of the whole person.

In fact, Bordwell does not claim that these alleged 'processes' are unconscious, for he rightly recognizes that narrative comprehension does require conscious inference-making on the part of a film viewer. Yet he erroneously bestows upon his description of the inference-making procedures the explanatory status of a theoretical generalization that constructivist psychology affords, rather than simply exploring the different ways in which understanding films does and does not involve the making of inferences. Thus he proposes that these inference-making procedures are simply non-conscious: while the spectators may be aware of these processes, they are not typically aware of them, unless, for example, the theorist points them out. Bordwell, in this context, actually uses the Freudian term 'pre-conscious' to describe them. But what is meant by the claim that the spectator may become conscious of these pre-conscious processes? Does this mean, for example, that the suitably informed spectator now consciously 'tests each event for its pertinence to the action' in a way that they didn't before, because they now recognize how this testing is enjoined by the text in order for them to understand it? A spectator, under the influence of the theory, may do this, but it could not be because such a conscious activity is enjoined by the text as that would contradict the theory that the processes that the text requires the spectator to engage in, in order to understand it, are non-conscious. The very point of claiming that these putative processes are non-conscious is precisely to recognize the fact that conscious understanding is often effortless! But to explain this effortlessness in terms of the non-conscious nature of these mechanisms is to misconstrue the character of effortless understanding. Effortless understanding, where it occurs, is not effortless because the effort is hidden, as if, when we were fully conscious of what understanding entailed, narrative comprehension would be effortful. Conscious understanding, at the level of narrative comprehension Bordwell is describing, is indeed often without effort. Of course, certain filmic narratives do require us to call into question our fundamental presuppositions about what it is that we are seeing and hearing and they may, as a result, call upon us to form hypotheses and make inferences about what it is that we see and hear. These films may, for example, call attention to our capacities to recognize objects or people and their relationship to one another that we take for granted. But it is a mistake to conceive experimental narratives as making explicit processes of 'narrative construction' that are implicit in watching all films. Rather they enjoin us to work out what it is that we see in a way that more conventional films simply do not.

This dismissal of Bordwell's theory of pre-conscious inference may seem to be too hasty. Surely there are certain cases in which it does make sense to speak of pre-conscious in the sense of tacit inferences about what we are seeing and hearing? Of course, but the claim only makes sense once the theory of perception as unconscious inference is abandoned. Visual inferences may indeed be pre-conscious in the sense of being made tacitly, but only where it is appropriate to speak of visual inferences taking place in the first place, and this depends upon context. One such context is Hitchcock's *Rear Window*. *Rear Window* provides an ideal example of the role that visual inference can play in the cinema, but it does not exemplify a general theory of narrative comprehension. Bordwell quotes from one point in the movie where the heroine Lisa (Grace Kelly) declares to her boyfriend L.B. Jeffries (James Stewart): 'Let's start from the beginning again Jeff. Tell me everything you saw – and what you think it means'. Bordwell comments: 'Her remark concisely reiterates the film's strategy of supplying sensory information ("everything you saw") and then forcing Jeff (and us) to interpret it ("and what do you think it means")' (Bordwell 1985: 42). Bordwell's characterization of *Rear Window* is accurate, and his analysis of the film insightful. We do infer, along with Jeff, that Lars Thorwald is a murderer on the basis of Hitchcock's carefully controlled 'visual cues': his wife's disappearance from the apartment, his mysterious comings and goings, his packing a big trunk (big enough to hold a body), his possession and wrapping of very large knives (suitable for cutting up a body), and the plethora of Hitchcockian stylistic cues (colour, graphics and sound design) that ambiguously prompt our sense that something is awry in this apparently everyday world. Furthermore, we are not necessarily or even characteristically self-aware that we are making visually-based inferences when we are making them. However visual inference, tacit or not, does not have the place in narrative comprehension that Bordwell ascribes to it. In *Rear Window*, the reason we make visual inferences, tacitly or not, is that such inferences are solicited by the film. *Rear Window* is structured as a detective film in which the problem of finding out what is going on from visual and aural clues is integral to the spectator's engagement with the plot. But it is comparatively rare for a film-maker to invite us to figure out what is going on in the narrative on the basis of visual and aural clues. Of course, understanding a film is always a question of understanding what we see and hear, and occasionally in the films of supremely visual directors such as Hitchcock or Lang, inferential processes that are distinctly perceptual may play a central role in understanding the film. But understanding what we see and hear is not, generally speaking, a matter of making inferences, and nor is it in the cinema.

Visual inference does not have the significance in understanding movies that Bordwell's cognitive psychology ascribes to it. But this does not mean that hypothesis formation and inference = making *per se* is not important to narrative comprehension. Bordwell writes that the film spectator 'uses schemata and incoming cues to make assumptions, draw inferences about current story events, and frame and test hypotheses about prior and upcoming events' (Bordwell 1985: 39). One of the great virtues of his theory of narrative comprehension has been to draw attention to ways in which we engage with narrative that were wholly ignored by film theorists held in thrall by psychoanalytic theory. Following Meir Sternberg. Bordwell shows the ways in which the temporal structure of narrative is predicated upon withholding information from the spectator, spurring curiosity about what has happened that the spectator does not yet know about or anticipation about what is to come. Detective films are built upon the concealment of narrative information and demand that we the audience alongside the detective protagonist piece together the story of the crime. The structure of suspense, so integral to popular narrative, is one in which the spectator is enjoined by the film to entertain the probability of a narrative outcome that is directly contrary to the one they would have wished for, even when they know that according to the conventions of popular narrative, there will be a happy end.[5] However, Bordwell's understanding of the role of non-visual inference is fundamentally distorted by the cognitive-perceptual psychology that frames it. For Bordwell tends to consider inference-making in general in cinema on the basis of his understanding of the way in which inference enters into perception.

I shall illustrate the problem by investigating Bordwell's use of a distinction that plays a central role in his account of the inferential basis of narrative comprehension. Bordwell rightly emphasizes the value of drawing a contrast between the order in which narrative events are presented to us in the plot or syuzhet and the reconstruction of those events into a linear sequence which makes up the story or fabula. Certain films mandate that we undertake the activity of reconstructing story from plot. As Bordwell writes:

> In *Rear Window*, as in most detective tales, there is an overt process of fabula construction, since the investigation of the crime involves establishing certain connections among events. Putting the fabula together requires us to construct the story of the on-going inquiry

while at the same time framing and testing hypotheses about past events. That is, the story of the investigation is a search for the concealed story of a crime.

(Bordwell 1985: 49)

Bordwell also brilliantly demonstrates how 'art cinema narration' seeks to convey the subjective, fragmented, 'psychological reality' of a protagonist by presenting narrative events in a disconnected, ambiguous fashion that requires effort on the part of the spectator to understand and piece together. He concludes that the art film is characterized by 'a highly self-conscious narration' that stresses 'the act of presenting this fabula in just this way' (Bordwell 1985: 211). Yet the distinction between plot and story is a heuristic device, a way of drawing attention to the ways in which a narrator such as Wilkie Collins in *The Woman in White* or Orson Welles in *Citizen Kane* deliberately parcels out, controls and withholds narrative information in order to engage the spectator in suspense, or perhaps to articulate deeper truths. Many narratives do present their events in linear sequence, whether a children's fairy tale like *Jack and the Beanstalk* or a Hollywood film like *My Fair Lady*, and most narratives manipulate the order in which they present story events or leave causal connections between events obscure only some of the time.

In his theory of narrative comprehension, Bordwell grafts the distinction between syuzhet and fabula onto the constructivist distinction between cue and schema. The syuzhet, for Bordwell, is defined as 'the dramaturgy of the fiction film, the organized set of cues prompting us to infer and assemble story information' (Bordwell 1985: 52). The fabula, by contrast is 'the imaginary construct we create, progressively and retroactively'. Bordwell continues,

The viewer builds the fabula on the basis of prototype schemata (identifiable types of persons, actions, locales, etc.), template schemata (principally the 'canonic' story), and procedural schemata (a search for appropriate motivations and relations of causality, time, and space).

(Bordwell 1985: 49)

Thus for Bordwell, the procedure of constructing the imaginary fabula out of the perceptual cues afforded by the dramaturgy of the film (the syuzhet) is a prerequisite for narrative understanding. Even the simplest, apparently linear tale requires us to undertake this process of narrative (re)construction:

No syuzhet explicitly presents all of the fabula events that we presume took place. A princess is born; in the next scene she is eighteen years old. In leaving a gap in the syuzhet, the narration implies that nothing extraordinary took place in those intervening years. We will assume that the princess had an infancy, a childhood and an adolescence.

(Bordwell 1985: 54)

In one sense, Bordwell's description of this narrative sequence seems innocent enough. Of course we assume that the princess grew up and did not, say, disappear after birth and reappear at age eighteen. However, in another sense, it is profoundly misleading, for Bordwell insists not simply that we take for granted that the princess did not disappear on the basis of our knowledge of princesses and other human beings, but that this eventuality is ruled out only by the creation of an imaginary construct, the fabula, that fills in what happened. This is absurd. Consider a second fairy tale: 'A princess is born; in the next scene she is an infant; in the next, a child; in the next, an adolescent; and finally we see her when she is eighteen years old'. This fairy tale, according to Bordwell, would pose exactly the same problem of narrative comprehension. So we fill in the gaps again, but when would we finally grasp the story? Bordwell contends that the fabula is not a 'whimsical or arbitrary construct' for reasons that the processes by which we construct fabula are intersubjective (Bordwell 1985: 49). However, it is precisely the possibility of intersubjective agreement that is ruled out by his account, for how can I be sure that my fabula is the same as your fabula and that we fill in the gaps in the same way?

The problem here, once again, stems from Bordwell's constructivist perceptual psychology. Once the plot is assimilated to a set of perceptual cues, these cues take on the underdetermined status of stimuli. Thus even the simplest story such as the story of the princess leaves a putative gap or ambiguity which we must fill in with an imaginary construction of what took place. But it is only meaningful to speak of a gap or incompleteness in a story where it is meaningful to speak of completeness. Yet in Bordwell's conception of the fabula nothing could count as a complete narrative. In fact, there is nothing incomplete about the story of the princess. There is a shift in time, but this shift in time is not a gap that requires to be filled in. This move is required only where a story makes a gap explicit. Another example Bordwell gives of a gap in the syuzhet is a question posed in *Rear Window*: 'What happened to Mrs. Thorwald?' Here we can legitimately speak of a gap in the syuzhet that requires us to fill it in with an hypothesis about what actually happened or why. A different telling of the narrative of the princess might pose a question like: 'What happened between the time of the princess's birth and her eighteenth birthday that made her this way?' Narrative events as they are presented to us are not ambiguous or incomplete judged in relation to an elusive fabula. The question of ambiguity or incompleteness only arises when a narrative purposively manipulates elements of the plot and withholds information. If plots do not typically consist of cues that are incomplete, nor are stories typically constructions or fabrications out of a set of (visual) cues. The terms 'syuzhet' and 'fabula' do not meaningfully designate items with a different ontological status: real and imaginary. Rather, the terms 'syuzhet' and 'fabula', or 'plot' and 'story', are simply terms we can use, contrastively, to highlight the way in which what is told partly depends on the form of its telling.

There is another way in which spectators approach a film with prior assumptions about what they will be seeing: through the knowledge spectators have acquired of narrative conventions. One of Bordwell's uses of the term 'schemata' is in the context of describing what he calls the canonic story format which, according to Bordwell, is roughly this: 'introduction of setting and characters – explanation of a state of affairs – complicating action – ensuing events – outcome – ending' (Bordwell 1985: 35). It is undoubtedly true that spectators approach fiction film with very broad expectations of this kind, though to specify narrative conventions at this level of abstraction is not very informative. However, an important achievement of Bordwell's book is to isolate and enumerate, in an illuminating fashion, the conventions that govern different forms of fiction film narration, such as classical cinema narration and art cinema narration. A spectator goes to a Hollywood action film with the expectation that the film will be readily intelligible with a minimal amount of effort, but ease of intelligibility of a Hollywood film is itself a complex achievement on the part of film-makers, and Bordwell has provided us with a canonical account of that achievement. Art movie audiences, to put it crudely, expect visual stylization, ambiguity and psychological complexity, and again Bordwell has provided a rich and complex account of the conventions that govern the European art film. In a similar way, we may enumerate the conventions and corresponding expectations that govern different kinds of genre film.

Not only do spectators typically approach a film with an understanding of these conventions, but they may be tacit rather than explicit. However, the spectator's tacit or implicit understanding of these conventions is misunderstood if it is conceived as a process in which 'the perceiver gauges how well the narrative at hand can be slotted into the schema' (Bordwell 1985: 35). The idea that a spectator, armed with knowledge of narrative conventions, tests out the 'perceptual input' of the film by applying a schema to see whether or not the film conforms to it misconstrues the relationship of conventions to the text. It is the film that possesses the conventions; narrative conventions are properties of groups of texts. Narrative conventions are not the property of a spectator or an attribute of a spectator's mind. A spectator is possessed with familiarity or knowledge of those conventions that is manifest in their capacity to respond and react appropriately; to react, that is, as an informed observer to works that possess these conventions. It is worth noting that when it comes to anatomizing in detail the conventions of different kinds of narratives, Bordwell abandons talk of schemata in favour of a more historical and text-based account of those conventions. Though Bordwell presents this move as something that is merely a methodological option, it in fact preserves his account of narrative conventions from the incoherence that besets the theory of narrative comprehension in other parts of the work.

Underlying Bordwell's theory of narrative comprehension and the cognitive psychology on which Bordwell draws is the metaphor of perception and cognition as a processes of construction out of perceptual cues. But what does the perceptual cue to which we apply schemata consist in? Bordwell writes: 'Taken as a purely sensory experience, seeing is a bewildering flutter of impressions', and yet, 'you "immediately" see a visual array as consisting of objects distributed in three-dimensional space through the (nonconscious) application of schemata that organize perception' (Bordwell 1985: 31–2). To pick out a bird, we require a bird schemata, which according to Bordwell is a visual image. But how can the bird schemata pick out the relevant data from the bewildering flutter unless the outline of the bird is, as it were, already contained within that flutter? The schemata will tell us what cues count as bird cues, but the 'cues' can only be picked out of the flutter if we already see them there. If the 'cues' already exist within the bewildering flutter, then the concept of a schemata is not required to explain perception; perceptions are not constructions: we simply perceive a bird. Furthermore, we do not perceive a bird on the basis of visual 'cues', for perceiving the bird is not something else that takes place alongside, or as a result of, the registration of an independent set of data that qualify as 'cues'; rather, we simply perceive a bird. If visual perception was framed by schemata in the manner characterized by Bordwell, then one could never step outside the schemata to match the template with data provided from the sensory array. Schemata theory, in spite of Bordwell's protestations to the contrary, leads inexorably to the idealist conclusion that the perceptual identification of material objects is merely a projection of the mind and its categories upon an unknowable reality.

Gregory Currie's theory of filmic perception and cognition

Bordwell's application of perceptual cognitive theory to narrative film is not the only version of cognitive theory that has been applied to the medium, though it was a founding moment in the cognitive study of film and has been widely influential. I shall now turn to the film theory of the philosopher Gregory Currie. Aside from the force and breadth of Currie's arguments, my major reason for addressing his writing is strategic. Cognitivist theorists such as Currie have sought to emphasize the diversity of cognitive theory: 'Cognitive science is not a doctrine', Currie writes, 'there is no one theory of mind which all or a majority of cognitive scientists accept' (Currie 1995: xv).[6] Furthermore, Currie has explicitly contrasted his own approach to cognitive film theory with the writings of Bordwell. Yet, I shall argue that while there is a diversity in cognitive film theory that is manifested (for example) in the contrast between the views of Bordwell and Currie, there remains, beneath surface differences, an underlying conception of the mind which supports the cognitivist programme in film theory, a conception which, if Wittgenstein is correct, is profoundly mistaken. My approach to Currie's work will be highly selective; my purpose is to illustrate the implication of Currie's views for Bordwell's views, and whether in the long run they really make a difference.

Currie's approach to the cognitive psychology of film is distinct from Bordwell's in the manner that he conceives of the rationality of cognition and the rationality of film viewing, and in the role he ascribes to the psychology of perception in an overall cognitive psychology. As we have seen, Bordwell initiated the cognitivist programme in film studies to counter the prevailing view of film spectatorship as an essentially irrational enterprise. According to Bordwell's cognitive theory, the rationality of the human agent is defined by the way that reasoning informs and defines the activities of the mind and, more specifically, film spectatorship itself. Furthermore, the cognitive psychology of perception, in which an inference is made on the basis of 'interpreting' a perceptual input in the light of background beliefs, is a model for all cognitive psychology. Thus for Bordwell, all operations of the mind involve the interpretation of sensory inputs in the light of schemata, and all operations of the mind salient to narrative comprehension are 'guided by organized clusters of knowledge' (Bordwell 1985: 31). Bordwell's cognitive theory is holistic in two related senses. First, he draws no sharp boundary between perception and cognition. Second, he draws no sharp distinction between the mandatory 'bottom up' inferential processes that are said to characterize perception and the 'top down' inferential processes that are explicitly informed by expectations and beliefs. Both types of processes for Bordwell are inferentially based and interact with one another. In Bordwell's psychology of film viewing, the activity of perception is informed by schema, tacit bodies of knowledge, that allow us to identify what we see as, say, 'buying a loaf of bread'.

Currie, in contrast to Bordwell, is profoundly influenced by a modular theory of the mind of the kind developed by Jerry Fodor (1983) and others. According to this theory of the mind, the systems of perception are relatively autonomous from the 'higher order processing' that defines the acquisition of beliefs. They are, as Fodor puts it, 'encapsulated'. This relative autonomy is illustrated, for Fodor, in the way in which the percipient of the Müller–Lyer illusion continues to see two lines of unequal length regardless of what they know to be the case. Thus from Currie's standpoint, Bordwell's holistic conception of the mind turns out to be a conceptual muddle, for Bordwell's theory of narrative comprehension blurs the line between those cognitive processes that do and those that do not require the application of tacit beliefs or systems of belief to 'perceptual inputs'. For Currie, the mechanism of perception is relatively insulated from belief and the network of inference associated with belief. Furthermore, Currie argues that not all higher level cognitive processes can be understood in terms of inferences from bodies of belief, for human skills and abilities are characterized precisely by the un-self-conscious effortlessness with which they are performed. Thus not only does Bordwell misconstrue perception as an inferential process, he misconstrues the extent to which we do not comprehend such things as narratives by inference from a body of propositions or a primitive theory about how such things as narratives work that are embodied in schemata. For, according to Currie, there are other human faculties aside from the perceptual-cognitive faculty that define the operation of human intelligence, in particular the faculty of mental simulation that plays a central role in narrative comprehension.

Currie's criticisms thus seem to echo some of the criticisms I have already voiced when I argued that forming hypotheses and making inferences form only one part, though an important part, of narrative comprehension, and are misunderstood if assimilated to a misguided theory of perceptions as unconscious hypotheses or inferences. However, whereas I based my criticisms upon a diagnosis of the 'theoretical' picture of the mind and its functioning that underpins Bordwell's account, Currie believes that the deficiencies in Bordwell's theory can be rectified simply by making the proper theoretical discriminations between cognitive processes that involve the application of bodies of belief and knowledge, and those that do not, whether because they are more primitive (such as the faculty of perception), or because they simply operate quite differently (such as the faculty of simulation). For Bordwell, conscious mental operations in narrative comprehension are the tip of an iceberg. Bordwell conceives the relationship between the bottom of the iceberg and the tip as a relationship between a body of unconscious propositions that frame perceptual inputs and conscious mental processes that are essentially similar in nature, one tacit, one overt. I have argued that this picture of narrative comprehension is incoherent on the grounds that the constructivist picture of perception as inference that underlies it is incoherent. There are no unconscious inferential processes hidden underneath the kind of inferential procedures that we may employ to understand a film. Our ability to understand a film is manifest in the practices that exhibit our comprehension of it. Narrative comprehension neither involves nor makes manifest hidden causal processes. Currie, however, remains wedded to the idea that conscious mental operations in narrative comprehension remain the tip of the iceberg, but he proposes a different picture of the iceberg. For Currie, the mind is comprised of a hierarchy of autonomous interacting units with consciousness at the visible surface. Although the parts below the surface interact with the part above (as well as each other), their operation is not governed in the same way as the visible part by explicit or implicit knowledge and beliefs. Our capacity to perceive and our ability to understand narratives where the 'effort to understand' is not explicit should thus be conceived not in terms of the application of a tacit body of beliefs to perceptual inputs but in terms of the operation of unconscious mental mechanisms.

Unlike Bordwell, Currie is a philosopher rather than a scholar of film and thus he approaches developing a cognitive psychology of film with philosophical problems in mind.[7] Because he is not concerned with philosophical issues *per se*, Bordwell, in his treatment of perception, makes very little out of the fact that films are depictions. He treats pictorial representations as 'inherently incomplete and potentially ambiguous' in the manner of other visual stimuli. Thus the problem for Bordwell, of 'constructing' an understanding of what it is that we see represented in a film, is treated as analogous to the problem of 'constructing' what it is that we see when we see something that is not a visual representation. Currie, in contrast, develops his account of perception in the context of explaining how it is that 'certain pictures and their subjects appear alike: that the experience of looking at the picture is in certain respects like that of looking at the subject' (Currie 1995: 80). According to Currie, in both cases I visually recognize something, but only in the case of the thing itself do I judge that I actually see something:

> my visual capacity to recognize a horse is the capacity to associate some visual feature of what I see with the concept horse, thereby enabling me to bring what I see under that concept. In that case, when I see that the picture depicts a horse, I must associate some visual feature of what I see, namely a picture, with the concept horse. What the picture of the horse has in common with the horse is some spatial feature which triggers my horse-recognition capacity.
>
> (Currie 1995: 81)

However:

> having your horse-recognition capacity triggered and judging that there is a horse in front of you are different things. They differ as to the level at which these operations are conducted in the mind. Judging that there is a horse in front of me is something that I do; it is an operation conducted at the personal level. Having my horse-recognition capacity triggered happens at a lower, subpersonal, level of functioning; it is something that happens within me.
>
> (Currie 1995: 83)

Currie continues:

> there is a not-very-intelligent homunculus in my visual system who
> is charged with the task of matching the visual input with a series of
> stored models of known objects and who is fairly easy to fool into
> thinking that the visual input derives from a horse, or whatever
> object is the best match he can find for the input.
>
> (Currie 1995: 86)

However, the conclusion of this encapsulated operational subsystem is
rejected and corrected by higher, more integrated processing that notes the
dissimilarities between horses and pictures of horses.

How does this theory of perception rectify the problems entailed by
Bordwell's application of a theory of perceptions as inferences to the analysis
of film? As we have seen, one of the central problems of Bordwell's appropria-
tion of constructivist theory is the equivocation evident in Bordwell's writings
and the writing of the cognitivist psychologists upon which he draws between
the concept of perceptions as unconscious inferences and the idea that we
identify what it is that we perceive on the basis of conscious inferences (tacit
or not). It is not clear that Currie would wish to abandon the idea of perceptions as unconscious inferences (Fodor does not), but he does wish to avoid
the equivocation that attends the concept and its use. By conceiving the visual
recognition system as a primitive self-contained homunculus that scans the
visual input in a manner that provisionally bypasses beliefs, Currie apparently
avoids conflating the activity of perceiving something with the conscious (tacit
or not) deployment of schemata. The visual processing system works 'not on
the basis of a detailed, comprehensive examination of the visual input in the
light of background belief and all the rest, but on the basis of just a few clues
extracted from the visual input itself' (Currie 1995: 85). Currie believes that a
second advantage accrues to his theory of perception from the fact that it
allows us to speak of actually seeing a horse rather than merely formulating
the hypothesis that we see a horse. In other words, Currie's theory seems to
avoid the spectre of idealism. Yet these theoretical advantages are purchased
at an extremely heavy price.

Currie speaks of a visual capacity to recognize something in a manner
that confuses the concepts of perception and recognition. He sets out to
explain how certain pictures and their subject matter 'appear alike' or how
the experience of looking at depictions is like looking at their subject matter
by 'our visual capacity to recognize' that he understands as the association
of a visual input with a concept. But we may look at a horse without recognizing that it is a horse, that is, without being able to classify or identify
what it is that we see as a horse. Seeing something does not presuppose
recognizing (in this sense) what it is. Furthermore, recognizing what something is is not the same as recognizing that something is like (or unlike)

something else, for I may perceive similarities and differences between two things without knowing what it is I am comparing. Perhaps all Currie means by our visual capacity to recognize is our capacity to point something out: to individuate it and compare it with other things. But such a capacity does not, as Currie contends, result in a confusion of one thing with another (horses and pictures of horses), quite the reverse. Currie seems to draw a distinction between seeing a horse depiction and seeing a horse on the grounds that while in both cases I visually recognize a horse, only in the second case do I actually see a horse. But this implies that I may 'visually recognize' a horse without seeing it, which appears, on the face of it, a nonsensical claim. Of course, Currie's locutions are motivated by his homuncular theory of the mind. But it is important to note, at the outset, just how much forcing of our mental concepts is already required in order to formulate this picture.

Here is Currie's most explicit statement of the homuncular picture of the mind:

> We can think of [a] person as constituted by a hierarchy (or complex of hierarchies) of intelligent creatures or homunculi. The farther down the hierarchy you go, the less intelligent is the homunculus carrying out the operations at that level, until we reach the ground floor, where intelligence bottoms out into straightforward causal interactions where notions of information, reason, evidence and inference play no role, and where everything that happens is driven by brute causal powers in accordance with natural law. The person or agent himself occupies the top level of the hierarchy and is more intelligent than any of the homunculi that operate at subpersonal levels...The primary insight of the homuncular or hierarchical view is that, when an operation is conducted below the personal level, we are not driven to describe that operation in purely causal, nomological terms. We can describe it as a task carried out for a certain purpose, employing information of certain kinds, and conducted within certain constraints of efficiency, reliability and so forth. That way, we describe it as a task performed by a subpersonal homunculus.
>
> (Currie 1995: 84)

While Currie rejects the idea that perceptual reports are dependent upon thought-like processes, he nonetheless enthusiastically embraces the idea that we can ascribe psychological predicates to a person's brain and parts of a person's brain. Currie asserts that the 'visual recognition system' 'recognizes something' that it 'sees' or at least that it identifies an object that is in front of it. Furthermore, this visual recognition system is capable of making a 'mistake', since, according to Currie's homuncular picture of the mind, one part of the brain visually recognizes a horse when it looks at the picture while another part of the brain corrects this perceptual error. This kind of talk is suggestive of and undoubtedly motivated by the analogy between computers and thinking creatures that is dear to the cognitive scientists upon which Currie (and indeed Bordwell) draws. Computers think like thinking creatures, therefore thinking creatures think like computers. But computers do not think, for in order to think one must be capable of following rules which are instruments that thinking creatures use, for example, to correct themselves when they wrongly identify something and to measure their mistakes. Rule following is a purposive activity undertaken to achieve a goal and the ways in which rules govern human activity are manifest in human activity. If a computer hooked up to a light-sensitive input misidentifies an object, the 'mistake' it makes is either a result of malfunctioning or an error in programming, unless the misidentification was planned. The computer that 'corrects' this mistake has not realized it has made an error, nor can it correct the error in the light of this realization. The 'correction' is simply an adjustment that has already been made in a pre-programmed, causally necessary, mechanical sequence of events. This is quite unlike the mistake made by an agent who uses a rule to achieve a certain end, realizes he has made a mistake by evaluating what he did, and justifies a new course of action by appeal to the rule he was following.[8]

In this passage, and elsewhere, Currie implicitly denies that there is a conceptual distinction between normative, rule-governed actions and causal mechanisms, and between persons and brains (or computers), there is just a hierarchy of more complex and less complex systems. Yet his theory depends upon the assumption that there is a conceptual distinction to draw between operations at the higher personal level and brute causal processes at the lower level. The distinction is blurred through Currie's use of the vocabulary of 'purpose'. It is of course possible to ascribe a purpose in the sense of a function, a telos, or a rationale to a causal system, and it may well be fruitful to conceive the interaction of parts of the brain in these terms. But the vocabulary of 'purpose' does not apply to an agent in the same way as it applies to a mechanism, and its application to a mechanism does not make that mechanism person-like or intelligent creature-like: we do not explain human agency in functional terms. A biological organism might be said to be purposive in the sense of functionally organized to bring about a certain end. But this is a very different sense of purpose than the purposiveness we ascribe to a human agent that is normative in character. By blurring the distinction between the functional purposiveness of an organ and the purposiveness of an agent, Currie mistakenly invites us to believe that human beings are simply highly complicated purposive (in the biological sense) organisms and that understanding the complexity of purposive human behaviour is an empirical matter awaiting the discoveries of cognitive science.

Let me now turn to the mental mechanism proposed by Currie to account for narrative comprehension. When Bordwell addresses the problem of narrative comprehension, what is particular to narrative comprehension is only that understanding fictional narratives mobilizes distinctive narrative schemata and makes explicit processes that are implicit. Currie's account of mental simulation is developed in the context of addressing a philosophical problem correlative to the problem of depiction; namely, how is it that we can emotionally respond to something that we know not to exist? The answer is, for Currie, that we possess a 'faculty of imagination' that allows us to simulate the mental processes that we would have if we were in a given situation, whether that situation is the experience of another person that we cannot literally have, or the experience of a fictional world that does not literally exist. When I mentally simulate, 'I let my mental processes run as if I really were in that situation – except that those processes run "off-line", disconnected from their normal sensory inputs and behavioral outputs' (Currie 1995: 144). Thus, for example, I do not acquire from the fiction a belief that the green slime is going to attack that causes me to respond emotionally, I acquire an 'imagining' that simulates the belief state and causes my emotional response. Fictions activate simulation in two ways: First, they require us to imagine those things that make the fiction fictional, for example, that Kane becomes an unsympathetic, cantankerous old man in *Citizen Kane* (Currie calls this kind of imagining 'primary imagining'). Second, they encourage us to imagine various things within the fiction that support primary imagining, for example, we identify with the sense of belittlement experienced by Kane's second wife, Susan Alexander (Currie calls this 'secondary imagining').

The broad significance of this theory for understanding narrative comprehension is suggested in an experiment Currie reports on to illustrate the rationale for his theory.[9] When a child is between three-and-a-half and four-and-a-half, it develops the ability to adopt the point of view of a third party. This is illustrated by the following experiment: the child sees Sally, a puppet, hide a sweet in box A. Sally leaves the room. The child sees another puppet move the sweet to box B. Sally returns. Question: where does Sally think her sweet is? Three-year-olds say box B. Five-year-olds know better and say it is box A. Now Bordwell, in accord with the cognitive theorists he cites, might claim here that the child has acquired a theory about what is going on that could be expressed in a principle of the following kind: under circumstances where the acquisition of knowledge is restricted to what somebody sees, when someone does not see something happen they usually will not know that it happened. He might formulate the following 'procedural schemata': 'If someone does not see something happen, treat it as something that the person does not know about'. However, Currie argues that the kind of knowledge at stake is a question of 'knowing how' rather than 'knowing that'. The child's ability is not explained by the fact that they have acquired a rudimentary theory (whether learned or innate), but that they are now able to mobilize an innate human capacity to imagine situations from the point of view of another through mental simulation:

> The Simulation Hypothesis says that we do have a reliable model of the mental processes of others, namely our own mental processes run off-line. Using the model, we are able to draw conclusions about other minds, without having a theory of how minds, including our own, work.
>
> (Currie 1995: 146)

Currie's theory of imagination as mental simulation is a very general theory of the mind with widespread ramifications. Here I am interested only in how Currie's approach to cognitive theory might account for narrative comprehension. When we see a person in a film buying a loaf of bread, we do not understand what this action is on the basis of testing perceptual inputs against a body of beliefs, we perceive a represented fictional action through the activation of our 'visual recognition system' and this prompts us to mentally simulate that someone is buying a loaf of bread. Furthermore, we may also be prompted to simulate the thoughts and feelings had by the character when they buy a loaf of bread, a secondary simulation that will nourish the primary simulation. Currie's theory therefore affords a general account of understanding fictional narratives that resists assimilation of narrative understanding to an explicit or implicit process of reasoning. Instead, narrative comprehension is a largely automatic, effortless process that is explained by the largely unconscious operation of the mental mechanism of simulation. We are enjoined to make an effort to understand, to form hypotheses and make inferences about what we see and hear, only under certain circumstances:

> Through incompetence and sometimes through design, the characters of fiction resist simulation: their responses to situations, their words, even their thoughts (in so far as the author lets us know what they are) seem not to be those we would have in their situations. In these cases, when we engage with the fiction, trying to guess what will happen, trying to fill in its background of unstated presuppositions and undescribed events, we may have to rely more than usual on inferences we make concerning the author's intentions or about constraints of form and genre the work conforms to.
>
> (Currie 1995: 155)

What justifies Currie's assimilation of the concept of imagination to the concept of simulation? To simulate something is to make a physical copy of it. We speak of simulation in the context of replicating or modelling one physical system by another, say a computer. The term 'mental simulation' is a term of art, a metaphor in which mental 'processes' are compared to physical ones. It is thus intrinsically misleading, for it begs the question as to whether psychological predicates can be explained in physical terms. Considered as a term of art the verb 'to mentally simulate' could perhaps be substituted for the verb 'to imagine' in contexts where visual imagination is required–such as when John Lennon invited us to 'picture yourself on a boat on a river with tangerine trees and marmalade skies'. But visualization is not a necessary accompaniment of imagination. I need not visualize something when I follow Lennon's injunction in another song to 'imagine there's no heaven'. It might be claimed that in this case we nonetheless simulate because if we follow Lennon's injunction we have, say, the emotional responses we would have had were there no heaven. But it is not the emotional responses that are simulated, according to the theory; they are real. It is the initial condition that causes the emotional response that is simulated, the condition of imagining there being no heaven. But in what, if not visual imagining, does this simulation consist? Furthermore, a central use of the verb to imagine is 'to imagine that something'. 'Imagining that p' is often a cognate of 'to think that p' as in 'I imagined that this paper would be finished by now'. But it makes no sense to say that when I imagined that my paper would be finished, I simulated that the paper would be finished. Yet 'imagining that p' is precisely what Currie claims is the form of mental simulation that is required for us to engage with works of fiction that invite me to imagine that such-and-such occurred.

Currie in fact explicitly disclaims that he is 'offering a piece of conceptual analysis' (Currie 1995: 151) when he equates imagination with simulation. Instead he claims that his proposal:

> has closer methodological affinities to such essentialist identifications as the claim that water is H_2O. This is not to be understood as offering an analysis of the concept of water; the claim is rather that water has a hidden inner structure that is explanatory of its more evident surface properties, and which may bring with it some surprising consequences – that water is not really a continuous substance.
>
> (Currie 1995: 152)

This claim is a classic illustration of the double reduction characteristic of theoretical explanations of the mind explored in the introduction to this volume. The concept of imagination, in spite of its surface diversity, Currie claims, is reducible to simulation. In order to make this reduction at all plausible, Currie claims that what the imagination really is is something hidden, something discernible only by the theorist. But while the analogy leads us to believe that conceptual investigation is being replaced by empirical inquiry in contrast to conceptual analysis, it turns out that the empirical inquiry does have a conceptual payoff, for Currie concludes that a result of empirical investigation is that water can no longer be defined as a continuous substance. So, in spite of Currie's disclaimer, the analysis of the imagination as simulation is, after all, a piece of conceptual analysis. But if his analysis of the imagination is a work of conceptual analysis then it is obviously inadequate, as I have suggested. If it is not a conceptual analysis but a putative empirical inquiry or theory of how the brain works, it has no bearing on our concept. The molecular structure of water does explain its surface properties, but it does not entail the consequence that water is not a continuous substance, as if the discovery of H_2O requires us to change the way we describe what we see when we turn on the tap. We may, under the influence of science, choose no longer to describe water as a continuous substance and discriminate between the discontinuity that characterizes the flow of water and the discontinuity that characterizes dripping water, but the value of such a conceptual innovation is far from obvious, and it has not been widely embraced despite the fact that knowledge of the molecular structure of water is one piece of scientific knowledge that is virtually universally held! This is not to deny the importance of discovering that the molecular structure of water is H_2O, it is to deny that this discovery changes the meaning, that is the use, of the word water. If we resist redefining water as discontinuous substance, consider the cost to the richness of our self-understanding if we were to reduce the myriad senses of imagination to that of mental simulation.[10]

Currie reiterates with disarming explicitness the incoherent conception of mind as a homunculus that underpins constructivist psychology. Currie's cognitive theory explicitly rehearses the erroneous assumptions about the mind that are merely implicit in Bordwell's theory. Currie attributes normativity to a mechanism, and he attributes psychological predicates to a part of a person that can only be coherently attributed to a whole. The fact that Currie explicitly embraces the homuncular conception of the mind only attests to the unquestioned status that this picture of the mind has for its adherents. The idea of the mind as a homunculus or as, in Currie's theory, a network of homunculi, deserves to be considered as much of an unquestioned doctrinal assumption for many cognitive (film) theorists as the picture of the mind as an unconscious mind is unquestioned dogma for many psychoanalytic (film) theorists. The redress Currie's theory offers to the flaws in Bordwell's account of perception and cognition is thus merely illusory, for Currie merely substitutes one set of unconscious mental mechanisms for another. Currie's 'visual recognition system' and 'mechanism of mental stimulation', replace the contructivist's conception that perception and cognition involve the application of tacit beliefs or schemata, and his account is prone to similar conceptual confusions. Furthermore, Currie's account of perception and cognition, focusing as it does on unconscious mental mechanisms that are different in kind from conscious levels of engagement solicited by films, detracts from the detailed analysis and understanding of the sensuous artefact, film, that lies at the centre of film scholarship and at the heart of Bordwell's achievement in spite of the incoherent theory he uses to support and motivate his scholarship.

Conclusion: cognitivism and humanism

In his recent discussion of cognitive film theory, Currie develops a contrast between cognitive film theory and psycho-semiotic Marxism and related theoretical positions. He astutely observes that a defining characteristic of theorization in the arts in general in the last twenty-five years by scholars working in the humanities has been a rejection of the idea of a humanistic study of the arts through appeal to a deep psychological theory:

> Much of the revolt against traditional humanistic studies of the arts has been based on a rejection of that tradition's casual assumption of a community of values, concerns, and interests – indeed of a whole conception of human flourishing – which many contemporary scholars reject as unsystematic, subjective and deriving from an unacknowledged hegemony of a certain class, race and sex. The 'common-sense' view of human beings having been unmasked as the insidious creature of interest, an alternative had to be found: thus the appeal of psychoanalysis and similar constructions.
>
> (Currie 1999: 108)

Thus, for example feminist anti-humanist film scholars turned to a combination of psychoanalysis, semiotics and Marxism to create a 'deep psychological' theory of the 'human subject' that purported to reveal the way that human purpose and motive is framed in advance by systems of signification and culture, such as film, that are bound by gender inequity (see, for example, Silverman 1983, 1988). Why the intellectual weed of theoretical anti-humanism found such fertile soil among the seeds of humanist film study in the 1970s had to do at least in part with the inherent weaknesses of an approach to film grounded in celebrating the director as auteur in an art form, film, that is primarily a mass art. Film is an art form that is easy to denigrate from a conservative humanist perspective, and thus it is not surprising that disgruntled humanities scholars could discover in the retrograde aspects of mass culture justification for theories that swept aside a humanistic understanding of culture *in toto*.[11]

However, Currie also argues that cognitive film theory serves as an antidote to theoretical anti-humanism:

> a point that seems to underlie a good deal of cognitivist work is this: it is a mistake to think that we can speak and write productively about the experience of film only by appealing to a 'deep'

psychological theory, that is one that postulates states, processes, and mechanisms not acknowledged by our quotidian psychological knowledge – the 'folk psychology' we unreflectingly use everyday in order to predict and explain the behavior of others and perhaps of ourselves... Folk psychology is, in fact, a subtle and successful instrument for helping us make sense of the community of minds in which we find ourselves immersed... While a cognitive film-theorist's official position is that we should use the best available psychological theory, her strong and well-founded impression may be that folk psychology fits that description very well.

(Currie 1999: 108)

Currie's assumption here is that our ordinary psychological vocabulary that informs the humanistic understanding of arts and culture is part of a rudimentary theory of the mind that, while it may be a superior theory to deep psychology, can and should be weighed against it as we seek to explicate and understand our responses to film. Although Currie contingently defends our ordinary psychological vocabulary, he nonetheless argues that it is, in principle, eliminable by a better theory. But to construe our ordinary psychological concepts as part of an, in principle, eliminable theory of the mind is to profoundly misconstrue their nature. And in misunderstanding the nature of our psychological concepts as in principle replaceable by a superior scientific theory, cognitive film theory unwittingly shares the same anti-humanism of the kind of psychoanalytic theory that it has tried to displace. For although driven by an ideological agenda, psycho-semiotic Marxism placed its faith in a version of 'science' to sweep away the naive impressionistic mumblings of humanistic scholarship. While a cognitive theorist such as Currie claims allegiance to 'folk psychology', it still 'must be regimented, refined, and indeed corrected by more academic constructions'.

What then is wrong with construing our ordinary psychological concepts as a rudimentary theory of human behaviour, and why is such a conception anti-humanist? The answers to these questions are already sketched in the introduction to this volume, and the first is addressed in the argument of this chapter.[12] They will be briefly sketched again here. Currie supposes that our ordinary psychological concepts are theoretical terms for unobservable states and processes. But many of our psychological concepts do not refer to states or processes of the mind, and many only in some of their uses. When we use a psychological verb in the first person – 'I liked that movie' – we are not entertaining a hypothesis about an inner mental entity, we are giving expression to or manifesting our love of the film. And our expression of liking the movie together with all the characteristic behaviour and attitudes that surround the expression are constitutive of our liking the movie. When we use a psychological verb in the third person – 'She liked that movie' – we are not making a hypothesis about or inferring the mental state of another on the basis of her behaviour, as if the true nature of the state could be discovered within, like Currie's mechanism of mental simulation, as if, after two millennia of waiting we finally can understand what our imaginative engagement with art really consists in! We may explain why someone saw the film a second time by saying that she liked it, but this explanation is not a theoretical explanation. The fact that she liked the film is a reason for seeing it again, not a cause, for it does not necessitate her action and it is perfectly possible that under the same circumstances she or someone else would not go to the movie. While we may form a generalization about her behaviour 'she typically goes to see a movie again that she likes', this is quite unlike a causal, nomological, generalization, for it helps define the concept involved in the generalization. Part of what defines 'liking and experience' is that experiences we like we often like to experience again.

The key point about our psychological concepts is that they are manifestations of our 'inner life' that are partly constitutive together with our expressions and behaviour of what that 'inner life' consists. Furthermore, it is this 'inner life', manifested in our immensely rich psychological vocabulary, that makes human beings distinctively human. To be sure, we can attribute primitive psychological concepts to animals – 'my dog wants to go for a walk with me' – but only human beings can entertain plans for the future and apply the lessons of the past to the present and future and only human beings can exhibit the finely nuanced and rich emotional life that language affords. The corollary of this view of human beings is that only human beings or creatures like them can develop and entertain the pleasures of art that serves itself to manifest distinctively human aspirations, achievements, and forms of life. To construe our psychological vocabulary as a primitive psychological theory is thus not only to misconstrue it, for to the extent that this confusion becomes endemic it threatens to reduce or impoverish human self-understanding which art and the criticism of art, including the art of film, manifests and reflects. This is not to suggest that cognitive theory is about to take over the humanistic study of film in the way that theoretical anti-humanism threatened to do, for, in the work of most cognitive theorists, the commitment to cognitive theory as a paradigm of explanation is tempered by their concern to understand and explicate the art of film. The work of David Bordwell is exemplary here of the way that a research programme framed by cognitivism can nonetheless yield extraordinarily rich insights into film. Nor do I wish to deny the central role of psychology in explaining the causal basis of our psychological capacities and the conditions under which we exercise them. For example, the psychology of film spectatorship promises to illuminate a great deal about the way in which films mobilize and constrain the mobilization of our natural visual capacities. In this sense, science and humanistic understanding do not conflict, the conflict occurs only when psychology confuses the task of empirical inquiry with the elucidation of our psychological concepts and their application to understanding our engagement with arts such as film. But I do want to affirm the intuitive sense of many scholars working in humanistic study of the arts, that scientific approaches to art, while they may be intrinsically valuable, can only have a circumscribed place in relationship to the main intellectual concerns of the humanist scholar.

Notes

1 Noël Carroll, in particular, has mounted a sustained assault on the mind/film analogy; see Carroll (1988, 1996a).
2 All subsequent citations in this section are to Bordwell (1985).
3 For a more extensive analysis of philosophical misconceptions regarding 'the inner', see Hacker (1990: 127–41).
4 All subsequent citations in this section are to Bordwell (1985).
5 See Carroll (1996b).
6 All subsequent citations in this section are to Currie (1995) unless otherwise stated.
7 There is not the space here to address the philosophical problems raised by Currie directly. I am concerned only with how Currie's solutions to these problems involve cognitive theory and to criticize the assumptions underlying the application of cognitive theory to film.
8 This is just a gesture towards the argument as to why computers do not think. For further argument see Hacker (1990: 59–82) and Hyman (1991: 1–26).
9 This experiment was developed by Hans Wimmer and Josef Perner (1983) and replicated in a variety of settings.
10 For a sustained analysis of the relationship between empirical discovery and conceptual understanding, and the confusions wrought by conflating normative understanding and empirical inquiry in the field of perception, see Hacker (1987).
11 There are thus startling affinities between the views of film of right-wing cultural elitists such as Roger Scruton (1983) and left-wing psychoanalytically-inclined film theorists (see Rosen 1985).
12 For a seminal analysis of methodology in psychology that has influenced both the overall argument of this essay and, especially, these concluding paragraphs, see Hacker (1996: 401–45).

Bibliography

Bordwell, D. (1985) *Narration in the Fiction Film*, Madison, WI: The University of Wisconsin Press.
—— (1989) 'A Case for Cognitivism', *Iris* 9 (Spring): 11–40.
Carroll, N. (1988) *Mystifying Movies: Fads and Fallacies in Contemporary Film Theory*, New York: Columbia University Press, 293-304.
—— (1996a) 'Film/Mind Analogies: the Case of Hugo Munsterberg', in *Theorizing the Moving Image*, New York: Cambridge University Press, 94–117.
—— (1996b) 'Toward a Theory of Film Suspense', in *Theorizing the Moving Image*, New York: Cambridge University Press.
Currie, G. (1995) *Image and Mind: Film Philosophy and Cognitive Science*, New York: Cambridge University Press.
—— (1999) 'Cognitivism', in T. Miller and R. Stam (eds), *A Companion to Film Theory*, Oxford: Basil Blackwell: 105–22.

Fodor, J.A. (1983) *The Modularity of Mind: An Essay on Faculty Psychology*, Cambridge, MA: MIT Press.

Gregory, R.L. (1973) 'The Confounded Eye', in R.L. Gregory and E.H. Gombrich (eds), *Illusion in Nature and Art*, London: Duckworth: 49–96.

—— (1990) *Eye and Brain: The Psychology of Seeing*, Princeton, NJ: Princeton University Press.

Hacker, P.M.S. (1987) *Appearance and Reality: A Philosophical Investigation into Perception and Perceptual Qualities*, Cambridge, MA: Basil Blackwell.

—— (1990) *Wittgenstein: Meaning and Mind*, Oxford: Basil Blackwell.

—— (1991) 'Experimental Methods and Conceptual Confusion: An Investigation into R.L. Gregory's Theory of Perception', *The Jerusalem Philosophical Quarterly* 40 (July): 289–314.

—— (1996) *Wittgenstein: Mind and Will*, Oxford: Basil Blackwell.

Hastie, R. (1981) 'Schematic Principles in Human Memory', in E.T. Higgins, C.P. Herman and M.P. Zanna (eds), *Social Cognition: The Ontario Symposium*, Hilldale, NJ: Lawrence Erlbaum, vol. I: 39–88.

Heath, S. (1981) *Questions of Cinema*, Bloomington, Indiana University Press.

Hyman, J. (1989) *The Imitation of Nature*, Oxford: Basil Blackwell.

—— (1991) 'Introduction', in J. Hyman (ed.), *Investigating Psychology: Sciences of the Mind After Wittgenstein*, New York: Routledge.

Kenny, A. (1991) 'The Homunculus Fallacy', in J. Hyman (ed.), *Investigating Psychology: Sciences of the Mind After Wittgenstein*, New York: Routledge, 155–65.

Rock, I. (1983) *The Logic of Perception*, Cambridge, MA: MIT Press.

Rosen, P. (ed.) (1985) *Narrative, Apparatus, Ideology: A Film Theory Reader*, New York: Columbia University Press.

Scruton, R. (1983) *The Aesthetic Understanding: Essays in the Philosophy of Art and Culture*, New York: Methuen.

Silverman, K. (1983) *The Subject of Semiotics*, New York : Oxford University Press.

—— (1988) *The Acoustic Mirror: The Female Voice in Psychoanalysis and Cinema*, Bloomington, Indiana University Press.

Wimmer, H. and Perner, J. (1983) 'Beliefs About Beliefs: Representation and Constraining Function of Wrong Beliefs in Young Children's Understanding of Deception', *Cognition* 13: 103–28.

Wittgenstein, L. (1953) *Philosophical Investigations* (PI), trans. G.E.M. Anscombe, Oxford: Basil Blackwell.

9

THE CODED-MESSAGE MODEL OF LITERATURE

Severin Schroeder

In memoriam Reinhold Vogt (1961–99)

A 'work of art', wrote Wittgenstein in 1947, 'does not aim to convey *something else*, just itself' (CV: 58). This is a response to Tolstoy's view that art is supposed to convey feelings. Wittgenstein's main objection to this arousal theory – an objection that has been widely accepted in philosophical aesthetics today – is that it would make the work itself in principle dispensable (BB: 178, LA: 29). And that seems wrong. Even if a drug were invented that gave us the same pleasant feelings as the *Eroica* Symphony, we would still want to listen to the music. For we value art not (primarily) as an instrument to an independently specifiable end, but for its own sake.

At least with respect to literature, arousal theories have gone out of fashion. But the academic study of literature seems to be dominated by a doctrine that is equally open to Wittgenstein's anti-instrumentalist objection. Twentieth-century literary theory is almost entirely ruled by the view that the value or interest of a work of literature consists in its conveying to us a certain message. This is quite obvious with those schools of literary theory that advocate a reading guided by some political ideology or concern. Marxist critics are naturally interested in what a given work tells us, intentionally or unintentionally, about class struggle, or the progression of society through various historical stages. And something analogous is true of psychoanalysis, poststructuralism, feminism, postcolonialism, lesbian/gay criticism and new historicism. There is not much to be gained from quarrelling with those whose 'theories' are just expressions of their ruling non-literary interests. Someone to whom class war (or the liberation of women) is of paramount importance will naturally focus on (or 'foreground') those aspects of literature that relate to it, rather than the traditional concerns of aesthetics. And why not? But there is no point in discussing aesthetic issues in literature with those who are not interested in the *aesthetics* of literature, but only in its political significance.

One major school of literary theory, however, seems concerned with literature for its own sake, and not just as a means to pursue other ideological

210

Literature for its own sake!

commitments; that is <u>structuralism</u>. But even in structuralism, the view that literary value lies in a work's message is <u>endemic</u>. And that is not surprising. For structuralism (or semiotics) is based on <u>linguistics</u>. As <u>linguists are concerned with the way words and sentences convey a particular meaning, structuralists investigate the way in which works of verbal art convey a particular meaning:</u> either in general (poetics), or in specific instances (interpretations) (see, for example, Culler 1981: 37). This meaning, or message, is usually taken to be <u>hidden,</u> written in a code that needs to be deciphered by <u>linguistically trained readers.</u> Indeed, this *coded-message* model has very much the status of an axiom in most versions of structuralism. In the words of the Franco-American structuralist Michael Riffaterre:

> poetry expresses concepts and things by <u>indirection.</u> To put it simply, a poem says one thing and means another…what constitutes [the poem's] message, has little to do with what it tells us or with the language it employs.
>
> (Riffaterre 1978: 1, 13)

Similarly, the Russian structuralist Yuri M. Lotman maintains that: '<u>literature possesses an exclusive, inherent system of signs and rules governing their combination which serve to transmit special messages</u>' (Lotman 1970: 21). Structural analysis will explain those peculiar 'signs and rules' and thus uncover the text's message, the meaning of the 'integral sign' as which a work of literature should be regarded (Lotman 1970: 22). Thus structural analysis brings to light a text's 'formerly hidden semantic content' (Lotman 1972: 36). It amounts to deciphering a code, <u>for in literature: 'Meaning is formed through…recoding'</u> (Lotman 1970: 35–60). Again, according to the American structuralist Robert Scholes, in poetic interpretation we are trying to discover 'new meanings' (Scholes 1982: 42–3) which the text contains only 'implicitly' (Scholes 1982: 56).[1]

Given a literary theorist's aspiration to something like the scientist's role and prestige, in conjunction with an insistence on the autonomy of poetics (perhaps as a new branch of linguistics), that basic assumption, the coded-message model, is readily understandable. Indeed, it seems almost unavoidable. For after all, science produces knowledge; hence literary theory, as a would-be science of literature, must do so too. Some of that knowledge may be fairly abstract: an explanation of the aesthetically relevant features of literary texts in general. But literary theorists will also be expected to have something new and worthwhile to say about particular poems and novels. They will be expected to give interpretations. <u>An interpretation is a paraphrase of the text's hidden meaning.</u> So there has to *be* a hidden meaning. In short, the literary text must be like a coded message awaiting deciphering. And it must have an unexpected solution. As Riffaterre says: 'the reader … solves [a] puzzle' (Riffaterre 1978: 165).

Rhyme and reason

How, then, does a poetic text acquire its implicit meaning? A prevalent structuralist answer to this question is derived from Roman Jakobson's doctrine of the poetic function, encapsulated in the slogan: 'The poetic function projects the principle of equivalence from the axis of selection into the axis of combination' (Jakobson 1960: 71).

What does that mean? For Jakobson (following Saussure), ordinary, non-poetic speech or writing is governed by two modes of arrangement: selection and combination. To produce the utterance 'The child is sleeping', the speaker first selects the words from classes of near synonyms. Thus he chooses a noun from a list containing 'child', 'kid', 'youngster' and 'tod'; and picks out the verb 'sleep' in preference to semantically close verbs like 'doze', 'nod' or 'nap'. In each case a word is selected on the base of equivalence, that is, 'similarity and dissimilarity, synonymity and antonymity'. Then these words are combined to form a sentence. This operation is based on contiguity. In poetic language, however, the formation of a sentential sequence is governed by the principle of equivalence. That is to say, in poetry one finds relations of equivalence among the words of a given sequence. First of all equivalence in sound (rhyme, assonance or consonance), which Jakobson calls the 'constitutive principle' of the poetic sequence (Jakobson 1960: 83). But then – and this is the crucial step – it is claimed that 'equivalence in sound…inevitably involves semantic equivalence' (Jakobson 1960: 83). And such semantic equivalence is the source of additional, implicit, meaning in poetry.

Note incidentally how nugatory the trimmings of linguistic theory are in terms of which Jakobson presents his doctrine. The combination of words to form a sentence is said to be 'based on contiguity'. Now, obviously, the words of a sentence do not usually denote objects that are literally *in touch* with each other. So all we can make of this claim is a vague and trivial metaphor: what the words of a sentence (particles apart) denote are *thematically connected*, or have *something to do with each other*. Again, in non-poetic texts 'the principle of equivalence' is said to govern 'the axis of selection'. That evokes the picture of a speaker equipped with *Roget's Thesaurus*, constantly pondering ranges of near synonyms. But of course speakers do not usually consider and choose from a list of related words. Most utterances do not really involve any act or axis of selection. There are, to be sure, equivalents (near synonyms and antonyms) for most words. But what is the '*principle* of equivalence'? Is it the rule that in each case one chooses a word to which there are equivalents? A vacuous rule, for what else could one do? In short, the high-sounding pronouncement that the principle of equivalence governs the axis of selection boils down to the trivial observation that for each word you could find other words similar (or dissimilar) in meaning.

Jakobson defines a poetic text as a text in which different expressions are equivalent in sound and meaning.[2] Hence, structural features of the text turn out to be meaningful in as much as they can be taken to represent semantic features. As Lotman puts it, in poetry, 'a text's formal elements are semanticized' (Lotman 1970: 17). The ordered repetition of combinations of phonemes yields 'additional meaning' (Lotman 1970: 22, 106–7). As an illustration of his theory, Jakobson discusses assonances and paronomasias in Edgar Allan Poe's 'The Raven' (Jakobson 1960: 86–7). For instance, in the following line: 'And the Raven, never flitting, still is sitting, *still* is sitting' – the ominous word 'never' is a phonetic mirror image of the preceding 'raven': /r.v.n/ – /n.v.r/. Thus phonetically, the weightiest two words of the poem are closely linked. Strictly speaking though, the example doesn't fit Jakobson's thesis. The phonetic equivalence of 'raven' and 'never' is not matched by semantic equivalence. Clearly, the two words are not semantically equivalent. They are neither near synonyms nor antonyms: they belong to entirely different categories. Nor could one say that in this (fictional) context there was a striking similarity or dissimilarity in their reference. For the word 'never' just is not a referring expression: it is not used to pick out an object of any kind. Still, the phonetic link corresponds nicely to the momentous combination of the two words in the narrative: The *raven* repeatedly answers '*never*more' to the narrator's questions, in particular to his anxious question whether he will re-encounter his deceased love in another world, and also to its being told to leave. And the *raven*'s apparent determination *never* to leave is once more described in the line quoted. Thus the sound appears as 'an echo of the sense' (Pope).

This is indeed an aesthetically relevant observation. But to what extent does it support the claims of Jakobson's theory? Such a phonetic equivalence does in no way add to the meaning, or information, conveyed by the poem. The consonance of 'raven' and 'never' does not tell us anything new about the raven's behaviour. Indeed, its very aptness, which makes it aesthetically pleasing, lies in the fact that the sound seems to confirm *what we already know* (that the *raven* enunciates '*never*more' and seems determined *never* to leave). A consonance that does not 'chime' in with anything fairly clearly expressed by the text will not give us such an impression of aptness, and, far from giving us new information, will not at all be seen in connection with the meanings of the words.

Consider the following two lines from the same poem: 'For we cannot help agreeing that no living human being / Ever yet was blessed with seeing bird above his chamber door'. The internal rhyme of 'agreeing', 'being' and 'seeing' does not reflect anything expressed by the poem. The poem does not present any non-trivial link between agreement, (human) being and visual perception. Hence any attempt to give a semantic explanation of this rhyme will appear far-fetched and fanciful.

213

Or will it? Lotman seems to think that phonetic equivalence can do more than just indicate or correspond to semantic equivalence; it can actually produce it: 'Sound repetitions may establish additional bonds between words, introducing contrasts and oppositions into the semantic organization of the text which are less clearly expressed or completely absent on the level of natural language' (Lotman 1970: 107). He tries to support this claim with the analysis of the first stanza of a poem by Lermontov (Lotman 1970: 108–11): '*Kak nebesá tvoj vzor blistáet/Emál'yu golubój,/Kak potselúj zvuchít i táet/Tvoj gólos molodój*'. (Like the heavens, your glance shines/ Like blue enamel,/Like a kiss sounds and melts/Your youthful voice). First, Lotman draws attention to the phonetic similarities between line 1 and line 3:

Kak *nebesa* **tvoj** *vzor* **blistaet**

Kak *potseluj* **zvuchit i taet**

On the background of these similarities, the phonetic dissimilarity of *nebesa* (heavens) and *potseluj* (kiss) is thrown into relief. The words form a 'semantic opposition'. This opposition carries over to what the two words are linked with in comparisons. Therefore: 'On this level of semantic construction, the opposition between *vzor* (glance) and *golos* (voice) takes form – an utterly typical opposition in the Romantic portrait of the enigmatic person' (Lotman 1970: 109).

However, Lotman hastens to qualify this observation – by combining it with the opposite one. The observed phonetic equivalences between lines 1 and 3 (reverse sound parallelisms /t.v.z/ – /z.v.t/, the rhymed endings *blistaet – i taet*) now lead to an equation of *nebesa* (heavens) and *potseluj* (kiss). He also points out phonetic similarities that yield the following semantic groups:

golu**b**oj – potse**l**uj – z**v**u**ch**it (blue – kiss – sounds)

t**voj** vzor – **gol**os – **m**olo**d**oj (your glance – voice – young)

Finally, lines 2 and 4 display the following cross phonetic assimilation:

Emal'yu golu**b**oj   /m – l g – l/

Tvoj go**l**os molodoj   /g – l m – l/

This, together with the conspicuous repetition of the letter 'o', allows us to equate *emal' golubaya* (blue enamel) and *golos molodoj* (young voice) in a 'semantic unity'. And Lotman concludes: 'Thus the phonological structure which is part of the plane of expression in natural language passes into the structure of content in poetry, forming semantic positions inseparable from the given text' (Lotman 1970: 111).

I have two comments on this analysis. First, Lotman uses the terms 'semantic', 'meaning' and 'information' extremely loosely. The meaning (in the ordinary sense of the word) of the first line of Lermontov's poem is *that the addressee's glance shines like the heavens*. No meaning of that kind seems to accrue from the verses' sound repetitions. Instead we are told, for example, that 'blue enamel' and 'young voice' form a 'semantic unity'. But what does *that* mean? Are we to take it that not only the person's glance, but also her (?) voice shines like blue enamel? Lotman does not say so. Presumably he does not want to go as far as that. But then what *does* it mean? Again, what are we to make of his talk of 'oppositions'? Considering someone's utterance: 'The sheep's in the meadow, the cow's in the corn', one can certainly observe that 'sheep' and 'cow' stand in opposition on the grounds that one is the subject of the first clause while the other is the subject of the second. But this is merely a formal feature, and it does not add to the meaning of the utterance. Similarly, Lotman just points out features of a poem's phonetic structure, in terms of equation and opposition (that is, similarity and dissimilarity). One could *imagine* them to carry meaning. But Lotman does not really show that they do, nor does he actually spell out any such additional meanings.

Secondly, Lotman's observations yield too many overlapping groupings for any one of them to appear particularly significant. *Emal'yu* sounds like *molodoj* (/m.l./), which sounds like *goluboj*, which sounds like *golos*; but *golos* forms a group with *tvoj vzor* and *molodoj*, while *goluboj* is grouped together with *poceluj* and *zvu it*. And it does not help either that *nebesa* and *poceluj* are first said to form an opposition, and then seen as equated. In short, all Lotman's analysis succeeds in demonstrating is that the words of this stanza are in various ways knit together by rhyme, assonance and consonance.[3]

Jakobson is wrong to say that equivalence in sound *inevitably* involves semantic equivalence (Jakobson 1960: 83). But perhaps that claim was no more than a careless exaggeration. For a little further on, Jakobson makes a more cautious statement: 'In poetry, any conspicuous similarity in sound is evaluated in respect to similarity and/or dissimiliarity in meaning' (Jakobson 1960: 87). And that is just what we did: we evaluated the rhyme of 'agreeing', 'being' and 'seeing' in respect of equivalence in meaning – and found that there wasn't any. Nor could we get any semantic mileage out of sound repetitions in the first stanza of Lermontov's *Kak nebesa....* Then the theory would be that in poetry equivalence in sound is *sometimes*, or perhaps often, combined with equivalence in meaning (or some other link between the contents of words). Now Jakobson's definition of poetry needs to be qualified too. The most he could say is that in poetry equivalence in sound *tends* to signal equivalence in meaning. And of course that is not a definition any more, but at best a partial characterization.

Perhaps then structuralists would want to say that in *good* poetry equivalence in sound betokens equivalence in meaning (c.f. Kraus 1927: 5ff). Our inability to find a semantic link between 'agreeing' and 'human being' just goes to show that this internal rhyme is a failure. But I do not think this is a very plausible criterion of good poetry. It oscillates uneasily between patent falsehood and triviality. Consider a random example (the first lines of Johnson's 'To Celia'): 'Drink to me only with thine eyes, / And I will pledge with mine; / Or leave a kiss but in the cup / And I'll not look for wine'. There is no semantic equivalence between the rhyming words 'mine' and 'wine'; nor between 'kiss' and 'cup' linked by alliteration (except perhaps that both are somehow related to the mouth). Taken thus at face value, Jakobson's thesis appears to be easily refuted by countless samples of respectable poetry. In fact, where it does hold–where rhyming words are closely related in meaning–the rhymes tend to be trite and of little aesthetic interest. This is illustrated further down in this same poem, where 'cup' is rhymed with 'sup', and 'mine' with 'thine'. If, on the other hand, we take the equivalence thesis with a pinch of salt (as we did above when dealing with Jakobson's own example of 'raven' and 'never'), and ask merely whether the rhyming (or consonant) words are also related in the presentation of the poem's content, the claim becomes trivially true of almost all rhymed poetry. In our example, *mine* eyes are used to pledge, the way one normally does with a glass of *wine*; and a *kiss* is considered as a substitute for wine, the normal content of a *cup*. Thus in any short text about one particular subject, most words will automatically be in some way 'semantically related'; after all, they are all used to talk about that subject.

To the extent to which we assess the aesthetic success of particular rhymes (rather than judge the sound and flow of the poem as a whole), I think we set much greater store by originality than by closeness in meaning of particular words. And in as much as a rhyme is original and unexpected, it is likely to pair words that are semantically *not* particularly close. This is the view of one of the great masters of rhyme and assonance, Vladimir Mayakovsky. In his 'How to Make Verses' (Mayakovsky 1926: 87–8), he writes that the device of an unexpected rhyme between entirely unrelated lines is necessary for the effect of, for example, the following quatrain:

Milkoj mne v podarok burka	The felt coat is a gift from sweetheart
i noski podareny.	and the socks too.
Mchit Yudenich s Peterburga,	Yudenich is fleeing from Petersburg
kak naskipidarennyj.	as if he were turpentined.

Nobody would guess after the second line that *noskí podáreny* (socks given) was going to rhyme with *naskipidárennyj* (past participle, derived from *skipidar*: turpentine).

So even as a criterion of aesthetic success in poetry, Jakobson's principle of equivalence in sound and meaning does not seem very convincing. Anyhow, it certainly does not lead to the discovery of additional and previously hidden meaning. For, even where equivalence in sound does correspond to some relevant semantic relation between the words, that semantic relation will be obvious independently of phonetic equivalence.

Poem as puzzle

I shall now turn to the work of the French structuralist, Michel Riffaterre. In his criticism of a showpiece of Western structuralism, Jakobson and Lévi-Strauss's notorious analysis of Baudelaire's 'Les Chats', Riffaterre showed some good sense. He convincingly pointed out that the wealth of linguistic observations presented by the authors was, for the most part, beyond the awareness of even an ideally attentive reader and anyway quite irrelevant to the poem's poetic qualities (Riffaterre 1966). Nonetheless, Riffaterre remained an enthusiastic structuralist himself and put forward his own version of the coded-message model of poetry. This is how, according to Riffaterre's theory, a poem is produced:

> The poem results from the transformation of the *matrix*, a minimal and literal sentence, into a longer, complex, and nonliteral periphrasis. The matrix is...the grammatical and lexical actualization of a structure. It is always actualized in successive variants; the form of these variants is governed by the first or primary actualization, the *model*. Matrix, model, and text are variants of the same structure.
>
> (Riffaterre 1978: 19)

'Decoding' the poem proceeds in two stages. At a first reading, language is taken as 'referential' or 'mimetic', that is to say as a literary representation of reality. But from this point of view the text displays 'ungrammaticalities'. Taken literally, it does not seem to make sense. Such ungrammaticalities force the reader, at a second stage, to regard the text as poetry: as an indirect way of saying something else. Eventually he recognizes 'that successive and differing statements, first noticed as mere ungrammaticalities, are in fact equivalent, for they now appear as variants of the same structural matrix' (Riffaterre 1978: 1–6). But not only are all the statements or expressions in a poem variants of an underlying matrix, moreover, each one of them is derived from some 'hypogram', that is another piece of language, either a passage in another work, or a cliché, proverb or idiomatic phrase. Thus intertextuality is a precondition of poeticity: a word or phrase becomes poetic when it refers to a hypogram (Riffaterre 1978: 23).

To see the theory in action, we shall apply it to one of Riffaterre's own examples, a poem from Baudelaire's *Les Fleurs du Mal*:

Alchimie de la douleur	Alchemy of Sorrow
L'un t'éclaire avec son ardeur,	One lights you up with his ardour,
L'autre en toi met son deuil, Nature!	Another puts his mourning in you, Nature!
Ce qui dit à l'un: Sépulture!	The same thing that says to one: Grave!
Dit à l'autre: Vie et Splendeur!	Says to the other: Life and Splendour!
Hermès inconnu qui m'assistes	Unknown Hermes, who assists me
Et qui toujours m'intimidas,	And yet frightens me,
Tu me rends l'égal de Midas,	You make me like Midas,
Le plus triste des alchimistes;	The saddest of alchemists;
Par toi je change l'or en fer	Due to you I turn gold into iron
Et le paradis en enfer,	And paradise into hell;
Dans le suaire des nuages	In the shroud of the clouds
Je découvre un cadavre cher,	I discover a dear corpse,
Et sur les célestes rivages	And on the heavenly beaches
Je bâtis de grands sarcophages.	I build large sarcophagi.

Taken literally, every line of this poem is baffling. Ardour does not literally illuminate; mourning cannot literally be put anywhere; who is it that says 'Grave' to one person and 'Life and Splendour' to another, and why? – and so on. Other features the first, prosaic reading may find incomprehensible are rhyme and metre (Riffaterre 1978: 2). But unlike Jakobson and Lotman, Riffaterre in his interpretations does not make much of phonetic structure. What matters to him is that the poem is an uninterrupted succession of metaphors, which seem to say one thing, which is usually quite absurd, but mean something else. And they all mean roughly the same, namely – and this is the poem's matrix sentence – *sorrow transforms a person's experiences from good to bad*. Its first actualization in the text, the model, is the title. It governs all succeeding variants of expressions of this one underlying thought by providing the key metaphor: of *alchemy*, that is, transformation into something more valuable; but since it is performed by *sorrow* it is inverted: transformation into something worse. This seminal metaphor is then developed in various ways. The entire poem is a series of figurative variations of one and the same theme introduced by the title, and spelled out by the matrix sentence. It is a dinner of one sort of fish served up in many courses with different cooking and sauce.

What are the hypograms referred to? Here are three examples. In line 9, we find an opposition between *gold* and *iron*, rather than between the more conventional *gold* and *lead*, 'because it reinforces one of the stereotypes of the theme of humanity's decline: the descent from the golden age to the age of iron' (Riffaterre 1979: 84). The clouds (in line 11) 'are invoked because they are a commonplace in literary representations of daydreaming' (Riffaterre 1979: 86). And the sarcophagi on the beaches at the end are an allusion to three passages in Virgil, where the body of a beloved companion is buried on the beach (Riffaterre 1979: 87).

So far so good. We have found a unifying thematic statement, a matrix, and there are some hypograms (though it seems doubtful whether hypograms could be found for *all* the poem's statements). There are also plenty of 'ungrammaticalities'; though perhaps this term is overly drastic. Most metaphors are immediately recognized and read as such and thus never perceived as ungrammatical. But that is of little consequence. More to the point, what we found true of this poem is certainly not applicable to all poetry. For in displaying so neatly what Riffaterre declares to be the essence of poetry, this poem is in fact rather exceptional. It is entirely metaphorical *and* expresses only one thought. Taking the latter point first: why *should* poetry always limit itself to the expression of a single thought? There is no convention to enforce this. Poems richer in thematic contents would not be banned from publication. So it would be extremely surprising if over two thousand years no poet had ever ventured to express more than one thought in one poem. But Riffaterre is not really interested in the actual way poems were written. Like other structuralists,[4] he evinces a fascination with a notion of transformation or derivation independent of human agency. Each line of a poem is said to be derived, on the one hand, from an underlying structure, and on the other hand, from some hypogram. Yet this is not supposed to be a hypothesis about the actual production of the text by the author (Riffaterre 1979: 185). So all it means is that the text *can* be derived that way. But again, why should we expect that to be the case if we have no reason to assume that poets are actually concerned about their texts being thus derivable? Are we to assume cosmic (or linguistic) forces that inevitably press poetic works into Riffaterre's patterns? Well, there are none. Although poetry tends to be poorer in thematic thoughts than prose (if only because poems are often so much shorter), it is clearly not always possible to find a single unifying thematic statement of which all the poem's statements are variants. Sonnets tend to be rather focused; but as often as not they express *two* thoughts, one in reply to the other. In Milton's 'On his Blindness', for instance, the octet (minus half a line) expresses a complaint, which the sestet answers with acquiescence in God's will. Keats's 'To a Nightingale' presents a sequence of daydreaming, one part leading on to the next. There are of course thematic links (flight, sorrow, death), but clearly the person's thoughts are not all equivalent. Riffaterre's generalization appears altogether absurd, however,

219

when we consider narrative poetry. Just try to find a statement that is equivalent to each single statement in 'The Rime of the Ancient Mariner'.

Similar considerations apply to the thesis that poetry is essentially composed of metaphors (or other 'ungrammaticalities'). There is no reason to expect that to be the case – and it is not. A.E. Housman's 'Farewell to barn and stack and tree', for example, contains not a single (living) metaphor, nor anything else the reader might at first find incomprehensible.[5] (No reader will ever find the euphony of metre and rhyme 'ungrammatical'.) On the other hand, figurative – or even quite literally ungrammatical – language is not uncommon in non-poetic texts. Just look at a few pages by Hegel or Heidegger.

Riffaterre's theory seems very much the result of a one-sided diet. It may appear fairly persuasive as long as one does not go beyond his very limited range of examples. The poems he discusses in *Semiotics of Poetry* are practically all by French romantics, symbolists and surrealists; they show not much development or narrative, and abound in images.

Riffaterre's theory serves well to highlight what problems beset 'coded-message' poetics. Wittgenstein objected to the arousal theory that it degrades art to a mere vehicle that has no value in itself. But at least the arousal theory has a persuasive explanation of why we care for art. For what it conveys, feelings and emotions, has in many cases an obvious appeal to us. By analogy, one would expect that according to 'coded-message' poetics literature provides us with some coveted pieces of information, yet what structuralists have to offer in this respect is a great disappointment. We did not get any message out of Lotman's analysis. Riffaterre is undoubtedly right in stating that *Alchimie de la douleur* conveys the thought that sorrow transforms a person's experiences from good to bad, but what is so wonderful about this thought? We have known that all along.

Wittgenstein argues that the arousal theory would make the work of art in principle dispensable. But that leaves at least room for the reply that it may not be dispensable in actual fact, for nothing has been invented yet that would give us exactly the pleasant sequence of feelings aroused by listening to Beethoven's Third Symphony. No such reply is open to the 'coded-message' theorist of literature. As Riffaterre himself demonstrated, the message of *Alchimie de la douleur* can easily be communicated by one plain sentence. So why bother about the poem? → the artistic form makes it *(more profound & enjoyable)*.

Lotman's answer to this kind of criticism is to deny that one sentence could ever fully capture what the poem conveys. In fact, spelling out a good poem's meaning in plain prose would require a text far longer than the poem itself, for art, according to Lotman, 'is the most economical, compact method for storing and transmitting information' (Lotman 1970: 23). However, as exemplified above, Lotman's analyses demonstrate merely that from a poem we can cull a lot of data about its various structural features;

data that are unlikely to explain our aesthetic interest in the poem. Why, for example, should we care to be informed about the recurrence of the letter 'o'? Besides, Lotman talks as if those data were stored in the poem as information is stored in an encyclopaedia. But that is misleading; for the poem does not *say* that it has those features, it simply has them, just as a tree has millions of geometrical, physical and chemical features, but doesn't *say* that it has them. Hence it does not say it in a particularly economical way either.

Again, if the point of literature is to convey a message, then once the message has been understood, the work will lose its interest. But that does not seem to be true. We enjoy rereading poems even if their contents are still fresh in our memory.

Riffaterre has a reply to these objections. He readily admits that the message conveyed by a poem, the matrix, tends to be trivial. What really matters is not the solution to the puzzle, but the enjoyable process of working it out; the way the text is not easily understood and holds the reader's attention, 'soliciting his ingenuity' (Riffaterre 1978: 115). But for one thing, this description is not even borne out by *Alchimie de la douleur*, which we found exceptionally congenial to Riffaterre's theory. The poem would not pose a puzzle to any moderately experienced reader of poetry. One might miss the allusion to Virgil; but ignorance on this point would not detract substantially from one's aesthetic enjoyment; whilst recognizing the allusion, though no doubt a mildly gratifying experience, would not exactly strain one's ingenuity. Furthermore, although it is true that puzzle solving to most people affords some pleasure (if they're any good at it), the fun of solving a cryptic crossword in *The Times* would hardly be classifed as an aesthetic experience and by writing my shopping lists in an elaborate code, I do not produce any works of art. Moreover, on the puzzle-solving account too it would be incomprehensible that we enjoy rereading our favourite poems. Having found the solution the first time, there would not be any further 'soliciting of our ingenuity'. If a particular message can't confer aesthetic value on a text, neither can it be done by making that message difficult to decipher.

In another passage, Riffaterre writes that what 'makes the poem endlessly rereadable and fascinating' is that it allows the reader a 'seesawing from one sign value to another' (Riffaterre 1978: 166). Thus the poem would provide the attraction of a puzzle picture in which we could switch from seeing a duck to seeing a rabbit. But this provokes two similar criticisms. First, not even Riffaterre's own examples satisfy this description. The seesawing is supposed to be between a literal and a metaphorical meaning. But many metaphors *cannot* be taken literally. There is no literal understanding of 'put one's mourning into nature': only as a metaphor do the words make any sense. In other cases, a figurative expression can be taken literally, but there is nothing to be gained from it, and hardly any reader would be tempted to do so. Reading lines 3 and 4 of Baudelaire's poem, you can imagine a person going round and literally pronouncing the word 'grave' to someone and the

*even we can imagine the metaphor, (the scene of it)
we are still conscious about it is only a metaphor*

words 'life and splendour' to others. The effect is slightly comical, and not at all conducive to a proper appreciation of the poem. Finally, there are extended images, as the 'building of large sarcophagi on heavenly beaches', in the last two lines. Here again it is impossible to form two opposing mental pictures, one of doing it literally, one of doing it metaphorically. A proper understanding of the metaphor involves the idea of someone literally building sarcophagi on beaches *together with* the understanding that this is to serve as an image for the subject's state of mind. The reader is of course free to visualize the picture and perhaps embellish the scene with further details. But that will not, and is not meant to, blot out the awareness that it is only a metaphor. For this awareness (as understanding in general)[6] is not another mental image that might come and go, like one's seeing the duck in a puzzle picture. Secondly, even if we imagine a case of real ambiguity where the reader can oscillate between two different readings, it is hard to see why this should in itself be of any aesthetic value. In all likelihood, it would at best be found mildly amusing, like a puzzle picture.

Two types of meaning

I said above that scholars of literature desirous of earning some of the prestige accorded to the sciences are under pressure not only to produce theories, but preferably theories whose application to texts will yield some new interpretations. And since an interpretation brings to light a meaning that was not obvious, this leads naturally to the coded-message model of literature. But the coded-message model has yet another source. It is likely to result from a failure to note an ambiguity in the use of the word 'meaning'. Wittgenstein illustrates this ambiguity in *The Brown Book*:

> A friend and I once looked at beds of pansies. Each bed showed a different kind. We were impressed by each in turn...
>
> I could have used the expression 'Each of these colour patterns has meaning'; but...this would provoke the question, 'What meaning?', which in the case we are considering is senseless. We are distinguishing between meaningless patterns and patterns which have meaning; but there is no such expression in our game as 'This pattern has the meaning so and so'.
>
> (BB: 178–9)

The word: meaning

Wittgenstein calls this an intransitive use of the word 'meaning', as opposed to its usual transitive use where one can answer the question what the meaning in question is (BB: 158, 161). How is the intransitive use to be explained?

First, consider the question of the meaning of life. This may be taken as asking for the *purpose* of life, and receive the answer that life is meant (intended) to glorify God. But this answer would satisfy only those who think that to glorify God is a good thing. And that brings out another implication in this use of 'meaning'. Those who inquire after the meaning of life are looking for reassurance that life has value, that it is worth living. Such an evaluative use of the word is also common in expressions like: 'It means a lot to me', which does not allow the question 'What does it mean to you?', for it is just a way of saying 'It's very dear to me', or, 'I very much care for it'.

Secondly, Wittgenstein discusses cases in which we experience something *as if* it said something; *as if* it had meaning in a transitive sense:

> The same strange illusion which we are under when we seem to seek the something which a face expresses whereas, in reality, we are giving ourselves up to the features before us – that same illusion possesses us even more strongly if repeating a tune to ourselves and letting it make its full impression on us, we say 'This tune says *something*', and it is as though I had to find *what* it says. And yet I know that it doesn't say anything.
>
> (BB: 166)

Note that this is not an error. We know perfectly well that in truth nothing is being conveyed. Still, we advisedly use the words 'meaning', or 'says something', for we experience the phenomenon as if it had a meaning, perhaps even as if we had understood a meaning – but could not articulate it. What in fact we perceive is a specific configuration, something striking, a *Gestalt*. But our paradigm for what is recognizably specific in faces and sounds is what has a specific meaning. A distinctive facial expression is usually the expression of a particular feeling, attitude of response (say, a particular shade of irony, or haughtiness). So we are naturally inclined to see a distinctive face as expressive of something even if as a matter of fact it does not express anything. Again, our paradigm of specific sounds are words that convey a particular message. Thus musical sounds, being also distinctly organized as a recognizable *Gestalt*, can easily create the illusion of a quasi-linguistic utterance.[7] And with verbal art, that effect is even more natural, but also more confusing. In the verbal sphere, a specific impression is normally created by the particular meaning words convey. Hence the specific aesthetic impression we get from certain words in a certain position, the unique physiognomy of a period or a poem, is easily experienced as an additional poetic meaning (c.f. PI §531).

Thirdly, in aesthetic contexts the word 'meaningful' can be used as the opposite of 'incidental', or 'arbitrary'. It is felt that certain features were meant to be as they are, and what is more, they were somehow prompted by other features, in music or literature typically those that went before. Thus, what has meaning appears to fit and make sense. In some cases, especially in music, such fitting seems inexplicable; we can only say that we experience *this* as a necessary consequence of *that*:

> The 'necessity' with which the second idea succeeds the first. (The overture to 'Figaro'.)... All the same, the paradigm according to which everything is *right* is obscure. 'It is the natural development'. We gesture with our hands and are inclined to say: 'Of course'.
>
> (CV: 57; see also 52)

Yet in other cases such aesthetic appropriateness is, up to a point, explicable. In Chekhov's story 'The Darling' (Dushechka), the telegram that informs the heroine of her husband's death contains a somewhat comical mistake: instead of the word *pokhorony* (funeral) one reads *khokhorony*, reminiscent of *khokhot* (laughter). The error seems strangely appropriate; and that can be explained in terms of a leitmotivic connection: earlier on the deceased predicted his own ruin and death 'with hysterical laughter' (*s istericheskim khokhotom*). The fusion of the words for funeral and laughter in the telegram appears as a reflection of the way death and laughter are conjoined in those earlier complaints. Thus it is aesthetically meaningful. Tolstoy, in a letter to Strakhov (April 1876), emphasizes the aesthetic significance of such concatenations of motives in *Anna Karenina*, and he judiciously notes the intransitivity of this kind of meaning: any thoughts one might try to extract from such concatenations would be dreadfully trivial. Literary critics should 'show up the nonsense of searching for thoughts in a work of art' and instead 'constantly direct the readers through the endless labyrinth of concatenations which forms the essence of art' (Tolstoy, LXII: 269).

So the word 'meaning' (and its cognates) can be used intransitively in three different ways, denoting (1) value, (2) a specific *Gestalt*, or (3) an (apparent) appropriateness. It may, however, not always be possible to keep those three uses neatly apart. For in aesthetics, *Gestalt* and appropriateness are likely to be regarded as valuable, and a specific *Gestalt* may be experienced as appropriate. It might be best to regard intransitive meaning in aesthetics (henceforth: Meaning) as just one concept to be applied flexibly with one or more of those three aspects to the fore.

It is easy to see how the ambiguity of the word 'meaning' fosters the coded-message model of literature. Naturally one would like to account for a literary work's *Meaning*, its aesthetically valuable characteristics, and so one does explain the work's *meaning* – its content. Failing to distinguish between the two, one easily slides from one to the other: from the Meaning one should like to explain to the meaning one knows how to explain. Trying to explicate aesthetic qualities we often don't even know where to begin; so we tend to fall back on what is common practice in the realm of language: interpretation, the paraphrase of linguistic meaning. This confusion is made less noticeable by the fact that interpretation too has its role in aesthetic discourse. One cannot properly appreciate a text whose contents one has not fully under-stood. So literary scholars will be expected to remove obscurities, particularly those that are due to conventions of symbolism, allusions to other texts or references to circumstances unknown to the common reader. Here an inter-pretation, though necessary, is a mere preliminary to aesthetic appreciation; and fortunately many of the finest works of literature require no such learned glossary. An interpretation of a different kind can indeed further the reader's appreciation and lead to a better understanding of the text's Meaning. By giving a selective paraphrase, the critic emphasizes aspects of particular aesthetic relevance. Still, the meaning spelled out by such an interpretation is not the Meaning. The content, thus reproduced by a paraphrase in plain prose, is not what makes the work valuable. Rather, the *way* in which the content is summarized can guide the reader to a better appreciation of the text. For literary value cannot be reduced to the things that are described and the opinions that are conveyed; it is always a matter of *how* certain things are presented and expressed. And this How cannot be reduced to another What.

Now the semiotic obsession to derive meaning from structure becomes readily understandable. Rhyme, for example, is certainly aesthetically Meaningful: it is essential to the physiognomy of a poem, and a clear example of one element being prompted by another one. But the struc-turalist mistakes this aesthetic significance for transitive meaning, and proceeds to investigate *what* it means; unsurprisingly, without any appre-ciable results. The most that comes to light is the occasional parallelism between phonetic and (broadly) semantic similarities, but this phenomenon is itself only intransitively Meaningful. It can reinforce the appearance of necessity with which one line follows another, but it does not *say* anything.

Another symptom of the leap from Meaning to meaning is the search for astonishing (new) interpretations. If extraordinary aesthetic signifi-cance is to be cashed out in content, that content had better be extraordinary too. Deeply impressed by *Anna Karenina*, people were prone to ask what profound message it might contain. Tolstoy replied that if he were to put into words what he meant to express by his novel, he would have to write down the whole novel again (Tolstoy, LXII, 269). Not – as Lotman understood this answer (1970: 11) – because only a work of art could convey that much information, but because the work's aesthetic Meaning does not at all consist in a message, which might be spelled out in other words. As noted above, aesthetic Meaning, according to Tolstoy, is found in 'concatenations' of motives that make each one appear as a necessary response to the other.

The triviality that typically results from an attempt to paraphrase the Meaning of a work of literature led A.C. Bradley to the famous (or noto-rious) claim that in art, form and content are identical, so that a work's content cannot be stated in another form (Bradley 1909: 572).[8] In this,

Bradley seems wiser than those who seek to match the extraordinary impression a work makes on them with an extraordinary interpretation. His denunciation of the 'heresy' of paraphrasing poetry rightly acknowledges that all attempts to account for a work's aesthetic significance by extracting from it a message are doomed to failure. But at the same time, Bradley is still in the grip of the misconstrual of aesthetic meaning as transitive. We cannot *paraphrase* the work's message, but it is there for the appreciative reader to understand. Nor is it ineffable, for the author has succeeded in expressing it: 'What that meaning is *I* cannot say: Virgil has said it' (Bradley 1909: 573). Now what is unsatisfactory about Bradley's doctrine is not that he talks of a poem's meaning while refusing to say *what* that meaning is. The problem is rather that he continues to talk as if there *was* a meaning of the kind that is normally given by paraphrase. Of course this is what it feels like. But the experience is an illusion.

Postlude

Post-structuralism is a kind of perennial schoolboy's philosophy that combines a taste for metaphysical profundity, paradox and *épater le bourgeois* with a blissful freedom from the trammels of conceptual clarity and precision. It is no coincidence that post-structuralism has flourished almost exclusively among those without any training in philosophical analysis. I shall not enter Derrida's stables, but finish with just a few words on deconstruction, the post-structuralist way of dealing with literature.[9]

From a distance, one might be inclined to expect that in moving on from structuralism to post-structuralism and deconstruction, theorists reacted to the detection of flaws and shortcomings in structuralism, among them the basic assumption I called 'the coded-message model'. One would be disappointed. Deconstruction is not semiotics overcome, but semiotics gone wild. It is still the same misguided game of deciphering messages. Textual details are pressed and twisted until they yield some extra meaning, usually calculated to surprise the 'naive' reader. Only two things have changed. First, the fashion now goes for a different kind of message. One is encouraged to 'read the text against itself', which means to excavate meanings that are not only different from what is readable on the surface, but contradict it. Whereas structuralists emphasize a poem's unity, post-structuralists are eager to destroy any semblance of such unity, by 'teasing out' the 'warring forces of signification within the text' (Johnson 1980: 5). The apparent aim of this exercise is to confirm the post-structuralist doctrine that all meaning is unstable and indeterminate. That of course leads to a somewhat tedious similarity of all literature. As Peter Barry puts it, 'after the deconstructionist treatment all poems tend to emerge as angst-ridden, fissured enactments of linguistic and other forms of indeterminacy' (Barry 1995: 77).

Secondly, once the goal posts had moved, the rules had to be changed too. In order to expose each text as self-contradictory, more flexible devices of 'uncovering meaning' had to be allowed, for example etymology. But above all, for meaning to be sufficiently unstable and open, it had to be made independent of authorial intention. In 1968 Roland Barthes earned himself the prefix 'post-' by pompously announcing 'the death of the author'. The short paper of that title is a hopeless muddle, devoid of serious argument and full of inflated rhetoric. Barthes welcomes literature's refusal to have an author, fixing its meaning, as ultimately amounting to a refusal of 'God and his hypostases – reason, science, law' (Barthes 1968: 171).

One might wonder how there can be a coded message without an author to send and encode it. As for the sender, Barthes solemnly proclaims that 'it is language which speaks' (Barthes 1968: 168). And of course the codes are provided by language too. Literary theorists are rather fond of this word and not too fussy about its different meanings. 'Coded message' is now taken as 'message to be read according to cultural codes'. Such codes are a mixed bag, containing socio-linguistic conventions, themes, semantic fields, items of knowledge, public opinions, customs and scientific procedures; anything, in fact, the reader might want to project into the text in order to elicit a hidden message.[10]

Notes

1 In this Scholes echoes the semantic definition of literature given by Monroe C. Beardsley: 'a literary work is a discourse in which an important part of the meaning is implicit' (Beardsley 1958: 126). Like a figure of speech, a poem must not be taken at face value. It has a real meaning that differs from what it explicitly says. Hence: 'A metaphor is a miniature poem, and the explication of a metaphor is the model of all explication [of literature]' (Beardsley 1958: 144).

2 Equivalences in position and grammatical form may also be relevant.

3 This is an older and less ambitious explanation of the function of rhyme and phonetic repetition: without it the lines would fall apart. See, for example, Mayakovsky (1926).

4 Notably V.I. Propp and C. Lévi-Strauss.

5 Jakobson draws attention to Pushkin's *Ya vas lyubil* (I loved you) as an example of poetry without images (1961: 128ff).

6 See PI §396.

7 'Mightn't we imagine a man who, never having had any acquaintance with music, comes to us and hears someone playing a reflective piece of Chopin and is convinced that this is a language and people merely want to keep the meaning secret from him?' (Z §161)

8 For a perceptive discussion of Bradley's doctrine see Kivy (1997: ch. 4).

9 For level-headed accounts of post-structuralism and deconstruction see Washington (1989: ch. 4) and Sim (1992).

10 I am indebted to Dr D. Maw for his comments on an earlier draft of this paper.

Bibliography

Barry, P. (1995) *Beginning Theory: An Introduction to Literary and Cultural Theory*, Manchester: Manchester University Press.

Barthes, R. (1968) 'The Death of the Author', trans. S. Heath in D. Lodge (ed.), *Modern Criticism and Theory: A Reader*, London: Longman, 1988, 166–95.

Beardsley, M.C. (1958) *Aesthetics: Problems in the Philosophy of Criticism*, Indianapolis: Hackett.

Bradley, A.C. (1909) 'Poetry for Poetry's Sake', in E.Vivas and M. Krieger (eds), *The Problems of Aesthetics: A Book of Readings*, New York: Holt, Rinehart and Winston, 1960, 562–77.

Culler, J. (1981) *The Pursuit of Signs: Semiotics, Literature, Deconstruction*, London: Routledge & Kegan Paul.

Jakobson, R. (1960) 'Linguistics and Poetics', in T.A. Sebeok (ed.), *Style in Language*, New York: Wiley; reprinted in Jakobson (1987: 62–94).

—— (1987) *Language in Literature*, ed. K. Pomorska and S. Rudy, Cambridge, MA: Harvard University Press.

Jakobson, R. and Lévi-Strauss, C. (1962) '"Les chats" de Charles Baudelaire', *L'Homme. Revue française d'anthropologie* 2(1): 5–21.

Johnson, B. (1980) *The Critical Difference: Essays in the Contemporary Rhetoric of Reading*, Baltimore, MD: Johns Hopkins University Press.

Kivy, P. (1997), *Philosophies of Art. An Essay in Differences*, Cambridge: Cambridge University Press.

Kraus, K. (1927) 'Der Reim', *Die Fackel* 757–8: 1–37.

Lotman, Y.M. (1970) *Struktura Khudozhestvennogo Teksta,* Moscow; trans. R. Vroon as *The Structure of the Artistic Text*, Ann Arbor, MI: University of Michigan Press, 1978.

—— (1972) *Analiz Poeticheskogo Teksta*, Leningrad; trans. D.B. Johnson as *Analysis of the Poetic Text*, Ann Arbor, MI: University of Michigan Press, 1976.

Mayakovsky, V.V. (1926), 'Kak delat' sticki' (How to make verses), in *Polnoe Sobranie So inenij*, Moscow: Khudozhestvennaya literatura, 1955–61, vol. 12, 81–117.

Riffaterre, M. (1966) 'Describing Poetic Structures. Two Approaches to Baudelaire's "Les chats"', *Yale French Studies* 36–7: 200–42, 1980.

—— (1978) *Semiotics of Poetry*, London: Methuen.

—— (1979) *La production du texte*, Paris: Seuil; trans. T. Lyons as *Text Production*, New York: Columbia University Press, 1983.

Scholes, R. (1982) *Semiotics and Interpretation*, New Haven: Yale University Press.

Sim, S. (1992) 'Structuralism and Post-structuralism', in O. Hanfling (ed.), *Philosophical Aesthetics: An Introduction*, Oxford: Blackwell, 405–39.

Tolstoy, L.N. *Polnoe Sobranie So chinenij*, Moscow: Khudozhestvennaya Literatura.

Washington, P. (1989) *Fraud: Literary Theory and the End of English*, London: Fontana.

Wittgenstein, L. (1953) *Philosophical Investigations* (PI), trans. G.E.M. Anscombe, Oxford: Blackwell.

—— (1966) *Lectures and Conversations on Aesthetics, Psychology and Religious Belief* (LA), ed. C. Barrett, Oxford: Blackwell.

—— (1967) *Zettel* (Z), ed. G.E.M Anscombe and G.H. von Wright, trans. G.E.M. Anscombe, Oxford: Blackwell.

—— (1969) *The Blue and Brown Books* (BB), Oxford: Blackwell.

—— (1980) *Culture and Value* (CV), ed. G.H. von Wright, trans. P. Winch, Oxford: Blackwell.

10

WITTGENSTEIN ON CONSCIOUSNESS AND LANGUAGE

A challenge to Derridean literary theory

Charles Altieri

I

It would be foolish of me to deny that the recent influence of serial structuralists like Barthes and Derrida has had an invigorating influence on
American literary criticism and has illuminated a wide variety of texts and
literary themes.[1] It is not so foolish, however, to decry the effects it has had
on American literary theory. Because it entered what was in a sense a
conceptual void and because its philosophical concerns seemed closely
parallel to much modernist writing, serial structuralism has popularized
sceptical perspectives on language, consciousness and meaning that have
been often ignored by critics with other commitments but rarely challenged.
Even if they are correct, the Mill in me finds this a bad situation. So I will
attempt in this essay to develop the position of the later Wittgenstein as a
direct challenge to their sceptical assumptions.

I am not yet sure that the Wittgensteinian approach I will be taking is an
adequate philosophy, but at the very least it can provide a direct and systematic contrast to concepts we seem to be accepting all too readily. Moreover, I
see this chapter as largely a prolegomenon to specific work in literary theory,
and will not here try to solve specific problems. Instead, I hope to take up
three general issues. First, I will compare a theory of consciousness implicit
in Wittgenstein with the theory of consciousness as a representational force
natural to literary critics and basic to Derrida's deconstructions. Then I will
pursue Newton Carver's suggestion that both Derrida and Wittgenstein
share a fundamental opposition to traditional essentialist forms of philosophy (1973: xix–xxix). Both subordinate a logic of reference to a rhetoric of
significations or speech acts, but the more closely we examine this common
point of origin the more the two men's differences emerge. Wittgenstein
indeed once intended to preface his *Philosophical Investigations* with a motto
from *King Lear*, 'I will teach you differences', but his reflections on differences help us to show that Derrida, in so much as he makes claims, remains
trapped like his master Nietzsche in an ironic or demonic version of the

logic he wishes to deconstruct. Moreover, by comparing Derrida's logical scepticism with Wittgenstein, we can dramatize Wittgenstein's claim that the activities of speculative philosophers provide the light which gives his mundane descriptions their significance (PI §109). Sceptical doubt applies a kind of pressure on familiar realities that can make us aware of how our ordinary activities are in fact anchored and of how we characteristically determine meanings and values. Then there is an easy transition to my third concern, for I want to show how the ontology implicit in Wittgenstein's work helps us recover the force of humanistic claims about literature that have come to seem mere truisms.

II

Let me try to give a brief summary of a theory of consciousness, ultimately derived from idealist thought, which I think underlies the work of most influential literary theorists today. It has two basic assumptions which take a variety of forms. First of all, it sees consciousness, or language as the medium of consciousness, as somehow a separate structuring force with its own contents. Consciousness does not mirror a world but represents and structures it. Trained as literary critics to articulate a variety of schemes for organizing experience, we find it quite natural to image reality as an unknowable flux and to attribute what order we experience to the power of consciousness to impose its structures on that flux. We often feel, in fact, that we only glimpse reality through the gaps or failures in any given representational scheme. Second, we tend to emphasize one particular problem central to representational schemes: the problem of personal identity or 'what you know too well about self-consciousness and never wanted to know'. The problem here is in essence the impossibility of making one's thoughts or fictions about the self correspond to what the self actually experiences and does. We find inescapable Paul de Man's restatement of Kant's distinction between conceptual and empirical selves. Or, now that we have come to prefer a problematic of language to one of self-conscious identity, we consider the self as lost among an endless play of impersonal signifiers. In both cases the problem comes down to one of negation. The agent seeking to locate itself, in experience or in a correspondence between signifiers and signified, is at the same time the agent of dislocation, the agent who must represent in an alien form what it seeks to find. In the classic terms of alienation, the spirit must posit as another's what it wants or should appreciate as its own. In order to represent his self to himself a person must posit as other, as a construct in the impersonal system of language, the very realm of pre-reflective experience which he wants to appropriate. Moreover, without the negation of the world as other, our symbolic system cannot define a self standing out against the world. The two themes ultimately come together in our sense that to be conscious, to be aware that one operates in an essentially arbitrary system distinct from an objective reality, leads inevitably to one's becoming self-conscious. One sees either his will or his linguistic acts as the source of the alienating powers of consciousness. No wonder that we find ourselves, like the literature we study, torn between two unacceptable poles. Always appealing and ever receding is the dream of a pure naturalism within which one can free himself from reflective consciousness and merge with the natural energies of the world and of his body. At the other pole, we can recognize the irony of the first dream and, embracing irony ourselves, devote ourselves either to Nietzsche's free play or to the more leisurely, and perhaps more decadent, free play of the intellectual, exploring the manifold fictions of consciousness while positing the empirical world as unknowable or, for Blakeans like Harold Bloom, actively demonic.[2]

The brief analysis I have just offered may be the clearest section in this paper, and for good reason, since its concepts come so naturally to one trained in literature. However, this may itself be sufficient reason for entertaining another perspective, even if the Wittgensteinian insights I will attempt to turn into abstract arguments do not directly connect with the thematic concerns that most interest literary critics. We must begin with an important proviso. Even if one is rash enough to claim that Wittgenstein's reflections can be turned into abstract arguments, one must realize that the first and perhaps most important move in his philosophizing is the refusal to posit an all-encompassing theory of any mental act. Instead he insists that there are only a wide variety of contexts in which we can glimpse, from different perspectives, the many ways it makes sense to speak of these acts. Perhaps the most pervasive theme in his specific treatment of issues relevant to the concept of consciousness is the need to define the reflective powers of the mind in a way not subject to the problematic of self-consciousness. This is most apparent in two interrelated recurring themes: the argument against private language and the insistence that truth and meaning do not depend on special forms of verification which exist beneath or behind the utterance, for example, in the speaker's intentions or in the intuition or sensation referred to. Wittgenstein argues that once the words are taken as primarily signs of something else, once verification depends on people's intentions or on their particular intuitions of the reality referred to, there will always be a gap between direct experience and linguistic expression, a gap which we try to fill with concepts of representation and of the necessity for a person self-consciously to mediate between signs and sources of meaning. But the terms by which one expresses his self-conscious awareness are always themselves mediated, impersonal and subject to the temporality of differing and deferring. Thus there is an inescapable infinite regress between expressions of consciousness and the necessary but unrecoverable grounds for certain direct knowledge. Both solipsism and scepticism, the demons with which Wittgenstein continually wrestled, derive from the logical impossibility of explaining how we move from representation to direct knowledge, whether in our own acts or in the doubly mediated process of interpreting the expressions of another.

The way out is to deny the way in, to refuse to grant that consciousness in any intelligible sense represents a reality independent of it and thus creates separate structures needing to be reconciled with immediate experience. G.E. Moore, especially in his disputes with idealism, realized this goal, but his arguments remain problematic because they try to establish an alternative general and abstract picture of the relationship between mind and world. Wittgenstein is more subtle and more willing to go beyond Moore's empiricism to incorporate some of Kant's insights, albeit on a very different foundation. The first move, as I have already suggested, is to stop talking about consciousness and examine specific forms of mental activity (PI §416). For our purposes, Wittgenstein's meditations on the process of 'thinking' will serve to delineate a clear alternative to models of the mind which see representation as transforming the content of some original relationship to reality.[3]

Two distinctions help clarify what is at play when we speak of someone thinking. The first is between dispositions and states of mind, and the second between situations in which we might describe someone as thinking and those where we would say he was acting without thought. The first distinction has been much discussed, but we can briefly characterize disposition terms as those expressing capacities or abilities, while terms referring to states of mind express specific modes of activity which have a duration and which are signified by characteristic marks (Z §72, §81). Knowing how to do something is a disposition term because it would be meaningless in ordinary circumstances to keep testing whether I knew how to play chess or to ask when I stopped knowing it. Expecting or fearing or, I think, thinking, on the other hand, can be considered states of mind since these verbs normally refer to specific durations, take direct objects, and are accompanied by characteristic behavioural traits while they are going on. Because thinking entails a relationship to an object and because it has characteristic behavioural signs, Wittgenstein feels that he can take on the Cartesian tradition. Thinking is not a separate act which takes place in addition to one's relationship to the object. It is not a mysterious inner process with its own rules and energies, but a particular way in which a person relates to his involvement in the world: 'Of course we cannot separate his "thinking" from his activity. For the thinking is not an accompaniment of the work any more than of thoughtful speech' (Z §101).

The most important single characteristic which indicates that one is thinking, and which determines the difference between thoughtful and thoughtless behaviour, is the phenomenon of paying attention to what one is doing: 'How can we learn the truth by thinking? As one learns to see a face better if one draws it' (Z §255). Closely involved with paying attention is the fact that thinking is often characterized by a reflexive testing of the process within which one is engaged:

> If he has made some combination in play or by accident and he
> now uses it as a method of doing this and that, we will say he
> thinks...He 'thinks' when in a definite kind of way he perfects a
> method he has.
>
> (Z §104)

The fact that thinking is not a separate activity but a way of proceeding
in other more specific activities has three important consequences. It
obviously suggests that thinking is not representation since thinking is a
style or mode of acting not the imposition of a separate set of forms.
(We may think within representations, for example, while looking at a
mimetic painting, yet in such situations the thinking occurs within what
we take as conventional processes not themselves constituted by thought
but guiding it.) Indeed Wittgenstein can avoid some of Moore's problems
here because by treating thinking as a way of engaging in other activities
he finesses the question 'what is the relationship between consciousness
and objects in the world'. Consciousness is essentially not a way of
relating to objects but of relating to actions we learn to perform. The
basic condition of human experience is not minds facing a world of
objects but a wide variety of activities constituting a complex interrelated web of cultural and natural forms toward which we can behave in a
creative way if we need or care to. As I will develop later, the relevant
alternatives here are not so much realism and idealism, as two versions of
Kantian thought: one positing a gap between representations and
noumena and the other insisting that the forms in human life are not
representations of consciousness but an irreducible web of activities and
language games which constitute human reality and beyond which there
is nothing for us to say: 'What has to be accepted, the given, is – so one
could say forms of life' (PI §226).[4] We do not usually think about objects,
but about the specific form of activity which involves us with these
objects at this time.

Second, because thinking is not a separate structuring activity, there is no
special subject of thought which one can seek by self-reflection. Compare
the approach in the two following statements to one like Poulet's, with its
endless and hopeless search for an original cogito:

> Ask: what result I am aiming at when I tell someone: 'Read atten-
> tively'? That, e.g., this and that should strike him and he be able to
> give an account of it. – Again, it could, I think, be said that if you
> read a sentence with attention you will often be able to give an
> account of what has gone on in your mind, e.g. the occurrence of
> images. But that does not mean that these things are what we call
> 'attention'.
>
> (Z §91)

It's true I say 'Now I am having such-and-such an image', but the words 'I am having' are merely a sign to someone *else*; the description of the image is a complete account of the imagined world.' – You mean: the words 'I am having' are like 'I say'...

(PI §402)

The self may be an object of consciousness but no requirement of authenticity tempts us to pursue it since the self does not here constitute anything. For if consciousness as thinking is a way of relating to specific activities, then all self-consciousness can give is awareness of the self acting in a particular way. It cannot give us any entity called the self. Indeed the very idea of a substantial, constitutive self to be discovered in reflexive thought is a residue of the essentialist thinking, the need to posit sources for phenomena, which Wittgenstein tries to escape. Given the difficulties in adequately conceiving what authentic knowledge of the self as an epistemological agent might consist in, one suspects, with Foucault, that our present concerns with discovering identity through self-consciousness are largely the result of specific historical forces. From an analytic perspective, it seems likely that our normal ways of acting in the world provide all the criteria we need for a sense of identity. As Sidney Shoemaker has shown, the most important source of our sense of identity is the way we use the spatio-temporal location of our body to make basic physical distinctions between here and there, in front and behind, and so on. Those who cannot make these distinctions and use personal identity in this way need therapy not self-reflexive philosophy. And this physical sense is supplemented on a public level, as J.F.M. Hunter has shown, by a wide variety of legal and behavioural constructs which define modes of seeing oneself as possessing an identity.[5]

Derrida, of course, would agree with this denial of a constitutive self definable through self-consciousness, but he goes on to make too easy a leap to denying any criteria of identity or possibility of self-knowledge. It seems likely, however, that if we cannot know the self as an independent entity, we can come to understand the various procedures it has for acting in the world and even for establishing emotional and conceptual attitudes toward its actions. Stanley Cavell, for example, has argued that Wittgenstein's way of investigating experiences in terms of established procedures and language games provides a basic source for enhancing human freedom by showing us what our commitments really are. Through these investigations we learn what we depend on in order to carry out the activities that give meaning and purpose to our lives, and, more important, we come to recognize that what is deeply personal is not therefore subjective and arbitrary. Literary experience is a relevant example. We can readily see that our reading is no less engaged for being dependent on conventional procedures. Moreover the kind of self-consciousness bred by literary texts is not of the self-reflexive sort propounded by theorists as diverse as Norman Holland and Jonathan Culler. Literary texts provide images of the various attitudes we can take up toward the world; they focus attention on the ways we normally engage in experience without reflectively attending to it. These texts do not lead us to consider the way we subjectively constitute our responses, but give us a perspective on and involvement in acts which can also take place without thought. (Consider the intuitive difference between describing a literary text and describing our subjective response to it.) Literature, one might say, interests us in our own interests[6] and thus encourages us to recognize, to enjoy, and to comprehend the many different selves we can be in different instances. The depth of our personal involvement in diverse literary attitudes leads not back into a particular self-consciousness, but into an awareness of the communal roles and modes of activity we share with others.

This capacity to respond to diverse attitudes leads to the third consequence of Wittgenstein's perspective on thinking, a different view of the popular insistence that whenever we try to understand an utterance or a phenomenon we must make an interpretation of it. If consciousness is a process of representing some external reality, it follows that consciousness is always interpretation, always the imposition of tenuous forms on an unknowable but felt flux. One need not follow Nietzsche and insist that interpretation entails a radical subjectivism. Karat and later idealists in different ways sought to deny the subjectivity of interpretation by positing forms of *a priori* mental structure, but then the possibility of a shared human world depends on tenuous metaphysical constructs readily susceptible to sceptical attacks. For Wittgenstein, the sense of the given as commonly held forms of behaviour greatly limits the sphere in which the problematics of interpretation apply. He does not deny that some modes of activity require interpretation, but he shows that interpretation, like other forms of behaviour, has characteristic marks. And more important, once he has called our attention to these marks, he can show that the theme of the instability of interpretation says less about the human condition than it does about the characteristic situations in which interpretation is necessary. It makes sense to talk about problematic situations; it makes no sense to generalize these situations as the basic reality for those cursed by consciousness and language.

Wittgenstein describes at least three distinct forms by which people make sense of situations (see PI section XI for a thorough discussion). The majority of cases we might call simply 'seeing'; one recognizes something by seeing its fit with rules, language games, or forms of life appropriate to the situation (PI: p. 201). 'Seeing as' occurs when a variety of possible contexts help shed light or significance upon an object or action. Here we still are not adding something not inherently a part of the 'internal relations' characterizing a situation (PI: p. 212). Finally interpretation in its traditional philosophical sense occurs when at least two characteristic signs are in evidence. There must be a feeling of doubt, a sense that the situation somehow does not allow us to respond to it in terms of our normal expectations (PI §652). And this feeling of having lost our way is complemented by a need to fill out the situation, to imagine a new hypothesis by introducing new terms which might synthesize the disparate elements (PI: p. 212).

> And if 'I have never read the figure as anything but an F [the figure is an inverted F in a mirror], or considered what it might be, we will say that I see it as F; if, that is, we know that it can also be seen differently. I should call it "interpretation" if I were to say "that is certainly supposed to be an F"; the writer does all his F's like that'.
>
> (Z §208)

It is crucial here to see that interpretations are problematic precisely because they are called for only when our normal procedures break down. Thus they cannot be applied to ordinary cases. On the contrary, they depend on a contrast with ordinary experience in order for us to recognize them for what they are. The problem of interpretation, then, has important similarities with the problem of doubt, a problem which Wittgenstein in *On Certainty* takes great pains to clarify because it is when this concept is misused that the sceptic gets his hold. I will develop his discussion of doubt later, but the following quotation should indicate how limits can be placed on both doubting and interpreting:

> What happens is not that this symbol cannot be further interpreted, but: I do no interpreting. I do not interpret, because I feel at home in the present picture. When I interpret, I step from one level of thought to another.
>
> (Z §234)

> If I see the thought symbol 'from outside', I become conscious that it could be interpreted thus or thus; if it is a step in the course of my thought, then it is a stopping place that is natural to me, and its further interpretability does not occupy (or trouble) me. As I have a time-table and use it without being concerned with the fact that a table is susceptible of various interpretations.
>
> (PI: p. 235)

Once we recognize a distinction between interpretation and knowledge as the ability to use established procedures, we can take a perspective on irony quite different from that shared by such diverse critics as Paul de Man and Northrop Frye. Both men see irony as essentially cancerous: as soon as we feel that one expression does not mean what it says, we find it hard not to scrutinize other statements, and once the process of doubting the correspondence of sign and referent begins, it is difficult to stop. But this concept of irony as breeding scepticism is too dependent on a representational theory of language not to incur suspicion. Of course if our grasp of reality must rely upon a tenuous link between words and world, any threat to the lines of projection between word and reference becomes dangerously general. Here, however, Wittgenstein's sense of the difference between seeing from without and seeing from within affords another way to view the role of irony. If we see from without, there is nothing matching words and things but some form of faith or abstract justification. If we see from within, we see our words as tokens in a complex series of customary actions and exchanges. If you call into question the words we use to describe the actions (as Wittgenstein himself often does), you do not seriously threaten the actions themselves or the natural and social history on which they are based. Irony, then, as Wittgenstein and as, I think, Socrates practiced it, does not make ordinary existence unstable; rather it makes it more secure by forcing us back on our natural history as the means to see the ironic contradictions in second-order statements about these processes.

Earlier I mentioned the fact that literary critics are tempted to representational theories of truth because they deal continually with different arrangements of experience. It may have struck some of you then that the same principle holds for philosophers even more strongly in fact, because in philosophy competing truth claims are rarely justified as expressions of different possible attitudes toward experience in which we are asked to participate attentively. Why have there been so many philosophies if not that Nietzsche is right in seeing discourse as the objectification of individual wills to impose their interpretive structures on experience? One possible answer helps clarify Wittgenstein's position on irony and on interpretation. Of course abstract philosophy is interpretation because it has traditionally been speech from the outside, from men who consciously reject a perspective from within ordinary experiences in order to put these experiences in another, more systematic and abstract light. Philosophy then has always been second-order discourse and thus has been doomed to the continual uncertainties besetting those who cannot rely on the secure stopping points and agreements experienced in ordinary behaviour.

Now what happens when a Socrates, a Lucian, a Hume or a Wittgenstein begins to poke irony at those structures? The structures grow problematic, but very little in ordinary behaviour is changed, even in the behaviour of living philosophers or critics who are the objects of irony. And the irony frees the rest of us from the doubts and uncertainties traditional philosophy has done more to foster than to check. Perhaps Wittgenstein's most significant achievement, through his articulation of the idea of justification by description, has been his ability to point out why traditional philosophy so vexes the world. He shows that the ground on which traditional philosophers try to construct their edifices is unstable precisely because they feel the need to alter the rough ground they find and to rearrange it into a foundation built upon a desired total interpretation of experience. But because interpretation inherently forces us to take up a position outside the justifications embedded in the way we live, it fosters the instability it is meant to overcome. Once we must interpret, we must hypothesize and be tentative: this is a grammatical fact about a language game or method of projection and not the ground for metaphysical statements. It has always struck me as illuminating that systematic philosophers like Kant read Hume as a scandalous sceptic while Hume's announced purpose was to put experience on a ground free from the attacks of scepticism.

III

I should now like to explore in a more systematic way the ontology which supports Wittgenstein's perspective on consciousness and his reflections on aesthetics. As my brief remarks on traditional philosophy may have indicated, there are here interesting similarities and contrasts with Derrida. These derive from both men recognizing that a representational theory of truth depends on problematic claims for permanent essential correspondences between mind and objects. Once words and things are seen as constituting separate, self-enclosed realms, one can only avoid scepticism by positing some metaphysical entity or 'origin', an absolute mind, a synthetic a priori, logical simples, or an idea of forms or essences, to explain how the two come together. Derrida sees the problem and (especially in his work on Husserl) makes the rejection of essences the cornerstone of his scepticism. But Wittgenstein takes a further step: he recognizes that scepticism is only the reverse demonic side of essentialist thinking and seeks to establish the grounds of knowledge in a new, less problematic way. He moves from the static concept of essence as a permanent correspondence of mind and world to a concept of human actions and the recurrent forms they take as the irreducible ontological base on which to construct his investigations. For Derrida, action as the play of signifiers destroys essentialist thought and leaves only free play; for Wittgenstein, action provides access to a different secure ground for philosophy to be found by remaining within the complex interrelationships of ordinary experience.

There are two traditional philosophic grounds given for a theory of essences, both of which depend upon the possibility of analyzing human experiences to find the deep structures which support them and allow us to distinguish truth from falsity. We might call the first mode Platonic because in a variety of ways it insists that the real is rational and that the test of truth is its correspondence to a deep rational or linguistic structure. The other mode is loosely speaking Aristotelian, since essences depend upon the internal forms and systems of potential relationships which inhere in objects. In modern forms of this mode, the test for one's knowledge tends to be some form of sensation or intuition.

Derrida attacks both modes, the first in his comments on Hegel and Lévi-Strauss and the second in his book on Husserl. But his deconstruction of these philosophers depends in large part on his accepting as true Lévi-Strauss's adaptation of Saussure's linguistics to all cultural modes of representation. That is, Derrida accepts the idea that essences must be express-ible in rational, self-justifying formal systems, then he proceeds to deny the possibility that such systems can even truly represent anything. If language, for example, is a self-contained system, we can never find any lines of projec-tion adequately linking it to the world. For all the projections we wish to apply to language must themselves exist in and be justified by the linguistic system. Lines of projection, the fields of force linking words and the world, then, are determined by linguistic acts of projection and any test of their validity leads us back to the slippery path on which language must continually justify itself. Each line of projection requires reference to an act of projection which can only be explained by another act of projection or signification *ad infinitum*.

In one sense, Wittgenstein begins where Derrida leaves off, convinced that truth theories based on ideal systems are doomed to infinite regress: 'If the world had no substance, then whether a proposition had sense would depend on whether another proposition was true' (TLP 2.0212). The impos-sibility of the Platonic way, however, only drove him deeply into the opposite camp. Despite his quarrels with Russell's logic, he found logical atomism the only possible secure basis for meaning, especially when he discovered in the idea of pictorial logical form a way to escape Russell's tendency to give logic independent ontological status. Atomism might be difficult to work out in specifics, but in principle it allowed him the security of locating the possibility of reference and of truth in the relationship between words, objects and a syntax mirroring the capacity for internal rela-tionships constituted by the form of objects. Each proposition could be measured on its own merits, as a picture of states of affairs, and need not depend on a total representational system. (Pictures are not representational in a Kantian way; they add no distinct content to what they image.) But even after greatly limiting the realm of possibly meaningful sentences to those that could picture facts, Wittgenstein could not successfully resist infinite regress. For what are the objects which guaranteed referring expressions? The sceptic in Wittgenstein soon realized that Russell's logical atoms, the simple objects constituting the world language pictures, were as difficult to locate as were the essential realities of a Platonic or Husserlian philosophy. He was still caught up in a situation where each apparent stopping place or moment of correspondence seemed to require further justification.

Despite the heroic efforts of the *Tractatus*, then, Wittgenstein found himself in the same impasse that justifies Derrida's sceptical claim that an honest philosophy can only express its nostalgia for a secure ground of objects or essences to check the infinite regress of language or learn to revel in the free play this multiplicity of signifiers affords. But his dissatisfaction with the logical atomism he took from Russell eventually brought him to a theory of meanings leading neither to nostalgia nor to free play. His basic discovery has been crucial to the spirit of postmodern literary thought, even if his particular solution has been largely ignored. What he saw, quite simply, was that the theory of logical simples assumed that there was a stable and static reality which language tried to label: propositions have sense when they provide a picture where the names pick out specific objects and logical form delineates a relationship between the names which can be tested for its truth or falsity. But why must we consider reality as primarily static configurations of objects? Suppose I want to tell someone, 'That is a cow'. How does he know I am speaking about the whole object and not its shape or colour or way of standing? (PI §§33–6). The theory of simples assumed that language had primarily an ostensive relationship to objects, but the example of the cow indicates that there is something prior to objects that enables men to make meaningful utterances. Language is woven into a context of actions (PI §7) which constitute the fundamental public norm for assessing statements, not simply as true or false but as appropriate to the procedures taking place: 'Only someone who already knows how to do something with it can significantly ask a name' (PI §31).

Wittgenstein's most suggestive metaphor for articulating the change in his perspective on the grounds of meaning consists in the opposition between lines of projection and methods of projection. He told Rush Rhees that in the *Tractatus* 'he had confused the method of projection' with the 'lines of projection'.[7] He had assumed that meaning and truth functions depended on specifying the lines by which propositions pictured states of affairs. He eventually saw that all the problems of logical atomism could be finessed if he made the methods of projection, the various ways we use names and expect them to be understood, the primary postulate of a theory of meaning. The *Tractatus* focused on explaining what is involved in testing whether we can know *that* something is the case. But knowing *how* is a prior consideration to knowing that, and this realization enables one to avoid any abstract ontology. The norms for understanding utterances are not the pictures they contain but the way they fit in the procedure, the knowing how to do something, that is relevant in a specific situation. This stress on knowing how not only frees Wittgenstein from a problematic ontology, but it also enables him to recover as philosophically significant and meaningful the multiple forms of human speech which he and, later, positivism had banished from philosophy as logically meaningless (though Wittgenstein, at least, never denied their importance for human life).

The later Wittgenstein's concentration on methods of projection establishes a new way of dealing with the concept of essences that, I think, successfully avoids the problematic relationship between signification and reference at the centre of Derrida's scepticism. Wittgenstein's basic epigram is, 'Essence is expressed by grammar' (PI §371), but this obviously will not get us very far without a good deal of analysis. Let us begin by setting another epigram against Derrida's insistence that there can be no secure concept of essence once we recognize the endless process of signifiers needed to supplement attempts to reach a secure signified. The relevant epigram is as metaphysical an utterance as Wittgenstein ever permits himself: 'If we construe the grammar of the expression of sensation as the model of "object" and "designation" the object drops out of consideration as irrelevant' (PI §293; contrast TLP 2.014–2.023). The point here is that some of the many ways we make meaningful statements correlate names and objects, but we recognize that and determine the specific reference from the form of the sentence and the actions woven into it, not from direct lines of projection between names and objects. We name objects because we know how words are used, not because sentences picture or correspond to independent facts (although 'independent facts' has a meaning in specific procedures that differentiate, say, hypotheses from what confirms them). This does not entail any metaphysical claim that objects either exist or do not exist; it simply claims logical priority for something other than objects. After all, the very terms 'object' and 'exist' change meaning as we employ different methods of projection. Moreover these terms are abstract and rarely used in ordinary discourse. Thus any analysis of them in ontological or epistemological terms is bound to be less secure and less convincing than the confidence we have in our established normal procedures for dealing with and discussing the public phenomena philosophers try to define abstractly. Two more epigrams make a clearer case than I can:

> Children do not learn that books exist, that armchairs exist, etc. etc., – they learn to fetch books, sit in armchairs, etc. etc....
>
> (OC §476)

> So one must know that the objects whose names one teaches a child by an ostensive definition exist! Why must one know they do? Isn't it enough that experience doesn't later show the opposite?
>
> (OC §477)

Wittgenstein's, as we will see more fully, is an ontology of what will suffice. The proposition that essence is expressed by grammar seeks to locate the possibility of philosophical certitude on a level of the surface purposes and actions that constitute ordinary experience. Instead of pursuing deep structures underlying appearances, it tries to make us see the necessity within these appearances and to disabuse us of the desire, always leading to nostalgia and to irony, of locating a true source of meanings beneath those we trust in ordinary actions. The corollary of this ontology is a different claim for philosophy: logical analysis gives way to describing the structures implicit in the many modes of projection we employ in carrying on our ordinary procedures for organizing and making sense of experience. The proper role of the philosopher of language, then, is to describe and reflect upon the characteristic way expressions are used (PI §43), upon our knowing how to manipulate language. Conditions of use, rather than the far more narrow and problematic conditions of objective reference, become the criteria for measuring successful achievements of meaning.

The implications for discussions of literary meaning here are far-ranging. First, since reference is not a primary criterion for successful public utterances, there is nothing scandalous or problematic about literary language. We understand what the various personages in a text (including the implicit author) are saying because we have at least two sets of characteristic uses to rely upon: our education in a culture which teaches us to connect certain assumptions and functions to utterances and our ability to see how the specific situation clarifies the action performed in the utterance. Moreover, as some critics have recently made clear, it is possible to see literary conventions themselves as characteristic uses of language we learn to understand as we do other language games.[8] And our response to these conventions need not be purely intellectual and analytic; emotional response or assessment of the qualities exhibited by an utterance can be as relevant and objective as any other way of responding to language when called for by the relevant method of projection. Finally, the role of methods of projection and the image of criteria for using utterances woven into the language help us see that there is something a little simplistic in two currently popular ways of discussing literary meanings. When Derrida distinguishes between the *sens propre* of a term as the only logical means for avoiding the ironic supplementary regress of signifiers, he ignores the possibility that methods of projection, our ways of producing meanings, are as publicly determinate as names which simply copy some ideal, static facts. And when critics like Stanley Fish make the slogan 'meaning as use' a principle to justify a radical process view of individuals creating meanings as they read, they make a similar mistake. They overlook the fact that methods of projection are no more indeterminate than ideal referring expressions. If meanings depend on a texture of actions, these actions are measurable by the conventions we master for achieving or responding to states of affairs that exist in a public realm. As Wittgenstein puts it, 'It is not because I mean it [an expression] that it makes sense' (PI §357), for meaning, like naming, is only possible when one already knows what to do with an expression in a given context.

Rather than enter the many specific arguments one would have to make to give a thorough justification for the claims I have just made, it is more economical to shift the plane of discourse back to the ontology that gives them logical support. Derrida and Fish, in their different ways, seem to assume that once one denies a ground for meaning in constructs like logical simples, one opens up a necessary relativism among competing ways to construe facts, none of which is secure without being itself construed from a relative point of view. The clichéd formulation of such procedures is that once we recognize the dependence of nature upon cultural systems, and not, as traditional Western thought had it, the dependence of culture on some ideal nature, then all cultural constructs must be arbitrary. The issue here is very close to the theme that all representational discourse consists in interpretive fictions, but now the focus is not on the nature of consciousness but on the ontological grounds we can use to discuss questions of meaning. We come then, with the issue of the possible arbitrariness inherent in replacing simples by methods of projection, to a topic where we can draw out the full impact of Wittgenstein's revolution in philosophy and of the gulf between his work and that of thinkers like Derrida who spin out ironic reversals on a theological dream of naturally guaranteed essences.

Paul Ricoeur provides a nice example of the way abstract metaphysics in the theological tradition poses the question of arbitrariness, later developed more fully by structuralists invoking Saussure. In comparing Wittgenstein and Husserl, he claims that Wittgenstein's emphasis on signs in use ignores the more fundamental issue of the ontological status of the sign. Wittgenstein fails to see that it is the arbitrary systematic quality of language which constitutes a 'sign as a sign' and determines the unbridgeable 'distance between thought and life'. This gap at once requires language and renders it problematic (Ricoeur 1967: 216–17). But from a Wittgensteinian perspective, defining the gap is more problematic than comprehending language in the only way it makes sense, in use. We can, of course, study language as a formal system, but how do we know what qualifies as language unless we concentrate on the uses it has? And how do we define such terms as 'life' or 'arbitrary' without seeing what they really mean in practice? Wittgenstein's strategy of posing intermediate cases provides a good example of the impossibility of satisfactorily defining terms like 'abstract', or the 'gulf between thought and life' without looking at the possible uses of such terms. The following remark echoes in its abstractness the pronouncements of Ricoeur and Derrida: 'But if you say: "How am I to know what he means, when I see nothing but the signs he gives?" then I say: "How is he to know what he means, when he has nothing but the signs either?"' (PI §504). But Wittgenstein then examines what possible opposite there could be to the practice of dealing in what might be arbitrary signs:

> I say the sentence: 'The weather is fine'; but the words are after all arbitrary signs – so let's put 'abcd' in their place. But now when I read this, I can't connect it straightaway with the above sense. I am not used, I might say, to saying 'a' instead of 'the', 'b' instead of 'weather', etc. But I don't mean by that I am not used to making an intermediate association between the word

'the' and 'a', but that I am not used to using 'a' in the place of 'the' and therefore in the sense of 'the'. (I have not mastered this language.)

(PI §508)

How easy it is to lose our place when we think from the outside. If the object can drop out as irrelevant then the whole problematic of arbitrariness cannot be resolved by abstract analysis. If the signs have a characteristic use they have the only kind of existence they need.

The possibility of defining language as arbitrary really requires the corollary possibility of standing outside language and judging it by reference to some more inclusive and more established form of certainty. In other words, we must be able to say 'arbitrary in relation to something'. The deeper issue here is the kinds of doubt that can possibly make sense in human experience. Descartes provides a prototype for a typical form of philosophy in his careful doubting of all the certitudes of ordinary experience in order to reach a deeper reflective ground for certainty. But this form of absolute doubt logically entails scepticism, since it begins by denying the only possible grounds for resolving doubt. If I want to suspect that everything may be arbitrary, how can I ever find a ground on which to stop doubting, without some recourse to faith? For a doubt really to make sense, it must itself accept its second-order status as a move within an established system for testing and confirming. Doubt only makes sense where certitude is possible; doubting the possibility of certitude is a doubt with no possible resolution, and hence not a doubt but an ungrounded metaphysical statement. The following quotation exemplifies Wittgenstein's many remarks on this subject in *On Certainty*: 'What would it be like to doubt now whether I have two hands? Why can't I imagine it at all? What would I believe if I didn't believe that? So far I have no system at all within which this doubt may exist' (OC §247; see also OC §115, §117). The doubt in such a case, we might say, has no meaning because it has no use.

The possible charge of arbitrariness then leads us back around to the kinds of ground we must be willing to accept for human actions. The fact that doubt itself requires a language game makes us realize more deeply the truth of Wittgenstein's contention that human actions form an enormous system and only within it do our actions make sense. Doubt presupposes certitude, so we cannot stand outside our forms of life to say that they are either arbitrary or not arbitrary:

You must bear in mind that the language game is so to say something unpredictable. I mean: it is not based on grounds. It is not reasonable (or unreasonable). It is there – like our life.

(OC §559)

If the true is what is grounded, then the ground is not true, nor yet false.

(OC §205)

...as if giving grounds did not come to an end sometime. But the end is not an ungrounded presupposition: it is an ungrounded way of acting.

(OC §110)

Such statements echo Kant's a prioris, but what if these are not forms of representation but a variety of established ways of acting which can be described and recognized without metaphysical or epistemological hypotheses? Here we reach the centre of Wittgenstein's implicit ontology. And the essence of this centre, with its claim that the irreducible bases for human certainty are a variety of ways of acting (PI §224), is the vision that there is no centre and need not be one. We arrive then at a perspective on origins which avoids the whole problem. Wittgenstein simply accepts the fact so much lamented in Continental thought that we are twice removed from the Christian doctrine of an original Logos. There is no divine word grounding the free play of human words, and there is no way to discover any luminously present object anchoring words to the world. But the alternatives remaining are not just nostalgia and free play, because these themes depend on the absence of what we never had. Instead, we can recognize the error so deeply embedded in traditional philosophy and try to restructure philosophy on the grounds of ungrounded but irreducible human actions. The hardest task in philosophy, then – one never achieved by French critics of the doctrine of essence from Bergson, to Sartre, to Derrida – is to stop asking the old questions. If we are to speak of origins at all we must learn to stop at what can be recognized as a valid beginning for philosophical reflection, and that beginning lies not beneath the signs but in the relationships and contexts of action which they carry with them:

It is so difficult to find the *beginning*. Or better: it is difficult to begin at the beginning. And not try to go further back.

(OC §471)

The real discovery is the one that makes me capable of stopping doing philosophy when I want to. The one that gives philosophy peace, so that it is no longer tormented by questions which bring itself in question. – Instead, we now demonstrate a method, by examples, and the series of examples can be broken off. Problems are solved (difficulties eliminated), not a *single* problem.

(PI §133)

IV

We have reached a point where philosophy and literature blend, for the only way to appreciate fully what Wittgenstein has achieved is to understand his own career as taking a dramatic form culminating in the metaphor of being able to stop doing philosophy. This achievement, moreover, helps clarify one crucial way literature in the Romantic tradition interprets its own humanistic role. I want to illustrate the dramatic structure of Wittgenstein's quest by showing how his implicit ontology comes to give a philosophical place to what he described in 1929 as his experience 'par excellence' of absolute values which he then felt were necessarily outside of his primarily positivist philosophy. The first is outwardly directed: a profound sense of wonder over the simple fact that the world exists. And the second expresses the psychological corollary of that state of wonder, an experience of a 'state of mind in which one is inclined to say "I am safe, nothing can injure me whatever happens"' (LE §8ff). The first is a vision of the world as a limited plenitude, the second is a feeling that one can accept that world and find it a secure home.[9]

In his early work, Wittgenstein developed the first experience, that the world exists, into the powerful idea that the mystical is the sense of the world as a limited whole, a sense of the world enclosed within all the possible forms of truth statements. As his vision of manifold methods of projection developed, the image of the limited whole gives way to the dream of a 'synoptic view' (PP §305) which recognizes but cannot enclose the virtually infinite possibilities for making sense of experience. The shift is most evident in the change from the metaphor of logic as 'an infinitely fine network, the great mirror' (TLP 511) to a metaphor for philosophical grammar as involving us in a complex tapestry or set of networks that continually expand (PI v; Z §§447, 568). Here then the world one must accept and the sense of the mystical can no longer be based on a single all-encompassing vision, but consists in an endless series of possibly significant arrangements of experience. When deep structures go, the only object of wonder remaining is a sense of multiplicity and an appreciation of the riches inherent in the surface structures of events. If we consider Wittgenstein's later work in these quasi-religious terms, it has clear affinities with Whitehead's aesthetic philosophy of constantly emerging multiple events, with Owen Barfield's insistence on the importance of saving the appearances, and above all, with Wallace Stevens's vision of resisting the pressure of reality by imaginatively participating in whatever occurs as it occurs. I would like to call this perspective phenomenalism, and to link Wittgenstein with the tradition of Romantic poetics by calling attention to his constant appeals that we use our imaginations to break the hold of traditional philosophical questions and the monolithic world views they entail. He shares, in short, the recurrent desire of the arts since Romanticism to define themselves in opposition to ideologies and to systematic and analytic models for discovering truths. These arts at their best, for example in the Romantic poets' continual testing of new states of mind from which to experience common realities, could themselves have employed Wittgenstein's projected motto from *King Lear*: their aim is to show us differences that make a difference, that are more than diacritical marks.

By investigating some of the implications of the concept of phenomenalism, we can clarify both Wittgenstein's own Romanticism and his articulation of a philosophical position that can provide a coherent secular defence for many aspects of the Romantic tradition. First of all, phenomenalism involves an ontology capable of demonstrating that most of the differences we see in appearances are irreducible differences in fact. Whitehead's organic atomism and his refutation of much analytic philosophy as based on the fallacy of misplaced concreteness exemplifies the kind of philosophy I mean, although Whitehead perhaps created as many metaphysical entities as he saved natural appearances. Wittgenstein is simpler and closer to empirical reality; differences matter because of the variety of games we play, and particular situations matter, even when they seem to be illusions, because it is only by examining the particular event that we can see the possible contexts which inhere in it.[10] Second, an adequate phenomenalism must be willing to stop at particulars and not seek some grounding origin, for the ensuing quest tends to displace the phenomenon. Here phenomenology also begins, but Husserl, Heidegger and Sartre could not ultimately resist the pull of metaphysics and essential realities. Husserl's concern for essence overwhelms his sense of phenomena; Sartre's concern for developing a theory of consciousness reduces his great gift for describing phenomena to the role of mere illustration; and Heidegger's religious and metaphysical concerns allowed him to pursue particulars only when they could be spoken of as disclosing the mysterious presence of being.

Finally, an adequate phenomenalism recognizes the role philosophy must play in relationship to causal explanations, especially scientific ones. Wittgenstein handles this by his distinction between description and explanation. Explanations seek to define phenomena in terms of categories derived from specific systematic constructs. They are concerned with giving reasons why things are the way they are, and they depend on specific needs and established ways of treating things from certain systematic perspectives. But, as we have seen, reasons depend ultimately on grounds which are not reasonable, grounds which simply are. And these grounds can only be described. We cannot be told why our fundamental views of things are the way they are, we can only be reminded of the grammar we have to deal with them. Moreover while explanations tend to appeal to specific systematic perspectives, descriptions appeal to the more fundamental testing ground of ordinary experience, to a perspective *within* the processes being reflected upon. Descriptions rely on the fact that we are all experts in the experiences that really matter and need only careful attention to our lives, not highly specialized forms of knowledge (PI §§124–8, 599).

The following reflection from the *Blue Book* illustrates both the difference between explanation and description and the dangers I have discussed in dealing with ordinary experience from a perspective outside it:

> We have been told by popular scientists that the floor on which we stand is not solid, as it appears to common sense, as it has been discovered that the wood consists of particles filling space so thinly that it can almost be called empty. This is liable to perplex us, for in a way of course we know that the floor is solid, or that, if it isn't solid, this may be due to the wood being rotten but not to its being composed of electrons...Our perplexity was based on a misunderstanding; the picture of the thinly filled space had been wrongly *applied*. For this picture of the structure of matter was meant to explain the very phenomenon of solidity.
>
> (BB: 45)

This sense of the fullness and the multiplicity of phenomena allows Wittgenstein a unique and important perspective on the relationship of philosophy to science, a perspective most clearly elaborated in the way Wittgenstein's heirs treat behaviourism.[11] As I see it, Wittgenstein's position is that philosophy neither applies nor rejects science. In some ways it tries to show what the grounds of science must be, but more importantly it proposes philosophy as a challenge to science. Wittgenstein in effect says to science, whether it be behaviourism or Chomsky's linguistic Cartesianism: 'If you want to extend your findings to the sphere of general human behaviour, I have described complex sets of behaviour which are undeniable and which any system must take into account'. He reminds us that the philosopher should keep the negative example of Kant's Newtonian categories in mind, and remember that the basic forms of human behaviour tend to be more constant in the face of cultural change than are the paradigms of science. The true antagonist for most ambitious systematic projects in philosophy is not another system, but a renewed awareness of the complexity of the obvious.

Wittgenstein's ways of recovering the obvious give concrete substance to the sense of wonder at what is the case which he could only state abstractly and place outside of philosophy in 1929. The generalization remains outside of philosophy, but now only because it is not needed. And Wittgenstein's phenomenalism also allows him to place within philosophy (though not subject to explanation or justification) the security he seeks. It is this concern with security which lies behind the need to find that one can stop philosophizing. Moreover, the need for security is met by the wonder he elicits at the familiar objects and ways of acting which define our intersubjective world and, as Stanley Cavell suggests, make us free by exhibiting our true commitments. Like so many modern writers, Wittgenstein's deepest quest, both philosophically and personally (since he was an alien), was to find a place or a home. And the grand testament of his work is that so long as one is alive to what constitutes the conditions of his existence and avoids the enchantment of deep structures, origins and essences, he need never find a home because he has never lost it. Yet at the same time he must find a way to lose it, if he is to recognize that it has never been lost. This is the key to his philosophical style and to one continuous project in modern literature:

> The feeling of 'familiarity' and of 'naturalness'. It is easier to get at a feeling of unfamiliarity and unnaturalness...
>
> (PI §596)

> The aspects of things that are most important for us are hidden because of their simplicity and familiarity. (One is unable to notice something because it is always before one's eyes.) The real foundations of his enquiry do not strike a man at all. Unless that fact has at some time struck him. And this means: we fail to be struck by what, once seen, is most striking and most powerful.
>
> (PI §129)

For Wittgenstein, to be happy always entailed that one make himself accept the world as it is and not try to impose his will upon it (NB: 73, 75). The poetry of his later writings offers a continually expanding testimony of how we can achieve this peace without surrendering our capacity for wonder or turning to the all too easy conundrums of metaphysics or the cheap sense of self-importance offered by alienated ironists.

Notes

1 I think that the term 'serial structuralism' nicely applies to Barthes and Derrida because both accept Lévi-Strauss on the nature of signification, but both deny that we can uncover beneath the signifying chain a single informing set of structural oppositions. See Derrida's comments on Lévi-Strauss (1972: 247–65), and compare Lévi-Strauss's (1970: 23–8) rejection of serial music with Barthes's (1972: 213–20) use of it as a model.

2 The conceptual self–empirical self distinction and the general structure of my account of representational versus empirical orders may be found in two of Paul de Man's essays (1967, 1970).

3 The most powerful statement of the concept of the tension between representation and some reality which is its other occurs in Michel Foucault (1970: ch. 10). I take his formulation as basic to a good deal of post-structuralist fascination with the limits of language, particularly that of Lacan and of Julia

Kristeva's pursuit of genotexts. For an interesting, if extreme, example following Kristeva, see Shoshannah Feldman's argument that woman may be defined as the other of the patriarchal representational order (1975: 2–10). I should add that there is an interesting argument for the need to conceive thought as representational and computational in Jerry Fodor (1975). Fodor, however, argues for a basic primitive language of representation not subject to infinite regress and thus is not fascinated by the other of representation. And he is not convincing in reducing semantic relations to computational processes.

4 Stanley Cavell (1968: 157–62) is very good on the relationship between language games and 'forms of life'. Below I will refer to this essay for its formulation of the parallels between Wittgenstein and Freud on the concept of freedom as depending upon self-knowledge.

5 Sidney Shoemaker (1963) and J.F.M. Hunter (1973: 38). I should confess here that I am troubled by one aspect of these Wittgensteinian approaches to identity. I do not see how we can avoid behaviourism if we do not posit a specific agent of choice who decides to initiate or change language games. Many philosophers who follow Wittgenstein handle this problem by discussing human actions as a specific form of life involving a grammar of terms like intention and purpose. While I agree with them, I do not see how to reconcile these action concepts with sheerly behavioural or public conceptions of identity. The same problem, of course, is even more pressing for structuralist denials of the whole notion of identity.

6 I am here combining Dorothy Walsh's (1969) fine Deweyian case for literature as eliciting 'the awareness of awareness' with J.N. Findlay's (1963: 251ff) argument for a dialectical process in which our interest in the interestingness of our experiences draws the mind out to a vision of Kant's absolute community.

7 Peter Winch makes very nice use of the distinction between lines and methods of projection (1969: 1–19). As one example of the difference between the two forms of projection, compare the *Tractatus* metaphor of logic as a ruler held up to the world (2.1512) with PI §430, where the ruler is 'in itself...dead, and achieves nothing of what thought achieves'. The best general treatment I know of the ontology of the *Tractatus* is the opening five chapters of Kenny (1973).

8 The two best Wittgensteinian approaches to literary theory are John Casey's *The Language of Criticism* (1966), and John Ellis's *The Theory of Literary Criticism* (1974). I might also cite three essays of mine on the subject: 'A Procedural Definition of Literature' (1978); 'The Poem as Act: An Attempt to Reconcile Presentational and Mimetic Theories' (1975), which deals briefly with speech acts and the institution of literary discourse as a language game; and 'Wordsworth's "Preface" as Literary Theory' (1976), which goes on at length about the difference between Wittgenstein and representational theories of literary language and elaborates the points about Wittgenstein and Romanticism that I will make in concluding this essay.

9 For Wittgenstein's early conceptions of value and of the mystical, see NB: 72–91; TLP 6.4–6.522; Jeremy Walker (1968: 219–32) and Eddy Zemach (1966: 359–75).

10 On the importance of understanding illusions in terms of their full contexts and the implications for this in refuting empiricist sense-data theories of knowledge, see J.L. Austin (1962: 20–54).

11 See especially John Cook (1969: 117–51), and for summaries of the anti-behaviourism growing out of Wittgenstein's phenomenalism, see Hannah Pitkin (1972: ch. 7) and George Henrik von Wright (1971).

Bibliography

Altieri, C. (1975) 'The Poem as Act: An Attempt to Reconcile Presentational and Mimetic Theories', *The Iowa Review* 6: 103–24.

—— (1976) 'Wordsworth's "Preface" as Literary Theory', *Criticism* 18: 122–46.

—— (1978) 'A Procedural Definition of Literature', in Paul Hernadi (ed.), *What is Literature*, Bloomington, IN: Indiana University Press.

Austin, J.L. (1962) *Sense and Sensibilia*, New York: Oxford University Press.

Barthes, R. (1972) 'The Structuralist Activity', in R. Barthes, *Critical Essays*, trans. R.H. Evanston, Evanston, IL: Northwestern University Press, 213–20.

Carver, N. (1973) 'Preface' to J. Derrida, *Speech and Phenomena*, trans. D.B. Allison, Evanston, IL: Northwestern University Press.

Casey, J. (1966) *The Language of Criticism*, London: Methuen.

Cavell, S. (1968) 'The Availability of Wittgenstein's Later Philosophy', in G. Pitcher (ed.), *Wittgenstein: The Philosophical Investigations*, London: Macmillan, 157–62.

Cook, J. (1969), 'Human Beings', in P. Winch (ed.), *Studies in the Philosophy of Wittgenstein*, New York: Humanities Press, 117–51.

Derrida, J. (1972) 'Structure, Sign, and Play in the Discourse of the Human Sciences', in R. Macksey and E. Donato (eds), *The Structuralist Controversy*, Baltimore, MD: The Johns Hopkins University Press.

de Man, P. (1967) 'The Rhetoric of Temporality', in C. Singleton (ed.), *Interpretation: Theory and Practice*, Baltimore, MD: The Johns Hopkins University Press, 173–210.

—— (1970) 'The Intentional Structure of the Romantic Image', in H. Bloom (ed.), *Romanticism: Theory and Practice*, New York: Norton, 65–76.

Ellis, J. (1974) *The Theory of Literary Criticism*, Berkeley, CA: University of California Press.

Feldman, S. (1975) 'Women and Madness: The Critical Phallacy', in *Diacritics* 5(4): 2–10.

Findlay, J.N. (1963) *Language, Mind, and Value*, London: George Allen and Unwin.

Fodor, J. (1975) *The Language of Thought*, New York: Thomas Crowell.

Foucault, M. (1970) *The Order of Things*, New York: Random House.

Hunter, J.F.M. (1973) *Essays After Wittgenstein*, Toronto: University of Toronto Press.

Kenny, A. (1973) *Wittgenstein*, Cambridge: Harvard University Press.

Lévi-Strauss, C. (1970) *The Raw and the Cooked*, trans. J. and D. Weightman, New York: Harper Torchbooks.

Pitkin, H. (1972) *Wittgenstein and Justice*, Berkeley, CA: University of California Press.

Ricoeur, P. (1967) 'Husserl and Wittgenstein', in E. Lee and M. Mandelbaum (eds), *Phenomenology and Existentialism*, Baltimore, MD: The Johns Hopkins University Press, 207–18.

Shoemaker, S. (1963) *Self-Knowledge and Self-Identity*, Ithaca, NY: Cornell University Press.

Von Wright, G.H. (1971) *Explanation and Understanding*, London: Routledge and Kegan Paul.

Walker, J. (1968) 'Wittgenstein's Earlier Ethics', *American Philosophical Quarterly* 5: 219–32.

Walsh, D. (1969) *Literature and Knowledge*, Middletown, CN: Wesleyan University Press.

Winch, P. (1969) 'Introduction: The Unity of Wittgenstein's Philosophy', in P. Winch (ed.), *Studies in the Philosophy of Wittgenstein*, New York, Humanities Press: 1–19.

Wittgenstein, L. (1958) *Philosophical Investigations* (PI), trans. G. E. M. Anscombe New York: Macmillan.

—— (1961) *Tractatus Logico-Philosophicus* (TLP), trans. D.F. Pears and B.F. McGuinness, London: Routledge and Kegan Paul.

—— (1965) 'Lecture on Ethics' (LE), *The Philosophical Review* 74(January): 3–12.

—— (1965) *The Blue and the Brown Books* (BB), New York: Harper Torchbooks.

—— (1969) *Notebooks, 1914–1916* (NB), trans. G.E.M. Anscombe, New York: Harper Torchbooks.

—— (1970) *Zettel* (Z), ed. G.E.M. Anscombe and G.H. von Wright, Berkeley, CA: University of California Press.

—— (1972a) *On Certainty* (OC), ed. G.E.M. Anscombe and G.H. von Wright, New York: Harper Torchbooks.

—— (1972b) 'Wittgenstein's Lectures in 1930–33' (PP), in G.E. Moore (ed.), *Philosophical Papers*, New York: Collier, 247–318.

Zemach, E. (1966) 'Wittgenstein's Philosophy of the Mystical', in I. Copi and R. Beard (eds), *Essays on Wittgenstein's Tractatus*, New York: Macmillan, 359–76.

11

WITTGENSTEIN, FREUD AND THE NATURE OF PSYCHOANALYTIC EXPLANATION

Louis A. Sass

Introduction

Ludwig Wittgenstein was of two minds about psychoanalysis, as he was about many things. Though generally dubious about the worth of psychology, Wittgenstein made an exception for Freud, whom he considered one of the few authors truly worth reading: 'Here at last is a psychologist who has something to say' (Drury 1984: 136). In the 1940s he went so far as to describe himself as a 'disciple' and 'follower' of Freud, and to speak of Freud's 'extraordinary scientific achievement' (LA: 41). Yet, all the while, Wittgenstein remained sharply critical of what he called Freud's 'fishy' way of thinking (Malcolm 1984: 100), and he generally suggested that psychoanalytic insights had more of an aesthetic than a scientific character. Freud he deemed more clever than wise, a man of formidable intelligence and imagination but also of 'colossal prejudice', a 'prejudice which is very likely to mislead people' (LA: 26).[1]

Wittgenstein's attitudes toward religion, science, and the arts are very much on display in his reaction to psychoanalysis, which he described as a curious amalgam of scientific or pseudo-scientific aspirations, of aesthetic effects, and of quasi-religious force and appeal. He recognized psychoanalysis's profound significance as both a symptom and a source of the contemporary sensibility, and was particularly concerned about the potential harm that the popularization of psychoanalysis could do, to individuals as well as to the culture as a whole (Malcolm 1984: 101). Wittgenstein acknowledged the pervasiveness of sexual motives and our powerful need to hide them from ourselves. He was, however, acutely aware of the potential for banalization inherent in psychoanalytic accounts. 'Freud's fanciful pseudo-explanations (precisely because they are brilliant) perform a disservice', he wrote in 1946. 'Now any ass has these pictures available to use in "explaining" symptoms of illness' (CV: 55). He considered the seductiveness of Freud's style of thought to be extremely dangerous. Though potentially a way of enriching self-awareness, psychoanalysis had, too often, proven itself an enemy of the two things Wittgenstein held most dear: clarity about one's own understanding, and a sense of awe about the world.

Whereas Freud was always emphasizing the resistance to his theories about sexuality and the unconscious, Wittgenstein was far more impressed with the meretricious attraction such ideas are likely to have: involving what he termed the 'charm' of the forbidden and of discovering things hidden, as in an underworld or secret cellar; the mythic appeal of seeing present events as repetitions of 'something that has happened before'; and the attraction of debunkingly reductionistic explanations which say that 'This is really only this' (LA: 24–5, 43).[2] He wrote that 'one must have a very strong and keen and persistent criticism in order to see through the mythology that is offered or imposed on one' by the psychoanalytic worldview (LA: 52). Although psychoanalysis might well teach a person things about himself, this was, at best, a mixed blessing: 'In a way having oneself psychoanalyzed is like eating from the tree of knowledge. The knowledge acquired sets us (new) ethical problems; but contributes nothing to their solution' (CV: 34). Wittgenstein believed, in fact, that the causal and scientific modes of understanding to which psychoanalysis aspired often had the insidious effect of *concealing* important questions by giving a false sense of inevitability and turning us away from the richness and multiplicity of the world: 'People who are constantly asking "why" are like tourists who stand in front of a building reading Baedeker and are so busy reading the history of its construction, etc., they are prevented from *seeing* the building' (CV: 40).

Wittgenstein was certainly well-positioned to witness the onset of the psychoanalytic era. Although he apparently did not read Freud before 1920, he came from a Viennese milieu steeped in psychoanalytic ideas, where interpreting dreams quickly became a sort of parlour game. His sister Margarete was an early defender of psychoanalysis, who knew Freud well and had herself been analyzed by him, largely for reasons of 'speculative curiosity' (McGuinness 1982: 29). Wittgenstein never wrote a sustained treatise on psychoanalysis, but he would not infrequently allude to it in his philosophical writings and more personal notes, sometimes as a model for escaping false analogies and other kinds of philosophical error, but more often as an example of the power and persistence of various sorts of illusion. It would be a long time, he believed, before we would lose our subservience to the psychoanalytic myth.

In this essay I shall offer a fairly comprehensive albeit somewhat idiosyncratic overview of the relationship between Wittgenstein and Freud. I shall emphasize Wittgenstein's attitudes toward several aspects of psychoanalysis: its scientific or aesthetic status, its implicit vision of human nature, the sources of its appeal, and its general cultural significance as a kind of modern scientistic mythology. In the course of my analysis, I hope to bring out major differences but also important similarities between these two thinkers, who could be described respectively as the greatest philosopher and

254

the most influential psychologist of the twentieth century. It is important to recognize the degree to which the acuity of Wittgenstein's critique stems from his recognition of profound affinities between his own and Freud's thinking, affinities that may have made him all the more sensitive to certain errors to which Freud too easily succumbed.

But in addition to presenting Wittgenstein's reactions to Freud and psychoanalysis, I will touch upon certain post-Wittgensteinian philosophical developments relevant to psychoanalysis, and will also broach a far more speculative topic: the question of what a Wittgensteinian style of psychoanalysis might look like. To treat these latter topics, it will be necessary to depart from the main theme, the comparison of Wittgenstein and Freud, in order to consider the views of several philosophers who have responded in influential but sometimes rather un-Wittgensteinian ways to issues that Wittgenstein raised about psychoanalysis (especially Donald Davidson and Richard Rorty) and those of another philosopher whose approach, I suggest, may be closer to Wittgenstein's true spirit (Friedrich Waismann). In discussing these thinkers, my primary aim is not to assess the internal coherence or cogency of their respective philosophical arguments, but to examine the general images of human nature and notions of human understanding which they espouse or imply, and to compare these with Wittgenstein's.

Arguments around psychoanalysis have been sharply, sometimes absurdly, polarized in recent years. Wittgenstein's comments on Freud may be unsystematic and unbalanced; they nevertheless point the way toward a more complicated as well as a healthier relationship to Freud and his legacy, one in which we can overcome our subservience without losing our appreciation, and in which we can better understand the rhetorical sources of Freud's sometimes mesmerizing power.

The craving for generality: hedgehog or fox?

Perhaps the most obvious feature of Freud's approach that offended Wittgenstein was Freud's predilection for grand generalization. In his interesting and useful book, *Wittgenstein Reads Freud: The Myth of the Unconscious*, the French philosopher Jacques Bouveresse remarks on the contrast between the caution and reticence of Freud's early collaborator, Josef Breuer, and Freud's own interpretative boldness and explanatory zeal.[3] Whereas Breuer was reluctant to fix on single explanations, preferring a modest eclecticism, Freud often seemed drawn like a sleepwalker toward sweeping generalizations and the assertion of single underlying essences. Thus Freud insisted on the fundamentally wish-fulfilling nature of all (or virtually all) dreams and the unconscious sexual meaning of all hysterical symptoms, on the way jokes always allow covert expression of repressed wishes, and on the primitive or regressive nature of all psychopathological conditions. A telling passage from Freud's *An Autobiographical Study* brings out this cast of mind very clearly: 'The state of things he [Breuer] had brought to light seemed to me so fundamental that I could not believe it would be absent in any case of hysteria, once it had been demonstrated in a single case' (quoted in Bouveresse 1995: 44–5).

But why, Wittgenstein would ask, should such an assumption be made? Why assume that what may be obvious, salient or central in one case is necessarily true of all cases of what we may term 'hysteria'? Hysteria, after all, might well be an instance of what Wittgenstein famously termed a 'family-resemblance concept', a loose grouping of individuals each characterized by one or another of a set of overlapping features or similarities, no one of which pervades them all. And why should dreams, or jokes, always have a single motivation, or always serve a single purpose?

If Freud exemplifies the hedgehog mentality famously described by Isaiah Berlin (1979) – the kind who 'knows one big thing', relating everything to a single central vision – Wittgenstein is far more the fox, moving on many levels, pursuing unrelated ends. Wittgenstein (BB: 18) was a persistent critic of what he termed the 'craving for generality' and its accompaniment, 'the contemptuous attitude towards the particular case', which he considered the most important sources not only of pseudo-science but also of much philosophical error and illusion. He was fond of the adage, 'Everything is what it is and not another thing' (LA: 27), and once thought of taking as a motto for his book a line he recalled (inaccurately) from *King Lear*: 'I'll teach you differences' (Drury 1984: 157). In a passage alluding to Freud's dynamic theory of dreams, Wittgenstein describes how this contempt for particulars comes about, suggesting its link with a belief in hidden essences:

> We now have a *theory*...but it does not present itself to us as a theory. For it is the characteristic thing about such a theory that it looks at a special clearly intuitive case and says '*That* shews how things are in every case; this case is the exemplar of *all* cases', – 'Of course! It has to be like that' we say, and are satisfied. We have arrived at a form of expression that *strikes us as obvious*. But it is as if we had now seen something lying *beneath* the surface.
>
> (Z §444)

Despite his suspicion of unrestrained cravings for generality, it should not be thought Wittgenstein was an enemy of generalization itself. He perfectly well knew that there is no thought, no explanation, and no understanding without generalization of some sort. He was also aware that his own method of philosophical criticism – which depends on an ability to discern recurrent patterns, offer similes, and discern orienting 'pictures' that underlie various modes of thought or philosophical traditions (such as the Cartesian picture of thoughts or sensations as inner objects) – bears more than a passing resemblance to some of Freud's own proclivities. Actually, Wittgenstein and

Freud have an important common ancestor in the romantic organicism of Goethe, whose approach to botany, colour perception and comparative anatomy was based on an aestheticized, intuitive discernment of subtle physiognomic similarities taken to indicate the *Urphänomen*, the primary phenomenon or prototype supposedly underlying all instances of a given type. It was Wittgenstein, however, who seems to have had greater critical distance from this intellectual ancestry.

Serious problems arise, in Wittgenstein's view, when a theorist's craving for generality conspires with the natural human tendency to ignore one's own role in the act of interpretation. The psychoanalyst – like the philosopher or would-be scientist – is inclined to forget how preoccupation with certain models can cause her to fix on particular aspects of a given symptom or event and to ignore all other features; to forget that, as Wittgenstein (LA: 27) put it, 'there are certain differences you have been persuaded to neglect'. This is what occurs, for instance, when the unconscious is treated like a person or a place, and also when unconscious processes are seen as having much the same kind of meaningfulness, deviously strategizing intentionality, or even logical articulation and coherence as may characterize our more lucid moments of conscious awareness (as in Freud's theory of the 'perfectly rational dream-thoughts' (SE 5:597) that supposedly underlie the manifest dream-content). Of the latter case, Wittgenstein (BB: 57) wrote, psychoanalysts seem to be 'misled by their own way of expression into thinking...that they had, in a sense, discovered conscious thoughts which were unconscious'. They treat unconscious experiences as if they were exactly like our most lucid, conscious ones; except for what seems the entirely contingent fact that these unconscious experiences were somehow happening in the dark.

Wittgenstein is not saying that such comparative, pattern-directed, similarity-seeking modes of thought could or should be avoided. His point, rather, is that only by recognizing them for what they are, can one avoid the effacement of differences – and consequent distortion, vacuity or dogmatism – that otherwise occurs. Freud's failure to demonstrate this kind of critical self-awareness is bound up with his commission of a closely related error that Wittgenstein viewed as perhaps the cardinal sin of the philosophical tradition: this is to confuse what is really a method of interpretation, frame of reference, or way of representing facts with a set of discoveries or hypotheses about the external world itself. The philosopher G.E. Moore reports that, in the early 1930s, Wittgenstein said that Freud's books were an excellent place to look for philosophical mistakes:

> because there are so many cases in which one can ask how far what he says is a 'hypothesis' and how far merely a good way of representing a fact – a question as to which [Wittgenstein] said Freud is constantly unclear.[4]
>
> (quoted in Bouveresse 1995: 51)

Wittgenstein likens psychoanalysis to (metaphysical) philosophy, to pseudo-science and to mythology. Psychoanalysis, in his view, is not so much a mode of discovery as of *persuasion*, far less a matter of uncovering new facts than of seducing us into seeing or representing the world in a new way.

Freud usually presents his views as bold empirical hypotheses, but, as Wittgenstein (LA: 44) noticed, many of his claims cannot be verified or falsified through empirical observation: 'Freud is constantly claiming to be scientific. But what he gives is *speculation* – something prior even to the formulation of an hypothesis', The notion of dream-as-concealed-wish-fulfilment, for example, is not a refutable claim. It actually functions as a principle that organizes and limits the *form* of discussion or reflection on the topic in question; it offers the criterion for what, out of an infinity of possible associations, will be allowed to *count* as the meaning of a dream, symptom or slip. It follows that what may seem to constitute potential counter examples to psychoanalytic claims, often turn out to be less a threat to the claims of the theory itself than a challenge to the ingeniousness of the interpreter. This is clear enough if one reflects on the impossibility (or, at least, extreme difficulty) of finding counter-examples, given, for instance, Freud's willingness to countenance the possibility of masochistic or self-punishing wishes and even of forms of anxiety that are supposedly pleasurable. (Freud, so much the hedgehog in his propensity to generalize, seems very much the fox when it comes to avoiding the possibility of discon-firmation or disproof.) One must also recall how much discretionary power the psychoanalyst really has in selecting his data. As one American psychia-trist remarked about his own experience of being psychoanalyzed by Freud:

> I would often give a whole series of associations to a dream symbol and [Freud] would wait until he found an association which would fit into his scheme of interpretation and pick it up like a detective at a line-up who waits until he sees his man.
>
> (Cioffi 1969: 204ff)

The wide variety of sources of empirical non-refutability in Freud's theo-rizing has been pointed out by Frank Cioffi, Sebastiano Timpanaro and others. Their arguments demonstrate the dubious nature of the philosopher Adolf Grünbaum's portrayal of Freud as a would-be empiricist or falsifica-tionist. They also tend to support Karl Popper's denial of the scientific status of psychoanalysis because of what Popper saw as its empirical unfal-sifiability. It is true that some of Freud's claims – such as Grünbaum's favourite example, Freud's association of paranoia with male homosexuality – may generate refutable predictions, a point Wittgenstein would not be likely to dispute; but there are many other claims that clearly do not generate such predictions. Freud sometimes compared his interpretative method with the challenge of solving a jigsaw puzzle. The analogy is misleading. Whereas the puzzle-solver is confined to a predetermined set of rigid fragments, all of which must enter into the eventual solution, the analyst is able to pick and choose the pieces he wishes to use; further, these individual pieces do not have a rigid and wholly predetermined shape. We might therefore echo Wittgenstein by saying that psychoanalytic interpretation is far more like having a dream in which one solves a jigsaw puzzle than it is like the actual solving of a puzzle in waking life.

Wittgenstein's remarks on psychoanalysis are occasional, unsystematic and primarily critical in intent; he never wrote a sustained treatise on the topic. (Many of the remarks come to us only through student lecture notes or the recollections of his friends.) Nor did Wittgenstein ever put forth an overall philosophy of science. It is not surprising therefore that we cannot say with confidence what his final assessment of the current or potential status of psychoanalysis as a scientific enterprise might be.

We do know that Wittgenstein harshly criticized the tendency to confuse 'grammar' or frame of reference (the rules of the game of our speech and understanding) with empirical findings about the world itself, a tendency he considered endemic to the philosophical tradition and that he also discerned in psychoanalysis. In the *Blue Book*, Wittgenstein (BB: 57–9) specifically likens psychoanalytic talk about unconscious thoughts or unconscious feelings to the vocabularies adopted by the realists, idealists and solipsists of the metaphysical tradition. But it is useful to consider as well some crucial ways in which psychoanalytic interpretation can also *differ* from the empty philosophical generalizations or hidden tautologies that Wittgenstein thought he recognized in the philosophical tradition.

Wittgenstein tended to see such all-inclusive philosophical viewpoints as solipsism, realism and idealism as involving rather empty transformations which he termed 'notations' (BB: 57). Adoption of a philosophical 'notation' can have the effect of effacing distinctions previously recognized. A subjective idealist, for instance, may deny that there really *is* any difference between what we naively term perception and hallucination. But more often, adopting a notation is like transposing a melody into a new key: despite a change in overall vocabulary or tone, all the familiar distinctions and relationships are allowed to remain in place. The problem in both cases, according to Wittgenstein, is that only pseudo-insights are likely to be generated; no *new* distinctions are being drawn or discovered. One may question whether metaphysical claims are necessarily as sterile as Wittgenstein seemed to think. But let us put aside this issue and ask instead whether a *psychoanalytic* perspective must necessarily be, in the derogatory sense, a mere notation.

It is true that Freud operates with grand and unprovable generalizations: all dreaming is wish-fulfilment, all motivation sexual in nature. But, once adopted, such a perspective would seem capable – in the right hands – of bringing out new aspects of people and events and of making us notice likenesses or contrasts we would not otherwise have seen. It may allow us to generate more specific hypotheses, perhaps even testable ones, concerning particular types of wish-fulfilling dreams or particular kinds of sexual predilection in relation to aspects of personality or child development. And these aspects, likenesses, or contrasts may well be neither trivial nor obvious. For as Wittgenstein recognized, 'Sexual motives are immensely important', and, 'Often people have good reason to hide a sexual motive as a motive' (LA: 26). Psychoanalysis may have often trafficked in tautology, reductionism, and cliché; its frameworks, however, are at least *potentially* fertile. Psychoanalytic re-descriptions are potentially capable of 'teaching us differences' – differences likely to be of considerable relevance in our lives.

It seems clear in any case that Wittgenstein's attitude toward frameworks of understanding that are empirically irrefutable is far more tolerant than that of either the positivist tradition or the 'critical rationalism' of Karl Popper, who spoke disparagingly of what he termed 'the myth of the framework'. Wittgenstein, after all, was a major source for the Kuhnian notion of the paradigm (Read and Sharrock, in press), and he once described the real achievement of 'a Copernicus or a Darwin [as] not the discovery of a true theory but of a fertile new point of view' (CV: 18). What Wittgenstein criticizes, then, is not the *adopting* of such frameworks but only the tendency – which he discerns in Freud and various philosophers – to mistake the frameworks themselves for something in the nature of empirical assertions or discoveries. It also seems unlikely that Wittgenstein would adopt a postmodernist relativism, arguing that psychoanalysis can, in fact, always and only be a form of rhetoric or persuasion, offering a merely mythological, narrative, or aesthetically pleasing account. But it is difficult to go much beyond these negative points – to say, with much confidence or specificity, what Wittgenstein would have advocated in place of positivism, critical rationalism and relativism.

Would Wittgenstein have recommended using psychoanalytic assumptions and frameworks to generate hypothetical generalizations of a genuinely scientific or empirical kind? Or would he have viewed the domain of human motivation as too particularistic and context-bound to allow for the possibility of meaningful, non-platitudinous generalizations about human motivation? On this last view, psychoanalytic explanations, like historical ones, might be real enough, even though necessarily *ad hoc* and elucidatory rather than rule-bound, general or predictive (see, for example, Louch 1966). Nothing in Wittgenstein's comments on psychoanalysis proves that he favoured one or the other of these last two views. My own guess is that Wittgenstein, the almost instinctual enemy of over-generalization, would have rejected any polarized choice. He might well have argued that psychoanalysis is really a heterogeneous perspective that involves purely hermeneutical elements as well as generalizations of a scientific – or at least proto-scientific – kind.

Reasons and causes

The question of the scientific status of psychoanalysis is frequently said to be bound up with the issue of what sort of explanation it offers; whether, to be specific, it accounts for human action by invoking reasons or by invoking causes. In *The Blue Book* and elsewhere, Wittgenstein (BB: 15) stresses the difference between what he called two 'grammars' or 'language games': one involving knowledge of efficient causation, the other, pursuit of teleological intelligibility. A cause, Wittgenstein argues, is something that cannot be known but only conjectured; it can only be established by observation of empirical correlations between a cause and its purported effects. Whereas a person's recognition or avowal is irrelevant to establishing the causes of his action, according to Wittgenstein, recognition and avowal do play an important role in the rather different language game of establishing reasons or motives. (In *The Blue Book*, Wittgenstein treats the grammar of 'motive' and 'reason' as being essentially similar.) The latter game is a process whereby we rationalize or see the point of our own actions, or else understand what the point of some other person's action must have been given his or her perspective; such understanding generally takes an *ad hoc* form, and does not require the establishing of empirical correlations.

As Wittgenstein notes, Freud generally portrays himself as a scientist pursuing the causes of psychological phenomena. Indeed, Freud often wrote as if such phenomena could be studied on the model of physical objects. In the *New Introductory Lectures*, he writes:

> [The] intellect and the mind are objects for scientific research in exactly the same way as any non-human things. Psycho-analysis has a special right to speak for the scientific *Weltanschauung* at this point, since it cannot be reproached with having neglected what is mental in the picture of the universe. Its contribution to science lies precisely in having extended research to the mental field.
>
> (SE 22: 159)

But Wittgenstein suggests that Freud's actual methods are, in fact, more akin to those of an aesthetic investigator who puts things side by side or strives to give a good simile, as when a critic of literature or art seeks agreement as to the aptness of certain comparisons or tries to sum up a complex artistic work or effect in a succinct expression (Cioffi 1969: 198ff). On this view, the significant similarities Freud emphasizes – between, say, infantile behaviour and adult sexual activity, or between a given manifest dream and a purported underlying wish – cannot be established by experimental or rigorously empirical methods of investigation. Rather, the phenomena at issue are placed side by side so as to elicit (an eventual) acknowledgment of these similarities by the person being interpreted. Such a method may be appropriate for establishing reasons or motives for particular attitudes or actions, says Wittgenstein (BB: 15), but it is a very dubious way of attempting to validate causal hypotheses.

Wittgenstein does not explain this asymmetry of reasons and causes in great detail. He does state that there may be no strict generalizations or deterministic laws that hold in the realm of motivations and feelings (LA: 42). Elsewhere he goes so far as to suggest there need not, in fact, be any correlations at all between thought processes and brain processes (Z §608–11): 'Why should there not be a psychological regularity to which *no* physiological regularity corresponds? If this upsets our concept of causality then it is high time it was upset' (Z §610). For Wittgenstein, a key difference between causes and reasons seems to be that, whereas causal explanation operates in the third-person realm of objective or objectifiable reality, there is something more first-person about the nature of reasons, some way in which reasons are intimately connected with the point of view of the person whose action is being accounted for. This is apparent in the fact that, as Wittgenstein points out, the self-ascription of motives will in many cases be sufficient and does not seem to require any justifying criteria or grounds. (Wittgenstein argues, however, that self-ascription should not be interpreted as involving private, introspective access to 'inner' mental states.) The implications of Wittgenstein's emphasis on self-ascription for the status of psychoanalytic explanation are problematic, however, given that psychoanalysis is in the peculiar business of postulating reasons of which the agent or subject is not consciously aware.

Despite his emphasis on the differences between giving causes and giving reasons, Wittgenstein does not deny a certain kinship between the two language games (Bouveresse 1995: 76). Wittgenstein did, however, believe that Freud's tendency to conflate these language games constituted a serious grammatical 'muddle' that had created an 'abominable mess' of theoretical confusion. There is also a more cynical interpretation of Freud's apparent muddling of reasons and causes. The philosopher Frank Cioffi (1969: 195) argues that (what he sees as) the illegitimate psychoanalytic tendency to speak of reasons as if they were causes has actually been 'ingeniously exploited' by Freud and his disciples in the interest of protecting psychoanalytic theory from any possible source of refutation. This conflation allows Freudians to treat a person's acknowledgment of an hypothesized motive as counting in favour of the hypothesis (since it *is* a kind of reason), without forcing the Freudians to treat refusal as counting *against* the hypothesis (since the hypothesized motive is also a cause, thus potentially independent of possible acknowledgment). And this, insists Cioffi, smacks less of grammatical confusion than of a certain grammatical flair, a flair for immunizing oneself against all possibility of epistemological risk.

Wittgenstein's remarks on reasons versus causes have given rise to a vast, intricately argued and highly technical literature on the distinction. Wittgenstein's own views remain, however, somewhat obscure. I would argue that a considerable amount of what has been written on the topic seems to miss either the spirit or the point of what Wittgenstein was getting at when he complained about Freud's tendency to treat reasons as if they were causes.

Theorists of a postmodernist persuasion might be tempted to take Wittgenstein's distinction between reasons and causes, along with his likening of psychoanalytic explanation to aesthetic similes, to have demonstrated the essentially non-scientific and wholly non-empirical nature of Freud's enterprise. If psychoanalysis, properly understood, trafficks in reasons rather than in causes, and if reasons are established merely through the actor's acknowledgment of similarities, it might seem to follow that psychoanalytic accounts are not, in fact, subject to any form of independent empirical confirmation or disconfirmation. Wittgenstein's distinction might therefore seem to support those who would deny that psychoanalysts can aspire to give veridical descriptions of some objective reality – the patient's psyche or past – and who believe that analysts should devote themselves instead to the only real option, the fashioning of appealing stories that can lend a sense of coherence to one's life history or foster a sense of control over one's fate.[5]

Whatever the merits of such a position (doubtful, in my view; Sass 1994b, 1995), this sort of relativism, scepticism or subjectivism is certainly inconsistent with Wittgenstein. The somewhat cryptic nature of Wittgenstein's remarks on the philosophy of action and mind may have allowed him to be interpreted, at times, as advocating a relativist attitude toward the explanation of human action (for example, Gergen 1994), but this is clearly a misreading.[6] In pointing out the role of avowal, Wittgenstein is speaking of what he characteristically called the 'grammar' of our concept of reasons. He is saying that it is intrinsic to our understanding of and way of speaking about reasons that they are the sort of thing that can usually or eventually be avowed, or, to put the point slightly differently, that avowal is generally *relevant* to the establishing of reasons. Although it is difficult to give a clear and succinct positive statement of what Wittgenstein means, it is clear that he does not mean to imply that having a reason and avowing that reason are one and the same thing. The fact that the possibility of avowal is part of the grammar of reasons does not imply that a reason must *always* be avowed; still less that avowal alone can *make* something a reason.[7]

In his 'Conversations on Freud' (LA: 43, 51–2), Wittgenstein does describe the powerful, and potentially therapeutic, effect that the acceptance of a psychoanalytic narrative can have, quite independently of its veridicality or truth value. But this is not the same as arguing that the goal of veridicality is either therapeutically irrelevant or, from an epistemological standpoint, futile to pursue; I doubt that Wittgenstein would have been inclined to argue in favour of either of these latter points. It is significant, in fact, that, just after mentioning the 'immense relief' a psychoanalytic narrative may provide, Wittgenstein immediately recommends a critical attitude that would help one 'recognize and see through the mythology that is offered or imposed on one' (LA: 52). Denial of the very possibility of aspiring to veridicality would make it difficult to see what this kind of critical attitude could amount to.

Perhaps the most influential analysis of the reason/cause distinction is to be found in the writings of the American philosopher Donald Davidson (Hopkins 1982).[8] In 'Actions, Reasons, and Causes' and a series of later articles, Davidson (1980) disputes the views of a number of followers of Wittgenstein by arguing that reasons can indeed be causes, and that reason-explanations are, in fact, a species of causal explanation.[9] Davidson's views have had considerable appeal, even to many who are generally sympathetic to Wittgenstein; his views have proved especially attractive to some philosophically minded psychoanalysts and psychoanalytically inclined philosophers (for example, Cavell 1993; Wakefield and Eagle 1997). Davidson's analysis seems to preserve the common-sensical assumptions that reasons are real things that can actually be discovered and not merely invented, and that reasons can have an efficacious role in the life of the mind; yet, at the same time, his analysis (like Wittgenstein's) rules out the possibility of *reducing* reasons to causes or the scientism this would imply ('scientism' here implies near-exclusive reliance on neo-Baconian empirical methods). Davidson's approach also suggests a way of conceptualizing motives that would seem to make them independent of avowal, and this is attractive for anyone who wishes to be able to speak of *unconscious* reasons.[10]

According to Davidson's view, reference to reasons (that is, to particular combinations of beliefs and desires) can indeed play a legitimate role not only in rationalizing or making sense of an action but also in giving a causal explanation of it. As he points out, to say that I crossed the road to buy a pack of cigarettes is to imply not only that I had a certain combination of desires and beliefs that are able to justify or make sense out of the action: the desire for cigarettes and the belief that I can obtain them by crossing the street. It is to say as well that this combination, this belief–desire nexus, was 'efficacious', that it actually caused me to cross the street; that is, that I was *in fact* motivated by this desire and did in fact do it *for this reason* (Davidson 1980: 232, 254). One can imagine situations where, even though the person had the relevant beliefs and desires, he nevertheless did not cross the street *because of* these particular mental states (Davidson 1980: 9). According to Davidson, the fact that a relevant belief/desire combination is assumed to have played some kind of actual causal role is what makes us speak of it not as *a* reason but as *the* reason for a person's action, or as one might also put it, as being an 'active' rather than an 'inactive' reason for the action (Thornton 1998: 181).[11] So far, all this accords with common-sense views.

The significance generally attributed to Davidson's intervention in the reasons-causes issue can, I think, best be described by contrasting it with two currently popular views. (Although these views are typically espoused by very different kinds of philosophers, they are actually mutually compatible and may even be complementary.)[12] Davidson's approach conflicts – or, at least, *seems* to conflict (see below) – with the kind of postmodernist scepticism and relativism that would ask us to consider reason-explanations to be mere *post-hoc* constructions that make no truth claim; and also with materialist approaches, such as epiphenomenalism and eliminativism, that would refuse to ascribe any causal or explanatory significance, or even reality, to mental phenomena such as reasons. Against the relativists, Davidson argues that, with regard to reason-explanations for human action, there is indeed a fact of the matter (or, at least, fact*s* of the matter). Against the eliminativists and epiphenomenalists, he seems to be arguing that these reasons do, in fact, matter; that they do, in some way (which I have not yet specified) play an 'efficacious' role (Davidson 1980: 232).[13]

It is not difficult to see why Davidson's position might appeal to many psychoanalysts. It promises to save them from the potentially demeaning (postmodernist or eliminativist) idea that psychodynamic accounts of motives and reasons can be nothing more than appealing stories or mere 'folk psychology', with no possibility of offering a true or a truly explanatory – i.e. a causal – account (see Cavell 1993: 86). It also countenances the possibility that the real or truly efficacious reason motivating an action might be something other than what the actor is able to recognize or to avow. As we shall see, however, it is questionable whether Davidson really delivers on these promises. (Actually, his position turns out to be more difficult to distinguish from epiphenomenalism and eliminativism, and perhaps also from relativism, than it initially appears.) But before addressing this issue, let us compare Davidson's and Wittgenstein's views on the role of reasons in psychological explanation, a topic on which they largely agree. Davidson does assert, *contra* Wittgenstein, that reasons can play a role in causal explanation. But on Davidson's account, reason-explanations are causal explanations of a rather special kind, a kind that differs from physicalistic causal explanation in very much the way that the reasons and causes to which Wittgenstein refers differ from each other.

Davidson (1980) states that reason-explanations, unlike the explanations of physical science, explain by 'rationalizing' or showing the point of something for the actor or agent. They lead us 'to see something the agent saw, or thought he saw, in his action – some feature, consequence, or aspect of the action the agent wanted...' (Davidson 1980: 3). Further, they operate in the realm of the mental, which Davidson views as having normative and holistic qualities (it is governed by constitutive principles of rationality) that preclude reasons from entering into the kinds of strict nomological generalizations that are possible in physics. According to Davidson's position, 'there are no strict psychological or psychophysical laws; in fact, all strict laws are expressible in purely physical vocabulary' (Lepore 1999: 207). Wittgenstein, too, saw reasons as making sense out of our actions; he too suggested that reasons could not be described in terms of strict generalizations or deterministic laws such as apply in the natural sciences or at least in physics. 'There are no strict laws at all on the basis of which we can predict and explain mental phenomena', writes Davidson. There are no 'serious laws connecting reasons and actions' (Davidson 1980: 224, 233). Compare this with Wittgenstein (LA: 42): 'Psychologists want to say: "There *must* be some law" – although no law has been found...Whereas to me the fact that there *aren't* actually any such laws seems important'.

So, on Davidson's account, a given reason may well illuminate the purported causal structure of a given series of events. However, it is highly context-specific and context-bound, and therefore unlikely to be generalizable beyond the given case; at least without watering down the generalization with a host of *ceteris paribus* or all-things-being-equal qualifications. Such a view has important implications for our understanding of psychology and other social sciences, of their potential to establish lawlike generalizations and their general contribution to the explanation of human actions. He claims that we can indeed regard someone's having a reason as the cause of his or her action.[14] But we should not conclude from this that the mental kinds that enter into reason-giving explanations (i.e. beliefs, desires and the like) are on a par with the kinds of phenomena that are cited in the causal explanations offered by the physical sciences. So far, what Davidson says concerning reason-explanations seems, then, to be not so very different from Wittgenstein's point when he reprimanded Freud for treating reasons on the analogy of causes operating in the physical world. As Marcia Cavell (1993: 57) puts it in a book that presents a Davidsonian reconstruction of psychoanalysis: 'Although reason-explanations are causal explanations, nevertheless no psychology which treats mental states *as* mental can be a science in the sense that Freud claimed for psychoanalysis'.[15]

I have been describing the agreement between Davidson and Wittgenstein concerning the rationalizing role played by reason-explanations. But what of Davidson's closely related, and avowedly *anti*-Wittgensteinian, theses that reasons *can* be causes and that reason-explanations can be causal explanations? What exactly is Davidson claiming when he says that reasons can play an actual causal role?

Regarding the nature of causality, Davidson accepts a neo-Humean or nomological position. On such a view, one can only speak of actual causal relations in the case of events that can be subsumed under fairly strict, predictive or covering laws. But I just noted Davidson's denial of the very possibility of 'strict' or 'serious' (Davidson 1980: 233) lawlike generalizations regarding mental events. How then, one may ask, can Davidson claim that a reason may not only rationalize an action, but also play an actual role in causal relations themselves? The answer lies in the doctrine of 'anomalous monism', which is Davidson's position concerning the mind-body relationship.[16]

According to anomalous monism, there is no type–type correspondance between mind and matter, no strict pattern of correlations between kinds of mental events and kinds of physical events in brain and nervous system. On this point, Davidson and Wittgenstein appear to agree, and probably for much the same reason (namely, that rationality and normativity play constitutive roles in the mental realm, and that there is no echo of these factors in the physical domain (Thornton 1998: 184; Kim 1985: 374, 377)). Davidson, however, asserts the token-identity theory, which implies a much closer connection between the two realms; namely, that even though there are no strongly systematic or strict relations between the two types of events, each mental event is nevertheless 'token-identical' with a physical event. According to Davidson's monistic view, each mental event just *is* a physical event, but one that happens to be described from a particular point of view. (Initially, Davidson also adopted a supervenience theory, according to which physical facts determine mental facts but not the reverse, a position that may well be incompatible with anomalous monism; later he seems to reject the supervenience thesis, but without explicitly acknowledging the shift (Davidson 1980: 214; 1987: 453; Evnine 1991: 70–1).) The fact that each belief-desire nexus is token-identical with some physical event means that it exists in a realm within which nomological generalizations (a requirement for actual causation) may hold. It is true that these mental events, when taken *as* mental events, cannot instantiate a strict causal law; these same mental events are, however, identical with physical events, and when considered *as* physical events, they may well instantiate such a law. This, according to Davidson, is the sense in which a reason can actually *be* a cause.[17] What justifies speaking of reasons as causes in our explanatory accounts is, then, that reasons have an indirect relationship to the realm of physical entities, a realm that *is* governed by the strict predictive or covering laws that define actual causation.[18] Various writers on psychoanalysis have accepted Davidson's argument and gone on to conclude that, contrary to Wittgenstein's claim, Freudians are justified in treating reasons as potential causes (Cavell 1993: 57, quoted above; Wakefield and Eagle 1997). But how compelling, and how helpful to the psychoanalytic project, is Davidson's position on reasons and causes, or the anomalous monism on which it rests?

This is not the place for a comprehensive critique of Davidson's approach. (Nor am I attempting to offer a synoptic reconstruction of Wittgenstein's position on reasons and causes.) It is worth noting, however, that many critics have raised what seems the rather obvious question whether Davidson's position on the mind–body relationship does not in fact end up depriving the mental realm (the realm of meaning or of propositional content) of any actual causal role (McGlaughlin 1993, 1999; Sosa 1984, 1993; Kim 1993a, 1993b, 2000; Johnston 1985; Honderich 1982; Stoutland 1985; Antony 1989). The critics' basic point is straightforward enough. If the mental realm is 'anomalous', that is, if no 'strict' or 'serious' nomological generalizations can be made concerning mental 'kinds' (as Davidson states), this would seem to imply that mental events, *qua* mental events, must be causally irrelevant (i.e., that they cannot be causes 'in virtue of falling under mental types' (McGlaughlin 1999: 690)); and that any causal powers a mental event may in fact have would be entirely dependent on its physical aspect. Davidson himself explicitly denies that anomalous monism implies that 'the mental properties of an event' are 'causally power- less' or 'make no difference to its causal relations' (Davidson 1993: 4, 13).[19] He often speaks as if a belief-desire nexus could indeed be causally effica- cious in virtue of its mental properties; that it could function as what Davidson terms a 'rational cause' (Davidson 1980: 233).[20] However, neither Davidson nor his followers have been able to explain how the thesis of the causal relevance of mental properties could be compatible with the non- reductive materialism of anomalous monism (McGlaughlin 1999: 691; but see Davidson 1993; LePore and Loewer 1987).[21] One commentator, gener- ally sympathetic to Davidson as a philosopher, sums up what he terms 'the rather aimless position one gets by combining the thesis that reasons cause actions with the admission that the mental properties of states are not causally relevant':

> [This] does not entail the falsity of the claim that reasons cause actions, but it does mean that we cannot say that a reason causes an action for which it is a reason because the mental states which constitute the reason have the propositional contents they do. And given this lacuna, it becomes doubtful how attractive the thesis is that reasons cause actions at all.
>
> (Evnine 1991: 161, 164)

Given Davidson's widespread influence, it is surprising how obscure, even 'opaque', most readers have found his arguments to be; even the general import of his views can be exceedingly difficult to pin down.[22] This makes it difficult to evaluate Davidson's position with much confidence. But if the above-mentioned criticisms are correct, then the import of his position on reasons and causes certainly does look rather different than it may first have appeared. Once the implications of Davidson's views are carefully traced, it is difficult to see how they provide any new resources that would help to justify the enterprise of psychoanalysis.

It certainly seemed that Davidson, in contrast with the Wittgensteinians, was according real causal significance to reasons. This turns out, however, to be largely illusory, or at least unrelated to their status *as* reasons in any usual sense. Despite Davidson's own explicit claims and apparent self-under- standing, nearly all commentators consider him to be ultimately committed to 'type epiphenomenalism', the view that 'no state can cause anything by virtue of falling under a mental type' and that the mental is causally inert

(McGlaughlin 1993: 27; 1999: 690; Kim 1993: 19). And, if mental content turns out to be causally inconsequential, or relevant only for the *post hoc* rationalizing of human action, then Davidson's actual position may even approach eliminativism:[23] his position seems to imply that beliefs and desires – the key elements of most psychoanalytic accounts – are nothing more than the paraphernalia of 'folk psychology' (the misleading and irrelevant stories we tell ourselves), and may therefore ultimately deserve, like phlogiston, to be eliminated from our fundamental ontology.[24]

Rationalism and the unconscious

There is an additional aspect of Davidson's understanding of reason-explanations that needs to be considered: its highly rationalistic flavor. This puts him at odds with the fundamental spirit of a Wittgensteinian approach, and in conflict as well with some of the more appealing aspects of psychoanalytic theory.

The Davidsonian approach to the explanation of human action is framed in terms of 'intentional states', that is, in terms of specifiable nexuses of belief and desire – propositional attitudes – that are described and imagined as having specific kinds of 'propositional content', and that play a logical but also causal role in what Aristotle called the practical syllogism. For instance, a person's desire to buy a pack of cigarettes, along with his belief that cigarettes are sold across the street – taken together with an indefinite number of other supporting beliefs – lead him to the practical conclusion of walking across the street. On this sort of account, the ensuing action is like the conclusion of a syllogism: it follows from it logically. 'For a desire and a belief to explain an action in the right way', Davidson writes, 'they must cause it in the right way, perhaps through a chain or process of reasoning that meets standards of rationality' (Davidson 1980: 232).[25]

Implicit in Davidson's account is the assumption that, for an interpretation to succeed in its explanatory task, the set of intentional states attributed to the agent, speaker or thinker must be to a large extent 'rational'. Davidson describes intentional interpretations (i.e., the ascription of mental states) as a process both normative and holistic that is guided by a principle of charity; namely, the constraint that we find a person's beliefs, desires, thoughts, etc., to be in large measure consistent with one another. In fact, he argues that unless we *do* attribute a large measure of rationality to a subject, we will have grounds for believing the subject in question may not be an intentional agent at all. And under such circumstances, one would, on the Davidsonian account, be obliged to give up on the project of interpretative understanding of a person's speech, action or experience, and to explain it instead in the starkly non-psychological vocabulary of physical science.[26] According to this view, 'inconsistency breeds unintelligibility' (Davidson 1982: 303).

One might have expected that the value of psychoanalysis resided in its ability to acknowledge the inconsistency or irrationality of the unconscious while, at the same time, finding a way to make this at least partially comprehensible. Davidson (1982) and other philosophers (for example, Cavell 1993) have argued, however, that there must be something incoherent about any concept, such as the psychoanalytic notion of primary-process thinking, that would allow one to attribute radically inconsistent, indeed mutually contradictory, beliefs to the same agent. (The very notion of incoherence is itself incoherent, one might say; for rationality, on Davidson's account, is 'the essential characteristic of the mental' (Kim 1985: 377).)

In 'Paradoxes of Irrationality' (Davidson 1982: 300–5), Davidson argues that, in order to explain many and perhaps all cases of irrationality, it is necessary to postulate a partitioning of the mind into overlapping but quasi-autonomous parts, each containing a considerable degree of internal logical structure and coherence, and which can interact more or less in the manner of separate minds. Following Davidson's lead, Richard Rorty (1991: 147) adopts what appears to be a more extreme position by claiming that many seeming cases of irrationality can only be understood if one adopts a homuncular account, a model of two or more distinct persons within the self, each having an internally consistent set of beliefs (and each of which is thus intelligible) but where these sets are somehow in conflict with each other.[27]

As the focus on the issue of coherence may suggest, Davidson's arguments concerning explanation are primarily driven by epistemological considerations. That is, they are driven by what Davidson takes to be constraints on an interpretation's making sense, rather than by a more immediate or direct concern with the intrinsic nature of the object that is *being* interpreted; which in this case is the human psyche, or a particular person's psyche. Davidson's project can be characterized as an attempt at 'rational reconstruction'. He describes it as an attempt to specify constitutive conditions that must be true for any psychological interpretation to get off the ground, and not as any kind of empirical or ontological project intended to specify the nature of the object of study, that is, the nature of the actual psychological realities that instantiate these conditions.[28]

To some readers, however, it has seemed that Davidson does in fact derive ontological conclusions from his epistemological analyses, given that he

> holds that what people actually believe and mean [and desire and do] is constituted by what, according to the 'epistemological' considerations included in the Principle of Charity, it is ideally rational for them to believe and mean [and desire and do].
>
> (Evnine 1991: 178, 168)

270

Evnine describes this as involving a 'penetration of the real by the ideal' (Evnine 1991: 168). Other readers of Davidson have gone further by arguing or assuming that his assertion of mental causation actually depends on a particular kind of 'realist' theory of propositional content, a view that treats beliefs and desires as 'intervening distinguishable states of an internal behaviour-causing system' (phrase from Dennett 1987: 52; Evnine 1991: 161, 178), that is, as 'separate entities that can cause actions', such as 'mental representations [existing] in my head' (Wakefield and Eagle 1997: 323).[29] But as I indicated, the position Davidson explicitly espouses is more tentative, and far more guarded concerning its implications at the level of actual psychological processes. Davidson himself describes his explanatory apparatus as offering no more than 'conceptual aids to...coherent description' (Davidson 1986b: 92).[30] He treats beliefs and desires as theoretical constructs, without suggesting they are entities or mental objects existing in or before the mind (Davidson 1986b: 165).[31]

Can we then speak of the ontological or metaphysical implications of a Davidsonian approach? I am not sure; the point is certainly debatable. But whatever one thinks regarding this question, I would argue that Davidson's philosophical position does at least have some important implications that go beyond purely epistemological concerns, beyond the understanding of the nature of psychological explanation and interpretation to affect our image of human nature itself. After all, to say that human beings can only be *understood* in a particular way (for example, as rational or consistent) is, at the very least, to accord a place of *privilege* to this vision. It is to say that, so far as *we* are concerned (and what else could possibly matter?), human beings must be understood in a certain light or according to a certain model.[32] In Davidson's case, this turns out to be a model that emphasizes logic or logic-like processes, and that dismisses the possibility, or at least the significance, of other modes.

In her Davidsonian reconstruction of psychoanalysis, Marcia Cavell (1993) argues that there is something incoherent about the very idea of attributing any significant degree of incoherency to a mental state; she goes on to draw conclusions that amount to a denial of the very possibility of forms of thinking – in early childhood or dream-states, for example – that are, in any significant sense, irrational. If this is to be taken as more than a merely semantic or notational issue (i.e., as amounting to more than a plea to use the terms 'thinking' or 'mental state' in an unusually restrictive way), then it does seem to involve implications about how we are to understand or imagine human nature and experience. Some of these implications emerge in especially clear, and perhaps exaggerated, form in Richard Rorty's essay, 'Freud and Moral Reflection', in which Rorty offers a highly rationalistic portrayal of human beings.

Rorty is a neo-pragmatist of an overtly constructivist, relativist, or postmodernist kind. He echoes Davidson's reticence about making ontological claims in exaggerated form. Thus in 'Freud and Moral Reflection', Rorty (1991) states that he fully approves of what he describes as the modern intellectual's 'increased ability to treat vocabularies [such as the Freudian] as tools rather than mirrors' of any objective reality (Rorty 1991: 158). He vigorously rejects what he calls the 'naturally metaphysical turn of mind', the sort of mindset that would insist 'on pressing the questions, "But what am I *really*? What is my *true* self? What is *essential* to me?"' (Rorty 1991: 146). But this does not prevent Rorty from going on to offer enthusiastic endorsement of a particular image of human beings.

Rorty claims that the Freudian unconscious, if understood properly (that is, in what he understands to be a Davidsonian fashion), can only be what he himself calls a '*rational* unconscious – one that can no more tolerate inconsistency than can consciousness' (Rorty 1991: 150). Rorty rejects Freud's vision of the unconscious as composing 'the deepest strata of our minds, made up of instinctual impulses', and in which 'contradictories coincide' (SE 14: 296; quoted in Rorty 1991: 150). He argues that one should instead think of one's unconscious mind as a kind of 'backstage partner', an alternative self some of whose beliefs, from the standpoint of consciousness, may be hopelessly 'whacky' or incorrect, yet who has 'a well-worked-out, internally consistent view of the world'. Our unconscious selves, he writes, are 'the intellectual peers of our conscious selves, possible conversational partners for those selves' (Rorty 1991: 149–50). On this view, the unconscious mind may well be mistaken about certain matters of fact; it cannot, however, be seriously illogical in the structure of its beliefs and desires.

It is striking to register the degree to which, at least in this particular version of a Davidsonian account, the nature of the human being approaches what one might have thought is peculiar to the logician or the philosophically inclined intellectual. Davidson claims to arrive at his position solely through an examination of the conditions of intelligibility; Rorty, however, is unabashed in acknowledging his preference for a certain vision of human nature. In 'Freud and Moral Reflection', Rorty lays his cards quite openly on the table, freely admitting that his enthusiasm for the reading of psychoanalysis offered in his essay is dictated by his assumption 'that the ironic, playful intellectual is a desirable character-type, and that Freud's importance lies in his contribution to the formation of such a character' (Rorty 1991: 158–9). One may wonder, however, whether this denial of irrationality is an instance of 'intellectualocentrism' or the 'theorization effect', Pierre Bourdieu's term for the theorist's tendency to slide 'from the model of reality to the reality of the model' by projecting onto actual practice or experience what is really the observer's theoretical way of understanding it (Bourdieu 1990: 29, 39, 86).

The unconscious, as Rorty conceives it, does seem to be a philosopher's not-so-secret sharer: he imagines the unconscious as a person with some strange intellectual commitments and peculiar intuitions, but who (sigh of relief) is just as committed as oneself to the rigours of logical form and the demands of consistent argument. Here it is worth recalling Arthur Lovejoy's (1936: 11) description, in *The Great Chain of Being*, of the 'diverse kinds of metaphysical pathos' that can be inherent in a theoretical description of the universe; implications that, apart from any more legitimate sources of validity, evoke congenial feelings and thereby incline a person to accept the view in question. Here philosophy is giving us a view of human experience that assimilates not only conscious thought but even the unconscious to the ideals of consistency and reason, the very concerns that are most salient for a philosopher in the logic-dominated tradition of analytic philosophy. The world echoes back what the philosopher feels to be his own deepest essence.

The merits of this rationalistic vision can be debated, of course. I think it is clear, however, that it is not one with which Wittgenstein, at least in his later thought, would have had much sympathy. I think it would have offended Wittgenstein's quasi-mystical leanings as well as his wish to ground human existence not only in the practical and the social, but also in the most creaturely and instinctual part of human nature: 'I want to regard man here as an animal', wrote Wittgenstein toward the end of his life,

> as a primitive being to which one grants instinct but not ratiocination. As a creature in a primitive state. Any logic good enough for a primitive means of communication needs no apology from us. Language did not emerge from some kind of ratiocination.
>
> (OC §62)

The whole spirit and thrust of the Davidsonian approach – so influential in contemporary philosophy – seems in fact to run at cross-purposes with that of Wittgenstein, whose own approach is far less programmatic or prescriptive in nature. Davidson wants to isolate the essence, and thereby prescribe the logic, of any acceptable account of human action or expression. Far more characteristic of Wittgenstein, by contrast, is the wish to warn us *against* the unrecognized and too-easy assimilation of a complex of ambiguous phenomena to the familiar and overly clear picture inherent in various theoretical accounts or ways of speaking. (This is part of what Wittgenstein means when he writes: 'And we may not advance any kind of theory...We must do away with all *explanation*, and description alone must take its place' (PI §109).) A good example of this assimilation was mentioned at the beginning of this essay: the way in which psychoanalysts seem, in Wittgenstein's words (BB: 57), to be 'misled by their own way of expression into thinking...that they had, in a sense, discovered conscious thoughts which were unconscious'. It is this very kind of assimilation, it seems to me, that occurs when the Davidsonians impose their rationalistic, explanatory conception of what can count as an acceptable intentional account, a conception that would treat even unconscious processes in terms of the practical syllogism.

273

Wittgenstein's distrust of the overly clear or overly simple, theoretical picture can be applied as well to some of his own distinctions, such as that between the language games of giving reasons and giving causes. Useful as Wittgenstein's distinction may be, for certain purposes, I do not think we must read him as implying that these two are the *only* language games having significant application to the understanding of human action and expression, or that there is only *one* way to capture intelligibility, or even that the distinction itself might not need to be transcended. (This would contrast with the Davidsonian position, which seems to assume that there are but two, radically different sorts of causal explanation: explanations referring only to 'blind' causal mechanisms, and intentional explanations involving reasons or 'rational causes' (Cavell 1993: 55–6).) I am not claiming that Wittgenstein actually does get around to calling into question his own reasons-versus-causes distinction. However, in his treatment of certain other psychological concepts, Wittgenstein acknowledges that similar distinctions sometimes do require just this kind of deconstructive critique. Consider, for instance, Wittgenstein's rich meditation on the phenomenon he called 'seeing-as' or 'aspect-seeing'.

The phenomenon of 'seeing-as' or 'aspect-seeing' includes experiences in which, in Wittgenstein's words (PI: p.196), one has the sense 'of a *new* perception and at the same time of the perception's being unchanged': for example, 'I contemplate a face, and then suddenly notice its likeness to another. I *see* that it has not changed, and yet I see it differently. I call this experience "noticing an aspect"' (PI: 193; on seeing-as, see Mulhall 1990; Sass 1994a). Wittgenstein's approach is not to assume that one or another clear theoretical picture from our repertoire of psychological concepts *must* apply to the experience in question, but to look carefully at a varied selection of examples against which he tests (and usually finds wanting) a set of relevant concepts. 'Seeing-as', for example, defies our usual ways of describing our understanding, for it lies between – it constitutes what Wittgenstein calls an 'amalgam' of – psychological concepts that we normally use to think about experience and the mind: it can equally well, or equally inappropriately, be described as a perceptual or as a conceptual process. 'Hence the flashing of an aspect on us seems half visual experience, half thought..."But this isn't *seeing*!" – "But this is seeing!" – It must be possible to give both remarks a conceptual justification' (PI: 197, 203).

This is but one example of a domain of experience where, as Wittgenstein remarks, 'Many of our concepts *cross*' (PI: 211); where insisting on too-clear or univocal a theoretical description would only mislead. In such cases we may indeed be justified in describing the same phenomena by using two inconsistent forms of description (for example, 'half visual experience, half thought') so long as we recognize just what we are doing, while continuing to attend to the phenomenon we are hoping to capture. Exactly this point is made, and with regard to reasons and causes, in 'Will and Motive', an essay by Wittgenstein's onetime disciple, Friedrich Waismann.

Fathoming motives: a principle of indeterminacy

A singular merit of Jacques Bouveresse's book, *Wittgenstein Reads Freud*, is to have brought Friedrich Waismann's work into the discussion of Wittgenstein and psychoanalysis. Unfortunately, however, Bouveresse is not very explicit about what he considers to be the precise relevance of Waismann's (1994) rich and lengthy essay, which was written in the mid-1940s. I would suggest that Waismann's arguments offer an interesting, quasi-Wittgensteinian way of understanding, and perhaps also of justifying, Freud's supposed conflation not only of reasons with causes but also of discovering facts with the projection of prior assumptions.

In the essay, Waismann challenges two distinctions that are central to Wittgenstein's critique of Freud: the distinction between interpretation and discovery and that between reasons and causes. His questioning of these distinctions, or at least of the dichotomies they might be taken to imply, is nevertheless in the spirit of the later Wittgenstein. It may even offer some hints of what Wittgenstein might have said if he had gone beyond his rather informal comments on psychoanalysis, taking it upon himself to define the proper way to conceive both the subject matter of psychoanalysis and the epistemological orientation appropriate for approaching it.

Waismann (1994) is particularly interested in the concept of motive or motivation, a notion that is obviously central to psychoanalysis. Motive, he notes, is really a kind of family-resemblance concept. It is a 'loose group without a sharp boundary' (Waismann 1994: 115) that embraces both purpose and drive, thus incorporating goal-directed concepts involving reasons as well as more causally oriented references to forces acting upon us. Bouveresse (1995: 79) describes this intermediary concept as 'indecisive and unclassifiable, situated between two seemingly heterogeneous extremes': that of the cause, lawlike and knowable from outside, and that of the purpose, constituted (and potentially observable) from within.[33]

Waismann's approach provides an interesting contrast with Davidson's. Unlike Davidson, Waismann does not begin with an abstract, epistemological analysis of what are supposed to be the *possible* modes of psychological explanation. He looks instead to the psychological realities at issue, subordinating his epistemological conclusions to these. And whereas Wittgenstein generally restricts himself to a purely conceptual kind of analysis (a clarification of what he calls the 'grammar' of the concepts whereby we negotiate the world), Waismann is more willing to combine conceptual or linguistic forms of analysis with a more empirical, phenomenological approach that aspires to elucidate psychological phenomena themselves. Waismann's general approach does, however, seem to be very much in the spirit of the famous passage on family resemblances in the *Philosophical Investigations* (§66), where Wittgenstein advises us not to think but to look:

> Don't say: 'There *must* be something common, or they would not be called "games"' – but *look and see* whether there is anything common to all...To repeat: don't think, but look!...observe what really happens when we act and then judge our own action.[34]

Also in contrast with Davidson, Waismann (1994) does not sharply distinguish between utterly distinct forms of explanation but, in a more Wittgensteinian spirit, tends to call into question the deceivingly clear models or pictures that, he thinks, are capable of distorting our understanding both of our own experience and of understanding itself. 'Our observations', he writes 'have shaken the belief that certain motives are present in us like so many distinguishable entities' (Waismann 1994: 131). Waismann generalizes his point, taking it to an all-encompassing (and therefore somewhat un-Wittgensteinian) extreme: 'any psychological explanation is ambiguous, cryptic and open-ended, for we ourselves are many-layered, contradictory and incomplete beings, and this complicated structure, which fades away into indeterminacy, is passed on to all our actions' (Waismann 1994: 134).[35]

Waismann also questions the reason/cause dichotomy, but in a more radical way than does Davidson. It is not merely that reasons can legitimately play a role in causal explanations, albeit one of an utterly different kind than blind physical causality. Waismann first contemplates the realities of psychological life, and notices the inseparability of motive and physical manifestations at the level of the actual psychological phenomena; for example, how certain attitudes and currents of feeling, such as hatred or desire, generally include bodily excitations, and how these excitations often pass naturally into action via a process of at least quasi-physical causation. In this sort of example, writes Waismann, we see 'how the concept of a motive merges into the concept of a cause' (Waismann 1994: 129–31). A parallel point could be made by thinking of the ways in which certain patterns of activity that may have had a distinctive intentional directedness when first initiated, can later become habitual. It may originally have made sense to analyze such actions in terms of the practical syllogism, as the outcome of particular propositional attitudes and beliefs. But the pattern may have long since been transformed into a more structural aspect of the person, something that has lost virtually all connection to any nexus of intentional mental states and that is now being propelled by the inertia of habit. This is not to say that it is now an entirely meaningless product of blind causality or a mere reflex. Rather, it should be seen as part or an expression of a person's *style* of acting or being, something that expresses the habituation of a general orientation to action and the world rather than the explicit, proposition-like goal-directedness of which Davidson speaks.

Waismann's point, then, is not that we can *tell* two kinds of stories – that of blind causality, that of reasons – but that what we actually refer to when we use the concepts of motive and of cause tend to merge with each other *in reality*, and that this merging is by no means unintelligible. Waismann rejects the dichotomy of reason-explanations *versus* brute-causal explanation; in doing so, however, he does not wholly reject the importance of the conceptual distinction to which Wittgenstein was calling our attention. For as Waismann acknowledges,

> The *closer* a motive is to a cause, the easier it is to recognize it from the outside and to subsume it under laws. The *farther* away it is from a cause, the more we have to rely on self-observation.[36]
>
> (Waismann 1994: 131, emphasis added)

'The difficulty of psychology', he writes a few pages later,

> is precisely that our ordinary concepts are too rigid; we need something looser, more indefinite. This brings out the fundamental character of the mental: everything is equivocal, indefinite, floating. In order to describe the mental we need a *language* that is just as flexible; which, of course, runs counter to our usual way of thinking.
>
> (Waismann 1994: 136)

Although Wittgenstein defended ordinary language, I think he would have agreed with the critique of 'ordinary concepts' that Waismann offers in this passage. For what Wittgenstein was really defending was ordinary language as it is ordinarily used. He well understood that ordinary concepts tend t become rigid, to lose their nuanced, fluid and context-embedded nature, when they are taken up into the technical vocabularies of philosophy or psychology.

The more one recognizes the potential 'ambiguity of the mental', Waismann argues, the more one will be forced to question the very possibility of any sort of straightforwardly 'objective self-knowledge' (Waismann 1994: 136), knowledge modelled on that we may have of middle-sized objects in the physical world. Waismann notes that motives are not, in fact, present in us like solid and distinguishable 'entities existing in us in isolation' (Waismann 1994: 126). They are *part* of an observer: they flow through him, leaving him altered, altering his perspective on everything (Waismann 1994: 110). To speak of *the* motive, or even of *a* motive, of a given action is often to concentrate on a certain grouping and a certain construal of what is actually a limitless set of forces as well as purposes operating at every level of conscious and unconscious awareness.

Waismann compares motives to clouds: they are intangible, unstable, tending to melt away on a critical view (Waismann 1994: 126, 129). A motive is 'never perfectly real and never perfectly unreal' (Waismann 1994: 136). He likens the difficulty of formulating motives to the difficulty of recounting dreams. As with dreams, it is hard to know how far one has really reproduced the original phenomenon and how far one has changed it in the telling: thereby removing 'some of its peculiar indeterminacy by putting it into words with definite meanings' (Waismann 1994: 111). The project of understanding motivation – one's own or that of another – also has much in common with that of artistic representation or appreciation, for it is something that demands active, imaginative interpretation or an attitude of subtle, connoisseur-like discernment toward the world. (As Waismann notes, the German word for motive, *Motif*, is in fact the same as that for an artistic motif.) This point is, of course, reminiscent of Wittgenstein's likening of psychoanalytic explanation to the aesthetic simile. The implication of both Waismann's and Wittgenstein's accounts, I would argue, is that understanding motives requires the ability to grasp patterns of expressive relations; and these are patterns that do not seem reducible to causal-deterministic forces or analyzable in terms of propositional attitudes or the practical syllogism (see Merleau-Ponty 1962: 160 regarding 'reciprocal expression'; Taylor 1993: 326; 1985b).

Does this mean that there is only interpretation, only subjectivism (Waismann 1994: 136), as many postmodernists have claimed? Another alternative would be to say that talk of the unconscious is nothing more than a 'convenient shorthand for describing a certain type of behaviour' (Waismann 1994: 96), as Gilbert Ryle and also various behaviourists have argued. Waismann (like Wittgenstein) would reject both these alternatives. Waismann accepts the reality of some kind of subterranean realm of experience, noting, in fact, that there are indeed moments when a repressed 'movement of the will' can break through into consciousness 'with all the signs of a soul-shattering experience'. And this, he says (echoing Wittgenstein's point about reasons) is 'the true criterion' which justifies our speaking of an unconscious motive or will (Waismann 1994: 97).

But none of this implies that our motives are not also, in certain respects, dependent on how we understand or describe them; not, of course, in the sense of being wholly *created* by our understanding, but in the sense of being thereby moulded or transformed. A motive 'thickens, hardens, and takes shape, as it were, only after we express it in words', states Waismann. 'Thus by expressing it, we *do* something to the motive; and this alone shows what difficulties we can run into in asking for a motive' (Waismann 1994: 112).[37] Here we might recall the philosopher Charles Taylor's (1985a) notion of 'self-interpreting animals': the selves or psyches of human beings are clearly affected by how they understand themselves; self-understanding does not simply reflect, it also constitutes and transforms.[38] But this is not to say we entirely create our selves through self-interpretation. Interpretations are not simply arbitrary (Waismann 1994: 132); there are limits to which interpretations are possible or plausible, partly because there are features of human nature and of one's individual personality and past that are prior to any interpretation and must be captured by it, and partly because interpretations themselves tend to solidify or take on a certain inertia. Hence the possibility of error in self-interpretation – of bad faith, self-deception, and so forth. So, to quote Waismann once again:

> There really is something like digging down to deeper layers, becoming more truthful, struggling passionately, while things become clearer and clearer. There is undoubtedly such a process of plumbing the depths in which one penetrates to one's innermost motives. So things are not entirely subjective; there *is* truth after all. And yet! When we want to put our finger on it, it will not stand up; when we look more closely at it, it looks different again. It is an interpretation and yet something more than an interpretation, knowledge and yet not quite knowledge: what are we dealing with?
>
> (Waismann 1994: 136)

Waismann's view suggests we might see certain of Freud's equivocations as reflecting not mere grammatical muddle or manipulation, but rather, certain potential ambiguities inherent in human existence itself. In the view of this onetime disciple of Wittgenstein, it is the basic character of certain mental or experiential phenomena that defies the rigid concepts so characteristic of both psychology and philosophy. To capture what it is to fathom a motive, that most central of psychoanalytic activities, we need to go beyond the familiar conceptual alternatives. We need something that equivocates between the avowal of reasons and the knowing of causes as well as between discovery and (mere) interpretation. We require a composite concept that combines 'knowing, acknowledging and interpreting. For fathoming a motive touches on all three' (Waismann 1994: 136).[39]

Conclusion: science and mystery

As we have seen, Wittgenstein was quite explicit in offering a critical perspective on psychoanalysis, for example, in pointing out its pseudo-scientific aspects and its affinities with metaphysical philosophy. What is more difficult to get clear about is the complex set of affinities and divergences of sensibility and ambition that made Wittgenstein feel not merely repulsed but also profoundly attracted by the Freudian perspective. As Wittgenstein himself realized, sometimes to his own despair ('I destroy, I destroy, I destroy', he wrote in his personal notebooks; 1980: 21), he is an exceptionally negative philosopher, far more inclined to criticize than to justify or defend. But this is no reason to ignore Wittgenstein's statements of admiration for and kinship with Freud, or to downplay the similarities that exist between psychoanalysis and Wittgenstein's own project of intellectual clarification and self-criticism.[40]

Wittgenstein did often warn against being preoccupied with depths, with what 'lies *beneath* the surface' (Z §444), stating that what he wanted to understand was 'already in plain view' (PI §89, §92). 'Philosophy only states what everyone admits', he wrote in another passage (PI §599). In fact, however, he himself was powerfully interested in delving below the surface of our ways of speaking and thinking in order to clarify – and ultimately, to dissolve – underlying pictures that captivate and mislead us. 'In our language there is an entire mythology embedded', he wrote (in Kenny 1994: 278). 'The problems arising through a misinterpretation of our forms of language have the character of *depth*. They are deep disquietudes; their roots are as deep in us as the forms of our language' (PI §111). All this is certainly reminiscent of psychoanalysis.

Other resemblances to psychoanalysis include Wittgenstein's fondness for illness metaphors; his predilection for constructing illuminating metaphors and similes; his inclination, at times, to connect philosophy with the personality that produced it; and his belief that the insight one seeks is ultimately directed toward a transformation of personality or self: 'A philosopher', he wrote,

> is a man who has to cure many intellectual diseases in himself before he can arrive at the notions of common sense.
>
> It is sometimes said that a man's philosophy is a matter of temperament, and there is something in this. A preference for certain similes...
>
> (CV: 44, 20)

In a passage from an unpublished manuscript, Wittgenstein explains why psychoanalysis, which he elsewhere compares with metaphysical philosophy, can also be likened to his own brand of philosophical clarification and critique:

> It is a principal function of philosophy to warn against false analogies. To warn against the false analogies which lie embedded in our forms of expression without our being fully conscious of them.
>
> I believe our method here resembles psychoanalysis which also makes conscious the unconscious and thereby renders it harmless, and I believe that this resemblance is not purely superficial.
>
> (Wittgenstein manuscript 109, 174; quoted in Hilmy 1991: 100)

In an entry from his diaries of the 1930s, Wittgenstein (in press, 9; 27 April 1930) expressed a parallel ambivalence toward Freud and toward himself:

> Freud surely errs very frequently and as far as his character is concerned he is probably a swine or something similar, but in what he says there is incredibly much. And the same is true of me. There is a *lot* in what I say.[41]

As I indicated earlier, one of Wittgenstein's deepest sentiments was his commitment to the ideal of clarity – clarity with regard to ourselves, to our own ways of speaking, understanding and acting. I believe that Wittgenstein did recognize Freud as sharing this ideal, even if he did not think Freud applied it sufficiently to his own intellectual approach. This helps to account for Wittgenstein's inclination to characterize his own philosophical method as a kind of psychoanalysis. It is with regard to Wittgenstein's second ideal, that of awe or wonder, that the sensibilities of Freud and Wittgenstein most truly and most sharply diverge. To appreciate this latter point, one must consider their respective attitudes toward knowledge, especially toward the enterprise of scientific as opposed to mythic forms of explanation.

Freud, at least in his ambitions, was a true child of the Enlightenment. Despite occasional gestures to the contrary ('The theory of instincts is, so to say, our mythology; instincts are mythical entities, magnificent in their indefiniteness', he wrote in the *New Introductory Lectures* (SE 22: 95)), he was, for the most part, deeply committed to causal-deterministic forms of scientific explanation, and inclined to scepticism about the claims of myth, morality and religion, which he dismissed as the 'attempt to procure a certainty of happiness and a protection against suffering through a delusional remoulding of reality' (SE 21: 28). Freud seems to have believed that virtually everything is amenable to deterministic forms of explanation; that, since everything has a cause, nothing could on principle lie outside the bounds of natural scientific knowledge. Even the characteristic human experiences that seem to point toward an unknowable or mystical beyond are, for Freud, but illusions to be accounted for by means of a scientific psychology. Thus the sensation of the uncanny is merely a sign of the partial return of repressed early memories; oceanic feelings are but recollections of the undifferentiated narcissism of early infancy. Psychology's triumph over religion is anticipated in a passage from *The Psychopathology of Everyday Life* in which Freud argues that most elements of the mythic or religious world views are not, in fact, really about the world at all, but, rather, a matter of 'psychology projected into the external world' – projections onto the universe of the psyche's awareness of its own structures:

> The obscure recognition (the endopsychic perception, as it were) of psychical factors and relations in the unconscious is mirrored...in the construction of a *supernatural reality*, which is destined to be changed back once more by science into the *psychology of the unconscious*. One could venture to explain in this way the myths of paradise and the fall of man, of God, of good and evil, of immortality, and so on, and to transform *metaphysics* into *metapsychology*.
> (SE 6: 256)

Freud's reductionistic project – his 'scientific' transformation of metaphysics into metapsychology as well as his relentless pursuit of the sublimations and parapraxes of daily life – would have been anathema to Wittgenstein, who took a far more critical view both of the scope and value of scientific explanation and of a culture overly dominated by scientific perspectives. Though Wittgenstein is in many respects the deeper sceptic of the two, his is a curious scepticism, profoundly dubious not only about science but about doubt as well, and curiously sympathetic to belief. 'What a curious attitude scientists have', Wittgenstein wrote in 1941; '"We still don't know that [they say]; but it is knowable and it is only a matter of time before we get to know it!" As if that went without saying', 'The insidious thing about the causal point of view is that it leads us to say: "Of course, it had to happen like that." Whereas we ought to think: it may have happened *like that* – and also in many other ways' (CV: 40, 37). Wittgenstein spoke more than once of his loathing and disgust for one style of thinking: 'a kind of idol worship, the idol being Science and the Scientist' (LA: 27–8). Although he had been trained as an engineer, he himself did not find scientific questions truly gripping; at bottom, he says, he was indifferent to them, though not to aesthetic or conceptual questions (CV: 79). Hypotheses, cause-and-effect relationships, even the sorts of insight psychoanalysis could offer: none of these seemed to him able to address the truly significant issues or existential dilemmas of our lives.

It is important to realize that 'mythology', for Wittgenstein, need not be a term of derision or abuse. Though not himself a religious man, Wittgenstein had the deepest respect for religion and mythology, and once said he could not help 'seeing every problem from a religious point of view' (Drury 1984: 79).[42] Wittgenstein argued that a truly religious belief should not be understood as a kind of empirical claim, a botched attempt to speak objective truths. Rather it is 'something like a passionate commitment to a system of reference...[it is] a way of living, or a way of assessing life. It's passionately seizing hold of *this* interpretation' (CV: 64). 'I understand that the state of mind of believing can make the human being blessed', he wrote in his diaries (in press, 219). Myth and religion provide a sense of orientation and they deepen a human being's appreciation of the seriousness and significance of life; for this, they deserve profound respect.

But what about psychoanalysis? Surely it, too, involves 'passionate decision in favor of a system of reference'. Surely its stories also provide a sense of coherence and meaning, as recent writers on narrative theory often remind us. In one set of remarks, Wittgenstein himself acknowledges this, noting that the psychoanalytic way of seeing, with its notion of a primal scene or *Urszene*, can impose a kind of tragic pattern on one's life, the salutary sense of being 'a tragic figure carrying out the decrees under which the fates had placed him at birth':

Many people have, at some period, serious trouble in their lives – so serious as to lead to thoughts of suicide. This is likely to appear to one as something nasty, as a situation which is too foul to be a subject of a tragedy. And it may then be an immense relief if it can be shown that one's life has the pattern rather of a tragedy – the tragic working out and repetition of a pattern which was determined by the primal scene.

(LA: 51)

But before pressing too hard the analogy of psychoanalysis with myth or religion, we need to consider the *kind* of system of reference or of narrative form, and the *sort* of passion, that psychoanalysis actually involves.

In another set of remarks, Wittgenstein (LA) focuses on a different aspect of psychoanalytic narratives: how they effect the alchemy of a debunkingly comic rather than tragic transmutation:

Freud shows what he calls the 'meaning' of the dream. The coarsest sexual stuff, bawdy of the worst kind – if you wish to call it that – bawdy from A to Z. We know what we mean by bawdy. A remark sounds to the uninitiated harmless, but the initiated, say, chuckle when they hear it.

(LA: 23)

Freud and his early followers thought they had access to deeper and more telling explanations, and to this end adopted an orientation of hyper-alert, almost paranoid suspiciousness toward human action and expression. The attitude is nicely captured in the psychoanalyst A.A. Brill's description of the early psychoanalytic circles:

We made no scruples, for instance, of asking a man at table why he did not use his spoon in the proper manner, or why he did such and such a thing in such and such a manner. It was impossible for one to show any degree of hesitation or to make some abrupt pause in speaking without being at once called to account. We had to keep ourselves well in hand, ever ready and alert, for there was no telling when and where there would be a new attack. We had to explain why we whistled or hummed a particular tune or why we made some slip in talking or some mistake in writing. But we were glad to do this if for no other reason than to learn to face the truth.

(quoted in Bouveresse 1995: 91)

It was not prudery that made Wittgenstein complain about 'the coarsest sexual stuff' and the chuckles of the initiated, but, rather, what we might term his respect for the sheer variety, irreducibility, unpredictability and wondrousness of Being. Wittgenstein had profound respect for any way of understanding that increases one's sense of the momentousness of human existence, inspiring emotions of humility and awe. In his 'Lecture on Ethics' (1993), he writes of an experience that was, for him, a paradigm of the sense of ultimate value: the sense of wonder at the very existence of the world itself. In a passage in his notebooks he speaks respectfully of the process of coming to understand the 'ordinary [as] filled with significance' (CV: 52). Psychoanalysis, by contrast, generally seems to undermine such feelings, to reveal the all-too-worldly sources of our mystical, religious, or aesthetic leanings, and to give its initiates a sense of knowing superiority. If psychoanalysis offers a mythology, it seems to be a mythology of a rather scientistic sort, one far better suited to an age of suspicion than to an age of awe.

Here, perhaps, lies the most significant contrast between Freud, child of the Enlightenment and would-be scientist of the mind, and Wittgenstein, the near-mystic and harsh critic of the present age. More than any other philosopher, Wittgenstein teaches us to suspect suspicion and our impulse to explain. At times he wrote of what he saw as the greater wisdom implicit in mythic as against scientific accounts of the world. If religious myths 'explain', it is by postulating entities that are flagrantly, even proudly, inexplicable, miracles, gods and the like; these do not dissipate our awe but merely focus it. By contrast, scientistic myths – and here Wittgenstein would surely have included many of the claims of psychoanalysis – leave us with the distinct impression that everything has been accounted for; they give us the illusion of explaining a world that we might do better to wonder at.[43] In his diaries of the 1930s, Wittgenstein spoke disparagingly of the 'irritation of *intellect*', the 'tickling of intellect', which he opposed to the religious impulse (in press, 239). 'Wisdom is grey', as Wittgenstein wrote in 1947. 'Life on the other hand and religion are full of colour', Whereas he considered faith to be 'a passion', 'wisdom' to him seemed 'cold and to that extent stupid': it 'merely *conceals* life from you', he wrote, 'like cold grey ash, covering up the burning embers' (CV: 62, 56).

This leads to a final difference between Wittgenstein and Freud, one that concerns the attitude each adopted toward his own distinctive framework or mode of understanding. Here, in fact, we encounter what is perhaps the central dilemma of modernist thought. Given the realization, ubiquitous since Kant, of the mind's role in constituting its world, what attitude should a thinker adopt towards his *own* frame of reference, the frame of reference he uses in understanding *other* minds, *other* frames of reference? The temptations toward epistemological arrogance, toward a kind of 'transcendental narcissism' (to borrow a phrase from Michel Foucault (1972: 203)), are considerable. The general realization of the perspectival nature of human reality would seem to demand, however, that one relativize one's own perspective as well; it would seem to demand recognizing that one's own point of view or theoretical perspective is also only a perspective, even if, in fact, it involves a perspective *on* perspectives.

The confidence with which Freud offered interpretations of the true meanings of symptoms and dreams and propounded grand meta-psychological theories suggests he was not terribly daunted by, or sensitive to, this latter concern. Wittgenstein's tone and attitude is very different. The ironic, self-cancelling quality of his early book, *Tractatus Logico-Philosophicus*, which ends by declaring its own nonsensicality; the absence in his later work of any straightforward philosophical theses: both are responses to this dilemma. Wittgenstein's concern is also expressed in his worries about the effects of his own teaching, which, he feared, could all too easily be turned into a way of debunking the sincere efforts of other thinkers. Instead of fostering a respectful and supple attitude distinct from dogmatism as well as scepticism, Wittgenstein thought that his own teaching, like Freud's, was in danger of being turned into some sort of 'formula' or 'rigmarole', and could end up by doing 'incalculable harm': 'The teachings, like wine, had made people drunk. They did not know how to use the teaching soberly...Oh yes, they had found a formula. Exactly' (quoted in Bouwsma 1986: 11–12, 36).

We must realize, then, how very different were Wittgenstein's and Freud's *motives* for their respective, and in some ways parallel, attempts to clarify analogies and pictures that underlie human thought and understanding. Both men did, in some sense, travel to the depths; but whereas Freud was searching for ultimate underlying truths, Wittgenstein's goal was to disabuse us of any such expectation. Among his most important targets, in fact, were precisely those images of surface and depth, of outer shell and inner essence, that have so often led human beings, especially intellectuals, astray. We might say, then, that Wittgenstein criticizes explanation in order to make way for wonder. Clarity for him was largely in the *service* of awe: his critical energies were directed at unmasking what he saw as the pseudo-explanations that tend to come between us and the world, blinding us to the sheer wonder of its existence.

Notes

1 The present paper incorporates some material that previously appeared in L. Sass (1998) 'Surface and Depth: Wittgenstein's Reflections on Psychoanalysis', *Partisan Review,* Fall: 590–9.
2 As Cioffi has noted, Freud sometimes admitted this. In 1893 Freud wrote to Fliess: 'The sexual business attracts people; they all go away impressed and convinced, after exclaiming: No one has ever asked me that before' (quoted in Cioffi 1969: 186n).
3 This essay has benefited considerably from my reading of Bouveresse's book, which (among other things) directed me toward relevant passages from Wittgenstein as well as to several secondary sources on Wittgenstein and psychoanalysis.
4 In Wittgenstein's view, there is nothing wrong with using a prototype as a way of generalizing about a set of particulars. But, Wittgenstein (CV: 14) warns us, 'the prototype ought to be clearly presented for what it is...so that its general validity will depend on the fact that it determines the form of discussion rather than on

the claim that everything which is true only if it holds too for all the things that are being discussed'. If 'we confuse prototype and object we find ourselves dogmatically conferring on the object properties which only the prototype necessarily possesses'.

5 Concerning the influence of Wittgenstein on discussions of narrative and of the reasons-versus-causes distinction in psychoanalysis, see Walkup (1990: 239–45). For discussion of postmodernist relativism in psychoanalysis, see Sass (1994b, 1995).

6 For arguments against the attribution of anti-realist and sceptical views to Wittgenstein, see Diamond (1995: 17, 243); Stroud (1996: 306); Collins (1992: 86).

7 In (PI §§683–4), Wittgenstein makes a related point in a somewhat different context: 'I draw a head...When I said it represented N. – was I establishing a connexion or reporting one?...What is there in favour of saying that my words describe an existing connexion? Well, they relate to various things which didn't simply make their appearance with the words...'.

8 I am grateful to Aaron Zimmerman and Ernest LePore for help in thinking about Davidson's views. Thanks also to Rupert Read, James Walkup, Malcolm Turvey, and especially Richard Allen, for useful comments and criticisms concerning various drafts of this article.

9 In one essay, Davidson (1980: 261) identifies his (and Hempel's) target as the 'very strong neo-Wittgensteinian current of small red books'. According to Rosenberg (1985: 400), these would include Peter Winch's *The Idea of a Social Science*, A.I. Melden's *Free Action* and R.S. Peters's *The Concept of Motivation*.

10 For statements re these supposed advantages of a Davidsonian approach, see Cavell (1993: 60 (conflict between Wittgenstein's avowability criterion and notion of unconscious reasons), 74 (psychoanalysis makes genuine discoveries), 81 (against neo-Baconian approach in psychoanalysis), 85–6 (versus postmodernist relativism; in favour of the objectivity and efficacy of reasons)).

11 Davidson notes, by the way, that the particular belief/desire combination has to play a particular *kind* of causal role: it is not sufficient that it *cause* the action; it must cause it in the right *way*. One can imagine situations in which the person had a related belief/desire combination, and in which this combination did indeed play an efficacious role, but where the causal relationship was not of the proper sort. Davidson (1980: 79) gives the example of a mountain climber who wishes to rid himself of the burden of another climber hanging onto a rope, and who may also know that loosening his grip will rid himself of this other climber. His awareness of having this belief and this wish may render him so nervous that he actually does loosen his grip, but without doing so intentionally. This is an example of a 'deviant' or 'wayward' causal chain. It shows that playing a causal role is not, in fact, a sufficient (though it is a necessary) condition for a reason to serve as *the* reason in a causal explanation of an action.

Given Davidson's emphasis on this actual causal role, one might have hoped that he would offer an analysis of the nature of this crucial causal connection, i.e. some description of what he terms 'the right sort of route' that 'the causal chain must follow' (Davidson 1980: 78). Davidson does not, however, believe that this is possible: 'I despair of spelling out...the way in which attitudes must cause actions if they are to rationalize the action' (Davidson 1980: 79).

12 Richard Rorty is one philosopher who has explicitly espoused both eliminative materialism and a form of postmodern relativism regarding interpretation.

13 In her Davidsonian account of psychoanalysis, Marcia Cavell (1993) writes: 'I want to argue, first...the psychoanalyst can arrive at true, objective interpretations of her patient's states of mind... and further, that the truth counts, both in

knowing why the patient behaves as he does and in helping him to change'
(Cavell 1993: 86).

14 It hardly seems likely, by the way, that Wittgenstein would have wanted to deny
that reasons can indeed play a legitimate role in causal explanations, if by 'causal
explanation' we are simply referring to instances when, in saying that a person
did something for a particular reason, we mean to imply that the reason was in
some unspecified sense 'efficacious' in common-sense terms – that is, that the
reason did somehow motivate the action and that, absent the reason, the person
would probably not have so acted. To issue such a denial would contradict
Wittgenstein's lifelong belief that ordinary language is 'in order as it is' (PI §98;
see also TLP: 5.5563), and would be inconsistent with his claim to be reminding
us always of what we already know (PI §89, §94). It would smack of the kind of
'metaphysical' philosophizing that Wittgenstein firmly rejected. When, in the
Blue Book (BB: 15), Wittgenstein says that reasons are not causes, he clearly has
in mind something akin to the nomological, covering-law notion of causation.
Elsewhere, however, Wittgenstein (CE: 373, 387, 389) acknowledges that causation is a heterogenous concept, and that a uniform account probably cannot be
given of its multifarious forms. His remarks on reasons and causes in the Blue
Book need not be taken to imply that Wittgenstein denies that reasons may be
causes in any of these other senses of 'cause' (see Thornton 1998: 194–6).

15 The implications of Davidson's position regarding the possibility of psychological science are controversial. Kim (1985: 383) argues that the 'view of
psychology that emerges from Davidson is one of a broad interpretative
endeavour directed at human action, to understand its "meaning" rather than
search for law-based causal explanations that are readily convertible into predictions; psychology is portrayed as a hermeneutic inquiry rather than a predictive
science'. But Davidson himself backs away from what he, rather oddly, terms the
'meretricious position' that 'psychology (the part with which we are concerned
(namely, the aspects that deal with propositional content)) is not a science'. The
appropriate conclusion, he writes, 'is rather that psychology is set off from other
sciences in an important and interesting way' (1980: 241).

Davidson has argued that psychology can be a science of non-strict laws.
However, his critics question whether this possibility is really consistent with
other parts of his overall philosophical position. Kim (1993a: 25) argues that
Davidson's arguments in favour of mental anomalism should banish non-strict
as well as strict laws. Others have pointed out that to acknowledge the possibility
of a psychology of non-strict laws (necessarily involving ceteris paribus or all-
things-being-equal clauses) is to deny the much-touted 'anomalousness' of the
mental, since it implies that psychology is in the same boat as all other sciences
with the sole exception of basic physics (Fodor 1987; also Føllesdal 1985: 319).
Evnine (1991: 23–4) points out, however, that the ceteris paribus conditions in
psychological generalizations reflect a deep fact about the mental (the constitutive role of normativity and holism), which is not the case in a special science like
geology (where these conditions simply reflect the diverse contingencies to which
geological regularities are necessarily subject). But this suggests that 'there is no
underlying mental reality whose laws we can study in abstraction from the
normative and holistic perspective of interpretation'; hence that psychology is a
hermeneutic rather than a scientific-nomological discipline. For related discussion, see McGlaughlin (1993: 39–40).

One critic (Rosenberg 1985: 402, 407) actually finds something 'meretricious'
in Davidson's refusal to recognize that his own arguments do indeed imply that
psychology cannnot in fact truly be a science. Rosenberg, who seems to share
Kim's view of the actual implications of Davidson's portrayal of psychology,

points out that Davidson's position is actually congruent with 'the neo-Wittgensteinian movement of the fifties and sixties' which Davidson was claiming to refute: 'A causal science of human action is [on Davidson's account] after all logically possible. But if anomalous monism obtains, it is just not practically possible. The irony therefore is that the followers of Wittgenstein were right after all, in all but the modality of their claims. I speculate that it is his discomfort with finding himself among such unlikely company that leads Davidson to deny that he has undermined the scientific prospects of intentional psychology' (Rosenberg 1985: 407).

16 Various commentators have remarked on what Føllesdal (1985: 317) calls the 'intimate connection' between Davidson's view on the explanation of action and his arguments for anomalous monism.

17 'All event causation is physically based...Since only physical predicates...appear in "strict" laws, every event that enters into causal relations satisfies a basic physical predicate' (Lepore 1999: 207).

18 Davidson draws a distinction between what he calls 'causal *explanation*' and the realm of actual 'causes' and 'causal relations' themselves (Evnine 1991: 33–8). 'Causal explanation' is what I have mostly been focusing on for the last several pages; it concerns how human beings *describe* events (Davidson speaks of it as concerning 'the features we hit on for describing events' (Davidson 1980: 155)). 'Causes' and 'causal relations' refer to relationships that actually obtain between particular events in themselves, regardless of how these events are described. But the two realms are not entirely distinct: if Davidson considers certain controversial forms of causal explanation to be legitimate (namely, those referring to reasons), this is precisely because he believes that the entities to which these explanations refer (i.e., reasons) can in fact play an actual causal role. As Føllesdal (1985: 314) notes, 'In ['Actions, Reasons, and Causes'], Davidson talks all the time about explanation, but his arguments turn on observations concerning causation...'.

19 In defending himself against criticism, Davidson distinguishes between claiming that mental properties '*make a difference*' as to whether events are causally related (which Davidson claims is true) as opposed to claiming 'that events are causally related "*in virtue of*" their properties' (which is how his critics sometimes speak, and which Davidson rejects as meaningless) (emphasis added). For criticism of what seems to be Davidson's distinction without a difference, see Mclaughlin (1993: 30).

20 Consider the sentence from Davidson that is quoted on the next page of the text; it begins: 'For a desire and a belief to explain an action in the right way...'

21 Davidson has attempted to suggest the causal efficacy of the mental by invoking both supervenience and the possiblity of non-strict laws. For criticism of these attempts, see Kim (1993a: 23–4); McGlaughlin (1993: 39–40); Sosa (1993: 47); Evnine (1991: 67–71, 161–4). See also Thornton's arguments regarding Davidson's inability to reconcile 'a nomological account of causation with anti-reductionism of the mental' (1998: 183), or to explain 'the general harmony of the rational and causal powers of mental states' (1998: 198).

LePore and Loewer (1987, 1989) offer an intricate argument to show that mental events can 'make a difference' to the physical in the sense that, if there is a change in the mental, there must also be a concomitant change in the physical. As Van Gulick (1993: 244) points out, however, the defence LePore and Loewer offer of the causal relevance of mental properties is 'tentative and hedged by a worry about whether [the kind of causal relationship they invoke] is sufficiently strong a relation to rebut epiphenomenalism'. Lepore and Loewer argue that alterations in the mental are always *accompanied* by alterations in the physical.

But a similar relationship of 'symmetric lawful covariance' holds between the shadow of a flagpole and the flagpole's actual height, and, as Van Gulick points out, this hardly implies that the shadow has real causal potency, i.e., that one could alter the flagpole's height by manipulating the shadow (1993: 246). See also Kim (1993a: 22–23) and Kim (1993b: 202, 206) regarding the absence of any possibility of 'downward causation' in the Davidsonian view.

22 Here is one representative reaction: 'there is little agreement as to exactly how [Davidson's arguments] are supposed to work. Many philosophers have an opinion about how successful these arguments are (the published verdicts are almost uniformly negative thus far), but most appear to feel uncertain about the accuracy of their interpretations, or think that the interpretations fail to make the arguments sufficiently interesting or plausible. Above all almost everyone seems to find Davidson's arguments extremely opaque; it is not difficult to discern the general drift of his thinking or pick out the basic considerations motivating the arguments; however, delineating their structure precisely enough for effective evaluation and criticism is another matter' (Kim 1985: 370). See also Føllesdal (1985: 320). Davidson (1993: 3) himself acknowledges that many readers have found his arguments exceedingly obscure.

Actually, not just Davidson's arguments, also his basic positions on key issues are remarkably difficult to pin down. For example, what *does* his position really imply about the scientific status of psychoanalysis? *Can* mental contents really have any efficacy in his account?

23 According to Johnston (1985: 417), anomalous monism is ultimately committted to 'exhaustive monism', the view that the physical facts exhaust all the facts. Kim (1993b: 202–9) argues that, since downward causation makes no sense in non-reductionistic physicalism (for example, in Davidson's perspective), mental properties are 'epiphenomenal danglers' which must ultimately be eradicated from one's ontology (since 'to be real is to have causal powers').

24 Davidson's claim that one of several possible reasons may in fact be *the* reason that actually caused a given action, distinguishes his position from that of the postmodern relativists. From a more practical standpoint, however, Davidson's position does not seem to contain any resources that would help a psychologist or psychoanalyst stave off the spectre of relativism in her search for reason-explanations. Davidson says, after all, that there is no way to specify the psychological characteristics necessary for a reason to be the reason for a given action (see note above). Presumably, the only feature that differentiates the reason that is a true cause of an action from other possible reasons for that action, is some unknowable, brute fact of physical causation. But, according to anomalous monism, this brute fact has no regular psychological correlate that might guide the analyst.

It does no good to imagine a day when an ongoing functional brain-scan might give the psychologist access to her patient's neurophysiological activity. Given Davidson's views, nothing yielded by these scans could be correlated in an interesting way with the patient's psychological processes. The sense in which reasons are causes for Davidson is, in fact, uncomfortably reminiscent of Kant's postulating of the noumenal realm: it seems to invoke something that is, on principle, beyond human knowing. A standard criticism of Kant is to question what sense it really makes to postulate such an unknowable realm.

25 This sentence is problematic. It uses the language of causation to refer to a relationship between mental contents endowed with propositional content; but, as indicated above, most readers of Davidson believe that his position implies the causal inertness of such mental events.

26 A good example of such a view (which I myself have strenuously disputed) is the standard, medical-model understanding of schizophrenic abnormalities of thought and language as being meaningless consequences of a 'broken brain' (see Sass 1992: 16–19, 374–97). John Campbell (1999: 624) reports that he has heard orthodox Davidsonians (though not Davidson himself) 'argue that since the schizophrenic is not rational, he does not possess propositional attitudes'.

27 Davidson (1982: 304): 'The analogy does not have to be carried so far as to demand that we speak of parts of the mind as independent agents'.

28 Some of the flavour of Davidson's approach is captured in the following quotation:

> claims about what would constitute a satisfactory theory [of interpretation] are not…claims about the propositional knowledge of an interpreter, nor are they claims about the details of the inner working of some part of the brain. They are rather claims about what must be said to give a satisfactory description of the competence of the interpreter. *We* cannot describe what an interpreter can do except by appeal to a theory of a certain sort.
>
> (Davidson 1986a: 10–11)

29 In a recent defence of the Davidsonian approach, Jerome Wakefield and the psychoanalyst Morris Eagle (1997: 323) describe the components of reasons as consisting of mental representations with particular (propositional) contents that have some kind of actual psychological existence in the subject's mind: 'If I say that my reason for drinking is that I am thirsty (rather than, say, because I have been told by my physician to increase my liquid intake), I am describing the content of the mental representation that was in my head before and as I drank and that played a role in causing me to drink' (Wakefield and Eagle 1997: 328, 355–56). This sort of 'intentional realism about propositional content' may well be incompatible with other aspects of Davidson's position (as Evnine argues, 1991: 155ff; see also Thornton 1998: 167).

Whatever the merits of this sort of account, it is worth noting that to postulate mental representations as 'intervening distinguishable states' certainly runs counter to the spirit of the later Wittgenstein. The *Philosophical Investigations* contains numerous meditations on such psychological concepts as 'understanding', 'expecting', 'intending', 'reading' and 'thinking'. In each case Wittgenstein is concerned to show that the use of these concepts is not linked to the presence of some essential or definitive inner experience or event. In one typical passage from his *Nachlass*, Wittgenstein dismisses 'the inner' as a 'delusion', explaining that 'the whole complex of ideas alluded to by this word is like a painted curtain drawn in front of the scene of actual word use' (LWII §84).

30 In this passage, Davidson (1986b: 92) is referring to the boundaries or partitions between sets of mental contents that, he says, are not discoverable by introspection but must be postulated as 'conceptual aids to the coherent description of genuine irrationalities'.

31 Davidson (1991: 205, quoted in Thornton 1998: 167): 'In thinking and talking of the weights of physical objects we do not need to suppose there are such things as weights for objects to have. Similarly in thinking and talking about the beliefs of people we needn't suppose there are such entities as beliefs'.

32 Thus I disagree with Bourdieu (1990: 29) when he suggests that things would be very much improved if only theorists would place an 'everything takes place as if…' before each such attempt at scientific discourse about the social world. Even if one adopts this kind of tentative vocabulary and attitude, one's theories can still have a profound effect on one's world view and image of human nature.

33 Whereas Wittgenstein (BB: 15) tends to equate the concepts of 'reason' and 'motive', Waismann exploits the term 'motive' to refer to something that has affinities with both 'reason' and 'cause'.

34 Wittgenstein does, in fact, have significant affinities with the phenomenological tradition in philosophy; see Gier (1981).

35 Wittgenstein would probably have preferred to speak of 'many' or perhaps 'most' psychological explanations.

36 Wittgenstein (BB: 15) would point out that this 'self-observation' should not be conceptualized as a kind of object-oriented or introspective form of awareness, as if we were speaking of a cause 'seen from the inside'.

37 In the *Investigations* (§682), Wittgenstein makes a similar point regarding meaning:

> You said, 'It'll stop soon'. – Were you thinking of the noise or of your pain? If he answers 'I was thinking of the piano-tuning' – is he observing that the connexion existed, or is he making it by means of these words? – Can't I say *both*? If what he said was true, didn't the connexion exist – and is he not for all that making one which did not exist?

38 Waismann's position has much in common with the ontological hermeneutic position of Hans-Georg Gadamer, and also with the hermeneutic phenomenology of Merleau-Ponty. For an overview of hermeneutics in relationship to psychoanalysis, see Sass (1998).

39 See Føllesdal (1985: 321) for a plea for a 'mixed psycho-physical theory' that, among other things, would reject Davidson's overemphasis on the maximizing of rationality in interpreting the mental life of others.

40 I would argue that Bouveresse makes this error. Bouveresse seems to have a distinctly anti-psychoanalytic bias, due in part to an animus against French Freudianism that he makes little attempt to conceal. It is this bias, perhaps, that prevents Bouveresse from exploring in more detail the interesting, albeit somewhat mysterious, question of how Wittgenstein could have considered himself to be, in any sense, a disciple or a follower of Freud.

41 In another passage from the diaries, Wittgenstein writes: 'Loos, Spengler, Freud and I all belong to the same class which is characteristic for this age' (in press, 29; 9 May 1930).

42 'All genuine expressions of religion are wonderful', Wittgenstein said once in conversation, 'even those of the most savage people' (Drury 1984: 93).

43 'Man has to awaken to wonder – and so perhaps do peoples. Science is a way of sending him to sleep again' (Wittgenstein 1980: 5).

Bibliography

Antony, L. (1989) 'Anomalous Monism and the Problem of Explanatory Force', *Philosophical Review* 98: 153–87.

Berlin, I. (1979) 'The Hedgehog and the Fox', in I. Berlin, *Russian Thinkers*, New York: Penguin, 22–81.

Bourdieu, P. (1990) *The Logic of Practice*, trans. R. Nice, Stanford, CA: Stanford University Press.

Bouveresse, J. (1995) *Wittgenstein Reads Freud: The Myth of the Unconscious*, trans. C. Cosman, Princeton, NJ: Princeton University Press.

Campbell, J. (1999) 'Schizophrenia, the Space of Reasons, and Thinking as a Motor Process', *The Monist* 82: 609–25.

Cavell, M. (1993) *The Psychoanalytic Mind: From Freud to Philosophy*, Cambridge, MA: Harvard University Press.

Cioffi, F. (1969) 'Wittgenstein's Freud', in P. Winch (ed.), *Studies in the Philosophy of Wittgenstein*, London: Routledge and Kegan Paul, 184–210.

Collins, A. (1992) 'On the Paradox Kripke Finds in Wittgenstein', *Midwest Studies in Philosophy* XVII: 74–88.

Davidson, D. (1980) *Essays on Actions and Events*, Oxford: Clarendon Press.

—— (1982) 'Paradoxes of Irrationality', in R. Wollheim and J. Hopkins (eds), *Philosophical Essays on Freud*, Cambridge: Cambridge University Press, 289–305.

—— (1986a) 'A Nice Derangement of Epitaphs', in E. LePore (ed.), *Truth and Interpretation: Perspectives on the Philosophy of Donald Davidson*, Oxford: Basil Blackwell: 433-46.

—— (1986b) 'Deception and Division', in J. Elster (ed.), *The Multiple Self*, New York: Cambridge University Press, 79–92.

—— (1987) 'Knowing One's Own Mind', *Proceedings and Addresses of the American Philosophical Association*, 441–58.

—— (1991) 'What is Present to the Mind?', in E. Villanueve (ed.), *Consciousness*, Oxford: Blackwell.

—— (1993) 'Thinking Causes', in J. Heil and A. Mele (eds), *Mental Causation*, Oxford: Oxford University Press, 3–18.

Dennett, D. (1987) *The Intentional Stance*, Cambridge, MA: MIT Press.

Diamond, C. (1995) *The Realistic Spirit: Wittgenstein, Philosophy, and the Mind*, Cambridge, MA: MIT Press.

Drury, M.O. (1984) 'Some Notes on Conversation with Wittgenstein, and Conversations with Wittgenstein', in R.Rhees (ed.), *Recollections of Wittgenstein*, Oxford: Oxford University Press, 76–171.

Evnine, S. (1991) *Donald Davidson*, Stanford, CA: Stanford University Press.

Fodor, J. (1987) *Psychosemantics*, Cambridge, MA: MIT Press.

Føllesdal, D. (1985) 'Causation and Explanation: A Problem in Davidson's View on Action and Mind', in E. LePore and B. McGlaughlin (eds), *Actions and Events: Perspectives on the Philosophy of Donald Davidson*, Oxford: Blackwell, 311–23.

Foucault, M. (1972) *The Archaeology of Knowledge and the Discourse on Language*, trans. A.M. Sheridan Smith, New York: Pantheon.

Freud, S. (1981) *The Standard Edition of the Complete Psychological Works of Sigmund Freud* (SE), trans. J. Strachey, London: Hogarth Press.

Gergen, K. (1994) *Realities and Relationships: Soundings in Social Construction*, Cambridge, MA: Harvard University Press.

Gier, N.F. (1981) *Wittgenstein and Phenomenology*, Albany, NY: State University of New York Press.

Heil, J. and Mele, A. (eds) (1993) *Mental Causation*, Oxford: Clarendon Press.

Hilmy, S. (1991) 'Tormenting Questions', *Philosophical Investigations* section 133, in R.L. Arrington and H.-J. Glock, *Wittgenstein's Philosophical Investigations: Text and Context*, London and New York: Routledge, 89–104.

Honderich, T. (1982) 'The Argument for Anomalous Monism', *Analysis* 42: 59–64.

Hopkins, J. (1982) 'Introduction: Philosophy and Psychoanalysis', in R. Wollheim and J. Hopkins (eds), *Philosophical Essays on Freud*, Cambridge: Cambridge University Press, vii–xlv.

Johnston, M. (1985) 'Why Having a Mind Matters', in E. LePore and B. McGlaughlin (eds), *Actions and Events: Perspectives on the Philosophy of Donald Davidson*, Oxford: Blackwell, 408–26.

Kenny, A. (1994) *The Wittgenstein Reader*, Oxford: Basil Blackwell.

Kim, J. (1985) 'Psychophysical Laws', in E. LePore and B. McGlaughlin (eds), *Actions and Events: Perspectives on the Philosophy of Donald Davidson*, Oxford: Blackwell, 369–86.

—— (1993a) 'Can Supervenience and "Non-Strict Laws" save Anomalous Monism?', in A. Heil and J. Mele (eds), *Mental Causation*, Oxford: Clarendon, 19–26.

—— (1993b) 'The Non-Reductivist's Troubles with Mental Causation', in A. Heil and J. Mele (eds), *Mental Causation*, Oxford: Clarendon, 189–210.

—— (2000) 'The Myth of Nonreductive Materialism', in J.S. Crumley (ed.), *Problems in Mind*, Mountain View, CA: Mayfield, 452–64.

Lepore, E. (1999) 'Donald Davidson', in R. Audi (ed.), *The Cambridge Dictionary of Philosophy*, 2nd edn, Cambridge: Cambridge University Press, 206–7.

LePore, E. and Loewer, B. (1987) 'Mind Matters', *Journal of Philosophy* 84: 630–42.

—— (1989) 'More on Making Mind Matter', *Philosophical Topics* 17: 175–91.

LePore, E. and McGlaughlin, B. (eds) (1985) *Actions and Events: Perspectives on the Philosophy of Donald Davidson*, Oxford: Blackwell.

Louch, A.R. (1966) *Explanation and Human Action*, Berkeley, CA: University of California Press.

Lovejoy, A. (1936) *The Great Chain of Being*, Cambridge, MA: Harvard University Press.

McGuinness, B. (1982) 'Freud and Wittgenstein', in B. McGuinness (ed.), *Wittgenstein and His Times*, Chicago: University of Chicago Press, 27–43.

Malcolm, N. (1984) *Ludwig Wittgenstein: A Memoir*, new edition with Wittgenstein's letters to Malcolm, Oxford: Oxford University Press.

McGlaughlin, B. (1993) 'On Davidson's Response to the Charge of Epiphenomenalism', in A. Heil and J. Mele (eds), *Mental Causation*, Oxford: Clarendon, 27–40.

—— (1999) 'Philosophy of Mind', in R. Audi (ed.), *The Cambridge Dictionary of Philosophy*, 2nd edn, Cambridge: Cambridge University Press, 684–94.

Merleau-Ponty, M. (1962) *The Phenomenology of Perception*, trans. C. Smith, London: Routledge and Kegan Paul.

Mulhall, S. (1990) *On Being in the World: Wittgenstein and Heidegger on Seeing Aspects*, London: Routledge.

Read, R. and Sharrock, W. (in press) *Thomas Kuhn: The Philosopher of Scientific Revolution*, Oxford: Polity.

Rorty, R. (1991) 'Freud and Moral Reflection', in R. Rorty, *Essays on Heidegger and Others*, New York: Cambridge University Press, 143–63.

Rosenberg, A. (1985) 'Davidson's Unintended Attack on Psychology', in E. LePore and B. McGlaughlin (eds), *Actions and Events: Perspectives on the Philosophy of Donald Davidson*, Oxford: Blackwell, 399–407.

Sass, L. (1992) *Madness and Modernism: Insanity in the Light of Modern Art, Literature, and Thought*, Cambridge: Harvard University Press.

—— (1994a) *The Paradoxes of Delusion: Wittgenstein, Schreber, and the Schizophrenic Mind*, Ithaca, NY: Cornell University Press.

—— (1994b) 'The Epic of Disbelief: The Postmodernist Turn in Contemporary Psychoanalysis', *Partisan Review* 1: 96–110.

—— (1995) review essay on Barnaby Barratt, *Psychoanalysis and the Postmodern Impulse, Psychoanalytic Dialogues* 5: 123–36.

—— (1998) '"Ambiguity is of the Essence": The Relevance of Hermeneutics for Psychoanalysis', in P. Marcus and A. Rosenberg (eds), *Psychoanalytic Versions of the Human Condition and Clinical Practice*, New York: New York University Press, 257–305.

Sosa, E. (1984) 'Mind–Body Interaction and Supervenient Causation', *Midwest Studies in Philosophy* 9: 271–81.

—— (1993) 'Davidson's Thinking Causes', in A. Heil and J. Mele (eds), *Mental Causation*, Oxford: Clarendon, 41–50.

Stoutland, F. (1985) 'Davidson on Intentional Behaviour', in E. LePore and B. McGlaughlin (eds), *Actions and Events: Perspectives on the Philosophy of Donald Davidson*, Oxford: Blackwell, 44–59.

Stroud, B. (1996) 'Mind, Meaning, and Practice', in H. Sluga and D.G. Stern (eds), *The Cambridge Companion to Wittgenstein*, Cambridge: Cambridge University Press, 296–319.

Taylor, C. (1985a) 'Self-Interpreting Animals', in *Philosophical Papers, Volume I: Human Agency and Language*, Cambridge: Cambridge University Press, 45–76.

—— (1985b) 'Theories of Meaning', in *Philosophical Papers, Volume I: Human Agency and Language*, 248–92.

—— (1993) 'Engaged Agency and Background in Heidegger', in C. Guignon (ed.), *The Cambridge Companion to Heidegger*, Cambridge: Cambridge University Press, 317–36.

Thornton, T. (1998) *Witttgenstein on Language and Thought: The Philosophy of Content*, Edinburgh: Edinburgh University Press.

Van Gulick, R. (1993) 'Who's in Charge Here? And Who's Doing All the Work?', in A. Heil and J. Mele (eds), *Mental Causation*, Oxford: Clarendon, 233–56.

Waismann, F. (1994) 'Will and Motive', in F. Waismann, J. Schaechter and M. Schlick (eds), *Ethics and the Will: Essays*, trans. H. Kaal, Dordrecht: Kluwer, 53–137.

Wakefield, J.C. and Eagle, M. (1997) 'Psychoanalysis and Wittgenstein: A Reply to Richard Allen', *Psychoanalysis and Contemporary Thought* 20: 323–51.

Walkup, J. (1990) 'Narrative in Psychoanalysis: Truth? Consequences?', in B.K. Britton and A.D. Pellegrini (eds), *Narrative Thought and Narrative Language*, Hillsdale, NJ: Erlbaum, 237–67.

Wittgenstein, L. (1922) *Tractatus Logico-Philosophicus* (TLP), London: Routledge and Kegan Paul.

—— (1953) *Philosophical Investigations* (PI) trans. G.E.M. Anscombe, Oxford: Basil Blackwell.

—— (1958) *The Blue and Brown Books* (BB), Oxford: Blackwell.

—— (1967a) *Lectures and Conversations on Aesthetics, Psychology, and Religious Belief* (LA), Berkeley, CA: University of California Press.

—— (1967b) *Zettel* (Z), trans. G.E.M. Anscombe, Berkeley, CA: University of California Press.

—— (1969) *On Certainty* (OC), trans. D. Paul and G.E.M. Anscombe, New York: Harper and Row.

—— (1980) *Culture and Value* (CV), trans. P. Winch, Chicago: University of Chicago Press.

—— (1992) *Last Writings on the Philosophy of Psychology: The Inner and the Outer* , vol. II (LWII), trans. C.G. Luckhardt and M.A.E. Aue, Oxford: Blackwell.

—— (1993a) 'A Lecture on Ethics' (LE), in J. Klagge and A. Nordmann (eds), *Ludwig Wittgenstein: Philosophical Occasions*, Indianapolis, IN: Hackett, 36–44.

—— (1993b) 'Cause and Effect: Intuitive Awareness' (CE), in J. Klagge and A. Nordmann (eds), *Ludwig Wittgenstein: Philosophical Occasions*, 371–405.

—— (in press) *Denkbewegungen – Movements of Thought: Diaries 1930–1932, 1936–1937*, ed. I. Somavilla, trans. A. Nordmann, to appear in *Public and Private Occasions*, ed. J. Klagge and A. Nordmann, Totowa, NJ: Rowman and Littlefield; German edn, *Denkbewegungen*, ed. I. Somavilla, Innsbruck: Hayman, 1997. (This is quoted, with permission, from the most recent version of the translation available to me.)

INDEX

Abstract Expressionism 97
Adams, L.S. 157
aesthetics 86–8, 92–3, 238, 278; 'science of' 86
Allen, R. 30, 33
Althusser, L. 175
Altieri, C. 34
analytic philosophy 57–8, 155, 234
animals 62–4, 69
anomalous monism 266–8, 288n.16
Antony, L. 267
Aristotelian concepts 46, 49–50, 86, 238, 269
Armstrong, D.M. 85
Arnheim, R. 30
art, appreciation of 101–3, 105–6, 108, 225; arousal theory of 210, 220; cognitive theories of 30–1; competent judges and 104–8; experience and 96; interpreting 117–18; kind of language 155–6, 159, 161, 165, 171–2; learning to see, value, and judge 100–5, 107; philosophy and 89–90; theories of 155; understanding 97–8, 110; unity of artworks 103; Wittgenstein's views 32, 210
artificial intelligence 58
avowals (first-person expressions) 16, 130–1

Bacon, F. 47, 52
Baker, G.P. 111–12, 124
Barfield, O. 246
Barry, P. 226
Barthes, R. 26–8, 175, 227, 229
Baudelaire, C.P., *Alchimie de la douleur* 218, 220–2; 'Les Chats' 217
Beethoven's Third Symphony 220
behaviourism 12–13, 18, 42;

computationalism and 54; logical 42; Watsonian eliminative behaviourism 42; Wittgenstein and 39, 248
Bell, C. 87
Bergman, I. 187
Bergson, H. 245
Berlin, I. 256
Blue and Brown Books (BB), arousal theory of art 210; criteria 131; explanation and description 248; generality 256; meaning 222–3; motives and reasons 261–2; psychoanalysis 257, 259, 273; reasons and causes 15; uses of language 119; words 76, 82–3
Boltzmann, L. 137
Bordwell, D. 30–1, 33, 175–80, 186–94, 205, 207; compared with Currie 195–9, constructivist cognitive psychology and 176–7 201, 204–5; inference 177–80, 188–90; *Narration in the Fiction Film* 176; narrative comprehension 186–94; perception 181–6; *Rear Window* 190–2; schema 177–8, 190–1, 193–6
Bouveresse, J. 19, 118, 256–7, 262, 283; *Wittgenstein Reads Freud: The Myth of the Unconscious* 255, 275
Bradley, A.C. 225–6
brains, human consciousness 13, 84
Breuer, J. 255–6
Brill, A.A. 283

Cage, J. 106–7
Carnap, R. 57
Carrier, D. 103
Carroll, N. 101
Cartesianism 12–14, 40, 47, 50–1, 84, 232, 248

Printed in Great Britain by
Amazon.co.uk, Ltd.,
Marston Gate.